Gerry Stahl's assembled texts volume #2

Tacit & Explicit Understanding in Computer Support

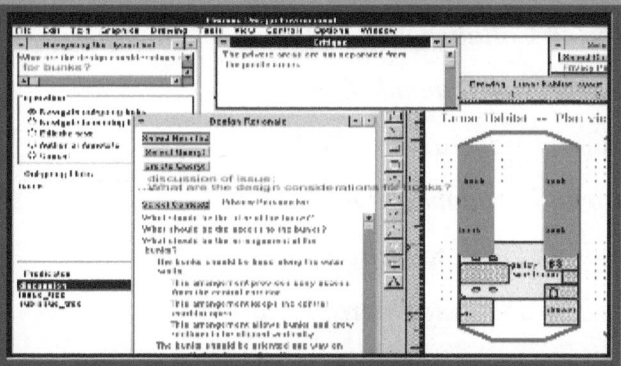

Gerry Stahl

Gerry Stahl's Assembled Texts

- *Marx and Heidegger*
- *Tacit and Explicit Understanding in Computer Support*
- *Group Cognition: Computer Support for Building Collaborative Knowledge*
- *Studying Virtual Math Teams*
- *Translating Euclid: Designing a Human-Centered Mathematics.*
- *Constructing Dynamic Triangles Together: The Development of Mathematical Group Cognition*
- *Essays in Social Philosophy*
- *Essays in Personalizable Software*
- *Essays in Computer-Supported Collaborative Learning*
- *Essays in Group-Cognitive Science*
- *Essays in Philosophy of Group Cognition*
- *Essays in Online Mathematics Interaction*
- *Essays in Collaborative Dynamic Geometry*
- *Adventures in Dynamic Geometry*
- *Global Introduction to CSCL*
- *Editorial Introductions to ijCSCL*
- *Proposals for Research*
- *Overview and Autobiographical Essays*
- *Theoretical Investigations*
- *Works of 3-D Form*

Gerry Stahl's assembled texts volume #1

Tacit & Explicit Understanding in Computer Support

Gerry Stahl

Gerry Stahl

Gerry@GerryStahl.net

www.GerryStahl.net

ISBN 978-1-329-85858-9 (ebook)

ISBN 978-0-557-69380-1 (paperback)

Note

This volume contains the doctoral dissertation of Gerry Stahl in Computer Science at the University of Colorado at Boulder. It was entitled: *"Interpretation in Design: The Problem of Tacit and Explicit Understanding in Computer Support of Cooperative Design"* and was defended on August 5, 1993.

The dissertation explored the implications of the theory of tacit knowledge for the problem of computer capture of design rationale. It discussed a software system for design by teams of NASA designers. The computer environment captured design ideas in a flexible system of professional perspectives. This research led to explorations after graduation in prototyping collaboration software incorporating mechanisms to support perspectives and negotiation.

INTERPRETATION IN DESIGN:
THE PROBLEM OF
TACIT AND EXPLICIT UNDERSTANDING
IN COMPUTER SUPPORT OF COOPERATIVE DESIGN

by
GERRY STAHL

B.S., Massachusetts Institute of Technology, 1967

University of Heidelberg, Germany, 1968

M.A., Northwestern University, 1971

University of Frankfurt, Germany, 1973

Ph.D., Northwestern University, 1975

M.S., University of Colorado, 1990

A thesis submitted to the
Faculty of the Graduate School of the
University of Colorado in partial fulfillment
of the requirement for the degree of
Doctor of Philosophy
Department of Computer Science
1993

This dissertation for the Doctor of Philosophy degree by

Gerry Stahl

has been approved for the

Department of

Computer Science

by

_____

Gerhard Fischer

_____

Raymond J. McCall, Jr.

Date: August 5, 1993

Dissertation Committee:

Gerhard Fischer,	Computer Science	(co-chair)
Raymond McCall,	Environmental Design	(co-chair)
Clayton Lewis	Computer Science	
Mark Gross	Environmental Design	
Michael Eisenberg	Computer Science	
Wayne Citrin	Electrical and Computer Engineering	

Stahl, Gerry (Ph.D., Computer Science)

INTERPRETATION IN DESIGN:

THE PROBLEM OF TACIT AND EXPLICIT UNDERSTANDING

IN COMPUTER SUPPORT OF COOPERATIVE DESIGN

Thesis directed by Professors Gerhard Fischer and Raymond McCall

Abstract

This work analyzes the central role of interpretation in non-routine design. Based on this analysis, a theory of computer support for interpretation in cooperative design is constructed. The theory is grounded in studies of design and interpretation. It is illustrated by mechanisms provided by a software substrate for computer-based design environments, applied to a sample task of lunar habitat design.

Computer support of innovative design must overcome the problem that designers necessarily make extensive use of situated tacit understanding while computers can only store and display explicit representations of information. The automation techniques used for routine design are not applicable: techniques are needed to support creative, tacit human understanding with explicit computer representations.

The process by which designers transform their tacit preunderstanding into explicit knowledge is termed "interpretation". Interpretation is necessary for solving design problems and collaborating with other designers. Considerable explicit knowledge is thereby generated in the natural course of designing. Often this knowledge includes the most valuable information that can be presented to designers who revisit these design projects or undertake similar projects in the future. If representations of this knowledge have been defined using computer-based design support systems, then the representations can be captured by these systems for the support of subsequent design work.

A theory of computer support for interpretation in design is presented in three stages. First, the role of interpretation in design is explored by reviewing descriptions of design by Alexander, Rittel, and Schön; by conducting a protocol analysis of lunar habitat design; and by applying Heidegger's philosophy of situated interpretation. Second, this analysis of interpretation is extended to define a theory of computer support. The features of this theory—support for the situated, perspectival, and linguistic characteristics of interpretation—are used to evaluate previous work on software design rationale systems. Third, design principles are discussed for HERMES, a prototype hypermedia substrate for building computer-based design environments to support interpretation in tasks like lunar habitat design. The hypermedia integrates a perspectives mechanism and an end-user language to capture and modify representations of the design situation, alternative perspectives on design tasks, and terminology for conceptualizing design issues.

Acknowledgements

The perspective on design methodology and the approach to computer support for design presented here grew out of the research of Raymond McCall of the School of Environmental Design, Gerhard Fischer of the Department of Computer Science, and other members of the Human-Computer Communication (HCC) group at the University of Colorado at Boulder. I have been privileged to work closely with Ray for three years as his graduate research assistant. My HERMES prototype began as a rewrite of his PHIDIAS project, and incorporated much of its approach. Even where my ideas have gone off in new directions, they have been helped along by Ray's unbounded interest and unstinting assistance. For the same three years I have participated in the HCC research group led by Gerhard, particularly the weekly seminars on computers and design. Gerhard guided me from vague interests in theoretical issues to a coherent view and a concrete dissertation project, using his characteristic style that provides a model of non-directive critiquing at its most effective.

Clayton Lewis' courses on AI and interface design raised many of the concerns I have tried to address in my dissertation. The HERMES language benefited not only from Clayton's programming language evaluation methodology, but more from his personal perceptive analysis. Michael Eisenberg also contributed to my understanding of the language, bringing his understanding of (and support for) the role of languages in programmable applications. Each member of my committee contributed his own strong perspective to my work. However, I was able to rely on Mark Gross for balanced reality checks. Mark placed each draft I gave him in the broader view of AI and design practice, and wondered in a friendly but insistent way what these esoteric notions really had to do with making better habitats. Although I have tried to address many concerns of my professors and fellow graduate students, I have used Mark to represent my target audience: skeptical but informed and interested. Wayne Citrin played a similar role as reader of this dissertation.

While individual professors had specific effects on my work, the most pervasive influence was that of the HCC research group as a whole, which included about twenty graduate students during my stay. They built the systems, gave the presentations, and made fun of my ideas. A series of student reading groups on situated cognition was particularly important in helping me start to grapple with the ideas of Schön, Suchman, Winograd, Ehn, and Dreyfus. Research groups like this where people's very different perspectives are brought together under the constraints of shared work and common vocabularies exert pervasive influences that are impossible to acknowledge in detail. Nevertheless, I must single out my beta-testers, Tamara Sumner, Jonathan Ostwald, and Kumiyo Nakakoji, who relentlessly critiqued drafts of every chapter. Many of the ideas and formulations in the dissertation arose during reviews of those drafts with them and with Ray McCall. Special note should also be made of the dissertation work of Brent Reeves, Kumiyo Nakakoji, and Frank Shipman, which is closely related to the themes of this dissertation.

Implicit in this dissertation is the question about the relationship of AI to philosophy, which has intrigued me since my undergraduate days at MIT. In 1966 I attended a debate between my teachers, Marvin Minsky and Herbert Dreyfus. Convinced by Dreyfus' arguments that the approaches of AI were fundamentally flawed, I wondered what an AI based on Heidegger's philosophy would be like. What I am proposing now is a partial answer to that question, although one quite different from anything I could have imagined 25 years ago. For my understanding of Heidegger and hermeneutics I am indebted to Sam Todes, Ted Kiesel, Hans-Georg Gadamer, and members of the Frankfurt School of critical social theory.

Writing a dissertation is part of living a life. Accordingly, this dissertation owes its existence to Carol Bliss, my wife, without whom I would never have moved West to pursue this study. She both tolerated my long hours at the computer and enriched the remaining times.

Johnson Engineering (JE) of Boulder contributed generously the time and expertise of Designer Mike Pogue and Vice President John Ciciora. They provided the primary source of information about lunar habitat design, its needs, and its methods.

The research in providing computer support for the task of lunar habitat design was supported in part by grants to Ray McCall from the Colorado Advanced Software Institute (CASI) for 1990-91, 1991-92, and 1992-93 in collaboration with IBM and JE. CASI is sponsored in part by the Colorado Advanced Technology Institute (CATI), an agency of the State of Colorado.

CATI promotes advanced technology education and research at universities in Colorado for the purpose of economic development.

Material from the following chapters has been previously published in different formats: Chapter 1 (Stahl, 1993a), Chapter 8 (Stahl, 1993b), Chapter 9 (Fischer, et al., 1993a, 1993b), Chapter 10 (Stahl, et al., 1992)

Contents

Introduction

"Not angels, not humans,

and already the knowing animals are aware

that we are not really at home in

our interpreted world."

> Rainer Maria Rilke
>
> *Duino Elegies*
>
> (1912, p.10)

A few words from the author's perspective may help to orient the reader for the task of interpreting the discussions that follow.

The focus of this dissertation is *interpretation in design*. This theme is motivated by the desire to provide computer support for the work of designers. The initial impetus for thinking about the support of design as the support of an interpretive process came from two sources (one theoretical and one empirical):

(i) I felt that a new theoretical perspective was needed on computer support of professional work, or more broadly human-computer interaction and computer supported cooperative work. The old view that thought was a form of computation—or that mind was functionally equivalent to software—has outlived its usefulness as a theoretical foundation for the design of software. I suspected that ideas from Heidegger's philosophy could help here. Readings of situated cognition theorists reinforced this suspicion.

(ii) After videotaping an initial session of lunar habitat designers at work, I was struck by how involved they were in processes of interpretation. In particular, issues of privacy in the habitat dominated their thinking and they concentrated on working out an interpretation of what privacy meant under lunar mission conditions and what implications that interpretation had for the habitat layout.

These ideas were only tacitly understood by me as I worked on the programming of the HERMES system, a software substrate for design environments to support the work of lunar habitat designers. I would have been hard pressed to state why I thought Heidegger was relevant or how design was a matter of interpretation. Above all, I could not articulate what implications this all had for the HERMES software. When my programming was done, I proceeded to try to put my implicit commitments into words and provide supporting evidence for them. I did this by writing the chapters of this dissertation, basically in their current order:

Chapter 1. Because HERMES was actually programmed before the issues about supporting interpretation were explicitly clear to me, the writing of the dissertation as a process of articulating my formerly tacit understandings in language has been a journey of gradual discovery. The HERMES system has served in this journey as an artifact to stimulate interpretation. The resultant dissertation is, to a large extent, a research document, sharing with the reader a contact with the raw phenomena that make its claims understandable. To some extent, I have attempted retrospectively to impose an argumentative structure on the text. So, for instance, Chapter 1 provides a road map through the other chapters, so the reader has a clearer sense of where the journey is going than the author originally did. Undoubtedly, I have failed to provide sufficient direction to make the long journey comfortable. I rationalize this by reminding myself that in order to accept new ideas each reader must have some contact with the phenomena themselves (hence the level of detail and proliferation of quotations), and that each reader will construct his or her own conclusions from the material I have offered (hence the lack of parsimony with respect to related thoughts and side paths).

Chapter 2. I turned first to three writers who I felt shed the most insight into *the nature of the design process*. As I tried to pinpoint their central ideas I was struck by the correspondence between these ideas and the three features of preunderstanding in Heidegger's theory. While Alexander, Rittel, and Schön discussed these three features in very different ways, they each paid special attention to one of them, and discussed the other two secondarily. I decided that these three writers could be taken as spokespeople for the three features of preunderstanding: its (a) *situated*, (b) *perspectival*, and (c) *linguistic* characteristics.

Chapter 3. In turning to the *videotapes of the lunar habitat designers*, I focused on a pivotal passage in which the direction of the rest of the designing was determined. Here the three features of interpretation could be seen at work: The designers were trying to design a *situation* for astronauts to live in where there would be a comfortable balance of private and public space. The emphasis on privacy defined a forceful *perspective* that determined their design work. Lengthy discussions among the designers articulated in *language* their tacit understandings of privacy and raised the question of how such understandings could be represented in design guidelines, including NASA's design standards.

Chapter 4. Heidegger's philosophy provided an *analysis of interpretation* that clarified many of the issues raised by the design methodologists and the video protocol analysis. It also offered a basis for a theory of computer support. *For Heidegger, interpretation is the process of transforming tacit preunderstanding into progressively more explicit forms*. In this process, the understanding is significantly altered; for instance, surprise discoveries may be made and the interpretive framework may require revision. The three features that are already present in tacit preunderstanding are each carried along and transformed in the more explicit forms of understanding: The *situation* is the tacitly preunderstood network of interrelationships, which may need to be revised as interpretation proceeds and discoveries are made that do not fit in. Interpretation always focuses on something as viewed from a particular *perspective*. As understanding becomes increasingly explicit, it can be communicated in *language*.

Chapter 5. *Applying Heidegger's analysis* of being-in-the-world to the imaginative realm of design clarified the structure of the successive transformations of understanding that Heidegger eludes to. Like a designed artifact, reality is socially constructed. Human intentionality *grounds* the interpretive construction of reality in tacit preunderstanding. *Transformations* of initially tacit preunderstandings can eventually be explicated and formalized so that knowledge can be reflected upon, communicated, documented, and stored in computer representations.

Chapter 6. Building on this analysis of interpretation in design, I sketched my *theory of computer support*. I argued that Heidegger provides theoretical grounds for requiring that computer systems for innovative tasks (like lunar habitat design) be subservient supports for the people who use them and who must make the critical decisions and judgments based on intentionality and understanding that computers cannot have. Such systems to support interpretation should support the three features of understanding discussed above: representing the situation, offering choices of perspectives, and providing linguistic expressions. Of course, software design environments could provide many other features, but these are the ones I focused on as illustrative of a *people-centered approach* to *supporting interpretation in design*. I extended the model of successive transformations of understanding to include a *model of computer support* for this process of interpretation.

Chapter 7. Previous software systems have suggested how to support particular points along the continuum between tacit and explicit understanding. At the other extreme, domain-oriented design environments provide direct manipulation representations of the tacit situation. Domain-independent design rationale systems propose explicit systems of perspectives, query languages, or explicit programming languages. Each of these ideas from *related work* have had their influence on the HERMES system. But none of them have tried to support *interpretation* in design in a theoretically motivated way. I explored a number of suggestions in the literature for providing *external media for designers* to work in, several *mechanisms for perspectives* to organize viewpoints, and some *end-user language* approaches. These led to ideas for ways HERMES could provide a proper mix of support for tacit and explicit understanding, and for the transformation of one into the other.

Chapter 8. Three key features of HERMES are discussed in the dissertation. They correspond to the features of human interpretation, which they are intended to support. (a) The hypermedia structure provides an *integrated knowledge representation* structure that incorporates (b) a perspectives mechanism and (c) expressions in an end-user language. It is intended to support tacit understanding of a design situation by representing that situation with multimedia elements that can be tacitly reused and modified. To the extent necessary, a designer using the system can make the representation structure more explicit in order to modify it to meet the needs of innovation. The hypermedia substrate provides functionality for a *computationally active medium*, on which *design environments can be built* for tasks like lunar habitat design.

Chapter 9. Design is generally a cooperative endeavor, involving the deliberation of multiple individual design perspectives and the construction of a shared perspective. HERMES supports this by organizing all knowledge in the system with a *hierarchy of perspectives*. While a designer is working, all knowledge retrieval and display by the system is done within a selected perspective, without the designer needing to be aware of this filtering of knowledge. However, designers can also use the perspective mechanism explicitly in order to incorporate knowledge from other perspectives or to create new perspectives that inherit information from existing ones. I described a *scenario* of how designers using HERMES could capture the knowledge that arose in the videotaped design session. The scenario included creation and merging of perspectives to support the *evolution* of knowledge. A discussion of the scenario presents the details of the *hypermedia implementation of perspectives*.

Chapter 10. *The HERMES language* supports tacit expression by providing a vocabulary of domain-oriented terminology that can be reused without concern for the (potentially quite complex) underlying definitions. At the same time, the interface to the language allows a designer to explore the definitions of particular terms and modify them in accordance with innovative needs, personal perspectives, or collaborative agreements. While the HERMES language serves as a programming language for communicating algorithmic definitions to the computer, many of the concerns that programmers must keep explicitly in mind when using conventional general-purpose programming languages are *encapsulated in tacit forms* and implicitly taken care of by the HERMES language. To test the power of the language, I worked out the definition of complex *interpretive critics for privacy issues* in detail.

Chapter 11. What has been accomplished here? I set out to define a new theoretical perspective for the computer support of professional work, taking lunar habitat design as my concrete example. I proceeded by trying to rethink recent attempts that were around me, notably the PHIDIAS and JANUS design environments developed at the University of Colorado. First, I programmed my own design environment substrate in order to work out implementation details for myself. Then I studied the design methodologists and situated cognitionists who had influenced the development of these systems. I also took time to familiarize myself with a particular design domain, that of lunar habitat design. Guided by Heidegger's analysis of interpretation, I tried to question as radically as I could the rationale given for the approach of PHIDIAS and JANUS. The theory of computer support I arrived at is, however, not so different. I concluded that the general approach of those systems was consistent with my theory.

What I feel I have achieved is not a recipe for a new kind of software, but a more carefully articulated way of thinking about the design of software for innovative, collaborative design as epitomized by lunar habitat design. Previous rationale for design environments did not explicitly recognize the centrality of interpretation in human-computer interaction or analyze the transformations from tacit human understanding to explicit computer representations. Not only does this dissertation work out these themes and their related issues in considerable detail, but it also provides technical descriptions of software mechanisms that extend previous design environment techniques in order to support interpretation in design.

CHAPTER 1. OVERVIEW

The following chapters present a *theory of computer support for innovative (non-routine), cooperative design* based on an *analysis of interpretation in design*. They will argue that the central impediment to computer support of innovative design is that designers make extensive use of *situated tacit understanding* while computers can only store and display *explicit representations of information*.

The process by which designers transform their tacit preunderstanding into explicit knowledge is termed *interpretation*. (See Part I for an analysis of interpretation in design.) Interpretation is central to the process of solving design problems and is part of the process of collaborating with other designers; the explicit knowledge that is generated by this interpretation is therefore a natural by-product of innovative, cooperative design. (See Part II for a theory of computer support based on this generated knowledge.) Representations of this knowledge defined using computer-based design support systems can be captured by these systems for the support of subsequent design work, including the maintenance and modification of the designed artifacts. (See Part III for details of a computer system for supporting interpretation in design.)

Chapter 1 provides a chapter-by-chapter overview of the dissertation. It discusses the claims, arguments, and themes that arise in each of the subsequent chapters, without going into the detail necessary to defend the claims, support the arguments, or work out the themes. Its purpose is to provide a readers' guide to the flow of the dissertation, motivating how one discussion leads into or provides the background for another. Section 1.1 offers a preliminary presentation of the central concept of interpretation, anticipating the analysis of this concept from various approaches in the dissertation. Each of the other sections provides an overview of a specific chapter.

1.1. Understanding Interpretation

To say that interpretation is central to innovative design is to stress that in order to design the designer must to some degree understand and be able to articulate the significance of the artifact being designed. This may include, for instance, understanding what is desired in a task specification, how possible composite parts of the artifact will function and interact, or how people can use the designed artifact. According to the analysis presented below, such understanding is possible for people but not for computers. People understand things because they are actively involved with them in the world. The significance of artifacts for a person is determined by the artifacts' relationships to other artifacts, activities, and people whose significance is already understood as part of the person's situation. Understanding combines personal and socially shared perspectives on the world. All of this takes place primarily in *tacit* ways, i.e., unverbalized. However, one's tacit understanding of something can be partially articulated or expressed *explicitly* in spoken, written, or graphical language—either to deepen one's own understanding or to communicate with others.

Two aspects of the process of interpretation can be distinguished.

(1) There is a tacit *preunderstanding* based on previous background knowledge; items from this preunderstanding can be articulated explicitly.

(2) There is the possibility of revising that preunderstanding based on *discoveries* that are opened up by it.

That is, one can interpret something *as* something that one already knows about, or *as* a variation that differs from that in ways that are discovered as a result of the breaking of one's tacit expectations. Accordingly, interpretation in innovative design involves both human understanding of extensive background and a creative ability to revise one's understandings iteratively.

The analysis of interpretation developed below distinguishes three characteristics of interpretation: being situated, having a perspective, and using language.[1]

---

[1] Note that the numbering scheme of 1, 2 and a, b, c is used consistently in this chapter as an organizing structure for the dissertation. It indicates correspondences among items listed; in particular, it indexes the way in which computer support features correspond to the characteristics of interpretation. Subsequent chapters are also organized around discussions of these characteristics and features, as emphasized in this Overview. Frequently, the numbering system is dropped and key terms are *italicized* as reminders that the discussion is focusing on (1) preunderstanding and (2) discovery, or on the (a) situated, (b) perspectival, and (c) linguistic character of understanding.

(a) *Being situated* means that what is to be interpreted is tacitly understood by virtue of its associations within an open-ended network of related artifacts, people, human purposes, and other concerns. All of these associations are themselves understood as part of one's background understanding of one's involvements.

(b) *Having a perspective* means that there is a focus on a certain aspect or that a specific approach is taken in interpreting something.

(c) *Using language* means that a particular vocabulary is available as part of a tradition that provides a conceptual framework for the interpretive task.

Each of these characteristics of interpretation is grounded in a form of preunderstanding that can be transformed through a corresponding phase of discovery. This two-dimensional structure is presented in Table 1-1.

Table 1-1. The structure of human interpretation.

	(a) situated	(b) perspectival	(c) linguistic
(1)pre-understanding	expectations	focus	conceptualization
(2) discovery	surprises	deliberations	refinements

In articulating tacit understanding, interpretation both discloses inherent implications and discovers unanticipated consequences in the situation. Through interpretation, designers might (a) try to externalize their expectations about a design situation by drawing a sketch and then discover surprises when they explore the sketch. Similarly, they might need to revise their understanding as a result of (b) shifting their focus on a problem and deliberating from alternative perspectives or (c) changing the way they conceptualize an issue and refining the definitions of terms in their language.

The structure of human interpretation carries over to design. The design process is a cycle or spiral of interpretation: (1) some item of the initial preunderstanding—the grasp of the design situation, the perspective for viewing, the language for conceptualizing—is made explicit, reflected upon, and further articulated in new design decisions. (2) This leads to the discovery of unanticipated consequences or contingencies and a new understanding that requires revisions to the understanding of the design problem, its viewpoint, or terminology. (1′) The new understanding then becomes re-submerged into a modified tacit understanding that forms the starting-point for the next iteration of interpretation and design.

The analysis of interpretation in design motivates a theory of computer support. According to this theory, computer support for interpretation in innovative design differs from autonomous software systems for routine design by focusing on supporting or augmenting human activities rather than automating them, because only people have the understanding and creativity required for interpretation. This computer support takes two general forms in order to support the two phases of interpretation:

1. It provides access to a wealth of information that might be useful as a basis for interpreting new design tasks. This information for *reuse* is culled primarily from previous design experience, and includes (a) partial representations[2] of design situations, (b) alternative ways of considering tasks, and (c) terminology helpful for conceptualizing problems.

2. It facilitates the revision of stored information so designers can tailor existing representations to novel problems and can capture innovative designs to extend the computerized knowledge-base and to communicate ideas to collaborators. This *plasticity* of representation— the ability to mold, form, adapt, alter, or modify the representations— applies to all design knowledge, including (a), (b), and (c) of point (1).

The proposed theory of computer support suggests an approach to building software systems that has been prototyped in a system named HERMES. HERMES is a substrate for building design environments to support interpretation in innovative design. Motivated by the analysis of interpretation, HERMES provides the following features to support reuse and plasticity of representations of each of the three characteristics of interpretation, being situated, having perspectives, and using language (see Table 1-2):

---

[2] Note that the computer manipulates symbolic *representations* of things in the situation, whereas the designer has a situated *understanding* of the things. According to Heidegger's philosophy, representations are explicit forms of information that only arise under certain conditions and on the basis of people's normally tacit understanding of things within the context of meaningful involvements. In Chapter 4, the *situation* is defined as this context of meaningful involvements, which provides a precondition for meaningful representations.

a-1. A persistent hypermedia network for storing partial representations of design situations and for browsing among them.

a-2. Efficient mechanisms for revising the representations (multimedia nodes) and modifying their associations (links).

b-1. A perspectives mechanism that organizes specialized or personal ways of filtering out information of interest

b-2. Procedures for switching perspectives or for creating new ones by merging existing perspectives and modifying their inherited contents in the new one.

c-1. An end-user language that provides useful domain terms, rules for critiquing designs, and queries for displaying stored information.

c-2. The ability to modify or generate new terms, critic rules, and queries or to use the language for defining computations.

Table 1-2. Computer-based mechanisms to support interpretation in design.

	(a) situated	(b) perspectival	(c) linguistic
(1) reuse	hypermedia network	perspectives mechanism	end-user language
(2) plasticity	revising representations	merging multiple perspectives	defining new expressions

Although computers cannot understand things the way people do, they can serve as a computational medium to support people's interpretive processes. The computer support mechanisms listed in Table 1-2 can augment cooperative design in a number of ways, including:

a-1 As a long-term memory or repository for information that was created in past designing and is now available to be shared by designers using the repository.

a-2 As an external memory for representing and revising designs to see how alternative variations appear.

b-1 As a retrieval mechanism for organizing and managing design knowledge and filtering through just what is relevant.

b-2 As a display mechanism to define new personal and shared views of designs.

c-1 As a linguistic medium for expressing knowledge in a canonical form that can be used for computations by the software.

c-2 As a communication medium to generate new knowledge to be shared with others.

A comparison of Table 1-1 and Table 1-2 shows that *the mechanisms of computer support are based on the structure of unaided human interpretation.* The computer support is intended to extend the power of designers to operate under conditions of "information overload," in which it is becoming increasingly difficult to work effectively without the use of computers.

Computer support will inevitably change the practices of collaborative design. This need not be considered harmful—particularly in cases where traditional procedures have become inadequate—if important factors like the characteristics of interpretation are preserved and adequately supported. Computational media have the potential for changing the activities of professionals even more than the media of written language did in the past, because of significant opportunities for the computer to play a computationally active role in organizing, analyzing, displaying, and communicating the information. The ways in which design tasks are accomplished will change dramatically as the computer augments and supports designers to do many of the same tasks they have done unaided in the past, like designing and modifying artifacts.

The proposed theory of computer support for interpretation in design goes to the root of the problem of tacit and explicit understanding. Designers approach their task with a background of skills, know-how, and experience that they are generally not aware of as they design but that is a necessary precondition of their work as trained professionals. For instance, architects have the ability to understand the situations people might face in the buildings they design, they know how to sketch and visualize relationships from the perspectives of different concerns, and they move freely between various frameworks or traditions that provide meaningful languages or metaphors for expressing their insights. Computers have no such tacit preunderstanding; they can only retrieve and manipulate what people have already formulated in explicit propositions or drawings. People and computers are not analogous processors of information. If computers are to support human cognition effectively, then these differences must be understood and taken into account.

By describing the transformation of tacit to explicit human understanding, the *analysis of interpretation* not only clarifies how human cognition differs from computer information processing, but also suggests how computers can support the way people think. Philosophically, the analysis of interpretation provides the key to a theory of people-centered computer support. Technically, the analysis enumerates the functionality needed for computer support of interpretation in design. Practically, it points out that the process of innovative design and the requirements of collaboration generate both the need for computer support and the sources of explicit knowledge that make it possible. For instance, large, multi-person design projects often confront the problem of information overload, where computers are required to manage volumes of technical knowledge. At the same time, these cooperative design processes naturally articulate much explicit knowledge that could prove useful in subsequent computer-supported design work.

The theory of computer support for interpretation in design is presented in three Parts: in Part I, Chapters 2, 3, and 4 develop the analysis of interpretation in design. In Part II, Chapters 5, 6, and 7 draw the consequences of the problem of tacit and explicit understanding for computer support. In Part III, Chapters 8, 9, and 10 describe how the technical features of the HERMES substrate support interpretation in collaborative design.

The analysis of interpretation is developed by reviewing insightful descriptions of design by design methodologists Alexander, Rittel, and Schön (Chapter 2). Characteristics of design enumerated in that review are then used to guide a study of transcripts of a design session involving a task of lunar habitat design (Chapter 3). The design process—as characterized by design methodology and as illustrated with lunar habitat design—is then conceptualized as a process of interpretation by using Heidegger's philosophy of interpretation (Chapter 4).

The consequences for computer-based design systems are drawn by further developing the analysis of tacit and explicit understanding in design (Chapter 5), and extending it to include a theory of the computer support of interpretation (Chapter 6). This theory is applied to evaluate traditions of software design environments and design rationale systems; useful techniques in these previous systems are explored and their limitations noted (Chapter 7).

The technical description of computer support for cooperative design describes the central functionality of HERMES. It has a hypermedia knowledge-base to support (a) the representation of design situations (Chapter 8). A virtual copying mechanism provides (b) perspectives on design knowledge (Chapter 9). An end-user language is used for (c) articulating formerly tacit understandings in explicit language (Chapter 10)

The order of presentation in the dissertation corresponds to the process of interpretation. First, in the Introduction and Part I a *preunderstanding* is sketched to provide a starting point for interpreting the problem of computer support for innovative design. A review of design methodology provides a *perspective* from which to understand design, formed by merging the perspectives of the three design methodologists. A lunar habitat design project provides a concrete design *situation* for grounding the developing understanding of design. Heidegger's philosophy provides a *language* and conceptual framework for talking about interpretation in design. Second, in Part II this preunderstanding is used to explore possibilities for computer support that are opened up by the preunderstanding. This is accomplished partially by drawing out the theoretical consequences in order to extend the analysis of interpretation in design to include a theory of its computer support. It is further accomplished by discovering the achievements and the limitations of previous software systems in providing the kind of support for design that is called for. Third, in Part III the arrived at understanding allows for a discussion of the HERMES system as an explicit illustration of possible responses to the problem of supporting interpretation in design .

Predecessor systems to HERMES (principally JANUS and PHIDIAS) were already headed in the direction that HERMES adopts. Discussions of these earlier design environments made frequent reference to Alexander, Rittel, and Schön, for instance, and insisted on supporting rather than automating design. The theory of computer support for interpretation in design presented in this dissertation extends this approach theoretically and practically. Its focus on interpretation *situates* its people-centered approach unambiguously in an analysis of human understanding. By providing a coherent *perspective* for viewing systems to support design, the theory suggests principled extensions to the functionality of design environments, such as those incorporated in the HERMES substrate. It provides an explicit *language* as a basis for a coherent conceptual framework.

Table 1-3. Correspondences among the chapters.
Note that the three mechanisms of HERMES *in Chapters 8, 9, and 10 correspond to the three characteristics of interpretation that permeate and structure the dissertation.*

Chapter	Theme	(a)	(b)	(c)
1	interpretation	situated	perspectival	linguistic
2	methodology	Alexander	Rittel	Schön
3	lunar habitat	privacy conflict	privacy concern	privacy gradient
4	preunderstanding	prepossession	preview	preconception
5, 6	computer support	represent situation	have perspectives	make use of language
7	previous systems	JANUS	PIE	PHIDIAS
8, 9, 10	HERMES software substrate	hypermedia network	perspectives mechanism	end-user language

Each section in the remainder of Chapter 1 provides an overview of a chapter of the dissertation. The first three sections each provide an argument for interpreting design as a process of interpretation. The other sections draw the implications of this argument for the computer support of design. The three characteristics of interpretation run through all the chapters. Table 1-3 shows the correspondences between the central themes in the different chapters. *These correspondences link the theoretical analysis of interpretation to the operational mechanisms that provide computer support for these characteristics.* For the sake of simplicity, the table does not indicate that each of the entries involves both reuse of past information and creative modification, however this is true both for the three characteristics of interpretation and for their corresponding software mechanisms, as already shown in Tables 1-1 and 1-2.

1.2. The Methodology of Design

A central claim of this dissertation is that design can be viewed as fundamentally a process of interpretation. In this interpretive process, elements of the designer's tacit background preunderstanding are made explicit. The first evidence in support of this claim is a review of the writings of three influential design methodologists. It is argued that their diverse but complementary descriptions of the design process highlight characteristics of what is here called interpretation. They recognize the importance of both tacit understanding and explicit representations, as well as the iterative movement between them. Among the three writers, the dimensions of (a) the situation, (b) perspectives, and (c) language are all stressed. Furthermore, each of these dimensions is recognized to entail both (1) traditions of past knowledge to start from and (2) an ability to revise that knowledge to promote and grasp innovation.

Alexander (1964) pioneered the use of computers for designing. He used them to compute diagrams or patterns that decomposed the structural dependencies of a given problem into relatively independent substructures. In this way, he developed *understandings of the design situation* for solving a task based on an analysis of the unique design situation.

Later, Alexander (1977) assembled 253 patterns that he considered useful for architectural design, based on an extensive study of successful past designs. These patterns were to be *reused* and *modified* to form personal pattern languages for expressing the individual perspectives of different designers. They were schematic enough to be adapted to a broad range of specific design situations.

Alexander felt that the design profession necessarily made *explicit* the understanding that was "unselfconscious" in traditional cultures in which everyone designed their own artifacts. His structures and patterns were meant to be tools for explicitly representing design situations for "self-conscious" design. However, he always also recognized the need for *tacit* or intuitive understanding as a basis for good design.

For Rittel (1973), the heart of design was the deliberation of issues from *multiple perspectives*. In a collaborative effort, each participant may bring different personal interests, value systems, and political commitments to the task. Also, people with different technical specialties or professional skills may contribute to a design. These are actually different kinds of "perspectives." The theory of computer support in Chapter 6 distinguishes three classes of perspectives that need to be supported:

*   personal or group perspectives

*   technical specialties (e.g., plumbing)

*   domain traditions (e.g., residential kitchens)

However, they all provide the same function of determining what issues will be addressed, what alternatives will be considered, and what criteria will be applied. Because they all determine the organization or relevance of information in a similar way, they can be discussed as one kind of determinant of interpretation and can be operationalized and supported with one software mechanism (a perspectives mechanism).

The important thing for Rittel was not the subjective character of interpretation deriving from its basis in personal perspectives, but the way in which deliberation among perspectives can lead to innovative solutions that would not have arisen without such interaction. Deliberation is an interpretive process in which understanding of the problem situation and of the design solution emerges gradually as a product of iterative revisions subject to critical argument from the various perspectives. This can take place for an individual designer as well if the designer consecutively adopts different perspectives on the issues. Rittel foresaw computer support for this. His idea of using computers to keep track of the various issues at stake and alternative positions on those issues led to the creation of issue-based information systems.

Schön (1983) argued that designers constantly shift perspectives on a problem by bringing various professionally trained tacit skills to bear, such as visual perception, graphical sketching, and vicarious simulation. The designer's intuitive appreciations shape the problem by forming a subsidiary background awareness of the design task's patterns, materials, and relationships. By then experimenting with tentative design moves within this tacitly understood situation, the designer discovers consequences and makes aspects of the problem explicit. As this is done, certain features of the situation come into focus and can be named or characterized in a *language*. When focus subsequently shifts, what has been made explicit may slip back into an understanding that is again tacit, but is now more developed.

Schön (1992) provided empirical evidence for the roles of the situation, perspectives for viewing, and conceptual frameworks in the iterative process of interpretation in design. His experiments showed how the designer uses tacit skills and preunderstandings to uncover unanticipated discoveries, to reflect upon them, and to develop new understandings, new perspectives, and new articulations of the evolving design situation.

1.3. The Example of Lunar Habitat Design

A second argument for understanding design as a process of interpretation is presented in Chapter 3. Here, a protocol analysis of designers collaborating shows that most of what went on was interpretation.

As part of the research for this dissertation, a study was undertaken of lunar habitat design. Lunar habitat design is a task that is not well understood compared to many other, more mundane design tasks. It is not a routine matter that can be done according to well-formulated rules or by applying available template solutions. Furthermore, it is representative of a broad range of high-tech design tasks. Such tasks typically involve extensive technical knowledge. They seem to call for computer support.

The volume of information available to people is increasing rapidly. For many professionals this "information overload" means that the execution of their jobs requires taking into account far more information than they can possibly keep in mind. The lunar habitat designers here provide a prime illustration of such professionals. In working on their high-tech design tasks, they must take into account architectural knowledge, ergonomics, space science, NASA regulations, and lessons learned in past lunar missions. These designers turn to computers for help with their complex, technical problems. That is why a group of lunar habitat designers initiated the software development effort that led to this dissertation.

Providing the computer support needed by lunar habitat designers is not straight-forward. Designers need to be able to consider wide varieties of experience, professional know-how, technical concerns, and previous solutions that are relevant to their current tasks. However, the problem is not so much one of storing large amounts of information as one of deciding what information to retain that might be relevant to novel future tasks and how to present it to designers in formats that support their mode of work. It is a problem of how to manage the information and present it so that it can usefully serve the design process. The necessary decisions must be made by the designers who are involved with these tasks. Computer techniques for capture and display of information must be under the control of people engaged in the interpretation of the information.

As part of the effort at developing computer support for lunar habitat designers, thirty hours of design sessions were videotaped and analyzed. The designers were asked to design a 23 foot long by 14 foot wide cylindrical habitat to accommodate four astronauts for 45 days on the moon. A protocol analysis of segments of the video recording was conducted.

The analysis of the videotape of the designers' activities shows that design time is dominated by processes of interpretation, i.e., the explication of previously tacit knowledge in response to *discoveries* of surprises. As part of the interpreting by the designers, graphical representations were developed for describing pivotal features of the design *situation* that had not been included in the original specification; *perspectives* were created for looking at the task in different ways; and *language* terminology was defined for explicitly naming, describing, and communicating formerly tacit understandings. The definitions of the situated understanding, perspectives, and language continually evolved as part of the design process in an effort to achieve an adequate understanding of the design task and the evolving artifact.

The nature of interpretation and the three dimensions of preunderstanding are illustrated in Chapter 3 with an example from the lunar habitat design sessions. This designing primarily consisted of sketching and discussion that explicated visual and conceptual expressions used for understanding, explaining, and guiding the emerging design. The example analyzed has to do with the tacit notion of privacy and a default perspective on bathroom design related to this notion. The following paragraph briefly summarizes the example.

The designers felt that a careful balance of public and private space would be essential given the long-term isolation in the habitat. This is an important concern that receives limited treatment in official NASA design guidelines. An early design decision proposed that there be private crew compartments for each astronaut. An initial sketch revealed problems with adjacencies of public and private areas, leading to an interpretation of privacy as determining a "gradient" along the habitat from quiet sleep quarters to a public activity area. In the process, the conventional American idea of a bathroom was subjected to critical reflection when it was realized that the placement of the toilet and that of the shower were subject to different sets of constraints based on life in the habitat. The tacit American assumption of the location of the toilet and shower together was made explicit by comparing it to alternative European perspectives. The revised conception permitting a separation of the toilet from the shower facilitated a major design reorganization.

In this way, a traditional conception of "private space" as a place for one person to get away was made explicit and explored within graphical representations of the design situation. As part of the designing process, this concept was revised into a notion of "degrees of privacy", which facilitated the design process. The failure of the NASA guidelines to provide significant guidance despite a clear recognition by NASA of the importance of habitability and privacy considerations raises the problem of how to represent effectively notions like privacy that are ordinarily tacit. This problem provides the central test case for this dissertation. In Chapter 9, a scenario shows how designers using HERMES can define interpretive critics to evaluate the distribution of public and private spaces in a lunar habitat. A detailed analysis of how these critics are defined in the HERMES language is then presented in Chapter 10.

In this and other examples, the designers needed to revise their representations to enhance their understanding of the problem situation. They went from looking at privacy as a matter of individual space to reconceptualizing the whole interior space as a continuum of private to public areas. The conventional American notion of a bathroom was compared with other cultural models and broken down into separable functions that related differently to habitat usage patterns. The new views resulted from argumentative discussions motivated by design constraints— primarily spatial limitations and psychological factors of confinement. In these discussions, various perspectives were applied to the problem, suggesting new possibilities and considerations. Through discussion, the individual perspectives merged and novel solutions emerged. In the process, previously tacit features of the design became explicit by being named and described in the language that developed. For instance, the fact that quiet activities were being grouped toward one end of the habitat design and interactive ones at the other became a topic of conversation at one point and the terminology of a "privacy gradient" was proposed to clarify this emergent pattern.

1.4. The Analysis of Situated Interpretation

Chapter 4 presents a third argument for focusing on interpretation in design: computer support of innovative design should be based primarily on an analysis of human understanding. As Norman (1993) puts it, "Without someone to interpret them, cognitive artifacts [like computer support systems] have no function. That means that if they are to work properly, they must be designed with consideration of the workings of human cognition." The philosophy of interpretation provides just such a consideration.

This contrasts with many previous approaches to computerization of design and to artificial intelligence, which lean toward theories on the natural science model (e.g., mathematical physics), like information theory and predicate logic formalisms. Human sciences (e.g., cultural anthropology or non-behaviorist psychology), however, necessarily center on human interpretation because their subject matter is defined by what people consider to be important and by how people construe things. As one moves from routine design to highly innovative tasks, the distribution of roles in the human-computer relationship shifts more onto the people involved, and it becomes increasingly important to take into account their cognitive functioning.

An initial framework for clarifying the respective roles for computers and people in tasks like lunar habitat design is suggested by theories of *situated cognition*. Several influential recent books[3] argue that human cognition is very different from computer manipulations of formal symbol systems. The differences imply that people need to retain control of the processes of non-routine design because these processes rely heavily upon what might be called situated interpretation. Computers can provide valuable computational, visualization, and external memory aids for the designers by supporting such interpretation in design.

Situated interpretation, as used here, refers to a view of human understanding as taking place within tacit contexts of background skills, human concerns, and linguistic traditions that provide its grounding. Interpretation is not just a function of a disinterested rational mind, but relies on the interpreting person or people being actively involved with the situation, which includes the artifact being interpreted and supplies the basis for that artifact's significance. (See Heidegger's fuller definition of situation below and in Chapter 4.)

Situated cognition theory disputes the prevalent view based on the natural sciences model that all human cognition is based on explicit mental representations such as goals and plans. Winograd and Flores (1986) hold that "experts do not need to have formalized representations in order to act" (p.99). Although manipulation of such representations is often useful, there is a background of preunderstanding that cannot be fully formalized as

---

[3] A series of publications in the last decade has, in effect, defined an approach to cognitive science and to the theory of computer support for design that goes by the name "situated cognition." These include Schön (1983), Winograd & Flores (1986), Suchman (1987), Ehn (1988), and Dreyfus (1991).

explicit symbolic representations subject to rule-governed manipulation. This tacit preunderstanding even underlies people's ability to understand representations when they do make use of them. Suchman (1987) concurs that goals and plans are secondary phenomena in human behavior, usually arising only after action has been initiated: "When situated action becomes in some way problematic, rules and procedures are explicated for purposes of deliberation and the action, which is otherwise neither rule-based nor procedural, is then made accountable to them" (p.54).

This is not to denigrate conceptual reasoning and rational planning. Rather, it is to point out that the manipulation of formal representations alone cannot provide a complete model of human understanding. Rational thought is an advanced form of cognition that distinguishes humans from other life forms. Accordingly, an evolutionary theorist of consciousness like Donald (1991) traces the development of symbolic thought from earlier developmental stages of tacit knowing (e.g., episodic and mimetic memory-based cognition). He shows how these earlier levels persist in rational human thought as the necessary foundation for advanced developments, including language, writing, and computer usage.

Philosophers like Wittgenstein (1953), Polanyi (1962), Searle (1980), and Dreyfus (1991) suggest a variety of reasons why tacit preunderstanding cannot be fully formalized as data for computation. It is too vast: background knowledge includes bodily skills and social practices that result from immense histories of life experience. We are unaware of much of it: these skills and practices are generally transparent to us. It must be tacit to function: the examples of biking, swimming or playing a musical instrument suggest that procedural knowledge at least gets in the way of skilled action if it is explicit. More generally, tacit knowledge is a precondition for explicit knowing: we cannot formulate, understand, or use explicit knowledge except on the basis of necessarily tacit preunderstandings.

The philosophical foundations of situated cognition theory were laid out by Heidegger (1927), the first to point out the role of tacit preunderstanding and to elaborate its implications. For Heidegger, we are always knowledgeably embedded in our world; things of concern in our situations are already meaningful before we engage in explicit cognitive activity. We know how to behave without having to think about it. For instance, an architect designing a lunar habitat knows how to lift a pencil and sketch a line or how to look at a drawing and see the rough relationships of various spaces pictured there. The architect understands what it is to be a designer, to critique a drawing, to imagine being a person walking through the spaces of a floor plan. Such tacit, background skills or preunderstandings of the design situation are necessary prerequisites for being able to design an artifact.

Heidegger defines the *situation* as a person's interpretive context— including the physical surroundings, the available tools, the circumstances surrounding the task at hand, the person's own personal or professional aims, and social or cultural relations. The situation constitutes a network of significance in terms of which each part of the situation is already meaningful. That is, the person has tacit knowledge of the situation as a whole; if something becomes a focus, it is perceived as already understood and its meaning is defined by its relations within the situation. Everything is tacitly understood in its relations to other things and to the whole.

According to situated cognition in contrast to rationalist views, to an architect a rectangular arrangement of lines on a piece of paper is not first perceived as meaningless lines that need defining attributes (to be determined by subsequent rational thought). Rather, given the design situation, it is already understood as (say) a sleep compartment for astronauts. The sleep compartment is implicitly defined as such by the design task, the shared intentions of the design team, the other elements of the design, the availability of tools for revising the drawing, the sense of space conveyed by the design, the prevailing NASA terminology. This network of significance is background knowledge that allows the architect to think about features of the design, to make plans for changes, and to discover problems or opportunities in the evolving design. At any given moment, the background is already tacitly understood and does not need to be an object of rational thought manipulating symbolic representations.

At some point the architect might realize that the sleep compartment is too close to some source of potential noise, like the flushing of the toilet. This physical adjacency would come into focus as an explicit concern against the background of relationships of the preunderstood situation. Whereas a common sense view might claim that the sleep compartment and toilet were already immediately and objectively present, and that therefore their adjacency was always there by logical implication, Heidegger proposes a more complex reality in which things are ordinarily hidden from explicit concern. In various ways, they can become uncovered and discovered, only to re-submerge soon into the background as our focus moves on.

In this way, our knowledge of the world primarily consists neither in mental models that represent reality nor in an unmediated and objective access to objects. Rather, our understanding of things presupposes a tacit preunderstanding of our situation. This is analogous to the view of Kuhn (1962), who argues that scientists' experimental observations presuppose their tacit ability to use their experimental equipment and to apply their frameworks of hypotheses and theory. Only by being already situated in our world can we discover things and construct meaningful representations of them by building upon, explicating, and exploring our tacit preunderstanding. Situated cognition is not a simplistic theory that claims our knowledge lies in our physical environment like words on a sign post: it is a sophisticated philosophy of interpretation.

According to the philosophy of situated interpretation, human understanding develops through interpretive explication involving both (1) preunderstanding and (2) explorative discovery of the situation. In Heidegger's analysis, interpretation provides the path from tacit, uncritical preunderstandings to reflection, refinement, and creativity. The structure of this process of interpretation reflects the inextricable coupling of the interpreter with the situation, i.e., of people with their worlds. One's situation is not reducible to one's preunderstanding of it; it offers untold surprises, which may call for reflection, but which can only be discovered and comprehended thanks to one's preunderstanding. Often, these surprise occasions signal *breakdowns* in a person's skillful, transparent behavior, although one can also make unexpected discoveries in the situation through conversation, exploration, or external events.

A discovery breaks out of the preunderstood situation because it violates or goes beyond the network of tacit meanings that make up the preunderstanding of the situation. To understand what one has discovered, one must explicitly *interpret* it *as* something, as having a certain significance, as somehow fitting into an understood background. Then it can merge into one's comprehension of the meaningful situation and become part of the new background. Interpretation of "something *as* something" requires a reinterpretation of the situated context if the discovery does not fit into the previously understood situation.

For instance, the lunar habitat designers discovered problems in their early sketches (their representations of the design situation) that they interpreted as issues of privacy. Although they had created the sketches themselves, they were completely surprised to *discover* certain conflicts among the functions of adjacent components, like the sleep compartments and the toilet. The discoveries could only occur because of their *situated* understanding represented in the drawings. The designers paused in their sketching to discuss the new issues. First they debated the matter from various *perspectives*: experiences of previous space missions, cultural variations in bathroom designs, technical acoustical considerations. Then they considered alternative conceptions of privacy, gradually developing a shared *vocabulary* that guided their revisions and became part of their interpretation of their task. They reinterpreted their understanding of privacy and articulated their new view using the terminology of a privacy gradient.

These themes of being situated, having perspectives, and using explicit language correspond to the three-fold structure of preunderstanding in Heidegger's philosophy. He articulates the pre-conditions of interpretation as: (a) *pre-possession* of the situation as a network of preunderstood significance; (b) *pre-view* or expectations that things in the world are structured in certain ways; and (c) *pre-conception*, a preliminary language for expressing and communicating. In other words, interpretation never starts from scratch or from an arbitrary assignment of representations, but is an evolving of tentative prejudices and anticipations. (1) One necessarily starts with a preunderstanding that has been handed down from one's past experiences and inherited traditions. (2) The interpretive process allows one to reflect upon this preunderstanding methodically and to refine new meanings, viewpoints, and terminologies for understanding things more appropriately.

The analysis of interpretation based on Heidegger's philosophy stresses the role of tacit preunderstanding as the basis for all understanding. Preunderstanding consists primarily of the characteristics of prepossession, preview, and preconception. It also implicitly incorporates the structure of "something *as* something." Through interpretation, this preunderstanding is articulated. The resultant explicit understanding can be externalized in discourse. This can be taken further through the methodologies of science to codify knowledge. Each stage in this process preserves the original structure of the preunderstanding. It is because of this structure that metaphors, speech acts, and scientific propositions have the structure they do of something *as* something, something *is* some predicate, or something *has* some attribute.

The process of explication through interpretation forms the basis for computer support by transforming tacit understanding into increasingly explicit forms that can eventually be captured in computer-based systems.

1.5. Tacit and Explicit Knowledge in Design

Heidegger's analysis of interpretation must be *applied* to the realm of design before it can be used as the basis for a theory of computer support of design. Three general problems must be considered:

*   First, although his philosophy is presented in a very general way, Heidegger's examples come primarily from people's relations to physical things in the world, rather than to imagined artifacts that they are designing.

*   Second, he stresses that things are always understood on the basis of preunderstandings we already have, which makes it hard to say how innovative design ideas are understood.

*   Third, of course, Heidegger (writing in the mid-1920's) did not address the issue of computer representations as a form of explicit knowledge.

Chapter 5 accomplishes the application of Heidegger's analysis to design in three steps.

*   First, it shows that Heidegger's philosophy can be extended naturally to design.

*   Second, it discusses the problem of application, which addresses the issue of how previously captured knowledge can be adapted to innovative new designs.

*   Third, it spells out a taxonomy of transformations of tacit understanding to explicit knowledge adequate for providing a basis for computer representations of normally tacit design knowledge.

Heidegger's concept of the situation transfers well to design. As the network of relationships in the understood world, the situation corresponds closely to the set of constraints and adjacencies that are of concern in design and that are sometimes even represented explicitly in design documents. Heidegger's definition of interpretation as the explication of tacit understanding, involving discoveries, is also applicable to the process of design, in which relationships are explored and discoveries made. Consideration of interpretation in the design context clarifies how breakdowns in action require repair to the tacit underlying understanding of the situation. Although Heidegger's examples focus on the individual, his recognition of the social dimension and the importance of shared understanding allows his analysis to be extended to design, which is largely collaborative.

Heidegger's philosophy occupies an important position in the twentieth century recognition that reality is socially constructed. People have access to their world (intentionality) because the world is in many ways a human, social creation. Of course, reality also has an immanence which can contradict our expectations and present surprises, just as we can make discoveries in designs of our own creating. The point is that an understanding of the world or of innovative designs requires the situated interpretation of a person: it cannot be reduced to a set of rules or a computer algorithm. The same goes for knowledge, which encapsulates understanding. To apply knowledge from past cases to a new design, one must apply it within a situated, perspectival, linguistic understanding. That means that computer software for designing should be people-centered and should support the situated, perspectival, linguistic character of human understanding.

Chapter 5 defines *tacit* as being expressed without words or speech, and *explicit* as being fully revealed or verbally expressed. It defines a taxonomy of forms of information along the continuum between these extremes and describes the transformations from one form to the next based on Heidegger's analysis. These transformations are summarized in Figure 1-1. Each transformation involves a reinterpretation of the informational content in a new medium. With that comes a gain in precision balanced by a loss of grounding. As a result of the increased clarity and the change of form, new discoveries are made about the content of the information.

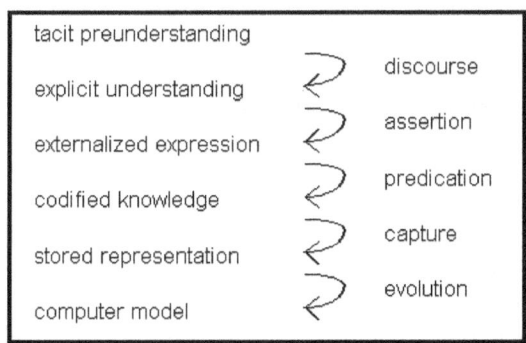

Figure 1-1. Transformations of tacit to explicit information.

The left-hand column lists consecutive forms of information. The right-hand column names the transformation processes from one form to another.

Heidegger uses the term *discourse* for the fundamental shift to putting one's understanding into words, even if the words are not yet *asserted* in speech to be shared with someone. After tacit preunderstanding is articulated in discourse as explicit understanding, this understanding can then be asserted and externalized in spoken or written language (such as documented design rationale). Such knowledge can be further codified in accordance with formal procedures (e.g., scientific methods). These are important transformations for creating widely shared knowledge. The movement from externalized to codified information can go from informal to formal (i.e., capable of being processed by computer). Shipman (1993) discusses this stage of formalization and methods for supporting it within computer-based design environments. This is relevant to the further stages of articulation, which involve computers: capture of the information in computer representations and modification of these representations to adapt them to new requirements. The theory of computer support for design proposed in Chapter 6 suggests that all stages of information articulation can take advantage of computer support. If designing takes place within a computer-based design environment, then designers can use and modify computer representations to support the design process from the start. As Reeves (1993) recommends, the design environment can serve as a medium of communication to support collaboration. In the process, design information can be captured automatically without becoming a burdensome task to be done in retrospect.

1.6. Consequences for a Theory of Computer Support

The ideas of situated cognition and Heidegger's philosophy of interpretation stress how different human understanding is from computer manipulations of symbols. These analyses suggest a *people-centered approach* of augmenting, rather than automating, human intelligence. According to this view, software can at best provide computer representations for people to interpret based on their tacit understanding of what is being represented. Representations used in computer programs must be carefully structured by people who understand the task being handled thoroughly, because the computer itself simply follows the rules it has been given for manipulating symbols, with no notion of what they represent. People (e.g., software designers or software users) who understand the domain must codify their knowledge into software rules sufficiently to make the computer algorithms generate results that, when interpreted by people, will be the desired results. Only if a domain can be strictly delimited and its associated knowledge exhaustively reduced to rules, can it be completely represented in advance (by the software designers) so that tasks in the domain can be automated.

Many tasks like lunar habitat design that call for computer support do not belong to well-defined domains with fully catalogued and formalized knowledge bases. These tasks may require (a) exploration of possibilities never before considered, (b) assumption of creative viewpoints, or (c) formulation of innovative concepts. Software to support designers in such tasks should provide facilities for the designers themselves (as the software users) to create new representations and to flexibly modify old representations. As the discussion of Alexander emphasizes, the ability *to develop appropriate understandings of the situation dynamically* is critical to innovative design. Because they capture understandings that evolve through processes of interpretation, representations need to be modifiable during the design process itself and cannot adequately be anticipated in advance or provided once and for all. Lunar habitat design is an example of an exploratory domain in two senses: (1) it is a new domain with relatively little in the way of accepted conventional knowledge, and (2) it involves continual innovation to meet novel, over-constrained, politically sensitive mission specifications.

The assumption of the existence (even in principle) of an objective, coherent body of domain knowledge that can be used without being reinterpreted in new situations and from different perspectives is misleading. As Rittel says, non-routine design is an argumentative process involving the interplay of unlimited perspectives, reflecting differing and potentially conflicting technical concerns, personal idiosyncrasies, and political interests. Rather than trying to supply all knowledge in advance, software to support this type of design should capture alternative deliberations on important issues as they arise and document specific solutions. Then, these can be available to support interpretive deliberations. Furthermore, because all design knowledge is relative to perspectives, the computer should be used *to define a network of over-lapping perspectives* with which to organize issues, rationale, sketches, component parts, and terminology to reflect the different viewpoints designers adopt. That will facilitate the retrieval of information relevant to a particular interpretive stance.

As Schön emphasizes, design relies on moving from tacit skills to explicit conceptualizations, and on the ability to reformulate the implications in linguistic expressions. Additionally, design work is inherently communicative and increasingly collaborative, with high-tech designs requiring successive teams of designers, implementors, and maintainers. Software to support collaborative design should provide *a language facility for designers to develop a sharable vocabulary* for expressing their ideas, for communicating them to future collaborators, and for formally representing them within computer-executable software. An end-user language that provides an extensible domain vocabulary, is usable by non-programmers, and encourages reuse and modification could help provide support for designers trying to express their interpretations..

Heidegger's analysis of interpretation says that new interpretations are based on preunderstandings developed in the past or handed down by tradition. In this sense, it is likely that the information designers need most when they reflect on problems may have previously been made explicit at some moment of interpretation during past designing. Accordingly, one promising strategy for accumulating a useful knowledge base is to have the software capture knowledge that becomes explicit while the software is being used. As successive lunar habitats are designed on a system, issues and alternative deliberations can accumulate in its repository of design rationale; new perspectives can be defined with their own modified representations, terminology, and critic rules; and the language can be expanded to include more domain vocabulary, conditional expressions, and query formulations.

This is an evolutionary, bootstrap approach, where the software can not only support individual design projects, but simultaneously facilitate the accumulation of expertise and viewpoints in open-ended, exploratory domains. This means that the software should support designers in formalizing their knowledge when it becomes explicit. The software should reward its users for increasing the computer knowledge base by performing useful tasks with the new information, like providing documentation, communicating rationale, and facilitating reuse and modification of relevant knowledge.

The theory suggested by the analysis of interpretation in design is diagrammed in Figure 1-2. As the cycle of interpretation proceeds, driven by the needs of designing and collaboration, explicit knowledge that is generated can be captured by the computer support system. The computer system relies on a combination of stored representations (for representing situations, defining perspectives, and articulating language expressions) and plasticity (for tailoring the existing representations to the requirements of the specific design process). This combination makes support of interpretation in design possible and simultaneously drives an evolution of the stored knowledge base.

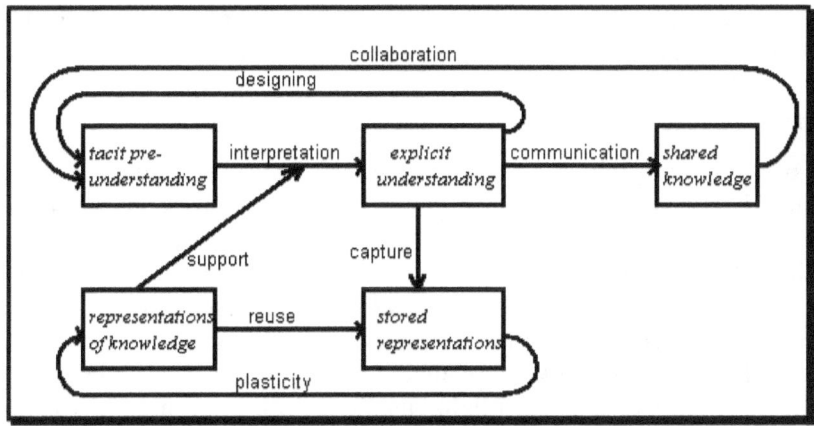

Figure 1-2. The theory of computer support for interpretation in design.

The cycle of human interpretation (illustrated on the top) is mirrored by a cycle of evolution of the computer knowledge base (below), that uses captured explicit knowledge to support future interpretation.

The theory proposed in Chapter 6 views the computer as a design medium. It is a multimedia device capable of representing the diverse forms of information used in design: text, graphics, pictures, pen sketches, numbers, voice, animation, and even video. It can use all these media to externalize design concepts and to store them for future use, serving as a medium of externalization and long-term memory. This means it can be used as a medium of communication among team members and a medium for embedding an artifact's design history within the design of the artifact itself—Reeves (1993) argues for the role of such a medium in supporting collaborative work.

The uses of the computer as designing medium mentioned in the preceding paragraph are primarily passive uses. The impact of written language on civilization shows that even passive media can be powerful. However, the computational power of the computer suggests using it as an active medium as well. Certainly, numerical computations can be left to the computer: calculate square footage of designs or total their costs. But information can also be made dynamic, with representations modified on the basis of the state of other parts of a design. Furthermore, the information stored in the computer can be managed by it, perhaps organizing and displaying information based on a structure of defined perspectives. A language can make the system programmable by designers, so they can adjust displays to their changing needs. Part III will show how HERMES accomplishes this by means of a computationally active form of hypermedia, that integrates a perspectives mechanism and an end-user programming language.

One of the most powerful consequences of designing in a computational medium is the possibility of integrating all the relevant information. An example of this is the mechanism of *interpretive critics* (see Fischer, et al., 1993a). It is an extension of *specific critics* (Nakakoji, 1993). Specific critics are critiquing rules that analyze the representation of a design situation and optionally display a message depending on the results of the analysis. For instance, if two appliances are closer than they should be in the design of a habitat, a critic might display a warning, suggest looking at related design rationale issues, and show similar stored designs that avoid the problem. The specific critics are dynamically computed based on the design specification that has been entered into the design rationale. The critic thus integrates information about the graphical design, the textual rationale, the computational critic rules, and other designs. It does this in a way that supports the needs of the designer without providing overwhelming amounts of information. Interpretive critics are even further embedded in the contexts of design because they can be defined differently in different interpretive perspectives. Their active behavior depends on the current perspective and the way in which terms in the language are defined in that perspective. They use the language that is being used for the particular design, they are tied to the currently active perspective, and they analyze the represented situation.

The view of computer support systems as computationally active communication media is consonant with a liberatory view of the role of computers in society. Feenberg (1991) argues that the expert system approach based on technical rationality philosophy is profoundly anti-democratic and that an alternative approach to computers as communicative media is needed to give people control over their lives:

> Systems designed for hierarchical control are congruent with rationalistic assumptions that treat the computer as an automaton intended to command or replace workers in decision-making roles. Democratically designed systems must instead respond to the communicative dimension of the computer through which it facilitates the self-organization of human communities, including those technical communities the control of which founds modern hegemonies. (p.108)

The theory of computer support presented in this dissertation pursues the democratic alternative, founding it on a respect for the irreducible nature of human interpretation.

The key is control. Computer systems are sophisticated tools for exerting control of information. As powerful as they are, computers have no understanding of the information they manipulate. Even in autonomous AI systems, all the interpretation is done by people—typically by the programmers who set up the system and the users who view the output. Innovative design is an arena in which the interpretation cannot be done in advance because this design requires understanding and interpretation at every step. Therefore, the role of computers in non-routine design must be to support designers. Human designers must retain control over (a) how things are represented, (b) which things are stored together, and (c) what terms are used to articulate ideas. Unless this control is vested in people who can use their interpretive skills, questions concerning what information might be relevant in a given context or in the future remain intractable for all but carefully delimited, well-understood, completely codified domains. The only heuristics proposed for the management of design knowledge are those tacitly followed by traditional design practice: (1) that knowledge represented, organized, and articulated in the past may be useful in the future, and (2) that designers will need to use their powers of interpretation to modify and apply reused knowledge in unique situations. (The problem of application addresses the fact that every situated, perspectival, linguistic understanding is unique and yet must be interpreted as similar to other cases; it is discussed in Chapter 5.)

The theory of computer support provides a principled basis for designing a computer system to support innovative design in such tasks as lunar habitat design. Before exploring the ideas suggested for such a system, the existing tradition of design environments is considered. This is a tradition of computer systems supporting the augmentation of human design efforts. It provides a basis upon which new ideas can be developed through extensions that are guided by the theory.

1.7. Previous Software Systems for Design

For thirty years now, at least since Alexander (1964), efforts have been underway to use computers to support design. Much work in the area of computer support for design has concentrated on two approaches that will *not* be explored here:

* Providing stand-alone tools for drafting and modeling, where the computer system has little or no representation of the semantics of what is being designed—e.g., so-called "computer aided design" (CAD).

* Automating the design process, where the computer is given a specification of a problem and is expected to produce a design with minimal interaction with a human user—e.g., an expert system for design.

Although these approaches have proven useful for certain tasks or within restricted domains, in general they have been shown to be quite limited. Winograd & Flores (1986) and Dreyfus & Dreyfus (1986), for instance, have argued that expert systems are in principle essentially limited when it comes to tasks like creative design. They have based their arguments largely on Heidegger's philosophy and other ideas that are discussed in this dissertation. Rather than duplicating their line of criticism, Chapter 7 will draw their positive implications for building software systems that can support innovative design.

There have always been some researchers who sought ways to use technology to *augment* human problem solving (e.g., Bush, 1945; Engelbart, 1963), rather than to model, simulate, or replace it. More specifically, there is a tradition in design methodology and design rationale capture efforts, going back to Rittel and his associates (Rittel & Webber, 1973; Kunz & Rittel, 1984) that advocates the use of computer-based design systems as cognitive aids for human designers.

Recent work in this tradition is reviewed in Chapter 7 and used as a starting point for designing a system to support interpretation in design. In particular, the design environments that will be reviewed (JANUS, MODIFIER, PHIDIAS) are *domain-oriented* in the sense that they try to embody generally accepted knowledge of their specialized design domains. In contrast, the domain-independent design rationale capture systems (KRL, PIE, DRL) focus on capturing and displaying potentially opposing perspectives on design issues. By synthesizing ideas from these different systems, the new approach will extend the notion of domain-orientation to support multiple interpretations of the domain as well.

The consequences of the theory of computer support for interpretation in design developed in Chapter 6 motivate and guide the survey of previous software systems. Established techniques implemented in the computer-based design assistants are reviewed and their limitations are critiqued on the basis of the theory. While mechanisms for representing situations, defining perspectives, and using language are found in some of these systems, the plasticity and integration of these mechanisms are quite limited. In many ways, these systems retain principles from expert system theory and are not oriented toward supporting interpretation in design even when they happen to provide some mechanisms that could be used for that.

JANUS (Fischer, et al., 1989) is a design environment combining graphical and textual representations of the design *situation*. It introduces a multi-faceted architecture that includes a palette of design components for building graphical representations of kitchen layouts, a catalog of stored design cases, an issue-base of design rationale, and a daemon mechanism for active critics. This system provides an important model of a design environment. Its lack of support for users to create new representations is recognized and addressed by a successor system named MODIFIER.

MODIFIER (Girgensohn, 1992) defines all the knowledge representations with parameterized property sheets. Then it provides a user interface to these system internals. While it offers extensive support for the user to modify representations, this still involves the user in modifying LISP expressions, altering hierarchical inheritance trees, and generally having to be concerned with system internals. Thus, it supports the user (with extensive help text, examples, checklists, and even critic rules concerning modifications) to engage in tasks of maintaining a sophisticated software system rather than supporting the user in interpretive tasks of design. Another problem with MODIFIER is that it provides no mechanism for organizing modifications into alternative versions to support personal and shared versions.

Several systems for knowledge representation and design rationale capture propose the use of multiple *perspectives*, a mechanism that this dissertation recommends. KRL (Boborow & Winograd, 1977) presents a sophisticated formal language for knowledge representation that incorporates a mechanism for perspectives. PIE (Boborow & Goldstein, 1980; Goldstein & Boborow, 1980a, 1980b) develops the ideas of KRL further as the basis for a design environment for software development. DRL (Lee, 1990; Lee & Lai, 1991) explores issues in design rationale capture using languages based on Rittel's IBIS as well as KRL and PIE. These systems provide invaluable experience in designing languages for knowledge representation and design rationale, and in using perspectives mechanisms. However, their implementations lack the generality called for in certain ways. Furthermore, they are not particularly appropriate to the kind of hypermedia structure that seems useful for representing a broad diversity of design information. They provide important examples and recommend useful principles for the kinds of languages and perspectives mechanisms useful in supporting design. The lessons from these systems are combined in Chapter 8 with two design criteria: (1) the implementations should be appropriate to a hypermedia structure of knowledge representation and (2) end-users should be able to revise and extend the vocabulary of the language and the structure of the system of perspectives.

PHIDIAS (McCall, et al., 1990) is another design environment like JANUS. It does not include as many components or a critiquing mechanism, but it does demonstrate the utility of a query *language* for users to define displays of design rationale. The PHIDIAS language has a number of important features: it is designed for navigation of hypertext and it is based on several syntactic characteristics of English. Vocabulary in the language can all be defined by users, so it supports adaptability. PHIDIAS uses a form of hypertext that has a fine granularity; thus textual displays of design rationale, for instance, may be computed dynamically through the use of queries defined in the language. The PHIDIAS language provides a good starting point for the design of a computationally powerful language that is appropriate to hypermedia and that can support interpretation.

In response to the shortcomings of previous systems, an integrated software prototype named HERMES is proposed. HERMES is a persistent hypermedia substrate for building design environments to support interpretation in design. Its mechanisms operationalize the positive design principles of the analysis of interpretation and the theory of computer support for interpretation in design.

1.8. Hypermedia in the HERMES System

In Greek mythology, Hermes supported human interpretation by providing the gift of spoken and written language and by delivering the messages of the gods. As part of the research for this dissertation, a prototype software system named HERMES has been designed to support the preconditions of interpretation (a) by representing the design construction situation to support prepossession, (b) by providing alternative perspectives to support preview, and (c) by including a language to support preconception.

HERMES supports tacit knowing by encapsulating mechanisms corresponding to each of the preconditions:

* Interpretive critics (Fischer, et al., 1993b) are used for analyzing the design situation, which is represented in arbitrarily complex hypermedia data structures. These critics are expressions in the HERMES language that perform an analysis of the current state of some representations and then optionally display a message. The evaluation of the critic expressions or rules is dependent upon the currently active interpretive perspective, which determines the versions of the expression, of its constituent terms, and of the representations being analyzed.

* Named perspectives (Stahl, 1993b) organize and manage alternative sets of information relevant to different purposes. By switching to a new perspective by selecting its name from a list, a designer can change how the representation of the situation appears, what interpretive critics are active, and in general what contents of the hypermedia network are "visible" from the viewpoint.

* Language terms (Stahl, et al., 1992) define computations across the knowledge base. While these expressions can be arbitrarily complex if viewed in complete detail, they are typically constructed in a series of stages. At every stage, the components of the term's definition can themselves be given names.

With each of these mechanisms, complexities are hidden from the user by being encapsulated in named objects. These complexities can gradually be made explicit upon demand so the designer can reflect upon the information and modify it. Together, these and other mechanisms make HERMES a *computationally active medium* in which designers can do their work.

HERMES is a knowledge-representation substrate for building computer-based design assistants like the Lunar Habitat Design Environment (LHDE) shown in Figure 1-3. It provides a hypermedia structure for designers to build representations of design knowledge.

The network of knowledge corresponds to the design situation. Multi-media nodes of the knowledge representation can, for instance, be textual statements for the issue-base, CAD graphics for sketches, bitmap images to illustrate ideas, or language expressions for critics and queries. The inter-linked hypermedia structure facilitates browsing by designers. It can also be used to support associative memory (Hinton & Anderson, 1989) or case-based dynamic memory (Schank, 1982; Kolodner, 1984). All displays are defined by queries that dynamically assemble arbitrary collections of multimedia items. For instance, the Design Rationale window in Figure 1-3 shows the textual issues, answers, and arguments that resulted from a query that was executed by a user's request to see the "discussion" of a previously viewed issue.

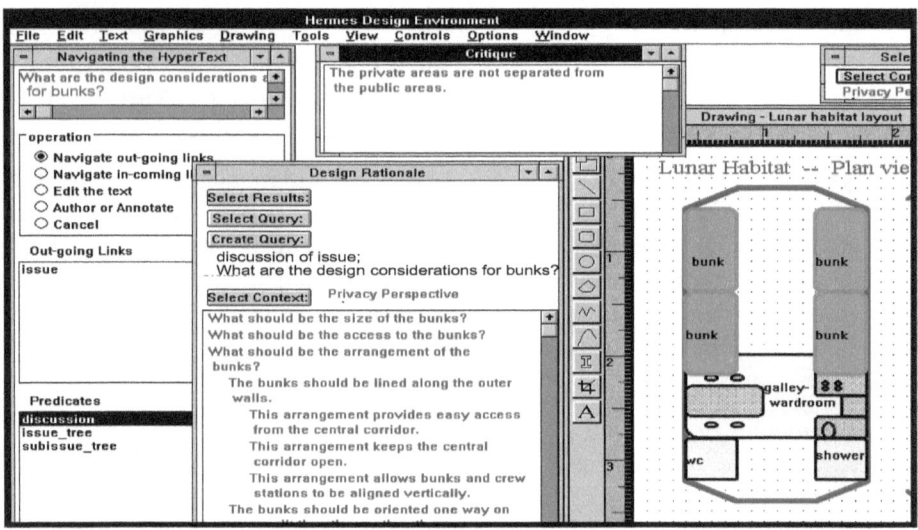

Figure 1-3. Arranging sleep compartment bunks using HERMES.

Windows shown (left to right) include a dialogue box for browsing the hypermedia content, a selection from the design rationale issue-base, a critic rule's message, a graphical sketching area, and a button for changing interpretive perspectives.

The hypermedia *knowledge representation* structure of HERMES is designed to facilitate the representation of design situations and to encourage their tailorability. Its generalized node and link structure models the network character of the situation as a network of inter-related, pre-understood significances and their associations. Its object-oriented implementation allows for the integration of information in different media—reflecting the need to bring together many forms of information in design. It provides graphics for sketching, text for issue-bases or design rationale, and other media for annotations to support the exploration of represented situations. All the media and mechanisms are designed to maximize plasticity of representation. The HERMES hypermedia structure incorporates a perspectives mechanism for managing and viewing all information and an end-user language for defining queries for displays, as discussed below.

Special emphasis is placed on the synergistic integration of the hypermedia, perspectives, and language mechanisms in the HERMES substrate. Definitions of perspective hierarchies and language expressions are stored in the hypermedia network so they can be browsed and modified like all other information. By using nodes of the hypermedia network to define the names of perspectives and links to determine the inheritance relationships among perspectives, the HERMES system can support annotation of these nodes to store information related to the purpose or origination of the perspectives. Similarly, the nodes that define terminology and expressions in the HERMES language can be linked like a semantic network (Quillian, 1967).

In turn, the definition of the hypermedia structure itself incorporates both perspectives and language expressions. Instead of having a fixed content in some medium, nodes can have their content defined by the evaluation of an expression in the language. Nodes and links can be conditional upon some computation defined in the language and involving other nodes and links. Furthermore, hypermedia information to be displayed is always dynamically computed in the currently active perspective—even language expressions can have different effects in different perspectives. In these ways, node contents can be dependent upon the state of other data in the hypermedia network. The interactions of the integrated hypermedia, perspectives, and language provide significant control and malleability for the designer. Design environments built on this substrate can have many features that support interpretation in design with consistent abilities to represent knowledge and to tailor the representations.

1.9. Perspectives in Hermes

HERMES includes a perspectives mechanism for organizing all knowledge represented in the system. This mechanism is general and can be used to define a variety of different kinds of "perspectives" for categorizing information and for organizing inheritance of information among perspectives. For instance, hierarchies of perspectives can be defined for technical specialties (e.g., plumbing, ergonomics), knowledge domains (kitchen design, partial gravity design), worldviews (Bauhaus, austere missions), specific designs (i.e., cases), individual preferences, shared team decisions, and experimental "what-if" versions. New perspectives can merge information from multiple existing perspectives and then modify the information as seen through the new perspective without affecting it in the original perspectives. This can facilitate periodic, non-disruptive reorganizations of the knowledge base as it evolves.

The perspectives mechanism of HERMES helps to support the collaborative nature of design by multiple teams. Drawings, definitions of domain terms in the language, computations for critic rules, and annotations in the issue-base can be grouped together in a perspective for a project, a technical specialty, an individual, or a team. A new perspective can be defined to archive a version of a design for historical purposes so it will not change as team members continue to work on new versions. Every action in HERMES takes place within some defined perspective, which determines what versions of information are currently being accessed. Perspectives can collect knowledge according to various categories. For example, there can be perspectives for individual designers or design teams; for technical or professional specialties; for traditional or cultural domains; for specific projects; or for historical versions of projects.

Since information in HERMES is always viewed through a perspective, switching perspectives can support the deliberation of alternative approaches. By redefining in different perspectives the same graphic objects or linguistic terms used in conditionals, queries, and critics, one determines how things will be displayed (interpreted) differently in different perspectives. Thus, as shown by a scenario in Chapter 9, critics in a "privacy perspective" might analyze habitat layouts using a concept of privacy gradient defined in that perspective, whereas the same critics would in effect have different definitions in other perspectives and would therefore produce different results. The interpretive critics for privacy that are used in the scenario are analyzed and explained in detail in Chapter 10 as a case study in use of the language.

The approach of HERMES supports communication among designers. The representations of the design situation may include documentation of design rationale by specifying resolutions of issues in an issue-base. For lunar habitat design, such documentation is contractually required by NASA. Requirements traceability and clear communication of rationale are necessary for a design to move from the original design team to subsequent groups for approval, technical elaboration, mock-up, and eventual construction. Documentation is notoriously difficult to produce. Design rationale is most effectively captured when it is an explicit concern. Formulations developed in the HERMES language by designers in the midst of designing can supplement the situation representations, stating for the benefit of future designers looking at their work what aspects were originally considered important and what rules of thumb were developed then. Viewing the design from the original team's perspective preserves their interpretation, while subsequent groups can define their own modified perspectives. Individuals in work teams can share ideas, viewpoints, and definitions by using group perspectives that inherit from and modify the contents of their different personal perspectives.

1.10. The HERMES Language

HERMES features a language for designers to use. The language is defined as a series of subset languages to facilitate learning by new users. First it should be noted that previously defined terms and expressions are used most of the time. These are simply selected from lists of relevant terms. Then there is a beginner's version of the language that is very similar to the PHIDIAS language, which proved easy to use for non-programmer novice users. This level of the language suffices for defining or modifying most common terms and queries. An intermediate level provides access to virtually all features of the language except those related to graphics. Finally, an advanced level can be used for graphics-related tasks, like defining interpretive critics. Most system displays and component interfaces are defined in the language, so they can be modified through use of the language.

The HERMES language defines domain vocabulary for referring to represented objects and their associations (the nodes and links of the hypermedia). It also provides expressions for stating queries to define displays and for stating rules to critique designs. The expressions fall into three major syntax categories: (a) definitions of lists of nodes, (b) expressions for filtering out nodes not meeting stated criteria, and (c) operations to traverse various kinds of associations. These support the situated, perspectival, and linguistic character of interpretation by naming representations of things in the design situation, filtering out objects for display based on viewing criteria, and providing expressions for exploring associations. Objects in each of these categories can be either (1) reused or (2) refined by combining expressions in useful ways. This defines the six primary syntactic classes in the language; four other classes provide auxiliary terms and features. The syntactic classes are listed with brief descriptions in Table 1-4.

Table 1-4. Syntactic classes of the HERMES language.

	syntactic class	description
a-1	Datalists	options for identifying hypermedia nodes.
a-2	Computed Datalists	permitted combinations of language elements that determine sets of nodes
b-1	Filters	predicates characterizing nodes for selection
b-2	Computed Filters	permitted combinations of language elements that define filter conditions
c-1	Associations	links and other associations of nodes
c-2	Computed Associations	permitted combinations of language elements that determine sets of Associations
d-1	Media Elements	nodes of various media: text, numbers, booleans, graphics, sound, video, etc.
d-2	Computed Media Elements	permitted combinations of media elements, e.g., arithmetic and boolean computations
e-1	Pre-defined Terminology	connective terms, measurement primitives, fixed values for attributes and types
e-2	Computed Terminology	namable quantifiers and numerical comparisons

The language provides a tacit form of language usage for non-programmers. Most of the sequential processing is kept implicit, due partially to the declarative form of the language structure. Also, expressions that were originally figured out explicitly are given names in domain terminology. In Figure 1-3, for example, the user clicked on an issue about sleep compartment bunks and then chose the "Predicate" (Computed Association), discussion. This predicate was already defined to produce a hierarchy of issues with their answers and arguments. The user did not have to be concerned with the recursive structure of this hierarchy or its iterations through multiple links. All of those computational matters were implicit in the definition of the predicate. The user could simply select the predicate by name. This example of choosing "discussion" from a list of predicate names in Figure 1-3 is typical of how the language is used in HERMES. Even when one is creating a new expression, one selects syntax options in dialogue boxes and selects predefined terms from lists. This minimizes the need to remember syntax and terms, prevents many kinds of errors, and avoids the impression that one can simply use free-form English to define expressions.

The HERMES language pervades the system, defining mechanisms for browsing, displaying, and critiquing all information. This means that designers can use the language to modify and refine the representations, views, and evaluations of all forms of domain knowledge in the system. All vocabulary in the language is modifiable by the designers. Every language expression (and every component of a larger expression) can be encapsulated by a name, so that many statements in the language can be defined with common terms from particular design domains. Considerable effort was put into the design of the language to make the appearance of expressions as easily interpretable as possible. Chapter 10 presents many examples and discusses the techniques used to achieve a readily interpretable appearance. This is just one way in which the language is designed to support tacit usage. Much of the knowledge that people must explicitly use in writing programs in conventional programming languages (assignment, variables, functions, quantification, etc.) has been hidden from the user in the HERMES language (see Chapter 10 for a detailed description of this). The power of these mechanisms is available through the language, but designers need not think in terms of the computational mechanisms. However, when it is necessary for a designer to explore the definition of a user-defined expression in the language in order to understand it more explicitly, this can be done.

Combined with the perspectives mechanism, the language permits designers to define and refine their own interpretations. This allows the HERMES substrate to extend systems beyond the domain-oriented approach of the knowledge-based design environments that HERMES grew out of, by supporting multiple situated interpretations of the domain. That is, the previous systems pre-defined most domain knowledge in a single, generic knowledge base. However, all representations are relative to human interpretation and interpretation is perspectival. HERMES lets designers reinterpret linguistic expressions of knowledge already in the system and store them in appropriate perspectives. This retains the relationship of design knowledge to interpretive perspectives. It also replaces the notion of a single body of domain knowledge (whether fixed or evolving) with a system of multiple perspectives on the domain. Furthermore, this extension encourages inter-related or relevant knowledge from diverse domains to be brought together in specific perspectives.

1.11.Conclusion

The analysis of situated interpretation argues that only people's tacit preunderstanding can make information meaningful in context. Neither people nor computers alone can take advantage of the huge stores of data required for many design tasks; such information is valueless unless designers can use it in their interpretations of design situations. The data handling capabilities of computers should be used to support the uniquely human ability to understand. The theory of computer support for interpretation in design suggests that several characteristics of human understanding and collaboration can be supported with mechanisms like those in HERMES for refining representations of the design situation, alternative perspectives, and linguistic expressions. The theory provides a coherent framework for a principled approach to computer support for designers' situated interpretation in the age of information overload.

In elaborating the argument of the previous paragraph, this dissertation seeks to make three kinds of contributions: to a philosophy of interpretation, to a theory of computer support, and to a system for innovative design.

*   It makes a philosophic contribution by clarifying the foundations of situated cognition theory in Heidegger's philosophy of interpretation and extending that philosophy through an analysis of interpretation in design and through a theory of computer support for interpretation in design.

*   It makes a contribution to computer science by arguing that systems to augment human skills in innovative design should be oriented toward providing support for the processes of interpretation.

*   It makes a practical contribution by prototyping three crucial mechanisms for design environments: a hypermedia substrate that integrates a perspectives mechanism and an end-user language.

These contributions reflect a belief that our age calls for alternatives to a technical rationality philosophy, an expert system approach to computerization, and a view of the designer as an isolated and unaided subject.

Part I. Interpretation in Design

"And to imagine a language
means to imagine a form of life."

Ludwig Wittgenstein

Philosophical Investigations

(1953, §19)

Interpretation is the process of understanding something in a specific way. That is, it is a matter of explicating a non-articulated (i.e., tacit) grasp of something. This may involve the phenomenon of seeing *as*: a closed line in a drawing is spontaneously perceived as (representing) a certain type of object. It may involve re-interpretation, in which a passage in a novel is seen in a new light on the basis of literary criticism. A psychoanalyst might interpret a patient's dream or behavior as an expression of deep-seated fears. A designer could construe an assigned project as a problem of creating a certain kind of space, light, or form.

An attempt will be made in the following pages to interpret interpretation: to articulate an increasingly more explicit understanding of what is involved in the process of interpretation and what role this process plays in design. What factors influence how things are interpreted? What prompts designers to reinterpret, and what cognitive function does this play? The purpose of this exploration is to determine how interpretation in design can be supported by computer-based systems, and why it might be useful to do this.

The next three chapters all argue that an essential feature of the designer's work involves processes of interpretation. Chapter 2 shows that three of the foremost analysts of design stress the role of interpretation (although they may not agree on much else). Chapter 3 presents original empirical evidence from a study of designers at work designing a lunar habitat. Chapter 4 offers a philosophical framework for conceptualizing interpretation as a fundamental aspect of human understanding.

CHAPTER 2. THREE METHODOLOGIES OF DESIGN

In each section of this chapter evidence will be presented in support of the claim that the process of understanding in design has the following three features:

(a) understandings of a design arise from interactions with the *situation* of the task in the world;

(b) the designer's unique interpretive *perspectives* grow out of traditions which pass on viewpoints for relating to the world, skills for behaving in the world and languages for talking about the world; and

(c) explicit articulations of interpretations in *language* emerge from situated, tacit understanding and then re-submerge (although they may be captured first).

This chapter will discuss the insights of three people who have provided insightful and influential interpretations of the design process: Christopher Alexander, Horst Rittel, and Donald Schön. Significantly, each has been concerned at some point with the issue of providing computer support for design. Also, they emphasize the themes of this dissertation: Alexander focuses particularly on the problem of representation; Rittel emphasizes the consequences of people's differing perspectives; and Schön is concerned above all with how explicit reflection arises from tacit understanding.

Alexander recognizes the need to combine mathematical methods and analysis of patterns with intuitive sense grounded in architectural practice. In pushing the paradigm of objective analysis as far as he can, he is nevertheless frank about the limits of empirical research and the importance of prioritizing human needs that are less susceptible to empirical evaluation. Finally, the pattern language he proposes is meant as a basis for every culture and every person to build their own unique and appropriate representations of design situations.

Rittel's analysis of the "wicked" problems of design does not suggest the elimination of method in favor of arbitrary personal whim. Rather, it stresses the complexity of continually framing the problem and solving it in parallel. One's interpretation of the problem must not only be based in the specifics of the situation, but must also grow out of the exploration of potential solutions. The argumentative process of design is not simply one in which everyone is entitled to their own opinion. Rather, it is a process in which initial prejudices are supposed to be subjected to critique from other viewpoints so that they will be refined. At the same time, Rittel recognizes that people have differing perspectives for various legitimate reasons, and that agreement will not always be possible even with the best processes of deliberation.

Schön can be seen as a resolution of the objective and subjective approaches, for he stresses the interplay or dialogue between the designer (who brings tacit skills and personal perspectives) and the materials of a design situation (which provides surprises for the moves of the designer that could not have been anticipated but that constrain the design). Schön's theories about the roles of tacit knowing and explicit reflecting, drawing upon important philosophical sources, flesh out both Alexander's notion of intuition and Rittel's sense of how judgments can be deliberated. Schön's theory of design focuses on the movement between the designer's skillful preunderstanding ("knowing-in-action") and explicit articulation ("reflection-in-action"). This is precisely the movement that is called interpretation in this dissertation.

2.1. Alexander: the Structure of a Design Situation

Deliberation on the question of whether and how computers should be used to support the work of designers has raged for several decades. In the beginning of the 1960's Alexander (1964) pioneered exploration of this possibility by running a series of computer programs for the hierarchical decomposition of systems into subsystems, diagrams, or patterns. This kind of decomposition was central to the methods he proposed for design, and it seemed logical and necessary to use computationally powerful equipment to implement such analysis. However, within several years, Alexander was discouraged about the use of computers to support design. He complained that, "the people who are messing around with computers have obviously become interested in some kind of a toy. They have definitely lost the motivation for making better buildings" (Alexander, 1971, p.309). In his 1971 Preface to the paperback edition of his original work, he characterized the problem with attempts at computer support in terms of a broader problem of separating the study of design methodology from the practice of designing (Alexander, 1964).

The issues surrounding the appropriate use of computers go to the heart of what design is and should be. In his now classic *Notes on the Synthesis of Form*—which presents his dissertation work incorporating the early computer programs—Alexander reviews the history and even the prehistory of design in order to argue that the field reached a second watershed in the mid-twentieth century. The profession of design had originally emerged when society started to produce new needs and innovative perspectives too rapidly to allow forms to be developed through "unselfconscious" activities of slowly evolving traditions. Now, the momentum of change has reached a second qualitatively new stage:

> Today more and more design problems are reaching insoluble levels of complexity. This is true not only of moon bases, factories, and radio receivers, whose complexity is internal, but even of villages and teakettles. In spite of their superficial simplicity, even these problems have a background of needs and activities which is becoming too complex to grasp intuitively. (Alexander, 1964, p.3)

Design problems are situated in "a background of needs and activities." These design situations are becoming so complex that the management of complexity must become a primary concern of the field of design. The level of complexity that Alexander had in mind is characterized by the fact that it exceeds the ability of the unaided individual human mind to handle it effectively. Various methodologies can help to decompose complexity, and this is where the mathematical structures, diagrams, or patterns that Alexander proposed come in. They provide the representational or computational basis today for computerization. In an obvious sense, computers are a natural tool for storing large amounts of information. But at a deeper level, computer languages and applications are designed to manage complexity. It is no coincidence that the movement toward structured programming was contemporaneous with Alexander's emphasis on functional decomposition.

Alexander saw a major advantage of the systematic use of structures or patterns in what he referred to as a "loss of innocence". When design first became a profession with rules that could be stated in language and taught, there was, according to Alexander's account, a first such loss of innocence. More recently, when Bauhaus designers recognized that one could design for mechanized production, another accommodation was made with changing times. The use of systematic methodologies to help manage complexity would, Alexander claimed, entail an analogous acceptance of the limitations of the individual designer's intuitive powers. This would bring with it a significant opportunity for progress of the profession. When the design process is formulated in terms of abstract structures it becomes much more readily subject to public criticism than when it is concealed in the mysteries of the lonesome genius' artistry, just as the earlier formulation of previously unselfconscious design into explicit plans, articulated processes, and stated justifications laid the basis for a science of design that could be refined through on-going debate. Loss of innocence entails the removal of an outmoded barrier to the kind of public critical reflection required for a profession.

But Alexander did not see the issue one-sidedly. Recognizing the power of both formal representations and non-formalizable tacit knowledge, he did not propose that design methods substitute for the practice of design or for the designer's practical intuitions. Rather, he recognized that intuition and rationalism were equally necessary, and argued for a proper balance: "Enormous resistance to the idea of systematic processes of design is coming from people who recognize correctly the importance of intuition, but then make a fetish of it which excludes the possibility of asking reasonable questions" (ibid., p.9). Alexander felt that the fetishism of intuition as some kind of inalienable artistic freedom of the designer functioned as a flimsy screen to hide the individual designer's incapacity to deal with the complexity of contemporary design problems. As a consequence of the designer ignoring these limitations, the unresolved issues of complexity get passed down to engineers who have been trained to work out details rather than to grasp complex organization synthetically; the product that results tends to be a monument to the personal idiom of the creator rather than an artifact with a good fit to its function.

The themes raised by Alexander three decades ago for design methodology generally still confront the particular task of figuring out how best to use computers to support designing. Consider his first example above, that of designing a moon base. This is a task requiring a significant amount of knowledge. One needs to take into account technical considerations about supporting humans in a vacuum, including issues that may not have previously been thought of and investigated (such as the practicality of using lunar rocks as building materials). One must also consider the mission goals of the base, both stated and implicit. Then there are social and psychological issues concerning the interactions among groups of people who are confined in an alien environment for a prolonged period of time. All of these factors interact with the more common issues of designing a habitat for working, eating, socializing, and sleeping—resulting in a design problem of considerable complexity. While computers may be necessary to manage this complexity, the tacit knowledge of human designers must also be brought to bear with their intuitions about what it would be like to live together in a lunar habitat.

Three themes can be mentioned from Alexander's discussion in *Notes*: (a) The point of his method of decomposition is to derive substructures through an analysis of the design problem so that the design process can be approached (understood) in terms that grow out of the problem situation and provide a basis for the solution. One problem of people who follow a methodology divorced from practice is that their representations are not based in attempts to solve concrete tasks. (b) The design profession has emerged from unselfconscious traditions. Rapid technological change has necessitated a multiplication of individual perspectives (and group movements) on design, but these perspectives need to retain ties to traditions in order to maintain goodness of fit and avoid academic or idiosyncratic arbitrariness. (c) Professional designing has evolved out of tacit knowledge of form. While we need to make things self-conscious or explicit now, we should remember the basis of such knowledge in tacit understanding: the kind of understanding that the traditional Slovakian shawl makers (see Alexander, 1964, p.53) had so they could distinguish good from bad designs without having any theory or rules to go by. Such tacit knowledge provides a basis for what Alexander calls *intuition*. These three themes reappear in Alexander's other writings.

It may sometimes seem that Alexander eschews personal interpretations and instead tries to compute mathematically determined structures, objective relations, and universal patterns. One can certainly view his work that way, in which case the problems he inevitably acknowledges represent a *reductio ad absurdum* of the attempt to define a theoretical basis for the automation of design. But it is also possible to see in his work the recognition that practice, perspectives, and intuition are as necessary as theory, objectivity, and rules. Certainly in *Notes* and in Alexander's reaction against the reception of *Notes* it was already clear that computerizable, mathematical methods of analyzing structural decomposition must be integrated with human design practice and intuition based on traditions and tacit knowledge.

In *The Atoms of Environmental Structure* (Alexander & Poyner, 1966), for instance, Alexander starts out by arguing for an objective approach to design, based on computations of relations that meet stated requirements. His first example of a requirement is to provide people working in an office with a view. How, he asks, does one know that people need or want a view? Alexander is frank about the complications involved here. He tries to operationalize the hypothesized need in terms of an underlying *tendency*. It is not sufficient to ask people, because their knowledge of their own needs is largely tacit. So experiments are needed to see if people choose desks with views, and under what conditions they do so. Further experiments are needed to rule out other factors, such as seeking better light or ventilation. Then "in order to make the hypothesis more accurate, we must try to specify just exactly what kind of people seek a view from their offices, during what parts of their work they seek it most, just what aspects of view they are looking for" (p.126). In the end, Alexander admits that "The ideal of perfect objectivity is an illusion—and there is, therefore no justification for accepting only those tendencies whose existence has been 'objectively demonstrated'. Other tendencies, though they may be speculative, are often more significant from the human point of view" (ibid.).

Another example where Alexander seems to be arguing for an objective approach, but in fact presents a case for supporting subjectivity is *A Pattern Language* (Alexander, et al., 1977). Here Alexander and his colleagues present 253 *patterns* for architectural designing and planning. Superficially, it may seem that these patterns are the kind of objective structures that might have been produced by computer analyses (as in *Notes)*, that represent the resolution of fields of relationships (as discussed in *The Atoms of Environmental Structure*), or that describe eternal, de-contextualized solutions (as implied by the title of the companion volume to *A Pattern Language, A Timeless Way of Building*). For instance, Alexander claims, "Many of the patterns here are archetypal—so deep, so deeply rooted in the nature of things, that it seems likely that they will be part of human nature, and human action, as much in five hundred years, as they are today" (p. xvii). However, a closer look shows that these patterns are intended as a basis (distilled from the traditions of world architecture) for people to create their own, situated perspectives on design: "Each solution is stated in such a way that it gives the essential field of relationships needed to solve the problem, but in a very general and abstract way—so that you can solve the problem for yourself, in your own way, by adapting it to your preferences, and the local conditions at the place where you are making it" (p. xiii).

In fact, the philosophy behind *A Pattern Language* is that every healthy society and every one of its members has their own perspective on design. These perspectives are shared and evolving; based on the constraints of the problems to be solved; and contributory to what it means to feel human and social.

> *A Timeless Way of Building* says that every society which is alive and whole, will have its own unique and distinct pattern language; and further, that every individual in such a society will have a unique language, shared in part, but which as a totality is unique to the mind of the person who has it. In this sense, in a healthy society there will be as many pattern languages as there are people—even though these languages are shared and similar. (p. xvi)

The 253 patterns given in the book are meant as templates to start building new languages. First one chooses the templates most central to one's project. Then one selects related patterns to the extent that they are appropriate or desired for the particular project. Extensions must be made to the list of patterns to cover missing topics, and one is always free to modify patterns and even rename them to make them more relevant. Finally, one's personal language can gain richness, subtlety, and "poetry" by compressing multiple pattern templates for a specific problem.

In the works just reviewed, Alexander is concerned with how to support interpretation in design. He successively suggests interpreting a design problem in terms of structures (of functional decomposition), relations (based on tendencies), and patterns (articulated in a language of design). In each case, he tries to push the notion of objectivity to its limits in terms of mathematical algorithms, operationalism and empiricism, or eternal paradigms. This would make computer support relatively straight-forward— that is, it would make sense to pursue the automation of design via expert system approaches embodying algorithms for decomposition, rules for relations, and templates of fixed patterns. However, in each case Alexander notes the limits to objectivity and the over-riding importance of tacit intuition, the human point of view, and contextual factors. Thereby, he has raised the issue of how to support interpretation in design, and even debated the use of computers in doing this. Whether one construes Alexander as ultimately arguing for or against objective methods, he has in the process provided arguments against both purely objective and purely subjective approaches.

2.2. Rittel: Deliberating from Perspectives

When Rittel declared in his *Dilemmas in a General Theory of Planning* that "planning problems are inherently wicked" (Rittel & Webber, 1973, p.160), he thereby spelled out that characteristic of planning and design tasks that has subsequently become the central source of perplexity in trying to imagine a computer system that can effectively support the challenging aspects of design. Computer programs have traditionally been devised in accordance with the classical example of *tame* science and engineering problems—precisely the paradigm that Rittel argued is not applicable to the problems of open societal systems with which planners and designers are generally concerned. This inadequate approach assumes that a problem can first of all be formulated as an exhaustive set of specifications. Then, based on such a problem statement, possible solutions can be evaluated to see which are optimal solutions to the problem. Computer programs based on this paradigm must represent in advance the space of problems and solutions for a well-defined type of design problem in an explicit, comprehensive, and non-controversial (objective) manner. However, as Rittel points out, in order to program such a computer system,

> you would have to anticipate all potential deontic judgments ahead of time before the machine could run. But if you did that you wouldn't need the computer because you would have had to have thought up all the solutions ahead of time. Therefore it is almost ridiculous to claim that there will be a designing machine if design is thought of in this sense. (Rittel, 1972, p.323)

Rittel claimed that the wicked problems of planning could not begin to be understood in the first place until one had already started to explore directions for solutions. He described what Heidegger calls the *hermeneutic circle* of understanding (see Section 4.3) when he argued, "that you cannot understand the problem without having a concept of the solution in mind; and that you cannot gather information meaningfully unless you have understood the problem, but that you cannot understand the problem without information about it" (Rittel, 1972, p.321).

Suppose, for instance, that you are asked to plan a mission to the moon for four astronauts for a period of 45 days. According to NASA, the purpose has been specified as: to explore long-term stays for crews of international backgrounds and mixed gender and to conduct some scientific research and some site work to prepare for future moon bases. In thinking about the design of the lunar habitat for this mission, you might begin to discuss the importance of privacy issues with other people on your design team. You might feel that not only was some physical privacy needed for cultural reasons, but psychologically there would be a need to structure a careful mix of public and private spaces and opportunities. These privacy issues might become paramount to your design even though they had not been included in the original problem statement. In this way, the set of issues to be investigated and concerns to be balanced would emerge and evolve as the planning process took place. Your ability to interpret the problem as one of privacy would have been based on your tacit preunderstanding of privacy as part of human life. On this basis you could then explicitly explore lunar privacy through discussion, simulation, or research on analogous situations.

In opposition to the then dominant methods of operations research that tried to compute optimal solutions from static and well-defined ("tame") problem statements, Rittel called for a model of planning as "an argumentative process in the course of which an image of the problem and of the solution emerges gradually among the participants, as a product of incessant judgment, subjected to critical argument" (1973, p.162). The language used in actual, significant planning processes is itself the result of discussion and debate among various parties, each of whom uses subjective judgments to criticize hidden assumptions and to reconstrue implicit meanings of terms. No one view of the problem or its solution has a necessary priority. The framing of problems and the judging of solutions arise through critique, deliberation, and reinterpretation, not by inference from an objective viewpoint. For Rittel, people's perspectives on problems are necessarily based on subjective conditions such as their individual value systems and political commitments or their personal roles *vis a vis* the proposed solutions:

> For wicked planning problems, there are no true or false answers. Normally, many parties are equally equipped, interested, and/or entitled to judge the solutions, although none has the power to set formal decision rules to determine correctness. Their judgments are likely to differ widely to accord with their group or personal interests, their special value-sets, and their ideological predilections. (p.163)

Consider again the concept of privacy in the lunar habitat. A design team might start from the idea of visual privacy. Through discussion of the implications of life in this confined space, they might want to include protection from the noise of flushing toilets and snoring neighbors. But then the design team member concerned with medical contingencies might introduce a notion of privacy for an injured astronaut who needs to recuperate. Psychologists, sociologists, engineers, and other members of the design team would each come to the common task with different perspectives. Given a methodology that builds on the strengths of design as an argumentative group process, these differences can contribute to a robust solution that takes into account a variety of competing and interacting insights, not all of which could have been anticipated in advance. Also central to Rittel's notion of argumentation or deliberation is the idea of *critique* as a driving force for improving one's thinking and designs. Thus an information system should not only confirm and add to one's knowledge, but also question and weaken elements of that knowledge and even delete some of it (Kunz & Rittel, 1984).

Wicked problems are open-ended in that there is no fixed set of objective criteria or procedures that can be applied to them. There is what Rittel termed the "essential uniqueness" of these problems:

> By "essentially unique" we mean that, despite long lists of similarities between a current problem and a previous one, there might be an additional distinguishing property that is of overriding importance. . . . There are no classes of wicked problems in the sense that principles of solution can be developed to fit all members of a class. . . . Despite seeming similarities among wicked problems, one can never be certain that the particulars of a problem do not override its commonalities with other problems already dealt with. (Rittel, 1973, p.164)

This creates a serious difficulty for supposed systems of domain knowledge. Rules, critiquing procedures, and design rationale cannot be applied to problems automatically based on their similarities to past problems or to prototypical problems of the domain. A given new problem may have some characteristic that makes the chosen rule irrelevant or inappropriate. The rule may need to be modified to fit the uniqueness of the problem. The problem with rules is that they always need meta-rules for applying them to cases. Algorithmically, this leads to an infinite regress which can only be circumvented by an act of human judgment of appropriateness (see Wittgenstein, 1953). Automated systems always rely in the end on a judgment by their designer that a certain measure of similarity will suffice; for the wicked problems of innovative design this is inadequate. Judgments of, for instance, the nature and priority of privacy under different conditions is a matter of interpretation. The situated, perspectival, and linguistic nature of interpretation means that each act of interpretation is essentially unique and its uniqueness must be taken into account. (See Chapter 5 for a discussion of the problem of application of rules and its implications for the computer support of interpretation in design.)

Somehow, the dimensions of the design problem must be allowed to emerge and change as different perspectives are brought to bear, as initial approaches are subjected to questioning, and as solutions gradually emerge. Rittel proposed systematic issue-based information systems (IBIS) to keep track of the issues that were being deliberated from various positions (Kunz & Rittel, 1970). Paper systems for organizing all the issues in complex planning activities soon proved unwieldy, so Rittel proposed computer support for them: "If, for example, you clearly organize a planning process according to such an argumentative model as an IBIS (issue-based information system), you will find that the bureaucratic effort of administering the process is abominable, and therefore one might look for administrative and monitoring computer aids to ease the process" (Rittel, 1972, p.324).

Rittel himself made some initial attempts to define issue-based information systems, leading to more recent computerized systems like MIKROPLIS (McCall, 1985), GIBIS (Conklin, et al., 1988), and other programs that will be reviewed later in Chapter 7. (Figure 2-1 shows a view of an IBIS display in HERMES.)

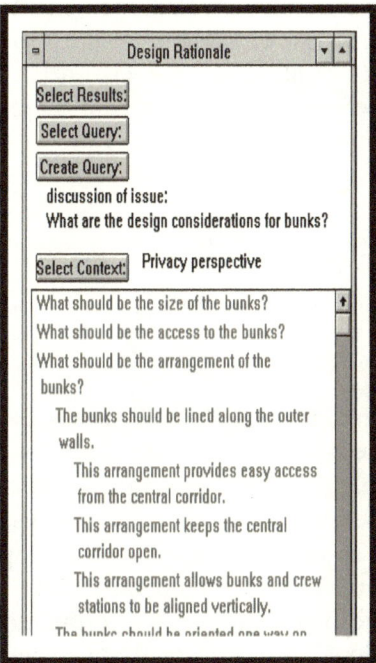

Figure 2-1. A view of an issue-based information system in HERMES.

Computer systems may be useful for storing, organizing, and communicating complex networks of argumentation—as long as they do not stifle innovation by imposing fixed representations of the ideas they capture or limiting diversity of interpretive viewpoints. Computer support for planning and design processes as Rittel conceived of them must allow team members to articulate their individual views and judgments, to communicate these to each other, and to forge shared perspectives. It must support deliberation or argumentation.

Rittel concluded that the proper role for computers and information systems generally is that of an enhancer of natural (human) intelligence, not an artificial substitute for it. In *Designing Crutches for Communication* (Kunz & Rittel, 1984), he uses the image of prosthetic devices like crutches or eye glasses: "The glasses do not see instead of you, or on your behalf. Neither does the automobile relieve you from traveling. They are prosthetic devises which support, reinforce, enhance some capacity or activity" (p.54). Because the role of information science is not to automate problem-solving but to augment human problem-solving, it must be based on an analysis of how people use information and solve their problems: "Here lies the central task of information science: to develop methods for exploring its users' knowledge and their modes of reasoning, i.e., the systems analysis of problem solving and information" (p.60). Given Rittel's view of design as argumentation from perspectives, this means computers should support people's perspectival interpretation processes.

2.3. Schön: Tacit Knowing and Explicit Language

Schön argues in his seminal work, *The Reflective Practitioner* (1983), that much design knowledge is tacit, rather than being rule-based. He views the design process as a dialogue-like interaction between the designer and the design situation, in which the designer makes moves and then perceives the consequences of these design decisions in the design situation (e.g., in a sketch). The designer manages the complexity that would be overwhelming if all the constraints and possibilities were formulated as explicit symbolic rules by using professionally-trained skills of visual perception, graphical sketching, and vicarious simulation. Note that these skills by-pass the process of analyzing everything into primitive elements and laying it out in words and propositions.

Schön recently addressed the question of computer support for design in an article descriptively entitled *Designing as Reflective Conversation with the Materials of a Design Situation* (Schön, 1992). He argued for a necessarily limited role for computers in design because one of the most important things that designers do is to construct the design situation itself. Not only is this something that computers cannot do by themselves, but it also precludes programmers of computer systems from pre-defining a generic design situation for the computer, prior to the involvement of the designer with the task.

To illustrate his claim that designers "construct" the design situation, Schön reviews an experiment in which several experienced architects are shown a 14-sided, dimensioned polygon with door locations indicated, and asked to design a library with that shape as its footprint. One architect saw the figure as two Ls back to back; another saw it as three pods surrounding a middle; a third saw it in terms of simple end entrances and complex middle entrances. Clara, another subject, discovered a five foot displacement in the layout which complicated the spatial relationships considerably for her. (See Figure 2-2.)

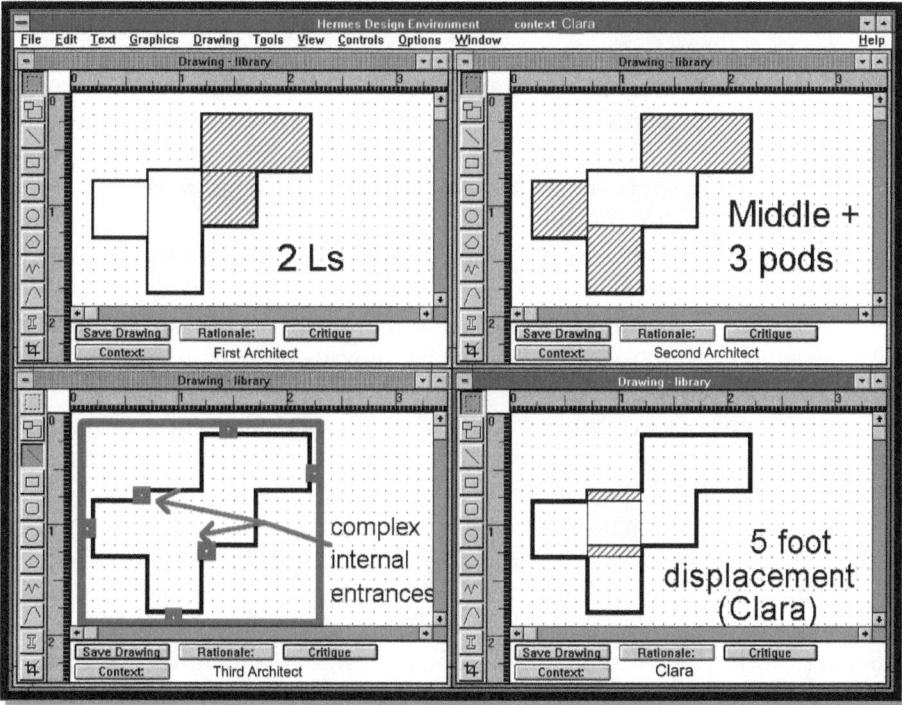

Figure 2-2. Four interpretations of the library.

Here the library is displayed in HERMES in four interpretive contexts, corresponding to the views of the four architects in Schön's study.

Schön concludes from these and other studies that designers construct the problem by seeing the situation *as* defined in a certain way:

> In one sense, the 5 ft displacement that Clara noticed is there to be discovered. However, not everyone who tried the library exercise discovered it. Clara did. She noticed it, named it, and made a *thing* that became critically important for her further designing. In this sense, her treatment of the library exercise shows her not only discovering but *constructing* the reality of a design situation. For designers share with all human beings an ability to construct, via perception, appreciation, language, and active manipulation, the worlds in which they function. . . . Every procedure, and every problem formulation, depends on such an ontology: a construction of the totality of things and relationships that the designer takes as the reality of the world in which he or she designs. (Schön, 1992, p.9)

What is Clara constructing here? She is not constructing the physical artifact (the actual library or even the drawing of it), but an *interpretation* of the problem situation *as* having certain crucial features, certain semantics, for her. Her awareness of the five foot displacement becomes increasingly explicit. She names it as a feature of the task and thinks about its relationship to possible solutions. Of course, the displacement was always physically present in the drawing, and the other architects may have had a subsidiary awareness of it. Maybe if they were questioned they would retroactively even be able to focus on it. However, it was not a focus for their designing the way it was for Clara's; they focused on other structures. Clara focused on the displacement. It became a problem for her. She reflected upon it as a central constraint of the design situation: she construed the situation in terms of this particular problem. Perhaps it presented an opportunity for her to do something with the library that she wanted to do; or perhaps it was a characteristic kind of feature she often exploited; or perhaps it stood in the way of her taking an accustomed approach. Whatever the details, she came to the task in her own characteristic way and constructed a design situation that differed essentially from what each of the other architects constructed. Each architect *interpreted* the given problem as a different task.

According to Schön, it is essential to recognize that the designer brings a creative constructive vision to the task. The problem of the library—the structure of the layout—is not explicitly given in the sense that an exhaustive specification of it could be given even in principle, but is experienced primarily in the mode of tacit *subsidiary awareness* (Polanyi, 1962). Nor does the designer impose a standard structure for interpreting the task. Rather, the designer approaches it with certain anticipations, conceptualizations, and background knowledge. Then the designer interacts with it to discover the basis for an understanding in terms of which the situation is framed or constructed. By attending to the displacement that others had ignored and naming it explicitly, Clara made it a crucial component of her design situation.

Schön's description of "construction" is very similar to Merleau-Ponty's concept of *creative discovery,* which is dependent on both the concrete individual and the specific task in their dialogical relation. Schön was undoubtedly influenced during his post-doctoral philosophy studies in Paris by Merleau-Ponty, the leading French philosopher teaching there at the time. Merleau-Ponty's *Phenomenology of Perception* (Merleau-Ponty, 1945) is perhaps the best analysis of Heidegger's philosophy (see Chapter 4 below) in terms of how we perceive our world. For Merleau-Ponty, the interpretive situation is neither simply objectively given nor subjectively represented, but creatively discovered. The dialectic of anticipatory framing and tentative setting of the object of perception *as* such and such a thing is elevated to an ontological principle by him at the same time as it is grounded in our corporeality as embodied perceivers. Perhaps more explicitly than any one else, Merleau-Ponty formulated a philosophy that explored the interplay of subjectivity and objectivity. By recognizing in detail how our body spans the subject-object dichotomy, he resolved at an abstract level the conflict that pervades late twentieth-century thought, including the design theory of Alexander, Rittel, and Schön. (The relevance of this conflict between the objectivity of artifacts in the world and the subjectivity of our interpretive perspectives for the question of computer support for design will be discussed at the conclusion of this chapter.)

Schön reviews other experiments that show that designers also construct the materials, site, and relationships in a similar way to how Clara constructed the crucial patterns of the project. In this sense, then, there is no given design problem that is explicitly and exhaustively defined before the designer comes to it. Correspondingly, there can be no well-defined problem space for the designer (or for some automated version of the designer) to search through methodically. Rather, the designer's subjective, personal or intuitive appreciations shape the problem by constructing its patterns, materials, and relationships. The design project is solved by the designer experimenting with tentative moves within the constructed design situation and discovering the consequences of those moves.

Clara made explicit the presence of the five foot displacement in the library footprint. As she works further on the library design, her awareness of the displacement may fade away, although it will have left its mark in the way she sees the structure of the building. This is one example of tacit knowledge becoming explicit for awhile during the design process, and then re-submerging into tacit, subsidiary awareness.

The movement from tacit to explicit understanding is an important and ubiquitous phenomenon, which Schön analyzes in more general terms in *The Design Studio* (Schön, 1985). Here he talks about the movement from *knowing-in-action* to *reflection-in-action*. For him, human action embodies tacit forms of knowledge: knowing *how* to physically do something without thinking about it or necessarily knowing *that* it may correspond to certain rules:

> To begin with, the starting condition of reflection-in-action is the repertoire of routinized responses that skillful practitioners bring to their practice. This is what I call the practitioner's *knowing-in-action*. It can be seen as consisting of strategies of action, understanding of phenomena, ways of framing the problematic situations encountered in day-to-day experience. It is acquired through training, or through on-the-job experience. It is usually tacit, and it is delivered spontaneously, without conscious deliberation. (p.24)

Schön's concept of knowing-in-action should be contrasted with the rationalist view of human action, which persists strongly into recent cognitive science. Rationalism (e.g., the tradition of Plato and Descartes) assumes that the basis of action is rational thought, that our behavior is caused by symbolic representations in our minds that could be articulated in propositions in language. Even in cases where we are not consciously aware of rational thought, it is argued, knowledge is at work unconsciously or in a "compiled" form and it could (at least in principle) be made explicit either by introspection of one's own motivations or by observation of rule-like regularities. Cognitive science makes the analogy between minds and software: our behavior, like that of a computer, is a matter of following computational rules that could be spelled out as an algorithm.

Polanyi, from whom Schön borrows an analysis of tacit knowledge, turns the traditional relationship between tacit knowing and rational thought around: "Tacit knowledge is more fundamental than explicit knowledge: we can know more than we can tell and we can tell nothing without relying on our awareness of things we may not be able to tell" (Polanyi, 1958, p. x). Our ability to use language and rational thought depends on more primordial skills and practices that cannot be clearly and exhaustively explicated: "We may say in general that by acquiring a skill, whether muscular or intellectual, we achieve an understanding that we cannot put into words and which is continuous with the inarticulate faculties of animals" (p.90). The priority of the tacit over the explicit does not mean that tacit knowledge is somehow better or more valuable, just that it is the precondition in terms of both ontogeny and phylogeny. That is, *for an individual person to articulate an idea, he or she must previously have possessed a tacit background understanding that led to the idea and grounded its meaning.* Similarly, for the human species to have developed sophisticated language and rational thought, it must have already evolved tacit forms of understanding such as those based on episodic (case-based) and mimetic (imitative) memory. Rational thought is still what distinguishes people from other animals, but that does not mean that rationality can exist without a foundation in tacit knowing-in-action.[4]

Polanyi provides the most concrete and detailed examination of tacit knowledge available. His analysis is strikingly close to that of Heidegger (see Chapter 4), as Polanyi acknowledges in his 1964 Preface: "All understanding is based in our dwelling in the particulars of that which we comprehend. Such indwelling is a participation of ours in the existence of that which we comprehend; it is Heidegger's *being-in-the-world*" (p. x). Unfortunately, Polanyi tends toward relativism, ending with a concept of "personal knowledge" that is too little grounded in the objectivity of a shared world. He emphasizes that everyone can have their own personal interpretations (assuming certain constraints of consistency, etc.), but lacks the sense of our embodiment (Merleau-Ponty) or situatedness (Heidegger) in a shared world, common traditions, social practices, and public language. (Compare Heidegger's views on a shared world in Section 4.2.)

Polanyi distinguishes *focal* and *subsidiary awareness*. His view of this is derived from the distinction between foreground and background in classical Gestalt psychology. Applying these terms, one could say that when Clara had a focal awareness of the five foot displacement, she also had a

---

[4] For a thorough discussion of the evolutionary basis for higher cognition, taking into account the latest findings of the cognitive sciences, see Donald (1992).

subsidiary awareness of the floor plan as a whole. It was only on the basis (background) of her tacit understanding of the problem as a whole (the floor plan) that the displacement could be taken as important and be understood as having certain implications—causing certain problems for the design. But, given this tacit knowledge of the whole, the focal part became the meaning of the whole: the design problem became a problem of resolving the issue of the displacement.

One can, according to Polanyi, only be focally aware of one thing at a time. When we switch our attention to something of which we have hitherto been subsidiarily aware, it loses its previous meaning. Consider the following three phases of Clara's attention:

Phase 1. She focuses on the plan as a whole, being only subsidiarily aware of the displacement (the way the other architects remained at best subsidiarily aware of it).

Phase 2. She focuses on the displacement. Now the displacement becomes the meaning of the whole floor plan. She becomes more explicitly aware of the displacement and starts to explore its details and implications. However, she can never achieve absolute explicit knowledge of the displacement issue because it involves and relies upon her tacit understanding of the general background problem.

Phase 1'. She returns her attention to the floor plan in general. Now her knowledge of the displacement becomes tacit once more. Of course, this tacit knowledge is much richer then it was originally, when she barely noticed it like the other architects. Now it can play an important role in her thinking about the floor plan.

How does Clara make these transitions? Why does the focus of her attention shift during the design process? Schön proposes an interesting theory of *breakdowns* to account for the shift from tacit knowing-in-action to an explicit focus and reflection. He argues that we can go along just *doing* what we are skilled at doing without much need for conscious thought. We are pretty much immersed in the doing, and any use of explicit language is more in the way of commentary than figuring things out. This can continue comfortably until we hit a problem that our skill cannot automatically resolve. Then, tacit doing suddenly breaks down and we have to think through the problem, explicitly focusing on the problem area:

> Sometimes, however, there are *surprises*. These take the form of unanticipated events which do not fit existing understandings, fall outside the categories of knowing-in-action. . . .

> There is a demand for reflection, through turning to the surprising phenomena and, at the same time, back on itself to the spontaneous knowing-in-action that triggered surprise. It is as though the practitioner asked himself, "What *is* this?" and at the same time, "How have I been *thinking* about this?"
>
> Such reflection must be at least in some degree conscious. It converts tacit knowing-in-action to explicit knowledge for action. (Schön, 1985, p.24)

We become aware of the problem and of what we have been doing that led us to the problem.

For instance, Clara was sketching in phase 1 above. She was exploring the approaches to the different entrances in the floor plan by drawing paths that users of the library would need to take. She was using her tacit architectural skills of sketching and vicariously moving through the spaces of the drawing. As she approached one of the interior doors, Clara suddenly remarked, "It's interesting that there's a five foot displacement here. I'm beginning to get more of a sense of those dimensions" (Schön, 1992, p.8). In the time it took her to say this, Clara passed through phase 2 and into phase 1'.

As Schön's commentary to this typical moment analyzes it, this was an instance of surprise or breakdown, which stimulated successful reflection-in-action. Clara had been pursuing a problem about the approach to the library. As she traversed one wall in her imagination she was surprised to find that it was longer than all the other (equal length) walls. Glancing across the interior, she saw the five foot jog in the opposite wall. These newly observed facts presented a problem for her attempt to find a comfortable approach to the building because they changed her understanding of the overall configuration. They showed that certain walls of interest were actually longer than other walls. Focusing on the five foot segments that made this difference gave new meaning to the whole building. As a trained architect, Clara could reflect on her discovery quickly, understand its significance and incorporate it in what she had been doing before.

Schön stresses that he is concerned with the form of reflection that actually takes place in the phase 2 moment of problem-solving—not what takes place retroactively long after the problem has been solved and the engagement with the process is broken. For Schön, reflection-in-action "must take place in the *action-present*—the period of time in which thinking can still make a difference to the outcomes of action. It has a *critical* function, questioning and challenging the assumptional basis of action, and a *restructuring* function, reshaping strategies, understanding of phenomena, and ways of framing problems" (Schön, 1985, p.25).

As a result of this moment of breakdown-reflection-repair, Clara's understanding of the overall problem has changed, as she immediately remarks. This does not mean she has an absolute and fully explicit understanding of the problem, but rather, as she puts it, she is "beginning to get more of a sense of those dimensions." The fact that she goes on to explore other issues and transfers her attention away from the displacement does not mean that the knowledge she gained from her momentary reflection-in-action is gone. It has just become subsidiary and tacit. According to Schön's description, later on in her designing, when she considered the entrance on the other side next to the five foot jog, "her discovery of the five foot displacement reemerges, and becomes central to her rethinking of spaces for circulation and use" (Schön, 1992, p.8).

Schön argues that a computer program cannot on its own construct a design situation the way an architect does, picking out, naming, and focusing upon critical patterns, materials, and relationships. The "construction" of a situation requires evolving a representation for it through the dialectic of creative-discovery or reflective conversation. It requires a subtle interplay between tacit knowing-in-action and more explicit reflection-in-action. To the extent that the role of a designer includes applying intuitive, perceptual, and linguistic skills to view the situation creatively and to converse with it reflectively, a computer cannot do what a human designer does. Assuming that Schön is correct that these skills are necessary for real design, a computer can also not accomplish the design task using alternative methods to those used by humans, because computer programs as we know them are ultimately based on predefined representations of fixed and strictly delimited ontologies. Computer programs for design are therefore limited to solving problems in well-defined "microworlds" (Papert, 1980) in which the framing of new problems is trivial, or else to working with human designers to augment their tacit skills and to allow them to define the perspectives and concepts in terms of which tasks are to be undertaken. Artificial intelligence (AI) projects have usually followed the microworlds option, trying to capture knowledge of a delimited domain in a symbolic representation that facilitates algorithmic computations. Schön calls for the alternative option of providing tools for people to define for themselves (within a computer system) representations of their own constructions or personal interpretations.

Ways must be found to support the interplay of tacit knowledge-in-action with more explicit reflection-in-action, which re-submerges into tacit awareness when the action-present passes. For a computer to process data, all information must be explicitly stated for it. A computer cannot slip facilely between the tacit and the explicit, the way people move from knowing-in-action to reflection-in-action. A person must translate the tacitly perceived world into a representation that makes explicit for the computer the person's partially implicit interpretation. Schön's theory of how designers are constantly making aspects of their implicit understanding explicit suggests that the computer should capture these explicit representations during the "action present" in which they can be most easily articulated. The implications of this for a theory of computer support are taken up in Chapter 6.

Three Perspectives on Design. The three writers just considered all present views of design as a process of *interpretation*. Alexander's tack of structural decomposition is one approach to interpreting a problem. For instance, the four architects in Schön's experiment interpreted their design situation differently by decomposing the library floor plan in four different ways: into a pair of "L" shapes, three pods around a middle space, a combination of simple and complex entrances, or a set of equal length walls complicated by a five foot displacement. Alexander recognizes how subtle even an objective seeming interpretation of a design can be, such as supporting people's tendency to want a view from their office desk. Finally, Alexander tries to provide a pattern language that people can use to articulate personal or group interpretations of buildings.

Rittel views the problems of planning and design as wicked problems largely because the participants in these processes bring conflicting interpretations to bear: they have different motivations, theoretical frameworks, and commitments. The notion of design as deliberation is an attempt to bring these differing interpretations into contact with each other in fruitful ways. Computer systems can serve as supportive crutches for such processes.

Schön emphasizes the variety of interpretations that an individual designer can pass through during a design session, as well as the differences in interpretation that different people are likely to come up with. One always sees something *as* something. This involves seeing a whole that one is subsidiarily aware of as meaningful in terms of a detailed aspect that is the momentary focus of awareness. When the evolving design artifact surprises the designer with something that stumps the interpretation projected by the designer's skilled, tacit knowing, then the designer is forced into a mode of reflection that transforms the interpretation. Interpretations are neither fixed nor arbitrary. They grow out of the traditions in people's backgrounds and they adapt to the constraints of the world to which they are applied.

These three writers provide important arguments about the three features of the process of design proposed in Chapter 1. They stress the roles of the situation, alternative perspectives, and explicit articulations. Furthermore, each of these is seen as essentially evolving, so that past understandings are built upon and modified. Despite their strong differences, each of these design methodologists describes design as a process of situated, perspectival, linguistic interpretation. Their emphases are different.

a. Situation. Alexander presents a strong case for deriving the interpretations in terms of which a design situation is to be construed from an analysis of the specifics of the problem. He claims that one must analyze the structure of the problem into patterns of components that are relatively independent. In a sense, this decomposition of the problem is a step towards solving it. In that sense, it is similar to Rittel's claim that the problem framing is inseparable from the problem solving. Schön echoes that sentiment by showing how the designer's understanding of the problem emerges from the dialogue with the design situation, which explores potential solutions.

b. Perspective. Rittel is the one who most emphasizes the uniqueness of the perspectives that designers bring to their work. Designers are as different as are problem situations; they have individual motivations, backgrounds, and commitments. At the same time, the factors that make people different each have a shared basis in their cultures, schools of thought, languages, and so on. While their perspectives may be irreconcilable in some ways, collaboration can critique and synthesize individual opinions to establish areas of consensus and to move beyond unreflective idiosyncrasies. Alexander recognizes the importance of different cultural traditions and tries to compile and organize patterns from diverse architectural traditions in order to provide a clearer basis for personal languages of designing. For Schön, individual interpretations can arise in the design process itself, regardless of personal differences among designers. In fact, a given designer will constantly be changing perspectives on the problem during the countless phases of the design process.

c. Language. Schön talks the most about how explicit interpretations emerge through articulating tacit knowing in language, and then re-submerge into the tacit. Alexander talks in much this way about the need for both intuition and analysis. For him, intuition is also associated with design practice. Practice is the necessary tacit element that is likely to be missing from considerations of explicit methodology. Rittel's emphasis on the role of personal prejudice recognizes the tacit basis of argumentation; yet his proposal of IBIS is very much a move toward making deliberation even more explicit than it is in less structured formats.

Computer support. Alexander, Rittel, and Schön have all taken seriously the question of computer support for design. They each wanted to use computers for their favorite part of the design process. Alexander used computers to analyze the decomposition of structures. Rittel used them to support the IBIS system of argumentation. Schön recommended using computer-based design assistants to create an environment in which a designer could explore design microworlds, reflect on knowledge, and enhance skills. None of them advocated an automated expert system approach. Alexander felt that such an approach led to people playing with computers like toys, divorced from the concerns of practicing designers. Rittel thought such systems would incorporate "freeze-dried prejudice" rather than stimulating the deliberative process of design. Schön argued that design requires human skills that computers could not duplicate, imitate, or replace by themselves.

Where Alexander was still struggling to maintain a sense of the possibility of objective methods in the face of problems that were becoming apparent in the 1960's, Rittel was formulating a clear call in the 1970's for an alternative use of computers to support human designing. In particular, he proposed supporting deliberation among opposed interpretive perspectives. Then in the 1980's Schön was able to describe the interplay between the human designer and the materials of the design situation as an interpretive dialogue. It remains for the 1990's to implement adequate computer support for this process of interpretation in design.

Objectivity and subjectivity. One could interpret Alexander and Rittel as occupying opposite ends of the spectrum. Alexander seems to long for the objectivity of mathematical decomposition analysis, empirical hypothesis verification, and a distillation of eternal patterns for building. Rittel, in contrast, stresses that similarities of pattern are a matter of interpretation and that all judgments are ultimately grounded in subjective prejudice. But first of all, there are historical differences. The late sixties, which separated most of the writings of Alexander and Rittel reviewed here, saw the widespread crumbling of faith in unified, objective science and in the mathematical methods of operations research.[5] And secondly, neither Alexander nor Rittel hold to simple, easily characterized views.

The question of how knowledge is objective and how it is subjective is closely related to whether design can be computerized or not. Certainly the expert system approach is one that assumes that design knowledge can be formulated in an objective way. The paradigm here is that one finds an expert who has somehow learned *the* knowledge of the relevant design domain: applicable regulations, rules of thumb, accepted wisdom, tricks of the trade, prototypical solutions, standard approaches. Through interview techniques, the expert's knowledge is made explicit and captured in a large set of rules, which are entered into the computer. Then, the specification for a problem in the domain is entered with sufficient detail and with all the relevant information so the computer can compute a solution that satisfies the specification by applying the set of rules to the specified starting conditions and goals. This approach should be contrasted with the view of design as interpretation. While it may work in certain narrowly-defined and well-understood domains, the expert system approach ignores the features of design that Alexander, Rittel, and Schön have argued are decisive for most innovative design work. Design knowledge cannot be formulated in abstract rules because it is dependent upon the situation, perspective, and language which are brought to bear in essentially unique concrete instances of interpretation. The rules of autonomous software systems can only work in narrowly defined realms in which a standard interpretation is accepted.

The design methodologists just reviewed present a strong case that computer systems should enable designers to define their own understanding of the structure of the design problem, to formulate their own perspectives based on traditional views, and to articulate their tacit knowledge in increasingly explicit forms. In this way, personal or group interpretations can build upon shared domain knowledge but also go beyond it. While a computer-based system can *support* such activities, it cannot *do* them without human participation. This is where the subjective aspect enters. As long as design is

---

[5] It would be simplistic to distinguish cause from effect by saying that, for instance, Rittel's writings either hastened or merely reflected the growing disillusionment with objectivist thinking. Alexander, Rittel, and Schön are important participants in this general movement. Within AI there have long been critics of the objectivist approach typified by expert systems, including Engelbart (1963), Dreyfus (1965), Weizenbaum (1976), and Winograd & Flores (1986). The systems discussed in Chapter 7 are also participants in this movement.

conceived as involving subjective aspects, it cannot be automated. Computers may be able to keep track of interpretive perspectives and even help to elicit tacit knowledge or subjective views, but computers cannot interpret. Nor can knowledge corresponding to interpretations be entered into computer systems in advance, the way that standard domain knowledge can (under the most favorable of conditions). By definition, domain knowledge is general and can be catalogued (although never exhaustively since it includes tacit background knowledge that cannot all be made entirely explicit). In contrast, interpretations are by nature innovative and go essentially beyond the standard domain traditions upon which they build—hence their characterization as "subjective". They can only be added to the computer knowledge base post hoc, in order continuously to expand the base upon which future interpretations can grow.

CHAPTER 3. INTERPRETATION IN LUNAR HABITAT DESIGN

Simon (1981) says, "Everyone designs who devises courses of action aimed at changing existing situations into preferred ones" (p.129). Design is a broad and diverse business. For the sake of concreteness, this chapter focuses on lunar habitat design and the problem of providing computer support for this task.

A number of characteristics of lunar habitat design make it an interesting candidate for studying the process of interpretation in design and the possibilities of providing computer support for interpretation. It is a high-tech undertaking requiring too much detailed information for an individual to keep track of without computer support. Significantly, although the field of lunar habitat design is so new that it must be considered an example of *exploratory* design, it also avails itself of extensive systematically codified domain knowledge. That is, lunar habitat design efforts necessarily innovate and explore new possibilities. Every effort at design is likely to make new *discoveries* that could not have been foreseen but that should be captured for future design work. At the same time, these efforts are obliged to take seriously design guidelines and technical studies compiled by NASA. There are so many social, technical, and bureaucratic constraints on the task of laying out a habitat for astronauts on the moon that it is a non-trivial—particularly wicked—problem. Yet it is specific enough that it makes for a realistic, but manageable case study. Its wicked nature is clear in the way the designers who were studied had to frame the problem of privacy in order to work out a layout solution.

A tool such as the proposed HERMES system is attractive enough to NASA contractors that cooperation was forthcoming for conducting a study of the work process involved in lunar habitat design. Specifically, approximately thirty hours of videotapes were recorded of an extended lunar habitat design effort. The sessions were structured as a conversation between pairs of designers in order to elicit verbally the knowledge-in-action that was at work tacitly as well as the more explicit reflection-in-action that emerged when problems were encountered. The following sections take a close look at two segments of the video recordings in order to observe the processes of interpretation at work in design..

Section 3.1 reviews a brief design episode that introduces the issue of privacy and proposes individual crew compartments to provide private spaces for the astronauts. The concept of privacy is a difficult one to represent objectively. It provides a challenging example for a theory of computer support. At first, the concept of privacy seems subjective, having a different meaning for every situation and every designer. Yet, it names a general issue that NASA recognized must be addressed.

Section 3.2 presents a longer transcript that reflects a series of design moves motivated by discoveries about the concept of privacy that resulted from deliberation of different perspectives on bathroom design. This process led to a concept of privacy gradient, that was recognized as an organizing principle for the evolving habitat design. Here the process of design can be seen to involve (a) a creative discovery of the situation, (b) views from different perspectives, and (c) the articulation of tacit understanding in language—both in traditional and in refined terminology.

Section 3.3 takes a look at NASA efforts to capture privacy considerations in their guidelines for manned-systems design. This suggests the difficulty of formulating important design concerns like privacy as generic domain knowledge. However, it also suggests the potential for capturing design ideas as they actually emerge during engaged design activities.

3.1. Situations of Privacy and the Problem of Representation

In the first design session the participants—a designer, who will here be called Desi, and an architect, Archie—sat down to design a habitat for four astronauts to stay in during a first "overnighter" on the moon. Two "days" and a "night" on the moon is about 42 Earth days. It was assumed that the crew might be of mixed gender and culture or nationality. The mission would include some scientific investigation and some preparation for future lunar stays. The habitat structure would, necessarily, remain on the moon and need to be adaptable to future missions. The habitat was to be designed to fit within a standard cylindrical module that is being used for Space Station and that can fit in the cargo hold of the Space Shuttle. This module is 25 feet long and 14 feet in diameter. Air locks can be attached to hatches at either end.

Desi is an industrial designer who has been involved with designing lunar habitats for NASA for a number of years. Archie is educated in architecture but has no experience in this specialized domain. Particularly in the beginning, the sessions provide an opportunity for Desi to teach Archie about the domain. The instructional nature of the sessions and the style of interaction between the participants serves well to elicit the design rationale that experienced designers might take for granted. In this way, the design of the study extended the basic technique of "constructive interaction" (Miyake, 1986), in which subjects are paired so that their processes of understanding will be verbalized.

The following excerpt is from the initial session. It is transcribed verbatim, except for the removal of an occasional "um" or "you know." Of course, it looks more formal and less spontaneous on paper with clear punctuation then when it was haltingly pronounced within the context of gestures, mutual interruptions, and sketching.

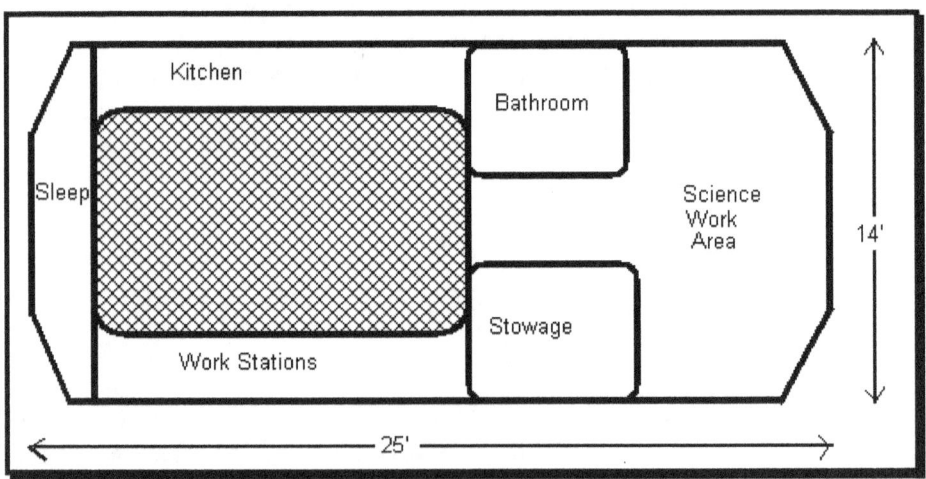

Figure 3-1. Initial design of a lunar habitat layout.

This is a complete graphics representation such as could be constructed in Hermes. It is meant as a guide to the reader. Desi's actual pen sketches evolved as he talked and are less useful as static representations.

This passage formed a critical turning-point in the whole design process. It is worth a close look even though it may not on the face of it appear that "real" designing is going on at the moment. Desi has just sketched his first sample lunar habitat layout, which is represented in Figure 3-1. He is emphasizing the large empty space in the center (shaded in the figure) that is available for a variety of uses, depending on the needs of the moment. For instance, beds can fold down into it from the small area marked Sleep at night. Exercise equipment can be set up at other times, or a table for meals and meetings.

Transcript of Lunar Habitat Design Session (Tape B, 33:00):

> Desi: You have a big "family room" or "den." And what they [the astronauts] do is either fold down the Murphy bed or set up cots. But for sleeping you don't dedicate space—since that's only used 8 hours a day and, face it, people's eyes are closed anyway. What you do is provide a place for sleep, an accommodation for sleep. All they need is a horizontal surface. They don't need a private room to sleep, if that's all you're providing.

> Archie: On the other hand, there are times when you're waking up or going to sleep and getting your clothes on or whatever, when a modicum of privacy can actually be treasured, and when some people read a book.

> Desi: That's another option that we can look at. When you talk about sleep compartments where you can read and work, change your clothes, and do all that, they [NASA] just call them "crew compartments" rather than "sleep compartments" because you're doing more than sleeping. It's just semantics.

> Archie: The idea is that it's intrinsically multi-functional?

> Desi: Yes. It's multi-functional. It's a crew compartment.

> Archie: Is that an accepted idea now? That they should be multi-functional.

> Desi: Well, it is an alternative. I'm not saying it's accepted or not. It is what they [NASA] originally pursued or conceived of for Space Station. Each astronaut had an individual crew compartment that had their audio, stereo, video. It had a computer. It had their

personal storage, their sleep [area]. It basically was their room where they could go in and work. And they could get away.

Archie: Have they [NASA] moved away from that now?

Desi: In the Space Station module they had about a third of the volume dedicated for sleep compartments only. And in the current configuration—with 25 foot long modules instead of 40 foot long— there is no provision for sleep compartments in the habitat. So it suggests they [the astronauts] are going to be stringing hammocks in the hallway or sleeping in the node. But there is no permanent, individual crew compartment. So they [NASA] have gone from one extreme to the other.

Archie: It's an interesting question. If you cross this 30 day limit, then it seems likely the sleep compartments suddenly become a dramatically higher priority. People start freaking out that they can't get away from other people.

Desi: I would think so. I would think that the idea of being able to get away would be nice. Having that privacy, the control, even if they don't use it.

A mini-drama of argumentation unfolds here around the issue of sleep accommodations in the habitat. Desi makes a first proposal in his initial concept sketch (Figure 3-1). It is to create a general purpose space in the middle of the habitat where beds of some kind could be set up during the sleep period and then cleared away for other uses. This is a relatively austere approach based on the idea that the astronauts will accept pretty much anything you give them. But Archie comes to this with a different perspective. He is not used to the military influence in NASA's attitudes and thinks it is nice to be able to get away by yourself and snuggle up in bed with a good book. Desi immediately responds that private crew compartments are definitely another alternative that they could look at. He points out that the design for Space Station—which offers the closest analog for lunar habitats—originally incorporated crew compartments, although the revised design does not. Finally, Archie argues that being confined together for over a month is qualitatively different from short term missions where lack of privacy can be tolerated more easily. Desi agrees that privacy will be important in designing a habitat for their mission.

Through this exchange, one of the crucial decisions of this design effort has been made: the decision to focus on habitability issues like the need for privacy. The next sections will explore in more detail how such decisions come about, and how they turn out to be important. For now, it might simply be noted that Desi starts the process by presenting an idea that was familiar to him from a tradition of past designs (e.g., recent NASA thinking about Space Station). Archie immediately brings his personal experience to bear, essentially asking, "What would it be like to be an astronaut living in this place for over a month? How would I like that?" Desi then switches to another experience case, the original Space Station module. By now Archie is imagining the social interactions in the confined space, and his notion of privacy grows from being one of life's little treasures to a dramatic necessity for the maintenance of sanity. Desi lets himself be convinced, and spends the next many hours trying to figure out how to carve some private sleeping quarters out of the tiny module (the size of a common living room) that had to contain all the facilities for life and work of four astronauts.

In this way, the framing of the problem and focus for solving it emerge through deliberation of different situations (related, historical, or imagined) from multiple perspectives (Desi's, Archie's, an astronaut's, NASA's, an emerging shared one). The interpretation of the design revolves around discoveries in the situation. The major discovery made in the transcribed episode is the issue of privacy. The on-going interpretation driven by the need to resolve this discovered issue will lead to many further discoveries. This is the nature of innovative design.

The need for privacy proves to be a major constraint in the videotaped design sessions. The primary problem for the design becomes the conflict between wanting to create a mix of private and public spaces and the need to fit a lot of equipment into a very small volume. Given the importance of privacy considerations in these sessions, it is natural to inquire how NASA's codified design standards handle the issue of privacy. This is closely related to the question of how an issue like privacy can be represented in a computer design environment. The problem is one of articulating the notion of privacy that everyone understands tacitly, but doing so in an explicit, objectified, and operationalized way.

NASA is a prime example of management by objectives, where issues are spelled out as explicit specifications and regulations. This accounts for its success according to Simon (1981), who contrasts the US's success in placing men on the moon with its lack of success in creating a humane society or a peaceful world. The social problems are truly wicked problems in Rittel's sense; they require deliberation by the many participants in the problem, who have different concerns and ideological commitments. Going to the moon had an unambiguous, highly operational goal enunciated by the

President of the United States. The space effort was judged a success in terms of this goal (p.162).

NASA is a major user of computers; the space program actually drove development of mainframe computer technology to a certain extent. One would think that if privacy is the first major issue to come up in the initial videotaped session of lunar habitat design then NASA must have long ago worked out ways of operationalizing this design goal and representing it in computerized design support systems. However, this does not seem to be the case. A first hint of this failure might be inferred from the history of the privacy issue in Space Station. In one design a major allocation of space was devoted to private crew compartments, and in the next there was absolutely no private space. Apparently, the original rationale for designing private spaces was completely ignored or forgotten.

NASA's major opportunity to explore what they call *habitability issues* was with Skylab, manned orbital missions during the early 1970's lasting up to two months long. In addition to providing a laboratory for studies of outer space, this program was meant to study problems of groups of people in space. Despite this explicit goal, the attempt to design the astronaut's physical environment to be more habitable was strongly resisted in NASA. As described in NASA's own history of Skylab (Compton & Benson, 1983), it was only through the consistent efforts of certain administrators over a period of years that any real design effort was put into this:

> Habitability, livability—or whatever name is given to the suitability of the environment for daily living—is, as one NASA designer remarked, 'a nebulous term at best,' one not usually found in the engineer's vocabulary. Besides factors within the engineer's usual responsibilities, such as the composition and temperature of the atmosphere and the levels of light and noise, habitability also encompasses the ease of keeping house, the convenience of attending to personal hygiene, and the provision for exercise and off-duty relaxation. Experience and intuition both suggested that these factors would become more important as missions grew longer. Looking ahead to space station, NASA designers needed basic information on these problems of living in space. (p.131)

During this process a designer brought in to study the Skylab layout from the perspective of habitability proposed the idea of a *wardroom*, a common space for eating, relaxing, meeting and socializing. The acceptance of this idea was an exception. In general, designing was done by engineers, who focused on purely technical issues. Along with the engineers on their staffs, many NASA administrators saw issues of habitability as threats to their budgetary and schedule goals. Skylab did not have a simple criterion such as the one attributed by Simon to the moon landing, and its planning process was a complex one of negotiation and political maneuvering, despite its confinement within the NASA bureaucracy.

Today, the planning process is even more complex. Architects, sociologists, and anthropologists are being involved. A recent survey was conducted of architecture professors to develop a set of criteria for planning a lunar base (Eichold, 1992). In contrast to the old engineering mentality, the architects felt that the issue of private space was very important. The highest statistic of the survey was that 85% of the respondents listed "balance between community and privacy" as their first or second design preference. The survey report concluded that this emphasis is supported by experience found in the closest analogs for extreme environments and isolation: submarines and Antarctic outposts (see Boeing, 1983; Bluth, 1984; Bluth, 1986). The perspective that Archie brought in the session transcribed above is clearly not idiosyncratic.

Although it is clear that privacy is an issue for NASA missions, it is not so clear that NASA has come to terms with the issue. The recent Endeavor flight launched on September 12, 1992, provides an amusing case in point. The goal of the flight could be characterized as "sex in space": frogs, fish, wasps, flies, and chicken eggs were taken up to be fertilized and reproduced in space. Yet there were no provisions for privacy for the first married couple to fly together as astronauts. Although NASA made an exception to its rule barring husbands and wives from flying in space together, they went out of their way to assure the public that there would be no human sex in space—a topic that has caused a certain amount of speculation in popular science circles. Press releases stressed that the couple slept on different shifts and were "too busy to even hold hands" on the flight.

NASA has published volumes of Man-Systems Integration Standards (MSIS), systematic compilations of design considerations and requirements for the development of manned space systems. The volume most applicable to lunar habitat design is Volume IV, which defines the firm requirements that are pertinent to Space Station. The most recent revision of this document (Revision A, December 14, 1989) defines *habitability* as the quality of life in an environment. The basic level of habitability stresses the traditional physical concerns for climate, food, noise, light, etc. But for Space Station, an extended level of habitability is introduced to "take care of the long-term condition of the on-orbit stay time and [to] support not only the individual's physical health but also the mental/psychological health because experience has shown that with the passage of time deleterious effects of isolation and confinement gain prominence" (NASA, 1989b, p.1-4).

Despite this explicit recognition of the need to support mental health under conditions of confinement, the standards provide little guidance for or guarantee of provisions for privacy and sociability. The only mention of *privacy* is in connection with crew compartments. The general requirement is "a dedicated, private crew quarter shall be provided for each crewmember" (ibid., p.10-8). The ten specific design requirements of the crew quarters are confined to physical, safety, and security concerns, with one exception: "h. Privacy—The individual crew quarters shall provide visual privacy to and from the occupant and acoustic privacy as defined [by reference to quantitative noise levels]" (ibid., p.10-8f). Spatial volumes are specified for allowing for sleep, stowage, dressing, working at a desk, and off-duty activities.

There is even less reference to *sociability*. The galley and wardroom are discussed solely in terms of food preparation and eating. It is stated that a table shall be provided for eating, but there is no suggestion that it be large enough to accommodate the whole crew at once. There is a separate requirement for a meeting room, although it is clearly intended that the wardroom would be converted to this use as required. Here it is stated that, "The meeting facility shall accommodate a meeting of the entire Space Station Freedom crew" (ibid. p.10-12). This single sentence (with no supporting rationale, references to psychological concerns, or further discussion) is all that exists to encourage designing for sociability. In the new Space Station design the crew compartments have been eliminated. The experience from Skylab shows that the crew often decides not to eat together in order to concentrate on work tasks. Thus, despite a token recognition of the importance of designing a balance of public and private spaces, the NASA requirements are ineffective in capturing this goal.

The need to plan for privacy and sociability arises repeatedly from the task of designing lunar or space habitats to be used for extended durations. It was a controversial priority in Skylab; it was recognized in the early designing of Space Station; it is emphasized by recent studies and surveys; and it came up right away in the design session transcribed above. Yet it has been just as repeatedly resisted by engineers, and is inadequately supported in NASA's requirements document. Even Desi—who prides himself in his concern for habitability issues—tried to end-run the topic in his opening presentation, until he was forced to admit that it was an option, and in fact an important concern.

The question is how a design consideration like establishing a healthy balance of privacy and sociability can be *represented* in a design support system, whether a manual of requirements or a computer-based system. It is easy for NASA to specify that 53 cubic feet (1.50 cubic meters) are required for sleeping or that noise levels must be kept below 85 dB. Regular CAD drafting programs can check the numeric dimensions of components of a design, and critic rules in a computer-based design environment like JANUS (see Chapter 7) can ensure that distances between components are within given quantitative limits. However, it is not so easy to see how concerns for privacy can be operationalized or encoded into requirements that can be supported by computer. It may have been relatively straight-forward to say that we want a man to step on the moon. It is more of a wicked problem to say that we want a diverse group of people to live on the moon for an extended period of time as part of a politically controversial long-range plan to land people on Mars. The problem of supporting privacy concerns in design provides a paradigm example of an interpretive issue that has resisted solution by traditional methods. It will serve as a key example throughout this dissertation.

3.2. Perspectives on Privacy

The concern for privacy in the lunar habitat came up again and again in the taped sessions. Several minutes after the discussion cited above, the following dialogue took place. In it, one can see the designers struggling to construct a *situation* of privacy by bringing different experiences and *perspectives* to bear and reframing the meanings of terms to develop a shared *language*. The transcript in this section is broken up for the sake of exposition, but it took place continuously except for pauses to sketch. The sketching was largely gestural, to accompany the discussion of specific features—the drawings below are more schematic and less dynamic, but should help the reader to visualize the layouts being discussed.

As shown in Figure 3-2, at this point in the designing private crew compartments have been added at the left end of the lunar habitat module. They are arranged like two bunk beds along the walls, providing accommodations for the four astronauts and leaving a corridor open through the center of the module for access to the hatches at the two ends. All the areas requiring plumbing have been located together along one wall, leaving a large area open for meeting, eating, exercise, and work activities. A table and chairs have been sketched in as a multi-purpose ward room, surrounded, perhaps, by work stations containing computer screens and panels for communication and control, or for other sit-down work. Another area has been left open for experiments, research, etc.

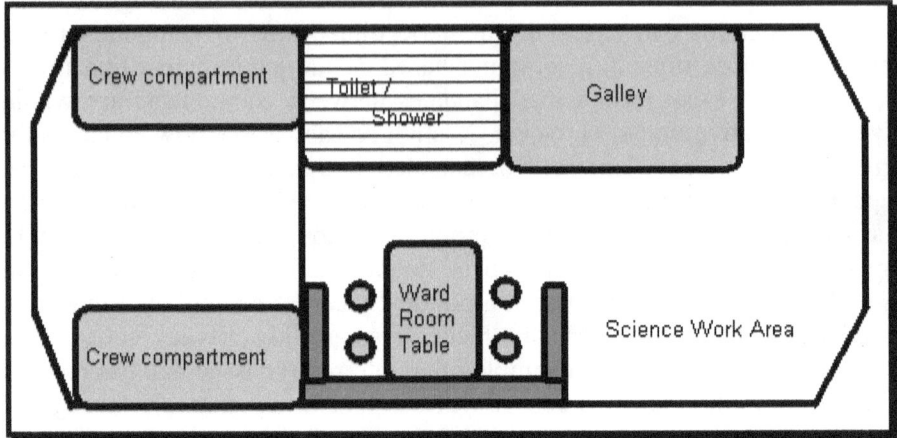

Figure 3-2. A layout for living and working.

Desi has placed the toilet, shower, and galley together to conserve on plumbing connections, which are more complicated in the moon's low gravity than on Earth. But he and Archie immediately discover some problems with this arrangement. Namely, the toilet encroaches too prominently visually on the eating area and acoustically on the sleeping area. They start moving things around in the layout. Buffers are added to provide visual and acoustic privacy, often by strategically locating storage closets. (Lots of storage will have to be designed in at some point anyway in order to hold all the provisions for a month and a half.)

Transcript of Lunar Habitat Design Session (Tape B, 42:00):

> Desi: Okay, this is the shower here. This is the galley. This is the toilet right here. [See Figure 3-2.] Assuming that the entrance in and out might be right here. One of the things about *privacy*...?

> Archie: Yeah?

> Desi: . . . One thing I hate about my office is that right out of the reception area, the secretaries are sitting there facing the bathroom door. It's like you're being watched.

Archie: Well I think *this* is problematic. Right here you've got the toilet right open into the open area, where meals are probably consumed and all.

Desi: That's awful! The potential here is that you could actually put a work station here. This might even be your galley here, with the plumbing back to back, But you've got a little equipment to create an acoustical/physical barrier and your open area is here.

Archie: Um hum. What about sound separation right here? When someone gets up to go to the toilet in the middle of the night and, bang, everyone else is woken up.

Desi: What's happening here is we're starting to see a separation of living and working as distinct ends. Potentially, quiet and noisy [areas].

Archie: We start to see some of the influences of the design. For one thing, separating those things allows you to get away from work. For, you know, you have different moods and different modes in which you behave. When you're in one side of the place your surroundings stimulate a certain kind of response, a certain kind of psychological response, whereas when you're on the other side, you're stimulated for another kind of response. . . . The danger of mixing them is that there is no place to get away, and every environment is stimulating multiple responses from you. So you don't have any support from your environment for your mood. It would seem to me that things like mood become pretty damn crucial when you're 45 days in a tin can with a bunch of people.

Experimenting with different arrangements—what Schön called making design "moves"—leads to a gradual differentiation of areas of the module. The designers make discoveries within the situation they have created. They discover that the constraints of the design situation (constraints that they have in a sense created by their concern with habitability and privacy issues) are leading to a "separation of living and working as distinct ends." This begins to solve the problem of being cooped up together: there are qualitatively different kinds of areas where one can go to relax, socialize or work. In this way, they "start to see some of the influences of the design": the constraints of the situation and the implications of their moves and concerns are starting to cause consequences that they notice. They start to discover in the sketch—as it evolves and as their interpretation or conceptualization of it evolves—that there are, "potentially, quiet and noisy" areas coming into definition. Now, a door can be closed to a crew compartment to provide a quiet area where someone can go to listen to music, tape-record one's thoughts, or study a training manual.

They focus on the placement of the toilet, which had served to sharpen their concern about privacy. Previously, Desi had argued for a design where the toilet, the sink, and the shower were combined in one unit to save space. He had supported his suggestion by talking about the bathroom ("the head") on a yacht, which squeezes all the functionality into a cramped space. He also recognized that combining the two in one room would cause accessibility problems, particularly first thing in the morning. Next, Archie brings in other concepts of bathroom design in which the shower or bath is located in a separate location. These different perspectives are introduced and kept in mind to determine alternative placements for toilet, sink, shower, and dressing area in the habitat, and to provide rationale for those alternatives. This allows the toilet and shower to be separated in Figure 3-3, removing the toilet from its acoustic and visual proximity to the sleeping and eating areas, while keeping the shower convenient to the sleep area.

Desi: Living/working; quiet/noisy. Now let's throw in that implication of some privacy when you go to the bathroom. If we're to say. . . .

Archie: Look, let's make the placement of the bathroom and shower a little more important. Or is the shower the same as the toilet and the sink? Could we separate them, have the shower a little more convenient to where you're going to change, get dressed. You get up in the morning, get dressed, change your clothes. Maybe that's a little more convenient.

Desi: You're not going to get up in the middle of the night and take a shower.

Archie: Here's an interesting analogy. America is, I think, the only one of the Western countries—I mean the countries of North America are the only ones—that have the toilet and the shower in the same room. Most of the European bathrooms have them in a separate room. Maybe that's changing as they're adopting some American style things over there. Certainly, in Germany it is no longer the case. But in England, I know, it's unusual to have the toilet and the shower in the same place. Americans use the term "bathroom" for the place where you go to the toilet. But the bathroom, if I'm not mistaken, in England means a separate room, which is connected. There is this separation. So maybe that becomes the model for what we should do. What that shows is there is a grouping of these activities which indicates sort of different levels of privacy.

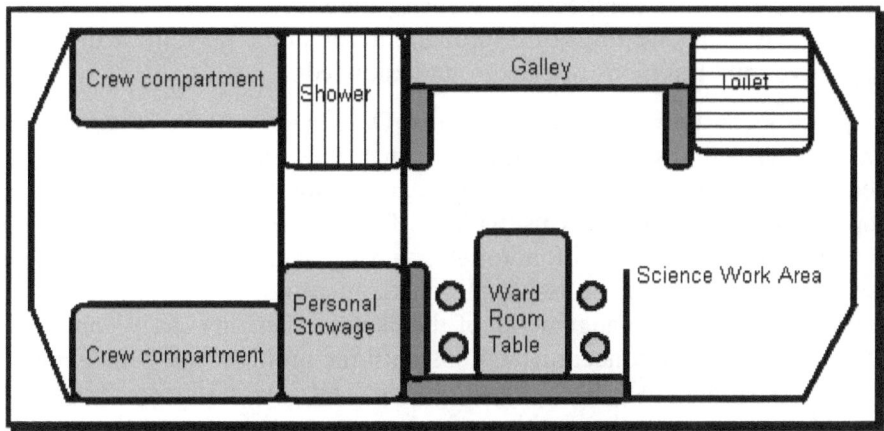

Figure 3-3. A private dressing area.

Here, the designers have adopted a perspective on privacy. They are creating this new shared perspective by not only incorporating their personal, tacit definitions of privacy, but by merging in ideas from other perspectives. By deliberating issues among themselves from different perspectives, they begin to build an agreed upon framework for looking at their problem and proceeding with the design effort. The privacy perspective guides their moves and makes possible new discoveries that would not otherwise have occurred.

It is interesting to note that the design process at this point thrives on the consideration of alternatives. First, at the level of rearranging the layout, the alternatives are tried out in a rapid succession of sketches to get a feel for how they work. Secondly, though, the designing does not consist solely of sketching. Most of the time, in fact, is spent in discussing the alternatives from various perspectives. The issue of separation of toilet from shower, for instance, was considered from the perspective of yacht and submarine examples as well as from the traditional American and European house design perspectives. In trying to define the European tradition that he was referring to, Archie even indicated that the European perspective is multi-faceted and evolving, a mixture of, say, German, French, and English traditions changing under American influence. It is not as though there is one rule from some supposed "domain of bathroom design"—like: the toilet should be near the shower—or even that one such rule applies in the context of lunar habitat design. Rather, the designers *deliberated* a number of possible (and mutually conflicting) rules and *tried them out.* They continually switched perspectives to view their design differently and to discover new understandings of it through interpretation from these different perspectives and traditions of background knowledge.

The process can be put in Schön's terms. Desi made a move (Figure 3-2). The designers reacted to the situation that they had created, and they discovered a serious problem (the adjacency of the toilet to the eating and sleeping areas), or "breakdown situation." They began to reflect-in-action on the issue of the location of a toilet. As they came up with justifiable alternative responses to the issue, they tried them out in little sketches (or gestures indicating rearrangements of the sketched layout). They continued to come up with new conceptualizations until the problem was satisfactorily resolved. What may look like a lot of obvious verbiage in retrospect, was an engaged struggle with the problematic design situation during the "action moment."

In Alexander's terms, the designers are continuously trying to represent the structural patterns of the problem: should a decomposition of the habitat include the shower and toilet in a unit, or should the shower be with the sleep area and the toilet elsewhere? Archie's last comment above suggests that the decomposition might be based on the European model he has presented, so that "there is a grouping of these activities [of daily life in the habitat] which indicates sort of different levels of privacy." This leads to the layout in Figure 3-3, in which the activities of getting out of bed, showering, and dressing are grouped together, while the toilet, which might interfere with sleep or the use of the shower, is grouped elsewhere.

For Rittel, this is a good example of the need to deliberate issues from a variety of perspectives; there is no single best rule, but an open-ended variety of approaches that can be used to critique and refine each other. Archie's lengthy discussions of people having different moods and different countries having different conceptions of bathrooms were not simply contributions of information, as though Desi did not already know these things. More importantly he was introducing new perspectives into the life of the debate and elaborating their rationale in an informal and abbreviated way. Deliberation is not simply a compiling of facts, but a subtle form of argumentation and persuasion through which a consensus might be reached and concepts of a shared language honed.

Schön, of course, adds the notion that the differing choices must then be tried out so their implications can be creatively-discovered. This takes place in the next two segments of the transcribed process, where the implications of Figure 3-3 are actively explored, leading to the design in Figure 3-4.

Desi: Oh yeah. So, what about the sleep compartments? As I said, chances are they are not going to get up in the middle of the night and take a shower. So we could probably safely put a shower next to a sleep compartment and create a zone where (this may be way out of scale) where you can have this privacy. Over here is the storage of clothes and stuff.

Archie: So that provides a buffer.

Desi: If you look at this elevation sketch, they all have their drawers along here for personal storage. You can get in to the drawers from this angle.

Archie: So you've actually got a sort of dressing, shower, change area as a buffer between that and the rest of the house. [See Figure 3-3.]

Desi: Right. The problem is if you want to change your clothes and take a shower, you're going to trap somebody back there and they can't get through. . . . What if you were to flip those? Say shower, storage here, and actually come in here and close this off. We've got this end-cone [of the tapered cylindrical module shell] geometry down here on the end which is a little awkward, where you could fit a lot of socks and underwear, as well as some plumbing. [See Figure 3-4.]

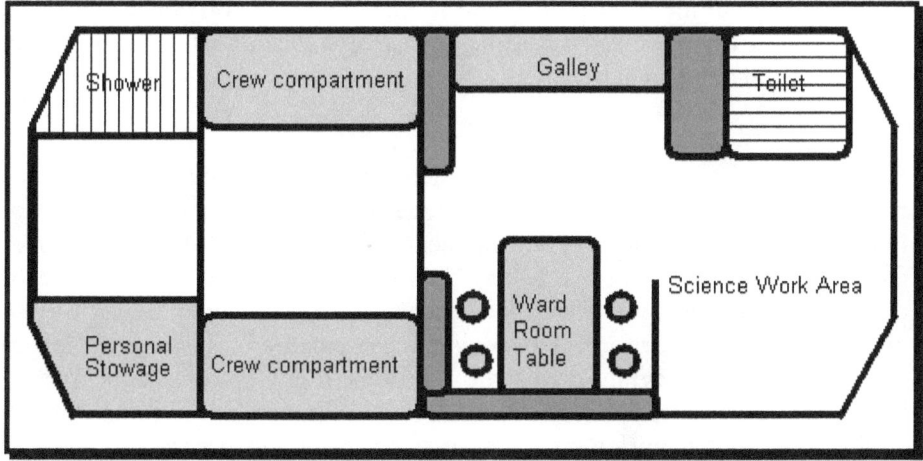

Figure 3-4. A privacy gradient.

Archie: So if you needed to take a shower or get to the storage you're going to have to walk through this sleep thing. Is there any danger. . . .

Desi: Well , you probably just shower once a day.

Archie: All right, the shower is probably not going to be a problem. But storage...

Desi: Storage? But this is clothes . . . personal effects. Stuff you need in the morning and at the end of the day, before you go to sleep and when you get up.

Archie: So if you forget something and you want to go back in you have to go past the sleeping people?

Desi: Yes, If they're sleeping. So anyway, the idea is that you could actually close this off and have a place to take a shower . . . come out here . . . change your clothes . . . and have relative privacy without obstructing circulation.

Archie: Then you do lose the buffer to the outside in the process. So there's a trade off. Also this storage thing here could conceivably be accessed from this direction, meaning that you wouldn't have to be in this area at all if you wanted to access it. The advantage there would be if you have some kind of tight corridor you wouldn't want to be pulling drawers out into it, but I suppose you could go inside. But I don't know how tight that is; a walk-in closet on the moon sounds like an extravagance.

Here Desi has grouped the shower together with the crew compartments because the preceding arguments suggested that the shower will not interfere with sleep the way an adjacent toilet might (and in fact did in Skylab). The shower forms a buffer between the sleep area and the rest of the module, which gives Desi the idea of creating a similar buffer on the other side of the corridor. He decides that can be a stowage (storage) compartment. To integrate it with the activities of getting up and showering, he says the astronauts will keep their clothes in drawers in the compartment. Archie sees that a buffer area has now been formed across the module. Adding doors to both ends of the buffer provides a changing room with access to the shower and the clothes storage. Desi likes the idea, but spots a traffic flow problem: when one person is changing, others cannot get out for their morning coffee. So he moves the changing area to the other end of the crew compartments, where it will not block traffic. (See Figure 3-4.) This move eliminates the buffer function, so Desi adds some small stowage areas to act as a wall and absorb sounds. He re-designs the shower and stowage to take advantage of odd-shaped spaces at the end, which had been wasted until now. Desi and Archie's understanding of the habitat design evolves as they create new features (verbally or graphically), discover consequences, deliberate implications from different perspectives, and develop terms for interpreting the design situation.

Archie repeatedly tries to test this new arrangement by imagining astronauts going about various activities in the layout. This is an important process, that requires a strong imaginative sense of what it would be like to live and move in the real physical spaces that are represented in the sketches. This ability is founded on the designer's understanding of what it is to *be* a person, to move about, to accomplish tasks, and to interact with objects, instruments, or other people. This ontological understanding allows people to adopt the interpretive perspectives of other people in other (even fictional) situations.

In addition, designers like Desi and Archie are constantly concerned with more quantitative issues, like 3-D volumes, adjacencies of different areas, and angles of access to spaces. To some extent these concerns relate to the human simulations: checking if a volume is adequate for pulling on clothes, if lights from one area will interfere with seeing things in another, or if opening doors will create safety hazards. In addition to spatial issues, designers must be concerned with lighting, noise, and dirt. In a lunar habitat, there will be no natural light and different areas will have to be illuminated differently depending upon their function. With a large number of mechanical and motorized systems at work in the metal module (circulating air, pumping water, etc.), noise and vibration are a serious problem. Lunar dust is very abrasive, so dust control systems are critical, especially when astronauts come in from working on the moon's surface.

The more they think about the way the lunar habitat design is working out, the more Desi and Archie discover that many of the issues of privacy, light, dirt, and noise have worked themselves out to form a gradient in which these problems are closely correlated.

Desi: But you know what? What we've created here is a changing area, without affecting privacy. So just by shifting this you lose the buffer. *Where this was leading is, I think,* that this is the quiet end. I'm also thinking this might be the emergency exit, not the primary air lock. We still have quiet activities here. Down here is the privacy. Here's your toilet. And if you think about stuff that's noisy, the idea of being dirtier, dustier . . . [at the other end].

Archie: *Are you talking about a kind of noise gradient?* Along this thing, in other words, one end might be noisy and the other end might be quiet.

Desi: As far as the planning issues, if you want to create some rationale as to why you plan or zone certain activities or adjacencies the way you do, you look at noise levels; you look at . . .

Archie: . . . light . . .

Desi: . . . light level; you look at dirt; dirty versus clean and all those . . .
.

Archie: Here's a basic point. One of the things you're short on in this place is distance. Okay? The one way, the one direction in which you have distance is along the axis . . . .

Desi: That's correct.

Archie: . . . of the things. Do you know Alexander's pattern of the long thin house? The idea is that to create privacy what you want to do is that you want to exploit distance, you want to make the house deliberately long and thin so people . . . . [Italics added.]

At this point a design has coalesced that has some satisfying coherence. It responds to the issues raised about privacy and arranges all the major necessary components of the habitat in a way which seems to make some sense. Of course, the design is far from final; in fact it will change considerably in future sessions, although some of its features will remain in place. So far, little thought has been given to determining sizes of things, and the drawings are not to scale. No storage space has been assigned for 45 days worth of food or other supplies. Space will obviously be extremely tight in the module—especially if so much room is permanently assigned to private sleep compartments—and too much space is wasted by the big corridor down the middle. There is very little space dedicated to the work of the mission, and not much thought given to room for exercise. But a start has been made.

This was a juncture of the designing process where there was a palpable sense of resolution for everyone. Major constraints imposed on the design— like the need for some privacy—and the secondary issues that arose in trying to solve them seemed fundamentally solved. The discovery of the privacy gradient concept (see italicized comments in transcript) resolved the prior discovery of the problem of privacy. It provided what designers call a *parti*, a guiding perspective for unifying a design. Now the designers felt that at last one had a place to go and relax in the habitat; this was finally becoming a home in which one could dwell, not merely function.

In a formal sense, the most satisfying aspect of the design is its consistent gradient character. This was an emergent property of the design process, with its concern for the creation of distinctly private and public areas. Desi observes that there is now a quiet end, which is also darker, cleaner, and quieter, in keeping with its private (and sleep oriented) character. The opposite end is where astronauts enter, bringing rock samples, equipment, and moon dust in with them. The noisy work takes place down there, with bright illumination for observing experiments. In the middle is a more moderate environment on each of the spectra, where the crew meets, prepares meals, eats, and socializes. This structure of the design gradually became explicit knowledge that could be shared in the transcribed dialog.

The privacy gradient that Desi and Archie came upon corresponds nicely with a chart in Volume I of NASA's MSIS, the volume of general design considerations and requirements for all manned space missions. This chart of adjacency design considerations contains the only specific guidelines related to privacy in the volume. Privacy is defined in terms of audio and visual privacy: that someone is not seen or heard by others. In NASA's terminology, "it has been found that a general sense of privacy increases when visual exposure of the individual is decreased and the individual has controllable visual access to the outside world" (NASA, 1989a, p.8-16).

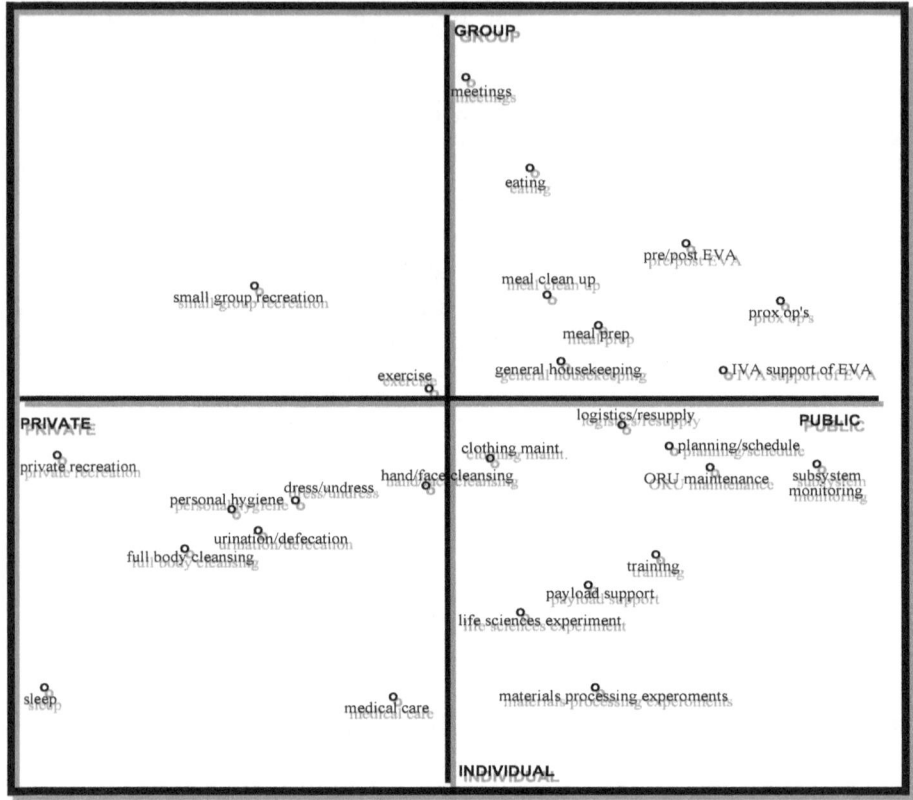

Figure 3-5. Relative adjacencies based on functional relationships.

The chart (reproduced as Figure 3-5) was constructed by analyzing the relationships among 27 typical functions of a space module crew according to 5 criteria and displaying something like a statistical cluster analysis. The criteria are: frequency of switching from one function to another; extent to which one function leads to performing another; percentage of support equipment shared by the functions; potential for noise of one function to interfere with another; similarity of audio and visual privacy requirements. The functions are then plotted on two scales: public/private functions and group/individual functions. The recommendation to designers is to group functions in the module similarly to how they are grouped on the chart. Note that in the chart sleep, showering, and dressing are grouped in one quadrant (private, individual); meeting, eating, and food preparation are in another (public, group); while experimentation and payload support are in a third (public, individual). This corresponds closely to the three areas of the lunar habitat design: sleep and dressing area, galley/ward room/meeting area; and science/entry area.

Of course, the lunar habitat functional decomposition grew out of the designing process, not from use of the NASA chart. Rather, the design discoveries remind Archie of the discussion of techniques for achieving a privacy gradient in Alexander's *A Pattern Language.* The principle of Pattern 109: Long Thin House there is, "The shape of a building has a great effect on the relative degrees of privacy and overcrowding in it, and this in turn has a critical effect on people's comfort and well being" (Alexander, et al., 1977, p.535). Alexander recommends creating a shape in which the mean point-to-point distance is high: "string out the rooms one after another, so that distance between each room is as great as it can be" (ibid., p.537). In the lunar habitat, this has been accomplished by massing components along the walls to make the open space narrow and long.

Later, in Pattern 127: Intimacy Gradient, Alexander recommends, "Lay out the spaces of a building so that they create a sequence that begins with the entrance and the most public parts of the building, then leads into the slightly more private areas, and finally to the most private domains" (ibid., p.613). The lunar habitat has in effect adopted this pattern even though Alexander's general pattern is primarily justified in terms of a spectrum of interpersonal relationships not relevant on the moon (strangers, friends, guests, clients, and family). The habitat grew into this pattern; there was never a conscious decision to make it conform to the pattern.

Suppose that Desi and Archie had first looked up the pattern and tried to decide if they should follow the rule of this pattern. How would they know if the rule was applicable? In the habitat, every crewmember has the same social relationships, so one might argue there should be no intimacy gradient. There is only a need for differentiation if one argues—as Archie in fact did when he introduced the need for privacy—that people have different moods and they want different relationships with the rest of the crew: sometimes buddies, sometimes co-workers, sometimes people to get away from. The question of applicability is a subtle one requiring complex human judgment. (The problem of applicability and its relation to interpretation will be discussed in Chapter 6.) How is a lunar habitat analogous to a home or office on the Earth? A traditional NASA engineering mentality would not make the analogy and would not see a problem with an undifferentiated, austere, work-oriented environment, as can be seen in the many factory-like designs for previous space missions.

The designs that Desi and Archie came up with at various stages contained striking parallels to many of Alexander's patterns. The multi-purpose galley and ward room combination as social center corresponds closely to Pattern 129: Common Areas at the Heart, Pattern 139: Farmhouse Kitchen, and Pattern 147: Communal Eating. For a while, the habitat design gave each astronaut a combination of a sleep compartment connected to a desk/workstation and a stowage cabinet. This was very much in the spirit of Pattern 141: A Room of One's Own. Later it was decided that this arrangement was too constraining on the arrangement of space, and the conceptual connections among the components was sacrificed.

Which of the patterns that Alexander culled from experiences on the Earth would make good rules of thumb for a domain of lunar habitat design? It seems impossible to simply list the applicable patterns. Rather, one might want to bring any of them into a particular deliberation when it seems appropriate, argue the pros and cons of applying it in the given design situation, perhaps try out some moves based on it, and see how things come out. Alexander's patterns provide yet another perspective for the argumentation, even if they are already the result of deliberations over the years incorporating many other perspectives, and so are relatively refined and general. This suggests a more eclectic approach than one that assumes a set of rules representing some compilation of domain knowledge. Such an approach does not avoid the problems of knowledge representation; on the contrary, it makes it more important than ever to capture knowledge of multiple perspectives, and to continue collecting new knowledge indefinitely.

3.3. Capturing the Language of Privacy

The analysis of the lunar habitat design process in this chapter confirms the importance of the ideas emphasized by Alexander, Rittel and Schön in Chapter 2 and the view of design as interpretation proposed in Chapter 1. This section will discuss some implications of the nature of lunar habitat design for computer support.

Problems of collecting knowledge have plagued attempts to provide computer support for design. Often it has been assumed that this is merely a practical problem, with no interesting theoretical aspects compared to the development of AI techniques for representing, accessing, manipulating, and displaying relevant knowledge. The expert system approach, for instance, assumed that a human domain expert, when interviewed, could spell out the important knowledge of the domain in a series of formalizable rules.

However, experience showed that professionals had surprisingly partial knowledge of their fields and relied heavily upon heuristics and access to other resources to work around or fill in gaps (Suchman, 1987; Winograd & Flores, 1986). Even what people did have working knowledge of they could not readily state explicitly or fully. Professional expertise relies heavily upon tacit background knowledge of the field that one picks up through apprenticeship-style training, not from the accumulation of rule-like information. This is emphasized by Kuhn (1962), Schön (1983), and Dreyfus (1985) in discussing how people develop expertise.

It may well be that the AI computational tricks are the easy part, for which much work has already been done and options are fairly well understood. The following questions may be more difficult. They have to do with the fact that knowledge is founded on interpretation and is not given independently of the knower's situations, perspectives, or language traditions:

1. What are the human cognitive processes involved in design?

2. What is the nature of the knowledge at work in these processes?

3. How can that knowledge be captured during the action present when it is available?

4. How can the often tacit knowledge be represented in ways which are explicit enough for computer processing?

5. How can stored information be supplied to people to support their current design efforts in a timely manner and a useful format?

These are the kinds of questions being pursued in this dissertation. The following paragraphs start to suggest responses based on observed characteristics of lunar habitat design. They will be returned to repeatedly, particularly in the discussion of the theory of computer support for interpretation in design (Chapter 7).

1. What are the human cognitive processes involved in design? Alexander argued that an important process in design was the decomposition of a problem into functional components, each component having more interactions among the items within it than with items outside the component. Rittel conceived of design as a deliberative process, in which people raised issues, made proposals from different perspectives, and critically debated each other's positions. Schön stressed the importance of active, creative involvement with the design artifact (e.g., sketching) in order to discover constraints and consequences of design moves. These different processes were apparent in the videotaped lunar habitat design sessions. The habitat was decomposed into private, group, and public areas based on functionalities of the items in the layout. Various perspectives on privacy were discussed and debated in verbal exchanges. Successive sketches were made, which formed the basis for discoveries and design decisions. Diverse cognitive processes were at work: analysis (decomposing into functional areas), recall (analogous situations: German bathrooms, Space Station crew compartments, submarines, Antarctic), simulation (imagining life in the habitat), argumentation (discussing the issues), gesture (pointing to drawn objects, indicating other arrangements, sketching), perception (seeing sketched lines as representations of a habitat).

2. What is the nature of the knowledge at work in these processes? Much of the knowledge involved in these cognitive processes of designing is tacit—far more than ever imagined in the heyday of expert systems. The notion of privacy is a good example. A designer's understanding of what situations are private and which situations require privacy is based on tacit understandings of what it feels like to be a human being in those situations. This understanding is used extensively by Desi and Archie in decomposing the functional areas, in deliberating adjacencies of items, and in seeing problems in layout sketches. What is interesting is that *much of this tacit knowledge becomes explicit during the designing*. It gets articulated in English statements in order to be introduced into the interpersonal argumentative process. For this period during which it is debated, which Schön calls the "action present", the knowledge is explicitly available. After the deliberation is resolved, the arguments and their basis in knowledge may sink back into a tacit understanding once more. So the optimal time to capture design knowledge is when it becomes explicit in the designers' language, while they are situated in the designing and have adopted the particular perspective.

3. How can that knowledge be captured during the action present when it is available? Information may be stored in a computer system in many ways. Some ways—such as textual formats in natural language—are more useful to human users, while others—like encodings in semantic networks or other formalisms—facilitate computer computation and manipulation of the information. However, all these forms are explicit forms of knowledge. Tacit knowledge, by definition, is not expressed in any way that could be stored on paper or in computer memories. It must first be made explicit. Because much important design knowledge is tacit, because it needs to be made explicit in order to be used in a computer-based system, and because tacit knowledge often becomes explicit during the action present of reflection during design, it can be helpful to capture the explicit articulation when it is available.

In general, lunar habitat design is more complex in its use of technical information than the episode transcribed in the preceding sections. Its high-tech nature means that technical data must often be looked up in manuals or even explored experimentally in subsidiary engineering studies. Contractual obligations to NASA and its subcontractors require documented adherence to voluminous specifications and requirements (including the volumes of the MSIS). The design of something like a lunar habitat passes through many phases, carried out by different teams. The capture and use of design rationale plays a variety of roles in this process, and should probably play even stronger roles in the future. Computer support systems could facilitate an increased role for stored design rationale if mechanisms are developed to capture knowledge as it becomes explicit in the design process.

The scenario in Chapter 9 shows how lunar habitat designers could use a software design environment as their design medium, rather than paper and pencil, even for design tasks like those presented in the transcript. If the computer becomes a medium for designing, then the knowledge that arises in the design process is largely already represented in the computer. Such knowledge can be stored for future use. Then the computer system functions as an external, shared memory. Knowledge captured there is available for the original designer to come back to later and for other designers to access as well. It becomes a medium of communication and collaboration, through which designers can share their ideas, approaches, rules, sketches, and interpretations. The computer can represent explicitly the relations that are normally tacit in situated interpretation, organize knowledge into different perspectives, and operationalize terminology of an interpretive language.

4. How can the often tacit knowledge be represented in ways which are explicit enough for computer processing? Lunar habitat design differs from design in simpler domains in a number of ways. For one thing, it is not a well-understood, mature field. One could not expect to interview an expert and come up with a set of formal rules and elements to define a comprehensive system of knowledge here. Workers in this field are attempting to explore a new domain and to begin to map out the potential problem space. A goal of researchers is to sketch in parametric curves that would indicate how designs have to change depending on such parameters as number of astronauts, length of mission duration, or payload delivery capacity (see, e.g., Design Edge, 1990; Moore, et al., 1991; Kazmierski, et al. 1992). This is a very preliminary step toward developing knowledge representations for this domain. Even the most important parameters remain undefined and open to interpretation and debate. For instance, few NASA guidelines cover privacy issues, even though this is an important concern of thoughtful designers and a topic for vigorous political debate and even power struggles within NASA (Compton, et al., 1983).

The MSIS was not able to define privacy well, except for some concern about visual and audio privacy as expressed in the graph of recommended adjacencies for different functions (reproduced as Figure 3-5 in the previous section). It does, however, indirectly recognize its importance when considering habitable volume requirements: "Sufficient habitable volume shall be provided and configured to decrease the possibility of degradation of crew performance due to detrimental psychological effects from feelings of confinement" (NASA, 1989a, p.8-17). Just as Archie noted that the need for private space becomes critical as the length of confinement exceeds a month, the MSIS states, "As the mission duration increases, there is a greater tendency for the crew to feel confined and cramped. This can affect psychological health and crewmember performance" (ibid., p.8-12). A graph of guidelines for determination of total habitable volume per person as a function of mission duration accompanies this statement (reproduced here as Figure 3-6).

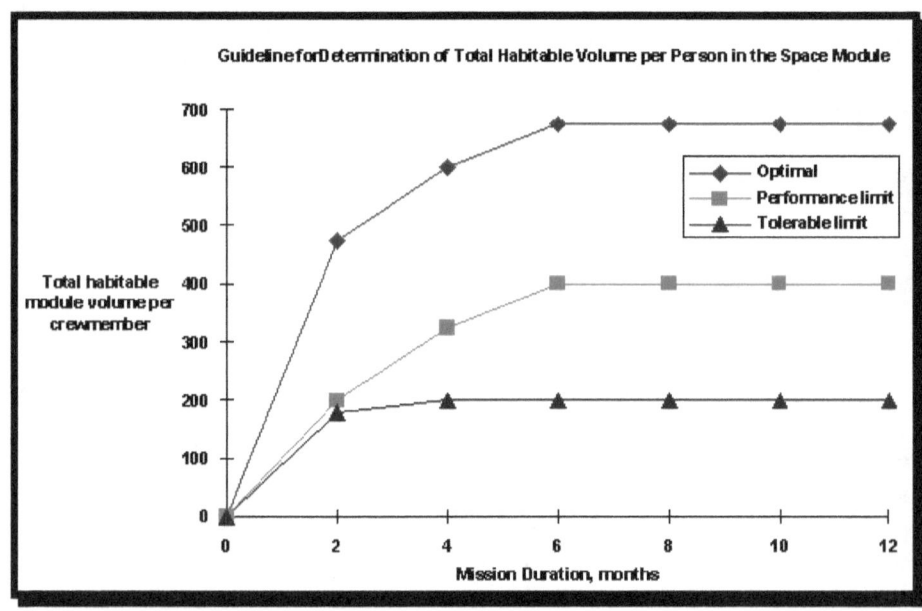

Figure 3-6. Required volume per crewmember as a function of mission duration.

It is an excellent example of a set of parametric curves to begin to define the problem space. NASA was able to represent knowledge about privacy here by reducing it to a matter of spatial volume. New methods are needed to allow designers to define less reductionist concepts of privacy and to capture knowledge related to such concepts.

In the lunar habitat design sessions, privacy issues due to prolonged confinement were the first real concerns to surface. They structured how the designers constructed their task. Related questions of social interaction dominated questions of physical layout, indicating that social planning was necessarily a significant aspect of the designing. When the geopolitics (or solar system politics) of NASA's goals are reflected in the deliberations, the result is truly a wicked problem in Rittel's full sense. It is not just that more study is needed to formulate objective rules for the field, but that decisions necessarily involve tacit understanding of inter-personal behavior and non-propositional recognition of political interests.

For relatively unexplored domains such as lunar habitat design, efforts at designing do not seek optimal solutions within a known problem space, but begin to mark out a solution space in the first place—as Schön says, to construct the reality of the design situation. The most important role of computer support for such domains is to capture the ideas that are being generated. Terms (like privacy) and patterns (like Figure 3-6) which are formulated on the spot during this design exploration process are expressions of what designers may want to pay attention to in the future as well. So, for instance, the important criterion for rules is not the rigor of their computations in the sense of some rationalist engineering ideal but their ability to convey the designer's interpretive intent. A computer system incorporating the knowledge should not be conceived primarily as an autonomous equation solver (or an expert system), but as a powerful medium of external memory to empower people's creativity. A software environment for this domain should be designed to capture new and evolving knowledge, rather than simply manipulate predefined knowledge representations and systems of production rules. This has been a primary concern in designing the HERMES software described in Part III.

5. How can stored information be supplied to people to support their current design efforts in a timely manner and a useful format? A high-tech design goes through many stages of development, involving different design teams. Architects, designers, a variety of engineers, and administrators all work on the designs from their own viewpoints. Successful designs are sent to other contractors around the country for detailing, mock-up, testing, and

construction. At each stage, the design is modified, based on people's understanding of the design and its rationale. If a creative design concept is to survive this argumentative process—with tight cost, weight, and volume constraints at every stage—strong *design rationale* must be communicated; a schematic diagram or a pretty picture will not suffice. In fact, a typical product of lunar habitat design consists of a small booklet predominated by textual explanations of rationale, not just detailed drawings. The important role that rationale plays in this extended design process should motivate designers to document their reasoning and interpretation more than they would in a domain like kitchen design. A logical step beyond a written booklet would be a computer system that integrates designs and rationale in useful, easily accessible ways.

Because designers lack personal experience living in lunar habitats, knowledge embodied in related designs (including Skylab, the Shuttle, Space Station Freedom, previous trips to the moon) is invaluable. Old designs are reused extensively. To the degree that design rationale of the old designs has been captured and augmented by subsequent experience, it can be vitally useful. Consequently, it is likely that design rationale will increasingly become an integral part of design. This should add tremendous power for practitioners who take it seriously and those who use computer tools that support rationale capture. Such a development represents a significant break with the tradition of CAD programs, which are purely graphical and embody very little semantics. However, it has impressive precedence in other fields like science, mathematics, and philosophy, where written theories, proofs, and arguments have been refined through processes of public critique and have grown into extensive bases of shared knowledge and accumulated commentary impossible in non-literate cultures.

The need for computer support of lunar habitat design was originally suggested by the sheer volume (and complexity) of knowledge required— far more than people could maintain in their heads or even locate easily in manuals. There are thick sets of NASA regulations for all Man-In-Space designs, ergonomic standards, and specific project contractual obligations that must be adhered to by designs. But the complexity of lunar habitat design is not just a matter of the volume of information. Requirements, components and rationale all have to be reinterpreted within the context of the evolving design. This is an application realm in which, for instance, most physical components require some degree of *customization*. Because of gravitational or volumetric considerations, one cannot simply select a stock sink or bed from a catalog. Even pumps and fans must be re-thought. Furthermore, there are many design interactions among components that are placed close together—partially because space is at a premium and also because things must work together to form a coherent environment for habitation. This means that design of a given part is very much situated in its context, in terms of neighboring components (e.g., sound buffers), design concerns (privacy), and projected usage issues (traffic flow). The computer representation of the design must function as the unique world in which representations of all the components and their relationships are appropriately situated so that design can take place effectively. One wants to start from existing components, but one then needs to be able to modify them freely to account for differences in the lunar setting. So representing standard parts with schematic icons or fixed items from a palette is inadequate. The idea that there is *a* definable domain with *its* primitive elements is too narrow a conception. All knowledge representations must be stored in *plastic* media, so they can be tailored to different interpretations.

Elements of lunar habitats should be similar to familiar products to facilitate manufacture and to give astronauts a sense of being at home, but they must also be different to meet the severe constraints of their context. This means that models and rules of thumb must be searched for in many other domains (houses, submarines, Antarctic labs) and then *applied* to the lunar setting. Such application must be done by the creative and synthetic minds of humans, with computer systems merely presenting the relevant elements. Even the determination of what might be relevant must involve the human designer, for this is also very much a matter of interpretation based on a deep understanding of the semantics involved. This means that computer-based systems for design should be *people-centered*, so that all interpretive judgments are under human control.

Desi and Archie communicate in English. They articulate and share their interpretations of what is going on in the design through the medium of *language*. To support the subtlety of communication between designers and a computer system, the designers should be able to develop a language that operationalizes their evolving interpretations in ways which can be used by the software. At the same time, the development of a language for interpretation can provide a basis for shared understanding among groups of designers, even if they are not working together at the same time or place. For instance, a designer who is considering an old design for adaptation into a new project can learn about the old design through the language which was developed with it—including the formulations of definitions and argumentation specific to that design. Providing some support for collaborative work among groups is particularly important in this domain because of the way each successful design must undergo the scrutiny of many teams. Generally, the only communication between these teams is the design document itself. To further mutual understanding, it is desirable that the design include effective documentation of the interpretive stance behind the rationale.

The computational platform within which design work is carried out can serve as a communication medium in which designs and related information can be viewed and interpreted by different people working together or working sequentially. Lunar habitat design is not a task for one person sitting at a computer. It is a *collaborative* process. It proceeds through the work of teams of teams, each viewing the common product through their own perspective. The essential communication is not that between a human and a computer, but among the design teams. What a computer system like HERMES can do is to provide an electronic medium to support this communication. It can do that by facilitating the development of a shared language of design interpretation and by providing a mechanism for the creation and sharing of interpreted designs defined using that language.

The example of lunar habitat design has illustrated the importance of *interpretation* in design. Desi and Archie interpret their task as one of creating a balance of public and private space. They spend much of their time developing an adequate interpretation of what privacy means in the context they are dealing with. A variety of interpretive perspectives are brought to bear and are deliberated. Finally, a shared interpretation of privacy guides the designing and provides a sense of resolution when the privacy constraints seem to be satisfied.

The interpretive processes draw heavily on *tacit* knowledge. During computations for decomposition, deliberation of relevant issues, or reflection-in-action, some of that knowledge becomes more explicit. The representations of the situation, perspectives on design, and guiding concepts that become manifest may be represented in calculations, arguments, or ideas—i.e., in formal or natural language. Unless these explicit forms of knowledge are made permanent in some external medium like annotations on paper or statements of rationale in a computer system, they may revert to tacit forms. Particularly in high-tech fields, it is important to capture design rationale knowledge to help people understand and reuse designs.

The following chapter explores the philosophy of interpretation in order to clarify some of the issues related to tacit knowledge, interpretive perspectives, and the explication of understanding raised by the study of lunar habitat design. The problem of computer support for interpretation in design is then addressed in Part II.

The discussion of lunar habitat design has highlighted a number of challenges for a theory of computer support:

(a) The concept of privacy is typical of a broad range of themes that are essential to habitat design but are hard to operationalize. Despite the fact that NASA epitomizes the effort to codify design issues as objective rules, after twenty years their success with the concept of privacy is definitely inadequate. It remains unclear how to represent situations in which privacy plays a key role. This poses a challenge for the design of computational support for interpretation in design. It will provide the key example for the utility of HERMES' mechanisms in Part III.

(b) Part of the problem with privacy is that different people have different ideas of what aspects are important in defining the concept. These differences may be due to concerns with varying technical specialties or simply to personal preferences. In any case, definitions of such concepts cannot be formulated as statements of necessary and sufficient conditions, but must be allowed to emerge in each situation through deliberation from multiple perspectives.

(c) Another part of the problem involves adapting the concept to the particular design situation. Fixed definitions from a body of domain knowledge can provide useful (even necessary) starting points for articulation of tacit understandings, but they must be capable of flexible modification to be applied appropriately in a concrete situation. This typically involves an iterative process of situated discovery and perspectival deliberation, as seen in the transcripts. Even where NASA has captured important information relevant to privacy (as in Figures 3-5 and 3-6), or Alexander has abstracted useful schemata in his pattern language, these representations must be applied to individual situations through human processes of interpretation. The language user must be capable of generating terminology and expressions whose meaning can be interpreted appropriately to unique situations.

CHAPTER 4. HEIDEGGER'S PHILOSOPHY OF INTERPRETATION

Chapter 4 explicates Heidegger's analysis of understanding and interpretation. It traces his discussion through the relevant sections of *Being and Time,* his major work that addresses these issues. Heidegger presents his analysis of interpretation through a discussion of the human understanding of artifacts in the world. This involves analyses of:

a. what it means for artifacts to be *situated* (Heidegger, 1927[6], §15 - §18; see Section 4.1 below);

b. how the situation is understood through shared traditions and personal *perspectives* (ibid., §26, §29 - §31; see Section 4.2); and

c. what the role of *language* is in communicating interpretations (ibid., §32 - §34; see Section 4.3).

This chapter uses examples of design from Chapters 2 and 3 to illustrate Heidegger's points. It explores his philosophic analysis just far enough to shed light on the role of interpretation in design. Then Chapter 5 will apply the analysis developed here more explicitly to design. That will form the basis for a theory of computer support for interpretation in design, presented in Chapter 6.

---

[6] Due to the intricacies of Heidegger's language and the unreliability of English translations, quotes from Heidegger's (and Gadamer's) works will appear in original translations, with references to the page (S.) or section (§) numbers of the German originals. The published English version of *Being and Time* includes the German page numbers in the margin.

Three points of background information are presented prior to beginning the Heidegger interpretation:

1. Heidegger's "hermeneutic" philosophy (or analysis of interpretation) is of central importance to people-centered sciences and other endeavors, including innovative design.

2. His philosophy provides the foundation for the recent approach to cognitive science known as "situated cognition."

3. Heidegger does not develop a theory of design, let alone a theory of computer support for design. Even his analysis of human understanding is developed to serve a methodological role in an argument about ontology (the philosophy of being) that is tangential to the interests of this chapter. His philosophy will have to be adapted to the analysis of design and its computer support in Part II.

1. Heidegger's hermeneutic philosophy is important to a people-centered science of design. Since Aristotle, the philosophy of interpretation has been known as hermeneutics. The term *hermeneutics* suggests the process of arriving at understanding, especially through language (Palmer, 1969). As such, it has long been associated with textual interpretation, such as Biblical exegesis. Etymologically, it derives from the Greek god Hermes, the wing-footed messenger, who was associated with the function of transmuting what is beyond human understanding into a form that human intelligence can grasp, and who was credited with the discovery of language and writing—the pre-computer tools humans have employed for grasping meaning and conveying it to one another.

In the nineteenth century, the hermeneutics of Dilthey and Schliermacher helped differentiate the *Geisteswissenschaften* (human sciences) from the natural sciences by contrasting the methods of (humanistic) interpretation and (scientific) explanation. Heidegger and his student Gadamer revived that orientation to expound a general theory of human understanding and interpretation. Today, hermeneutics refers primarily to this philosophy of interpretation as fundamental to human existence, which Heidegger (1927) formulated and Gadamer (1960) further expounded.

This chapter culminates the argument that design is to be understood as fundamentally a process of interpretation. That is, innovative design tasks such as lunar habitat design cannot be reduced to sets of explicit rules that are taken to be independent of the situations in which they are applied and the perspectives of the people who interpret them. To understand design, one must take into account the role of human interpretation. This means that a science of design—or, for instance, a theory of computer support of design—should be conceived on the model of the human sciences more than on that of the natural sciences (Figure 4-1). This is contrary to the traditional approach of AI attempts to automate design with rule-based expert systems, that look primarily to the mathematical sciences rather than the interpretive sciences for their model of scientific method. The subjective human aspects they often dismiss as incidental to design or view as unfortunate limitations are here taken as being of the essence.

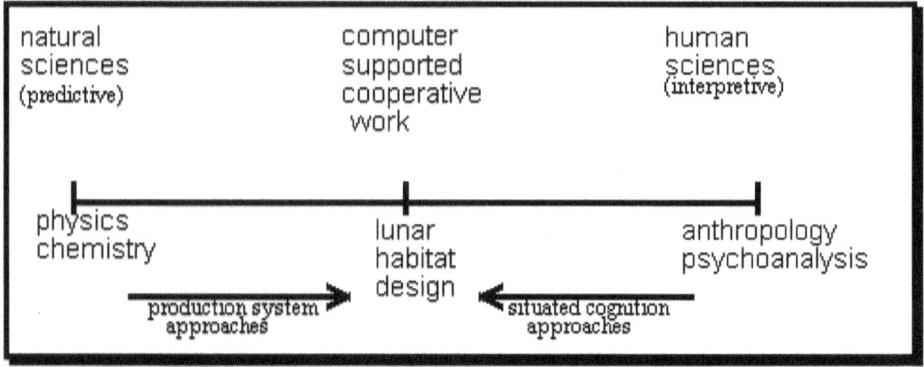

Figure 4-1. Hermeneutic versus natural science approaches to design.

Heidegger's philosophy of human interpretation occupies a pivotal role in this dissertation because innovative design is here approached from the perspective of the human sciences. This contrasts with, for instance, the influential approach of Simon (1981), who starts from a computational natural sciences outlook and then points out its bounds or limitations in design in order to arrive at a "science of the artificial."

2. Heidegger's ideas are fundamental to situated cognition. The power of Heidegger's writings to inspire critiques of rationalist outlooks can scarcely be over-estimated. In particular, the approaches of design theory, AI, and cognitive science that are important for this dissertation are philosophically close to Heidegger. His influence is, for instance, traceable via Dreyfus to the major spokespeople for situated cognition: Suchman, Ehn, Winograd, and Flores (Figure 4-2). Their relevance to the analysis of interpretation in design was discussed in Section 1.4 above. The parallels of Heidegger's thought to other important writers like Rittel, Polanyi, Kuhn, and Schön are striking. Without understanding Heidegger's alternative to the rationalist tradition, it is easy to misunderstand and trivialize the novelty and importance of situated cognition theory.

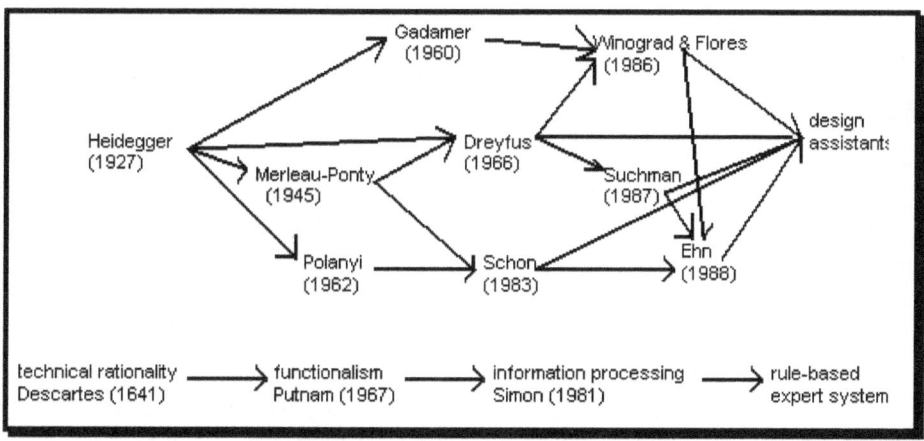

Figure 4-2. The two mainstreams of contemporary philosophy.

Their influences on theories of design and computer support for design can be traced back to Heidegger's philosophy or to rationalism.

3. Heidegger's analysis must be adapted to a theory of computer support. *Being and Time* (Heidegger, 1927) presents an "existential analytic". By this Heidegger means a hermeneutic interpretation of what it is to be human, to be involved with one's world and concerned with one's self. Along the way to his explication of people's understanding of themselves, Heidegger analyzes the ways that people can be involved with things other than themselves in the world—for instance, by using tools like hammers. It is this secondary analysis of artifacts that will be of primary concern for the following discussion of interpretation in design. Heidegger's presentation will need to be reinterpreted along these lines and fleshed out with observations about the involvement of designers with design artifacts. It is entirely in keeping with the spirit of hermeneutics that Heidegger's writings be construed in accordance with current concerns, because interpretation is always necessarily from a perspective of specific human interests.

To understand Heidegger's view, it is important to place his analyses of understanding within his methodological context, even if these notions are eventually to be applied in a quite different context here. The ideas presented in this chapter form the analytic core of the first step in

Heidegger's project: to explicate the meaning of being. Roughly, his general question is, what does it mean to say that something *is*? —what is it to *be* a person, a hammer, a lunar habitat? It is hard to say more precisely just what Heidegger means by the *meaning of being*, even after he spent a lifetime struggling to articulate it. This difficulty is due to peculiarities of the history of Western thought according to Heidegger. While the early Greeks had a tacit understanding of being, even that vague grasp became increasingly obscured from the time of Plato to the present. So Heidegger's task is to regain the original tacit understanding and explicate it. This is a matter for interpretation, and that is precisely how Heidegger treats it. He argues that it is methodologically possible to pursue this question only because people do have a vague, tacit sense of the meaning of being. The question can be pursued by gradually explicating this sense. So the problem of tacit and explicit understanding is central to Heidegger's task, just as it is to the task of providing computer support for design.

Heidegger's argument is, in a way, circular. He first postulates that people have this sense of the meaning of being and that they have the ability to explicate their tacit senses through interpretation. They have a sense of the meaning of being because they exist in a world where they are involved with and concerned about beings: artifacts, other people, and themselves. Heidegger takes these postulates as phenomenological givens of human experience. For him, understanding never starts with a blank slate, but always with some meaningful content that can then be explicated: what was tacit can be stated, discoveries can be made, and terminology can be iteratively revised. From this starting point, he develops a coherent theory of interpretation that justifies his approach, provides an original philosophic outlook, and explains the ways in which traditional views obscured our relation to being.

Heidegger's thought can be viewed as a philosophy of interpretation or hermeneutics (although it is ultimately concerned with a very abstract form of interpretation: the philosophic understanding of being). His analysis of what it means *to be human* is inseparable from his analysis of what it means *to interpret*. The "hermeneutic circle", according to which "any interpretation that is to contribute understanding must already have understood what is to be interpreted" (S.152), is symptomatic of our relation to our world: "In every understanding of the world, [our] existence is understood with it and vice versa" (ibid.). Heidegger's writings are notoriously abstract, abstruse, and difficult to interpret. In order to concretize his ideas—including the analysis of the hermeneutic circle and of our relation to our world—the following sections will focus their attention on Heidegger's analysis of the three features of understanding that have already been considered in the previous chapters: its situated, perspectival, and linguistic nature.

4.1. Definition of the Situation as Basis for Tacit Understanding

Heidegger wants to get at the being of beings. But his methodological access to this (at least at this initial stage of his investigation) is via the human understanding of artifacts. So the question, what is a hammer? becomes, for instance, the question, what is a hammer for a person? —say for the person who is using it to nail something together. Heidegger looks at the tacit sense that we have of a hammer when we are using it. He points out that when we are hammering we are focused on the nail or on the pieces of wood that we are joining or on the project we are building, and not directly on the hammer itself. There is only what Polanyi calls a subsidiary awareness of the hammer as part of the background of the activity that we are focused on. In fact, for the act of hammering to take place effectively, we must be unaware of the hammer; we must be primarily concerned with the task we are pursuing, not with the tool we are using to pursue it. This is part of what is meant by saying that our understanding of the hammer is necessarily tacit: that its use requires that we not focus our attention on it.

When we are engaged in hammering, the hammer is not there in the sense of an object that we relate to as a subject—a subject who might, for instance, formulate propositions about the hammer, like: I am lifting the hammer; the hammer is heavy; the hammer is made of metal and wood. The hammer is only there as part of what Heidegger calls the "totality of equipment" that is available to us and that we make use of in our work. When we are at work hammering, we are in a situation where the hammer, nails, wood, and other tools are available for our use. The hammer is available in order to drive nails, and the other tools are similarly related to their uses. All these references (e.g., hammer to nails for driving them) form a totality of significance, that is definitive of our *situation*. So the hammer is accessible to us in terms of this *system of references* among the tools we use. The references inter-relate the tools in terms of their possible utilities, and also refer to people as those for whom the uses are ultimately intended.

Figure 4-3 is meant to illustrate that the hammer is tacitly understood in terms of its relations to other artifacts, concerns, and people. The totality of these things *as understood* in this interrelated way is the *situation*. To say that interpretation is *situated* is to say that everything is interpreted as part of this understood totality, as having these relations.[7]

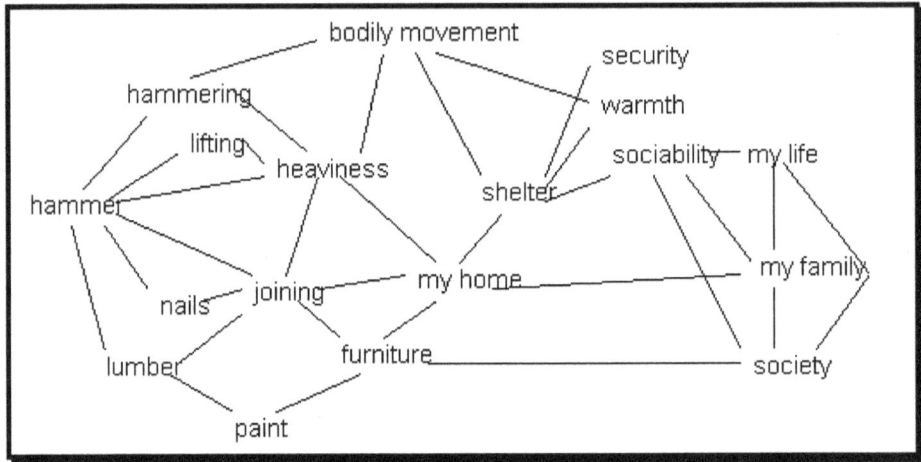

Figure 4-3. The network of references for tacit understanding of hammering.

The entities presented in this figure are involved in many different kinds of relations. For the sake of simplicity, the various kinds of relations have not been identified here.

Heidegger stresses that our understanding of the situation, defined as the totality of references, is necessarily prior to our understanding of the individual tools. We are only aware of the hammer as part of the available situation that defines it via the references to something for driving nails, etc. In this way, we can *understand* the hammer *tacitly* only because we always already understand our situation as a significant totality.

Our tacit situated understanding provides a space (a stage or "clearing") within which elements can be discovered and brought to a more explicit form of knowledge. This process is a central concern because it involves the

---

[7] Recently, in his book rejecting functionalism, Putnam (1988) expressed this idea in the following way: "If I say, 'Hawks fly,' I do not intend my hearer to deduce that a hawk with a broken wing could fly. What we expect depends on the whole network of beliefs" (p.9).

bridging of tacit understanding (the normal mode for people) and explicit knowledge (required for computer representations). Within the space of understanding given by our being tacitly situated, we can discover new things and understand them in relation to what we already understood. In some cases, this subsumption of new understanding involves us in making our understanding explicit by formulating it linguistically. In this way, explicit knowledge may emerge from tacit understanding when we are situated. However, we can never make all our tacit background understanding explicit.[8]

Heidegger's difference from all *objecti*vistic philosophies is already clear here. The world does not consist of a fixed set of multiple objects that we can come to know by staring at them and explicitly noting their attributes. Rather, to *be* human means to have *disclosed* (opened up) a situation or world within which and in terms of which things can be *discovered* as already significant. The issue of intentionality, epistemology, or mind/body (that poses the question of how mental activity can gain access to physical reality) is a non-problem for Heidegger because we are already understandingly involved with things when we first discover them (see Heidegger, 1975, and Dreyfus, 1991).

According to Heidegger (1927), our tacit understanding of things is founded upon our situatedness. Understanding can then become more or less explicit on the basis of this tacit understanding:

> Involvement in the immediate work-world has a function of discovering such that the beings brought along with the work (i.e., in the references that are constitutive for it) remain discovered in various degrees of explicitness and to various extents of insight, depending upon our mode of involvement in the work. (S.71)

This explains why we understand best when we are properly situated in the context of an issue we are trying to understand. That is when we have access to the associations that are related to the topic of our concern and that define its meaningfulness. It is our involvement with the topic that makes manifest the things, issues, and concerns that are related to it and whose mutual associations constitute our situation.

---

[8] As Polanyi (1958) put it, "Tacit knowledge is more fundamental than explicit knowledge: we can know more than we can tell and we can tell nothing without relying on our awareness of things we may not be able to tell" (p. x).

In Heidegger's philosophy, to say that we are situated means that we are involved with things in the world and can discover things based on our tacit understanding of what we are involved with. The situation is neither a set of physical circumstances in the objective world nor a model representing such objects in a subjective mind. Heidegger overcomes the separation of world and mind by focusing on the situation as the understood world itself in which we are involved, not a re-presentation of it "in the head." Of course, we can subsequently represent the structure of the situation in explicit terms: words, graphics, computer symbols. But in our tacit involvement things are there as meaningfully related to our concerns; they are available to us in ways that are not mediated by symbols or re-presentations.

The next question is, then, how our understanding can become more explicit. This is important for Heidegger from a methodological perspective. In order to answer the question of being, he needs to take our tacit understanding of being and make it explicit. To show that it is possible to bring to light the structures that ordinarily operate tacitly, Heidegger gives three examples of cases where an artifact like a hammer stops functioning invisibly in the background and becomes explicitly manifest. These cases are when a hammer is conspicuous, obtrusive, or obstinate. For instance, (i) if a hammer that one wants to use to drive a nail is encountered as unusable, damaged, or unsuitable (too large, broken, or the wrong style) then one discovers its usability for hammering in a conspicuous way. Similarly, (ii) if a tool that one reaches for turns out to be missing, then one becomes conspicuously aware of it as necessary but unavailable. Finally, (iii) if something is in the way of what one wants to do, then that thing is discovered as obstinate. When one discovers the hammer under such circumstances, it is not discovered as a raw physical object, but as an unsuitable driver of nails (or whatever) and the situation in which one is desirous of driving the nail—the related and referenced other tools and human purposes—also rises to a more explicit presence. The situation comes to light as a network of artifacts; it is disclosed as a context of significance that is then seen as having already been familiar as the basis of the tool and its references.

This is a very different view from the usual cognitive science approach in terms of explicit goals, according to which a carpenter who has the goal of producing an artifact formulates propositional sub-goals like joining two pieces of wood, and sub-sub-goals such as lifting the (explicitly considered) hammer and swinging it at the nail with adequate force. In the Heideggerian view, the tool and the goals are only tacitly available by implication or reference as long as everything is going smoothly. It is when the references are disturbed that they become visible. When some tool is missing whose ordinary availability was so obvious that we never even took any notice of it, then this absence creates a break in the totality of references. Our awareness runs into unexpected emptiness, and discovers for the first time the (now broken) references connecting the anticipated tool with the other tools and goals of the situation. Whereas the rationalist tradition tends to think of the being of things as a simple form of physical presence, Heidegger has a more complex view of things being ordinarily hidden in various ways, having to be uncovered and disclosed, only to then re-submerge into tacit, subsidiary awareness. In the hammer example, the hammer itself is hidden when it is normally available, useful, or in use; it becomes explicitly visible to us precisely when it is physically absent or otherwise unavailable.

It should be noted that Heidegger has *not* claimed that things *only* become explicitly manifest when there is a *breakdown* of normal activities. This is a suggestive claim offered by Dreyfus (1991), Schön (1983), and others influenced by them—but it is a stronger claim or a narrower theory than Heidegger's. Also, it is open to misinterpretation of what the phenomenon of breakdown is all about. One could, for instance think that a breakdown in design is when a designer gets stuck in the flow of designing *activity* and has to stop to think of a solution. In fact, Schön's concept of reflection-in-*action* might suggest this idea, even though Schön himself knows better. This is a point where it is important to understand what Heidegger is up to methodologically in order to understand what his analysis is about. The three examples he gave are just sample cases and by no means rule out other paths to making things explicit. When Heidegger presents them, he is making a methodological point presenting phenomenological evidence for the structure of the situation as prior to the artifacts understood by it. Here he is not proposing a general theory of explicit knowledge or reflection. Even later, when he does discuss explication, he develops his analysis only to the extent needed to make his points about the possibility of explicating the vague sense of the meaning of being. The breakdown examples make manifest the structure of the situation—that is why Heidegger refers to them. What is important is not that tacit involvement in the world is broken, but that the structure of the *situation* is broken. That is, the network of references is suddenly inadequate for making sense of the world because the references anticipated one thing and something else was discovered in the world: i.e., the hammer was unusable, missing, or in the way.[9]

---

[9] Heidegger's example of hammering is often cited. However, it is in some ways too pat and raises a difficult question concerning its generalizability. For instance, it conjures up visions of the craftsman's workshop where, as

The important phenomenon is not a matter of psychological consciousness: that one suddenly has to become more conscious about what one is engaged in. Rather, one has to *reinterpret* in the sense of reorganizing the network of references that define the situation so that circumstances that have been discovered make sense in the revised situation. Heidegger is interested in this phenomenon from an ontological, rather than psychological perspective. The discovered artifact that causes the breakdown loses its ontological status as available to the person's tacit understanding because that status was conditional upon the situation. Heidegger's ontological analysis need not be pursued here. The important point for computer support is that a breakdown

---

in an obsolete blacksmith's shop, one automatically reaches out for hand tools that extend the limbs of one's body. This is an enticing image, given Heidegger's argument. But one must ask—as do Adorno (1964), Stahl (1975b), Habermas (1985), Lefebvre (1991), Bourdieu (1991) and others—if this is not a romantic vision longing for a return to pre-industrial forms of labor. Is Heidegger insightfully characterizing a primordial foundation of human existence throughout history or is a different analysis of our being-in-the-world needed in an industrial or computerized age? In particular, are Heidegger's analyses relevant to contemporary design of high-tech artifacts, with or without computer support? Is the individual craftsman the appropriate paradigm for analyzing collaborative design in the contemporary world?

Two general arguments in support of using Heidegger's approach suggest themselves. The first is the argument from evolution: that advanced forms are built on earlier stages. Donald (1991) and Polanyi (1953) argue that primate-level episodic (tacit) understanding still provides the necessary basis for human consciousness and theoretical knowledge. The second argument is that the medieval workshop is not an anachronism, but still provides the preferable model of organization of learning and work, at least for certain fields. Budde and Züllighoven (1990), for instance, claim that the tool/workshop structure is superior to the CASE/industrial model for software development, and they therefore apply Heidegger's categories in their hermeneutically-based concepts of software tools for programming workshops. Similarly, Schön (1985) argues that the apprenticeship model of the design studio is more important than the engineering ideal of theory application for the teaching of architecture. Because Heidegger's examples are suspect, it is important to turn now to concrete examples of interest. In Part II Heidegger's analysis will be extended to collaborative design to overcome the danger of an ahistorical, asocial interpretation.

is a rupture of the *situation* as the network of references for *understanding*, and not simply a difficulty in action involving some artifact.

In the cases of designing discussed in the previous chapters—the library footprint and the lunar habitat layout, for instance—tacit situated understanding played a crucial role. The situation for Clara, the architect in Schön's study (Section 2.3 above), is the library as she understands it. This situation is disclosed to her through her study of the line drawing, which she interprets as a library footprint. Within this situated understanding, Clara can discover things: like the anomalous walls or five foot displacement. Things discovered in the situation are discovered *as* already having some meaning (a jog in the wall, a deviation from uniformity of lengths, a long way for a library user to walk, a dimension with a certain architectural sense) by virtue of their relations in the situation. When Clara notices the displacement, she is already situated in a world that is meaningful for her. The displacement is noteworthy in terms of its relations to the other walls, to the areas that are defined within the library (especially those affected by the five foot irregularity), to the surrounding lawns or streets, and to the approaches that a visitor could take to the library. It is only within this network of significance that the displacement can be discovered as an object of interest. Perhaps the other architects in the experiment saw the library plan as a different complex of relationships in which the displacement could not be discovered as a significant feature.

One can, of course, ask how Clara's understanding of the drawing originally gained the significance that it had for her. Heidegger's point is that one does not first "decide" to understand something—as though one had to label objects with values through rational judgments—but always first discovers things within contexts that are already meaningful (i.e., already related within the situation). In some cases, the discovered meaning can be modified through reflection and judgment, but this is not as common as rationalist theories assume and it is always done on the basis of prior situated understanding. This takes place through the explication process called interpretation (see Section 4.3, below). When, for instance, Clara is first shown the line drawing and told that she is to design a library using the drawing as a footprint, she discovers the drawing within the larger context of her professional life. She already understands what it means to *be* an architect, to design a building, to visit a library, to participate in an experiment, to study a floor plan, to sketch alternative approaches (Figure 4-4). She dwells in a world in which the drawing and its associated task are already meaningful, in which significant relationships can be explored, and in which discoveries can be made, understood, and further interpreted.

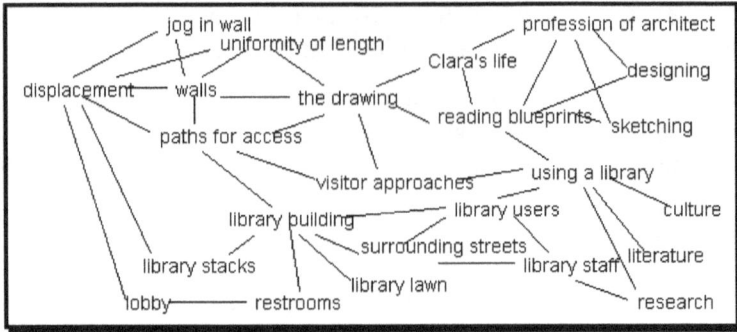

Figure 4-4. The network of references that define Clara's situation.

Ultimately, the various kinds of spatial and functional relationships of the situation point to people: the future library staff who manage the entrances and exits, the stacks, and the offices; the potential library users who walk in from the street, orient themselves after entering a door, search for books or magazines, and use the other facilities. Clara understands these relationships because she has a tacit understanding of the meaning of human being: of what it means to *be* a person working in the library, a person using the library, a person appreciating cultural artifacts, a person negotiating pathways among physical walls.

The situation as meaningful network of physical, functional, and human relationships plays a central role in Alexander and Rittel's theories as well as in Schön's analysis of the library experiment. Alexander is particularly concerned with finding the best decompositions of such relationships in a design, so that the definition of components in terms of their most important or tightest network of interconnections is not disturbed when design decisions are made that rearrange less tightly bound components. Alexander's analysis of unselfconscious design reveals a strong sympathy for the rootedness of artifacts in the worlds of their creators. Artifacts like native houses serve obvious needs in the physical environments and daily lives of their inhabitants, and their designs function centrally in the local cultures and traditions as well. All aspects of their design are immediately meaningful in terms of the understood world. For Alexander, to decompose a design problem in a way that ignores the ties of structural form to social "fit" is to destroy the integrity and value of the artifact being designed.

Rittel also takes a relational view of design, but he focuses more on the level of rationale for self-conscious design. To argue that design is a deliberative process is to say that a given claim does not stand on its own self evidence, but that it is tossed upon a sea of conflicting opinions. The value of an item of rationale results from the way it swims among the other items and how it survives the buffeting by criticism and argumentation. Ultimately, the significance of design justifications are relative to other design decisions, individual modes of reasoning, and personal or group interests or predilections That is, they are always already primarily understood within a broader perspective of understanding, on the basis of which opinions may occasionally be swayed subsequently. The Rittelian issue-base representation captures the structure of the situation's inter-relatedness as explicitly as Alexander's decomposition patterns or Schön's library experiment.

The role of the situation is perhaps clearest of all in the example of lunar habitat design. Here, two concerns dominate most of the discussion in the videotapes: adjacencies and functional relationships. At the level of analysis reported in the transcripts of Chapter 3, the designers are working with a set of components (sleep compartments, galley, toilet, table, stowage, etc.) that are fairly well determined by general mission requirements. Their efforts are aimed at arranging these component volumes so that their mutual relationships define a meaningful situation for life and work on the moon. So the designers—who understand things from within *their* situation—are trying to design a *different* situation that will serve as a world for the astronauts (Figure 4-5).

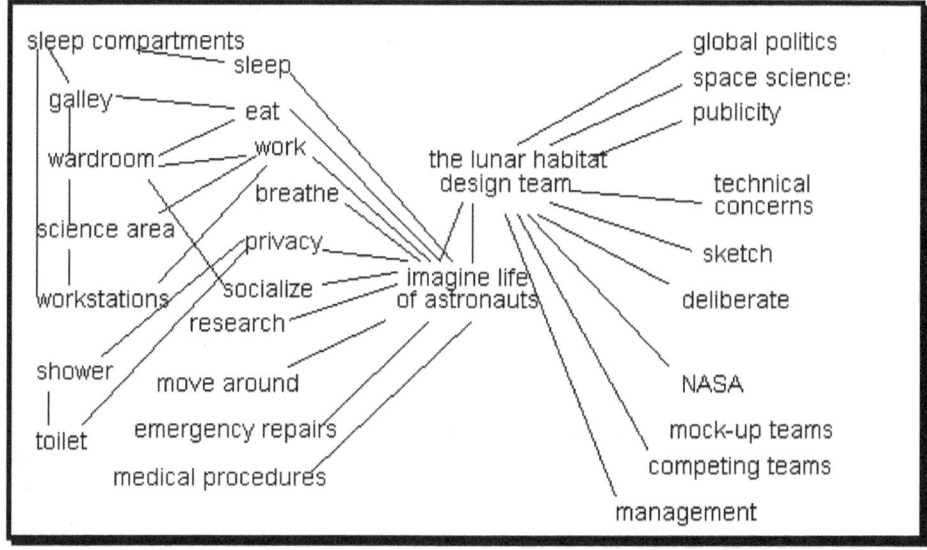

Figure 4-5. The network of references in lunar habitat design.

It defines both the lunar habitat design situation that is being designed and the situation of the designers designing it.

The designers' world includes their sense of what it is to be human in a variety of situations, as well as their knowledge of technical information and regulations. They understand, for instance, what it is to get out of bed in the morning, to sit down with other people at breakfast, to yearn for privacy. As designers, they are experienced at using this tacit understanding to project themselves into the situations they are designing and to understand what it would be like to understand things from within that situation. They know (whether or not they articulate it) that this kind of design hinges on the establishment of a coherent network of significance that can support a meaningful life for people in the situation. They structure and rearrange the physical, functional, and interpersonal relationships of the habitat until they have established a nexus in which dimensions of life like privacy and sociability are defined.

The designers project themselves into the world disclosed by these relationships in order to *discover* the meaning of things for astronauts in that situation. If they discover something that does not work properly, they try to redesign the relationships. When they finally feel comfortable in their new world, then they have reached a satisfactory resolution of the manifold design constraints and they can move on to another level of design. At the conclusion of the design session transcribed in Chapter 3, the designers felt a sense of resolution. They had reached a plateau in their interpretive process at which all the major things they discovered fit comfortably into the network of relationships of the evolved state of their tacitly understood situation.

The lunar habitat design session provides a particularly clear example of how the situation, that is always already understood in a tacit way, provides the working basis for discovering meaningful things within its context— whether one looks at the situation of the designers or at the design of the situation. The lunar habitat design is understood by the designers as a situation incorporating multiple functional relationships. It is designed to be a situation that will be understood by astronauts living in it. But as it exists on a piece of paper or represented in a computer memory as data for a CAD program, it is not understood; it is not a situation; it is not meaningful. Only people can understand.

When NASA compiled the chart of functional relationships and relative adjacencies shown in Figure 3-5 (Section 3.2 above), it may have looked like they recognized the role of architecture to structure human situations. But actually that chart analyses the habitat components as physical objects with functional characteristics that imply certain adjacency constraints. It analyses the habitat as a physical environment that has to function efficiently, without ever explicitly taking into account the fact that most of the functions have to do with people pursuing human aims. The chart of functional relationships does not directly represent the experiential relationships of a situation, but rather incorporates formal, explicit relationships of adjacencies and functional inter-dependencies. However, the chart is similar to an analysis of the designed lunar habitat situation because the formal interpretation necessarily grows out of tacitly understood experiences.

The underlying situation is not to be taken as a physical environment of spatially juxtaposed objects, but as a network of relationships that characterize how one thing is understood as useful to another, ultimately in terms of human purposes. As the basis for tacit understanding, the situation serves as a precondition for understanding from various viewpoints (see Section 4.2) and for more explicit understandings (see Section 4.3).

4.2. The Role of Shared Traditions and Personal Perspectives

The situation is a complex network that can be understood (tacitly) from various perspectives, that is, with various focuses. The meaningful situation is in the first place a *shared* world. It can also be one with *personal* significance.

Shared perspectives. For Heidegger, human being is fundamentally a being with others, and this interpersonal existence takes place through the medium of a shared world. The relationships of significance that constitute the situation of an artifact point to other people and open up a realm in which they can be encountered as fellow ends for whom the artifacts are useful. So, for instance, the chairs around the habitat's wardroom table are there not only for the individual astronaut who discovers them, but for others as well and for the group of astronauts all together. The one astronaut experiences the chairs as part of a public space and knows that this understanding of its public character will be shared by others. The astronaut's own sleep compartment is understood as private in the privative sense that it is *not* for others, and that the others will recognize and acknowledge its shared private significance.

The relationship of interpersonal and personal understanding is important for analyzing collaborative design; but it is also complex, as can be seen from Heidegger's treatment of the issue. Heidegger recognizes the fundamentally interpersonal character of the situation, but he also presents a critique of the public realm (shared "common sense"). He is interested in uncovering the meaning of being that has been lost sight of in our culture. The common sense traditional views that pervade a culture contribute to the cover-up, more than they contribute to the ability to explicate the meaning of being. "Public opinion," according to Heidegger (1927), "regulates from the start all interpretation of the world and human existence. . . [but it] obscures everything and presents what has been covered up as familiar and universally accessible" (S. 127).[10]

The role of shared understanding is clear in the lunar habitat design sessions. The discussion of bathrooms in the videotape illustrates the complexity of the shared world. There is a publicly defined understanding of what constitutes a bathroom. Yet, if one looks closely at the concept—particularly under pressure from design constraints to rethink the concept creatively—it becomes clear that there are really many variations on the notion. There is, for instance, the British WC. One can trace the history of the concept, relating it to the development of mechanical devices and indoor plumbing, and noting its continuing evolution under international influences (Americanization). Other notions of bathrooms can be considered, such as the nautical "head", designed under severe spatial constraints for use in a boat's unusually confined environment.

---

[10] The conservative culture critique of inauthenticity that Heidegger developed from this was a questionable move (see Adorno, 1964, and Stahl, 1975b), that he dropped in his subsequent writings. In fact, his later thought increasingly emphasizes the historical character of the meaning of being, an emphasis that calls for a deeper respect for the positive role of tradition. Gadamer (1964), building on Heidegger's later writings, tries to rehabilitate the role of historical authority, tradition, and prejudice as the necessary foundation for understanding—including for any critical reflections that go on to reject the accepted views (see the debate on this point between Gadamer, 1967, and Habermas, 1967).

The discussion of bathrooms in the transcribed design session serves a double purpose: (1) to problematize the inherited tacit understanding of bathrooms and (2) to establish a new shared understanding. Because the tacitly assumed character of the bathroom as a single room containing a toilet, a sink, and a shower was obstructing the ability to design in response to certain constraints that were arising, Archie started to reflect on the common conception. He discarded it in favor of a multiplicity of notions of bathrooms, named several, and explicitly described some of their characteristics. At the same time as this argued against the original public conception, it served to establish a new definition of bathroom as a shared understanding between Archie and Desi. Their new conceptualization was promptly incorporated in designs that featured a separation of toilet from shower. The new way of thinking about bathrooms corresponds closely to the NASA terminology that discusses "personal hygiene" and "human waste management" as separable functions. Desi was, in fact already familiar with this terminology as a shared understanding among lunar habitat designers, so he could easily make the transition from the public way of thinking in the civilian world to that of the NASA establishment. Archie and Desi started out from different traditions. They deliberated by switching to views from several other perspectives and eventually merging a variety of considerations to define a new, shared perspective. We know how to live in many worlds, to act in numerous situations, and to move freely among them. We understand things from a variety of shifting perspectives that we share with other people as a result of complex social histories and continuing negotiations. [11]

---

[11] Because understanding is founded on social conventions, Dreyfus (1991) goes so far as to identify Heidegger's concept of being with social practice as defined by Bourdieu (1974). He uses examples of body language, like our tacit understanding of interpersonal distance, to illustrate how we know how to be in the shared world in countless ways of which we have no explicit knowledge. While these culturally transmitted understandings provide insightful illustrations, Dreyfus' interpretation of Heideggerian ontology threatens to collapse into anthropology (albeit one with strong ontological roots). Even this paradigm of tacit understanding has been subjected to explication and operationalizing as part of the space effort. In particular, the weightlessness of outer space and the confinement of lunar habitats transform the accustomed situations of social interaction in ways that have been made explicit and studied. (See Raybeck, 1991, and Tafforin, 1990, for example.) However, the meaning of being is arguably more pervasive and less obtrusive than even social practice. It includes, for

Personal perspectives. Understanding has its personal, as well as its interpersonal aspects. Just as society projects the conventional understanding of the shared world, so individuals project their own perspective on their situation. Heidegger uses the German term *Stimmung*—that can be variously translated as mood or tuning [12]—to characterize the sense we have of being in our own particular world. To say, as Heidegger does, that we are *thrown* into a world with a certain *mood* is to state that we always already find a world disclosed for us and it has a particular character that colors our perceptions of what we discover in the world. The mood is not something we explicitly think about or choose. Rather, it determines in the first place how we can direct ourselves toward things that we discover and interact with tacitly or that we can then in exceptional cases think about or make decisions about. The mood determines the way in which things are discovered as mattering to us. It defines our personal perspective on the world. For instance, things might seem threatening if we are in a state of fear or paranoia. It is neither a matter of first ascertaining a possible evil nor of first observing a neutral object and then judging it to be fearsome. Rather, if one is in a fearful mood then one may discover fearsome things. Our

---

instance, the way nature has been encountered in different historical epochs as, e.g., the creation of gods, or the way artifacts are encountered as market commodities in industrial society.

Heidegger sees the epochs of being as historically given; however he does not think they are reducible to culture, but rather that culture reflects changes in the history of being. Although it is possible to propose a materialist critique of this view (see Adorno, 1966, and Stahl, 1975a) one cannot simply reduce Heidegger's radical rethinking to commonsensical categories. Again, it is necessary to distinguish Heidegger's methodological (ontological) arguments from the applications (e.g., a theory of human interpretation) that one would like to garner from his discussion. Regardless of what one thinks of Heidegger's history of being, the point for now is that all understanding involves from the start a sharing of interpersonal meaning and an initial acceptance of received opinion. Some of the perspectives we bring to bear in trying to understand the world are idiosyncratic interpretive "moves" with which we explore possible new views; others are the results of thousands of years of cultural history.

---

[12] See Stahl (1976) for a development of the metaphor of attunement to being.

mood is a way in which our understanding of our world is *filtered* or colored for us.

Mood is correlative with understanding. Understanding is the disclosure of the network of relations of significance. This disclosure always has its specific mood. The situation is always disclosed as a *possibility* of being. For instance, fear is a possible way of being in which things can possibly be discovered as fearsome. The mood of fear thereby opens up the possibility of understanding things as fearsome. Heidegger (1927) emphasizes the way in which understanding is a matter of opening up possibilities. Through one's understanding one discloses what one is able (capable, possible) to be and what can possibly be discovered:

> As disclosure, understanding always pertains to the entirety of being-in-the-world. As a potentiality for being, one is always being-able-to-be-in-the-world. Not only is this, *qua* world, disclosed as possible significance, but when things within the world are themselves freed, they are freed for their own possibilities. Things are discovered in their service*ability*, us*ability*, and detriment*ability*. The network of references reveals itself as the categorical totality of a *possibility* of interconnectedness of things. (S.144)

People are constantly projecting these possibilities of understanding and then seeing the world in terms of them. We always *anticipate* the next moment's world, and we can only discover it through this anticipation. For instance, if we project a fearful mood then we can discover things that are fearsome, but we can also discover that there is nothing fearsome there. This is not a matter of explicit planning. We do not decide to anticipate the fearful. It is more like Schön's designers, who project a design decision not because they know what the consequences will be but rather because they anticipate some general results and want to see what really ensues in detail. In fact, Heidegger's word for projecting, *Entwurf*, in addition to meaning throwing something ahead of oneself can mean designing or sketching a project. So it is appropriate to think of this in terms of moves in design. In this kind of understanding as projecting, there is not an explicit, thematic grasping of the possibilities upon which the understanding is projected. That would destroy the very character of the projection as possibilities and reduce it to specific given, intended contents. So projecting must remain tacit in order to throw before itself possibilities as possibilities and thereby let them be possible. To make an explicit choice is to limit oneself to a single, fully specified option, whereas the tacit projecting that is characteristic of understanding is an opening up of a (structured and delimited) range of possibilities for human being toward that which is understood.

Perspectives for discovery. Heidegger differentiates (1) the *disclosure* of a world from (2) the *discovery* of things in that world. Our shared perspective (traditions) or personal perspectives (moods) open up ranges of possibility. They do this by defining our understood situation as a network of significance. Within this situation, we can discover contingencies. The things we discover are always discovered as meaningful in terms of the situational network of relationships that associates the discovered thing to already tacitly understood other things. *The disclosure of the situation is the opening of a range of possibilities for discovering things and understanding them.*

Schön's view of design provides a metaphor for Heidegger's characterization of life as interpretation. For Schön (1983), the reflective practitioner projects a framing of the design problem by making design decisions or moves. This imposes a structure on the situation and determines the kinds of things that can take place. But it does not fully determine what does take place: that must be discovered by paying attention to the reaction of the situation. "In the designer's conversation with the materials of his design, he can never make a move which has only the effects intended for it. His materials are continually talking back to him, causing him to apprehend unanticipated problems and potentials" (p.101). One can almost understand this literally in terms of a question and answer conversation. The designer poses the question, how would things work out if I make such and such a design move? The designer can choose the question, based on personal interests, intuitions, aesthetics, training, experience, anticipations. (This is the subjective or creative aspect.) But the designer does not choose the answers. (This is the objective aspect of creative discovery.) The answers are discovered, and may be surprising—despite the fact that they could not have been discovered if the question had not been posed. This is a subtle point: through the designer's transaction with the situation, "he shapes it and makes himself a part of it. Hence, the sense he makes of the situation must include his own contribution to it. Yet he recognizes that the situation, having a life of its own distinct from his intentions, may foil his projects and reveal new meanings" (p.163).

For Heidegger, the situation is always disclosed from a certain perspective. The perspective or mood is like a questioning: how does the situation look to a fearful person? But, of course, we do not choose our moods, even if once in a mood we can try to change it. So the metaphor of interpreter as designer is limited to the extent that designers are thought to make volitional, explicit choices. But the parallel holds in that once the situation is disclosed as a network of mood-influenced meanings, the things that can be discovered within that situation have not been determined. To some extent, their possible character to us might be delimited by our anticipations, but things discovered can completely surprise us. For instance, the lunar habitat designers may have projected a certain understanding of what it is to live in the habitat while they arranged modules along one wall to keep the other side of the habitat open for group activities like eating around a table. Then they discovered that the bathroom opened onto the eating area. This was a surprise that they had not anticipated as part of their design decisions. However, the fact that they could then discover this as a new problem in their design was based not only on their having tried out an arrangement and having sketched it so they could see its implications, but also on their continuing to look at the new design with their sense of living in it. Desi actually talked about the situation that he was living in his imagination in terms of past situations that he had experienced in his office, where the bathroom opens onto a public area.

So the possibility of discovering surprises, constraints, and problems in a design is a function of the understanding of the situation and would not exist for someone who lacked such understanding. The projecting of a situation (with its mood and its understanding) is the posing of a question. Gadamer (1966) formulates this connection between the answers that can be discovered and the questions we come to the world with in linguistic terms: "The most fundamental phenomenon of hermeneutics is this: that any statement that is possible can be understood as an answer to a question—and in fact that is the only way it really can be understood" (S.107).

This sketch of Heidegger's interpretation of the phenomena of the public realm and of personal moods shows that understanding is neither objectively determined nor a matter of unfounded whim. Rather, it is based on the projection of a world of *specific possibility* that has the character of a shared world and/or a personal mood. Understanding is founded on the disclosure of a network of references that point to the person who understands the situation and also point to other people as those who share the meaningful world. The situation is not a physical collection of objects that can be investigated scientifically,[13] but a structure of significance in which things can be discovered as already meaningful within the projected nexus of possible ways of relating to other things and serving human aims. The phenomenon of mood provides phenomenological evidence that in

---

[13] Of course, some things in the situation can become objects of scientific investigation. But this is only possible on the basis of pre-scientific, situated understanding. Scientific methodology is a derived form of understanding according to Heidegger's analysis (see next Section).

understanding one always finds oneself already anticipating distinct kinds of things in terms of the network of significance in which one is situated. One always understands from within some *perspective*, whether this perspective is primarily public or personal. Although understanding is only possible from within a mood (Heidegger), a conversation (Schön), or a questioning (Gadamer), one can subsequently modify, shift, or change perspectives within a situation.

4.3. Interpretation as Explication in Language

To understand, according to Heidegger, is to be tacitly situated. This philosophy of understanding could be contrasted with Descartes' "I think, therefore I *am*," by saying, "I *am* situated, therefore I understand." This would not be meant as a logical existence proof, but rather as a description of human existence as always being in a world that is already understood as meaningful and that opens up possible ways of understanding oneself, artifacts, and other people. Nor would this yet involve any explicit cognitive act in the sense of Descartes' propositional *cogito*. Furthermore, it avoids the trap of post-Cartesian philosophy, the problem of how subjective mental acts can understand objects in the world, because such understanding is given with human existence. Also in contrast to Descartes, human existence is not a "clean slate," but always understands from some concrete perspective, that incorporates shared traditions and personal anticipations as part of its being embedded in an understood situation.

One way of looking at this contrast is to say that Heidegger has described tacit situated understanding as the *precondition* for explicit knowledge in Descartes' sense. Heidegger then goes on to show how everyday knowledge and even scientific knowledge are built upon such understanding through processes of interpretation. In general, *interpretation is simply the further development of understanding*. Through interpretation, what was understood tacitly comes to be known explicitly. Such knowledge is not the acquisition of information in the form of propositional facts (although it can eventually be developed into that form), but the working out of the possibilities that were inherent in the understanding. This "working out" is a matter of interpretation. As discussed in the previous section, such working out can produce unanticipated surprises and require a reinterpretation that revises situated understanding.

In German, the word for interpretation is *Auslegung*: literally the laying-out of something. This is similar to the English word, *explication*, that is derived from the Latin for un-folding. Interpretive explication unfolds, lays out, or develops the implications in tacit understanding. This happens in the discovery of artifacts in the situation. When an artifact is discovered *as* a hammer, the references in the network of significance concerning the hammer (illustrated in Figure 4-3 of Section 4.1) are taken apart, laid out, or un-folded; thereby they become explicitly understood. The artifact is seen *as* a hammer, as a tool for pounding nails, as a means to the building of a structure, as something useful in pursuing human projects. This is the structure of explicit interpretation: something *as* something.

The "as" makes up the structure of the explicitness of something that is understood. It is known as the *hermeneutic as*: the as of interpretation. To simply use the artifact as a hammer is to understand it tacitly, but to articulate it as a hammer is to interpret it explicitly. According to Heidegger (1927), this is, in turn, a precondition for being able to formulate propositional knowledge (and ultimately methodological scientific facts) about the thing as a hammer:

> In the mere encountering of something, the thing is understood in terms of a totality of references, and the encounter hides within itself the explicitness of the assignment-relations that belong to that totality. That which is understood gets articulated when the entity to be understood is brought close interpretively by taking as our clue the "something as something"; and this articulation comes before our making any thematic assertion about it. In such an assertion the "as" does not turn up for the first time; it just gets expressed for the first time, and this is possible only in that it lies before us as something expressible. (S.149)

That is, tacitly understanding something *as* something on the basis of references in the situation is what permits one to interpret the thing explicitly *as* something subsequently and eventually to name it *as* something in linguistic discourse.

Section 4.1 suggested that in various kinds of breakdown cases—where an artifact is, for instance, conspicuous, obtrusive, or obstinate by being damaged, missing, or in the way—the implicit working of some of the references in the network of significance may be broken and as a result these references come to prominence. In such a breakdown case, the role of interpretation would be to mend the referential breaks by creating new reference links to the artifact within the situation. As depicted in Figure 4-6, the process of understanding would proceed through the following stages:

* An initial preunderstanding discloses a world from a certain perspective of possibilities.

* The artifact is discovered and understood as something in terms of the situational network of references.

* However, the references are inadequate for understanding the artifact and there is a breakdown in the network.

* The artifact is interpreted by laying out the implicit references and repairing the break in them.

* This makes explicit the understanding of the artifact as such and such a thing.

* The new understanding can then be asserted in language and communicated or it can revert to tacit understanding.

* The revised tacit understanding forms the preunderstanding for any further interpretation, completing the hermeneutic circle of understanding.

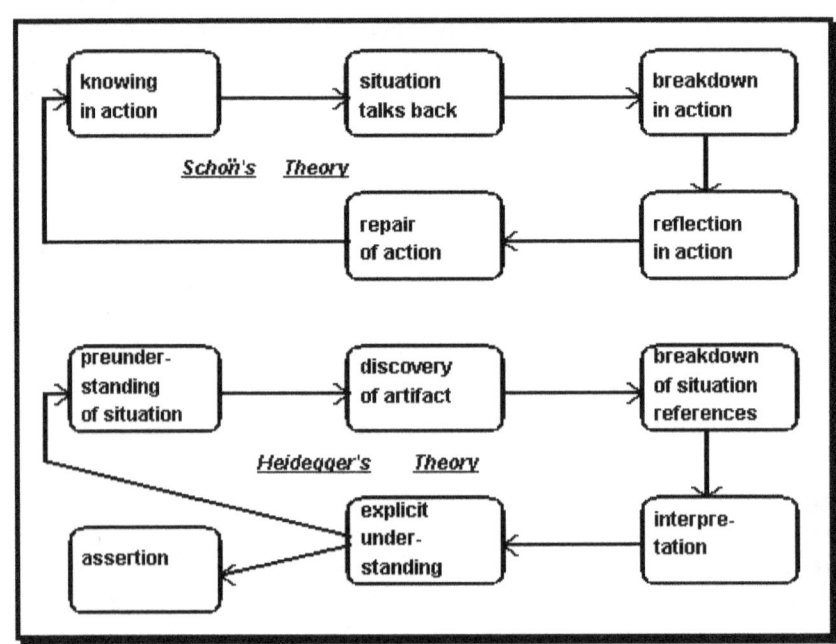

Figure 4-6. Two similar theories of breakdown.

A comparison of Heidegger's hermeneutic circle with Schön's theory of reflection-in-action shows strong parallels. For Heidegger, the breakdown occurs within the network of references that constitute the situation.

Note that although this process is similar to Schön's (1985) theory of breakdown and repair, for Heidegger the breakdown is in the situational preunderstanding, not in the activity itself.

Actually, if one reads Schön carefully, it is apparent that he also views breakdowns as taking place at the level of understanding, even though his terminology is open to the misinterpretation that the breakdown is at the action level. As quoted in Section 2.3, Schön (1985) says, "Sometimes, however, there are surprises. These take the form of unanticipated events which *do not fit existing understandings*, fall outside the *categories* of knowing-in-action. . . . There is a demand for reflection [that] converts tacit knowing-in-action to explicit knowledge for action (p.24; italics added).

At the corresponding point in *Being and Time*, where he is formulating his general theory of understanding and interpretation, Heidegger does not limit himself to cases of breakdowns in action. Rather, he emphasizes the tacit basis of all understanding of artifacts. The grounding of all understanding in a tacit grasp of the significant references of the situation provides the first of three important characteristics of interpretation. According to Heidegger's analysis, there are three preconditions of interpretation, here referred to as pre-possession, pre-view, and pre-conception.

(a) Artifacts are always understood in terms of the totality of references of the situation. This totality is generally not explicitly grasped through a thematic interpretation. In fact, if it has once been grasped that way, it tends to return again to a tacit understanding. It is in this tacit mode that understanding is the essential foundation for everyday interpretation. In other words, interpretation of something as something is always grounded in a situatedness or *pre-possession*: the interpretation already *possesses the situation* through an understanding of the totality of references, and it moves within this understandingly in order to develop the understanding into a more explicit form.

(b) Interpretation is also always grounded in a *pre-view*. The development of understanding of something that is still veiled takes place through an unveiling that is always guided by a *point of view* that fixes that with respect to which the thing should be interpreted. The preview carves up that which the prepossession has in terms of a specific interpretability; it specifies what are to be viewed as the things and what are the joints dividing them. This basis of interpretation was taken up later by Kuhn (1964), who argued that even the natural sciences viewed reality through paradigms that institutionalized this kind of preview. An indication of the importance of preview can be seen in the way that both Schön (1983) and Kuhn (1964) claim that a major outcome of professional schooling is the transfer (tacitly, through apprenticeship relationships) of modes of preview that are definitive of schools of science, technology, or design.

(c) Interpretation is grounded in *pre-conception* as well. Interpretation has always already chosen a way of conceptualizing whatever is being interpreted. The choice need not be a final decision; it can be tentative and subject to future change. The *conceptual framework* can either be created appropriately through articulation of the thing being interpreted, or the thing can be forced into a conceptualization that contradicts its nature. But some framing of the interpretive effort in terms of a system of concepts must be chosen. To interpret x as y is to choose a conceptualization of x in terms of something like y. Even if this is not an explicit choice, but happens spontaneously or implicitly, it opens a range of possible interpretations and excludes other ways of grasping x.

Table 4-1. The three aspects of interpretation.
They are grounded in the three-fold preconditions of all understanding.

	(a)	(b)	(c)
preunderstanding	prepossession	preview	preconception
interpretation	situated	perspectival	linguistic
Chapter 4	Section 4.1	Section 4.2	Section 4.3

The characteristics of prepossession, preview, and preconception make up the three-fold preconditional structure of interpretation in Heidegger's analysis. The understanding that has this three-fold structure will be referred to as *preunderstanding* to distinguish it as a stage of the more general term, "understanding", and to emphasize that it forms the initial precondition for the development of any interpretation. The character of interpretation as situated, perspectival, and linguistic is derived from the three-fold structure of preunderstanding (see Table 4-1).

The three aspects of preunderstanding can be illustrated with the example of interpretation in design given in Section 3.1, where Archie and Desi begin to discuss privacy issues. The action in that opening scene of the transcripts is propelled by a tension between Archie and Desi's two different understandings of the proposed design. They start out with somewhat different prepossessions, previews, and preconceptions. Desi starts off trying to orient Archie to share his prepossession of the situation represented in the sketch (Figure 3-1): "You have a big 'family room' or 'den'. And what they do is either fold down the Murphy bed or set up cots...." Archie gets the picture—i.e., he starts to have the same understanding of the situation in the habitat—but he has a different preview or slant on it. Desi views the design as meeting the need to provide a minimal accommodation for sleeping: a place to stretch out one's body during the period set aside for sleep. Archie, however, views it on the basis of his own personal experiences. In his view, "There are times when you're waking up or going to sleep and getting your clothes on or whatever, when a modicum of privacy can actually be treasured, and when some people read a book." While Desi is quick to respond to Archie's concerns, he does it while remaining within a preconception that he has adopted from NASA. That is, he had started with an austere, military view of providing a minimal "accommodation for sleep" and then he switched to discussing "crew compartments", a term used within NASA to describe private sleeping cubicles for astronauts in Space Station.

The initial discussion of privacy ends with agreement about the importance of privacy for a long mission:

> Archie: It's an interesting question. If you cross this 30 day limit, then it seems likely the sleep compartments suddenly become a dramatically higher priority. People start freaking out that they can't get away from other people.

> Desi: I would think so. I would think that the idea of being able to get away would be nice. Having that privacy, the control, even if they don't use it.

Here it is clear, first of all, that Archie and Desi each have an understanding of the situation that goes far beyond what is explicitly drawn in the sketch to include a sense of what life would be like in the nexus of artifacts, meanings, and relationships that are implied there. Secondly, they view this from specific perspectives, whether based on personal experiences of feelings of privacy or on traditions passed down by other designers. Thirdly, they bring to bear conceptualizations such as "crew compartment" in order to understand the given possibilities and to share this understanding.

The preconditional structure of understanding—the fact that interpretation always already has a prepossession of the situation, a preview of a perspective, and a preconception in specific language—means that interpretation is never a presuppositionless apprehending of something pre-given. Rather, all interpretation that is to contribute to understanding must have already understood the thing that is to be interpreted. The interpretation process must understand the context of significance in which the thing is situated; it must know how to carve up the matter appropriately; and it must use suitable terms to interpret it as something. The circularity of this undertaking is known as the *hermeneutic circle*. It is a well-known phenomenon in literary interpretation and in holistic disciplines: one cannot, for instance, interpret the line of a poem without understanding the context of the whole poem, the poet's other works, or the poet's life; but the interpretation of the line may be needed in order to understand these very contexts.

Such circularity cannot be avoided. It is part of the structure of human existence and of interpretation. It does not mean that things cannot be interpreted appropriately, but just that this is not automatic. The circular structure must be taken into account. In it, according to Heidegger (1927), is buried "a positive possibility of the most primary kind of knowing, that, however, can only be grasped if the interpretation has understood that its first, last, and constant task remains to make sure that the prepossession, preview, and preconception are not given by fancies and popular conceptions, but that the scientific theme is secured by working them out from the things themselves" (S.153).

One necessarily starts with sets of prejudices that have been handed down historically. However, the interpretation process allows one to methodically reflect upon these prejudices and develop new understandings, perspectives, and words for carrying on the interpretation. *Being and Time* is itself a model of such a process, beginning as it does with the vague, confused, and obscured historical sense of the meaning of being and explicating the way that it is understood in order to develop a new viewpoint and vocabulary for interpreting being. Of course, the danger exists that one will not pursue this effort and will remain with the prevailing prejudices. (This is the basis for Heidegger's critique of the understanding defined by the public realm and of the corresponding inauthentic existence that does not strive to develop beyond such understanding.)

The way the hermeneutic circle works can be seen in the way Desi and Archie develop their understanding of the location of the toilet in Section 3.2. They start with a set of prejudices that have been handed down in the preconditional structure of their understanding. Desi bases his first design on the wet-wall principle, the idea that all appliances needing plumbing should be located together to facilitate the supply and removal of water. Archie starts out his thinking with the conventional (at least in his culture) idea that the toilet and shower are located in a single room, the bathroom. But then they both begin to reflect on the role of each item in the unique situation that is being designed. If the toilet is too close to the sleep compartments, then people may be disturbed by it during the night (as they in fact were in Skylab). On the other hand, as Desi points out, "You're not going to get up in the middle of the night and take a shower." So Archie suggests, "Could we separate them, have the shower a little more convenient to where you're going to change, get dressed?" The idea of separating the shower and toilet arises out of the process of interpretation, and then motivates the subsequent thrust of the design effort to establish a public-private gradient across the habitat.

For both Desi and Archie, the understanding began with an assumption that the shower and toilet would be located together. They were able to get beyond this starting-point only on the basis of starting there and then reflecting on the problems that they could see in the consequences of this starting-point. (In Schön's terms, they had to make a design decision and then let its implications talk back to them.) Then they were willing to make their initial assumptions explicit and to criticize them in terms of the things themselves: in this case, the functions of the shower and toilet in the life of the habitat. Their designing necessarily begins with uncritically accepted popular prejudices (the preconditional structures of understanding), but it then works out more appropriate interpretations through an on-going analysis and critique of the specific relationships of the situation, of their own perspectives, and of the conceptual framework being used.

The first two components of the preconditional structure of interpretation have already been discussed in the preceding presentation of Heidegger's philosophy. The prepossession of a situation was considered in terms of the situated cognition of artifacts in Section 4.1, and the preview of public and personal perspectives was presented in terms of public opinion and moods in Section 4.2. However, the conceptualization or language of preconceptions has not yet been examined. Heidegger discusses it in terms of *assertion* and *discourse*.

Assertions are familiar from the rationalist tradition as propositional judgments (statements of the form: "x is a y" or "x as y"). Heidegger reviews three basic meanings of assertion: (a) assertion means *pointing out*, (b) assertion means *predication*, (c) assertion means *communication* (Table 4-2). In each case, Heidegger argues that assertions are not fundamental, but are derivative of understanding and interpretation.

Table 4-2. The three aspects of assertion.
They are grounded in the preunderstanding that belongs to discourse. Discourse, in turn, is grounded in the preunderstanding of human involvements.

preunderstanding	prepossession	preview	preconception
discourse	situation	view	shared language
assertion	pointing out	predicating	communicating

(a) When someone asserts, "The hammer is too heavy," this is a pointing out of an artifact that has already been understood as a hammer and has been interpreted as too heavy. The assertion is not about some kind of representation of a hammer (where the status of the representation and its relation to the assertion are problematic), but about the hammer artifact itself, as it is discovered in the understood situation.

(b) In predication, we assert a definite character of the thing discussed. But this is simply a variation on pointing out. We point out the thing in a way that restricts our view of it, for instance, to its heaviness. By this explicit restriction of the view, that which is already manifest may be made explicitly manifest in its definite character. So predication is a development of tacit understanding into a more explicit form.

(c) As communication, assertion is letting other people see with us what we are pointing out, and letting them see it as explicitly restricted. It is a sharing of the more explicit interpretation of something in the world whose understanding is already shared as part of a shared situation.

Because it is derived from interpretation, assertion has the three-fold preconditional structure. The pointing out requires a prepossession of what gets pointed out. The predication that narrows the view is a development of the preview, that had already narrowed the view in that direction. The communication takes place within a language that inconspicuously implies a preconception, because language already hides in itself a developed conceptualization.

However, assertion (that rationalist philosophy focuses on as the basic form of objective knowledge) may also entail an essential transformation from primary interpretation, from which it is derived. The hermeneutic-as can become transformed into the *apophantic-as* of discourse, and ultimately into the copula ("is") of propositional assertions. This happens through a process of decontextualization; the artifact that is the subject of the assertion losses its embedding in the situation. The prepossession no longer has the situation with its nexus of references that determine the artifact's significance (the basis of the hermeneutic-as). Now the thing is simply present as an isolated object, which can have attributes. The assertion still points out the thing in a definite way, but now the definiteness is associated with an attribute, rather than with an aspect of the situation. The binding of the object to its attribute can be further formalized into a calculus of relations. In this way, situated understanding can eventually develop through interpretation into theoretical knowledge, which can be represented in formalisms. As the interpretation draws further and further from its original concrete embedding in the situation, it becomes increasingly abstract.[14]

Despite the importance of language in Heidegger's philosophy of interpretation, he is very sketchy in his discussion of the various layers of abstraction through which understanding can be transformed (Table 4-3) and the way each successive level in grounded in previous levels (Table 4-2). The transformations of tacit preunderstanding into increasingly explicit and formalized knowledge will have to be further worked out in Chapter 5 in order to provide a basis for the theory of computer support of interpretation in Chapter 6. Thereby, the entries in Table 4-3 will be clarified in Part II.

---

[14] The term abstract comes from the Latin *abstrahere*, to draw away.

Table 4-3. Increasing abstraction of the preconditions of understanding.

preunderstanding	prepossession	preview	preconception	implicit as
interpretation	situated	perspectival	linguistic	hermeneutic as
discourse	identify	filter	associate	the word "as"
assertion	name	clause	adjective	apophantic as
predication	object	modifier	attribute	the copula "is"
logical calculus	variable	conditional	operator	relation

Like all interpretation, assertion has its dangers. Assertions can become abstracted from their basis in the preunderstanding of discourse. Communication in the public realm can degenerate to hearsay, where the grasp on the original phenomena becomes veiled. As assertions are passed on in re-telling, there is a widening of the range of shared interpretations, as Plato (348 BC) had already remarked in his famous seventh letter where he discusses the potential dangers of written language. Whenever something is uncovered in a process of explication, there is the possibility or even likelihood of its becoming covered up again in various ways. Such is the dialectic of tacit and explicit. This need not be considered a problem in every case. It is often necessary that our explicit interpretations re-submerge into tacit understanding in order to function effectively. Heidegger (1951) provides a good example of this in his later writings on poetry interpretation. Literary interpretation is a process of explication whose goal is to be absorbed into a deeper, but tacit understanding of the work:

> Whatever else a commentary may or may not accomplish, the following is always true of it: in order to make what has been composed in the poem somewhat clearer, the commentary must always shatter itself and what it is trying to do. For the sake of what was composed, the commentary to the poem must strive to make itself superfluous. The final, but also the most difficult step of every interpretation consists in disappearing along with its commentary in favor of the pure presence of the poem. The poem, that then stands under its own law, itself directly shines a light on the other poems. Then, during repeated readings we believe we had always already understood the poems that way. It is good that we think that. (S.7 f)

Heidegger's point here is simply to show that the basis of all knowledge is in situated understanding and in its explication via hermeneutic interpretation. He notes that many intermediate gradations are possible between the primary form of engaged understanding that is absorbed in the situation and propositional assertions about objects of theoretical study that have distanced themselves from their situatedness. There are, for instance, assertions about what is happening within the situation, accounts concerning artifacts being used, reports on things discovered in the world, the recording and fixing of "facts", descriptions of states of affairs, or narrations of events that have transpired. Such assertions have their basis in our understanding of the world; to take them as propositions whose meaning is traced back to theoretical observations would be to pervert their origin and misconstrue their derived status.

An interpretation or assertion can be articulated as discourse, which is expressed in *language*. The existential foundation of language is *discourse* and *hearing*: our ability to talk and to listen form the basis of our ability to use language to articulate the meaning of our understanding or interpretations. For instance, the articulation of the interpersonal shared world gets constituted in speech acts like assenting, refusing, demanding, warning, and so on. Discourse and hearing make it possible to communicate a shared world, and thereby to grasp it as truly shared. They also make it possible (e.g., through intonation) to communicate one's personal mood. So discourse and listening are the way in which we are open to other people and to our shared being together.

Once more, Heidegger (1927) reverses the priority of phenomena from the scientific view. When we hear sounds, we do not first hear tones and then subsequently interpret them as signifying something—as though we apprehended the tone as a neutral object and then associated an attribute with it. Rather, we first hear meaningful, understood artifacts, that we can later abstract to pure sounds and facts: "What we 'first' hear is never noises or complexes of sounds, but the creaking wagon, the motor-cycle. We hear the column on the march, the north wind, the woodpecker tapping, the fire crackling" (S.163).

When Desi and Archie look at the sketch reproduced in Figure 3-2 of Section 3.2, with the rectangle labeled "toilet" near the rectangle labeled "ward room table", they do not observe a series of lines forming rectangles, etc. Rather they directly perceive a public meeting and eating area with a bathroom opening onto it. Desi immediately starts to talk about this (sketched) situation as being like the (real) arrangement at his office, where the bathroom faces the reception area. Archie also points to the situation as being problematic. He *perceives* the habitat *as* consisting of meaningful areas interacting, he does not have to deduce this fact from an analysis of coordinates of points and distances between lines—the way a computer would have to. Furthermore, the language for talking about his understanding and sharing it with other people is immediately available as part of his linguistic traditions.

When Archie tries to rethink the concept of bathroom and to suggest to Desi that other definitions might be worth exploring for the sake of the design, he does all this in language. It is clear from the videotape that his chain of ideas follows haltingly, as one link after the other is brought out as a follow up to what came before. It is not that Archie had an argument all logically thought out in his mind that he then telegraphed to Desi. Rather, he thought out the relationships of the different national models of bathrooms by linguistically pointing out different aspects. Desi followed the discussion, not by translating sounds into symbols and deducing consequences for some representation of bathrooms in his head, but by seeing their shared notion of bathroom develop as its various aspects were unveiled through discourse.

Language is the medium in which our understanding of our world is interpretively explicated. Whereas animals exist in the wilderness of environments that are simply understood in unmediated, instinctual ways, people dwell in richly interpreted, socially-mediated worlds thanks to language. As Heidegger (1947) puts it, "Language is the house of being" (S.188). Gadamer (1960) attributes an even more universal role to language, simultaneously stressing that it is a medium of discovery as well as of projection: "Being that can be understood is language" (p.xxiii). For Heidegger and Gadamer language is not an arbitrary system of symbols for representing things (the way a programming "language" is), but the embodiment of historical tradition, the constantly evolving encapsulation of mankind's understanding of the being of the world, artifacts, and people. In this sense, "being is not experienced where something can be constructed by us and is to that extent conceived, but it is experienced where what is happening can merely be understood" (ibid.). Thanks to our dwelling in language, we can understand, discover, interpret, and share whatever can *be* that can be understood.

Part II. The Problem of Tacit and Explicit Understanding

"The predicate calculus is often treated by philosophers
as if *it* were the universal language; but to put beliefs
expressed in a natural language into the predicate calculus
format, one must first *interpret* them—that is, one must
deal with the very problem we wish to solve."

> Hilary Putnam
>
> *Representation and Reality*
>
> (1988, p.88)

CHAPTER 5. GROUNDING EXPLICIT DESIGN KNOWLEDGE

Part I presented several analyses of the process of interpretation in innovative design. The various analyses were not always entirely consistent with one another and were open to a variety of misinterpretations. Despite the effort to view them from the perspective of this dissertation, they retained the influences of their sources in very different enterprises: Alexander's focus on patterns, Rittel's on deliberation, Schön's on discovery, Archie and Desi's on habitability issues, and Heidegger's on ontological concerns. Although most of them (except Heidegger's) were related to attempts at computer support for design, the analyses did not explicitly address issues of computer support. In order to provide a foundation for the development of a theory of computer support of interpretation in design in Chapter 6, a number of open issues need to be clarified in the present chapter. Inconsistencies should be resolved and misinterpretations guarded against.

In Part I, evidence was presented in Chapters 2 and 3 to show that design is an interpretive process. Then in Chapter 4, the character of interpretation as situated, perspectival, and linguistic was explicated using Heidegger's philosophy. Although some examples from the earlier chapters were used to illustrate Heidegger's ideas, the relation of Heidegger's analysis of interpretation in general to interpretation in design specifically still needs to be addressed (Section 5.1). Here it will turn out that the domain of design fits Heidegger's analysis particularly well in several interesting ways.

A theory of computer support for interpretation in design centers on human-computer interaction and the role of the people whose interpretive processes are to be supported. The distribution of roles between the computer and the people is determined by how interpretation is socially grounded (Section

5.2). This includes the way in which the understood reality is socially constructed and how people have intentional access to that reality. It has implications for the problems of application and relevance, which are critical for a theory of computer support.

The theory of computer support is based on the transformations of tacit to explicit forms of knowledge (Section 5.3), by which people's preunderstandings can be articulated and represented in a computer. Definitions of tacit and explicit must be developed. The different forms explicit knowledge can take must be distinguished and the processes by which one form is transformed into another identified.

5.1. Applying Heidegger's Philosophy to Design

Heidegger's philosophy offers what is arguably the most thorough account of the process of human understanding available. Although his analysis of interpretation is useful if one is to understand activities like innovative design, it never addresses the realm of design directly. Heidegger discusses interpretation at a high level of generality and chooses his examples from interactions between people and physical artifacts, like the use of hammers by carpenters. He is concerned with the nature of understandingly being in the world. While a person's world includes conceptual and imaginative realms like design, Heidegger's examples primarily come from the world of physical artifacts which can be encountered perceptually.

Design is distinctive. It has its own existential structure and characteristics. Heidegger's philosophy must be adapted to the realm of design by reflection upon how design differs from Heidegger's examples, and by modifying or extending his theory accordingly. Specifically, such an extension must address five concerns:

1. Design is different from direct action in the world. It has to do with plans on paper as its artifact, rather than with the object that might someday be built with bricks and mortar in the world based on those plans. Interpretation in design differs from interpretation of one's involvements in the world.

2. Heidegger emphasizes that interpretation is a matter of working out what is implicit in the tacit preunderstanding that provides the necessary preconditions for interpretation. Schön, in contrast, emphasizes the role

of discovery, through which designers creatively discover surprising consequences of their design moves. These two components of interpretation must be integrated in a comprehensive theory.

3. Schön argues that breakdowns in action function as catalysts for interpretive reflection. Heidegger also recognizes the role of breakdowns, but he sees a break in the references of the situational network of significance as the underlying phenomenon. Accordingly, an adequate theory has to take into account the need to repair the network of significance through interpretation, and not just to repair the problem with the action.

4. Heidegger's example of the craftsman using a hammer may appeal to the ideal of the designer as solitary artist, but it conjures up a different social setting than that of a design team working on a stage in the development of a high-tech artifact like a lunar habitat. In particular, collaborative design places more stress on cooperation and communication mechanisms than does design by an individual. Collaborative design that takes place over decades—as do many NASA projects—requires communication among people who cannot directly talk to each other.

5. Heidegger was concerned with the ontology of interpreted things—what it is to be something that is tacitly preunderstood versus what it is to be something that is explicitly codified in formalized propositions. His philosophical distinctions must be recast as operational mechanisms that can be incorporated in computer systems.

Consideration of these five concerns leads to a more comprehensive and appropriate theory of interpretation in design.

1. From artifacts in the world to artifacts on the drawing board. In common sense terms, there seems to be a world of difference ontologically between artifacts and designs. However, in important senses Heidegger treats artifacts in the world the same way he would treat design artifacts on the drawing board. That is, he is not really concerned with them as physically present objects of perception. On the contrary, his main effort philosophically is to distinguish artifacts-in-use from traditional conceptions of physically-present-objects (as discussed in point 5 below). For example, a hammer in use is not understood by the carpenter as an observed object with physical attributes, but is skillfully applied to the activities of the current situation. Furthermore, this skillful use takes place within the context of future-oriented plans and desires, such as the anticipation of the item that is under construction. This is similar to components of a design, which are skillfully arranged in terms of their relationships to other design components and within the context of the anticipated final design. Marks in a design sketch, for instance, are important for their roles within a network of significances, rather than for their physical properties as lines. Interpretation of both physical artifacts and designs is situated.

By abstracting from the world of physical artifacts, designs, in fact, present the structure of the Heideggerian situation even more clearly than it is apparent in the physical world. Designing can be a way of directly working out the situational references that are of interest. Here it is clear that the designer has created the relationships in order to achieve future-oriented goals. That is, in creating a design, the designer discloses a network of significance. Within this network, discoveries can be made and problems can be uncovered.

The situation is the context of interpreted meaning within which understanding takes place. Normally, this network of significance operates tacitly in the skilled use of artifacts. However, in design work features of the situation that emerge explicitly during phases of interpretation can be expressed in the representations of the design medium. For instance, the distinction of two independent functions within an artifact being designed can be symbolized by distinct graphical icons and by separate entries in an issue-base. Design media provide external memory mechanisms for expressing and retaining explicit by-products of interpretive reflection, such as conceptual distinctions.

The fact that designing presents the structure of the Heideggerian situation more clearly than other activities in the physical world provides an important opportunity for computer support of design. If the design work can take place within a computer system that represents the relationships properly, then such a system can provide support for the network of significance: for the semantics of the design, not just its syntactic outward structure. This opportunity will be pursued in Section 5.3, where the model of interpretation is extended to include computer support.

2. From laying-out implications to creative discovery. In the domain of design—in which the designer creates the structure of a world—it is particularly clear that the discoveries that can take place within the disclosed situation are results of the creative activity of the designer. Viewed this way, interpretation in its literal sense of laying-out (*Aus-legung*) the implicit meaning is seen to be congruent with creative discovery because the structure whose implications get laid out is one that was created by the designer. The interpretation process makes discoveries within a creatively constructed context by laying out the implications of that context.

In adapting Heidegger's philosophy to design it is necessary to consider the relationship between Heidegger's analyses and those of the design methodologists. In Section 4.3 of Part I, a contrast was made between Heidegger's and Schön's discussions of breakdown. Figure 4-6 of that section is reproduced as Figure 5-1 with minor changes to show the contrast between their analyses.

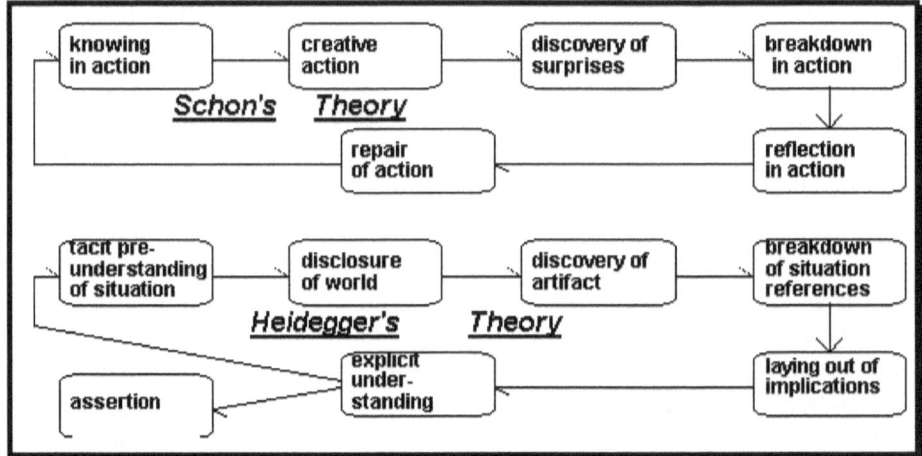

Figure 5-1. Two different theories of breakdown.

A contrast of Heidegger's hermeneutic circle with Schön's theory of reflection-in-action shows a difference of emphasis. For Heidegger, the implications of the disclosed world get laid out; for Schön, creative action leads to discovery.

Here it is clear that the two theories are describing much the same process, but emphasizing different moments within the cycle of interpretation. Putting aside for now (until point 3) the differences in their concepts of breakdown, one can see that creative discovery in Schön's theory plays the same role as disclosure in Heidegger's. For the sake of clarity, this process can be broken into two moments—as is done by both Heidegger and Schön. Heidegger distinguishes disclosing a world (as a context for things to exist meaningfully within) and discovering things (e.g., artifacts, other people, and oneself) within that world. With Schön, one can distinguish between creating the design structures and discovering surprises within them. Whatever the terminology, the important thing is that both aspects of interpretation be included: (1) the idea of creating a structure of significance or a disclosed world and (2) of discovering things within it that were implicit but not foreseen or intended.

Figure 5-2 shows the model of interpretation in design that is being proposed here and in the next chapter. First, the world is disclosed. This disclosure takes place on the basis of tacit preunderstanding, and is thus not a beginning *ex nihilo* but a continuation of the hermeneutic circle of understanding. Within this disclosed world, creative discovery (as the second moment) reveals discovered things that exist in the situation. Surprise discoveries can lead to a breakdown of understanding, requiring the interpretation of new meanings.

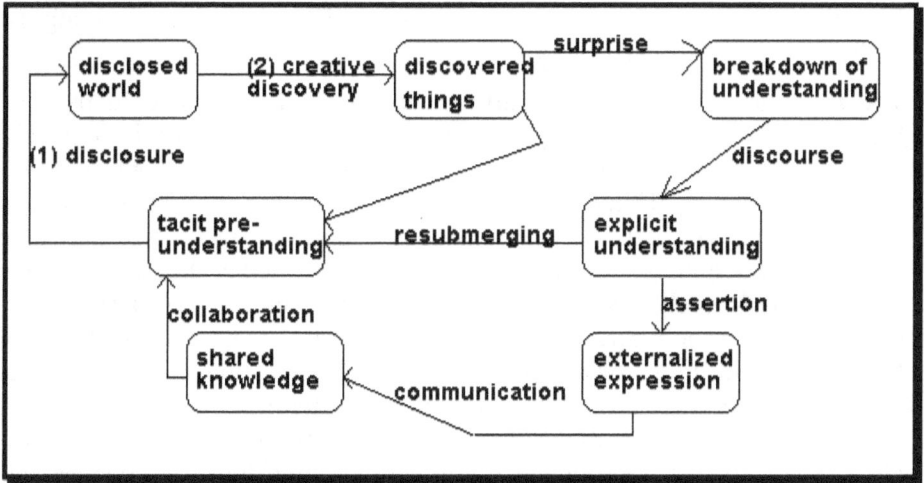

Figure 5-2. The model of interpretation in design.

The rectangles represent stages of understanding within the cycle of interpretation. The arrows represent transformations from one stage to another. The hermeneutic circle appears at the top of the figure. Below, the basis for collaborative design is shown.

The process of breakdown and the other pictured stages will be discussed in the following numbered points. In particular, the role of discourse and assertion as transformations related to explicit understanding will be discussed as further developments of the laying out of tacit understanding, based on Heidegger's analysis of language in Section 4.3. The fact that understanding can become more explicit and be externalized provides the possibility of developing a computational medium for externalizing design understanding.

3. From breakdown in action to repair of situated understanding. The notion of breakdown in action plays a rather small role in Heidegger's analysis of human understanding. As discussed in Section 4.1, Heidegger uses examples of breakdown in order to make explicit the network of references among artifacts that are only present tacitly under conditions of normal use. Yet, the notion of breakdown has been elevated to central importance in the theories that have tried to adopt Heidegger's analysis to a theory of design and to operationalize this theory for computer support. Thus, breakdown plays an important role in Schön (1985), Winograd & Flores (1986), Suchman (1987), Ehn (1988), Budde & Züllighoven (1990), McCall, Morch, & Fischer (1990), Dreyfus (1991), Coyne & Snodgrass (1991), Fischer & Nakakoji (1992).

The fact that so many writers influenced by Heidegger have focused on breakdown does not provide multiple independent support for this emphasis. As can be seen from Figure 4-2 in Chapter 4, most of these writers have been influenced by Heidegger only indirectly—either through Dreyfus or through Schön. If one looks closely at the discussions of breakdown in Dreyfus and Schön, one can note an ambiguity in whether they are speaking about a (ontological) breakdown in the network of references or a (practical) breakdown in action. Dreyfus is certainly aware of the ontological role of breakdown, but he is concerned to make his presentation acceptable to an American audience, trained in the rationalist tradition. For the sake of concreteness, he uses examples that stress the breakdown in action. Schön is also aware of the ontological ramifications, but he has couched his discussion in terms of action (e.g., knowing-in-action, reflection-in-action), so it often seems that his examples of breakdown exemplify breakdowns in action rather than breakdowns in situated understanding. Given that it is easier to operationalize breakdowns in action than breakdowns in situated understanding, it is not surprising that people interested in producing practical results from Dreyfus or Schön's theories would tend to emphasize the action-oriented reading of the ambiguous discussions.

Breakdowns of action and breakdowns of understanding both call for repair. However, the repair of understanding is more complex to support. To repair a breakdown in action, it is only necessary to propose a new action. For instance, in Chapter 7 a critiquing mechanism in the JANUS system will be discussed that causes breakdowns in designing activities by flagging design constructions that violate rules in the domain knowledge. Early versions of this mechanism merely displayed a message indicating the rule that was violated. Thus, if in laying out a residential kitchen one located the stove in front of a window then one received a message that the stove should not be in front of a window. The repair for this breakdown in design action was to move the stove. In more sophisticated subsequent versions of the critiquing system, the designer is given information relevant to understanding the reasoning behind the rule. Then the designer can make a reasoned decision as to how to repair the breakdown. This is a step toward repairing the understanding that led to the breakdown.

In Chapter 3, a more complex breakdown was illustrated from the transcript of the lunar habitat design sessions. Here, the designers recognized that the arrangement they had sketched in with a bathroom opening onto an eating area was problematic. To repair this situation, however, required a reinterpretation of their concepts of privacy and of the functionality of bathrooms. This involved consideration of their conceptualizations from various perspectives (e.g., the European WC) and the development of new terminology (e.g., the privacy gradient). The repair of this breakdown meant a restructuring of the designers' understanding of the situation, perspective, and language. To provide computer support for such a process would necessitate empowering the designers to explore the interpretive network of significances they are using, to review alternative viewpoints, and to generate innovative conceptualizations through reuse and modification. This would necessarily involve representations of the perspectives and language used in the interpretation, and not just the graphical representations of objects manipulated in the action within the represented design situation.

To support the repair of breakdowns in the interpretation of the situation, a computer system needs to facilitate the representation of interpreted meanings. This involves a medium for maintaining externalized expressions of the designers' explicit understandings that emerge from their repair of interpretive breakdowns. Part III will suggest mechanisms for doing this.

4. From individual design to collaboration. The representation of explicit understanding is not something new to computer support. It is an historical product of the development of design from a craft to a technology—from "unselfconscious" to "self-conscious" activity in Alexander's terms. Taking Heidegger's example, a carpenter skillfully wielding a hammer does not need to keep in mind conceptualizations having to do with the hammer's characteristics. To use Alexander's illustrations of unselfconscious design, an Eskimo patching an igloo or a peasant selecting colors for weaving a scarf does not explicitly follow a theory of construction or aesthetics. People who work by themselves or with personal apprentices can proceed without developing systems of explicit rules and terminology. Expertise can be passed on face-to-face through concrete demonstration. However, when the contexts of skilled activity change rapidly and involve complex social interactions, then design necessarily becomes self-conscious, requiring theories for understanding, coordinating, and communicating.

As design becomes increasingly explicit and interpersonal, it becomes an argumentative process. As Rittel described it, design becomes a matter of deliberating issues from the perspectives of various stakeholders. Using Heidegger's concepts from Section 4.3, the designers engage in discourse and assertion. *Discourse* is the formulation of meanings in explicit terminology. This is integral to the process of interpretation, in which breakdowns in tacit understanding lead to repair through explicit understanding. For an individual designer, this explicit understanding tends to resubmerge into a modified stage of tacit understanding in which the former breakdown has been repaired. However, in a group design context, the explicit understanding can be expressed in an assertion. The assertion is external to the individual and available for deliberation by others in the group. *Assertion* is the expression of discourse in an external medium.

As indicated in Figure 5-2 above, the assertion, as an externalized expression, serves as a medium for communication among design participants. The communication leads to shared knowledge, forming the basis for collaboration. Just as individual design leads through interpretation to the tacit understanding needed for further design work, so in collaborative design the shared explicit knowledge generated by deliberation on externalized assertions leads to a shared tacit knowledge that provides the preunderstanding of a shared design world. Assertion makes it possible for the hermeneutic circle to expand from individual understanding of being-in-the-world to shared understanding of social being-with-others. This extends Heidegger's analysis of interpretation from individual being-in-the-world to collaborative design.

Heidegger and the three design methodologists all recognize the social basis of explicit understanding. For Heidegger, social being-with-others is an important constituent of individual being-in-the-world. Alexander sees the emergence of self-conscious design as a social phenomenon, tied to specific stages of increased societal complexity. For Rittel, deliberation is a social activity, essentially conditioned by the social roles of the participants. Although Schön often focuses on the work of the solitary designer, he is vitally concerned with the social context in which the designer acts and in which design practices are taught. They all recognize the role of external media of design—whether assertions, patterns, debated issues, or reflective categories—both in the work of the individual designer and in collaborative interactions.

The transformation of tacit understanding to explicit understanding via interpretation makes possible many developments that go beyond the unselfconscious skilled activity of the traditional individual designer. By externalizing explicit understanding in the assertions of explicit language, possibilities for communication, extended reflection and conceptual formalization are all opened up. Communication means that communities of design can be established, in which rules of design can be formulated and terminologies developed. The externalization of knowledge also augments the individual's abilities by overcoming the severe limitations of human memory, so that ideas and experiments can be brought into contact with other ideas and can be reflected upon over extended periods of time. Media of communication and externalization also encourage formalization. Explicit, externalized assertions can be gradually formalized to increase interpersonal clarity and computational power, as discussed in point 3. Finally, the externalization of understanding makes possible the capture of this understanding in computer systems, providing the key to a theory of computer support. The assertions that Heidegger discusses are primarily speech acts in natural language. However, these expressions of understanding can be further transformed for use with forms of external memory offered by computer technology.

5. From ontology to computer support. Heidegger's central concern is ontological, to determine the being of things. His discussion of human understanding focuses on the distinction between artifacts-in-use (ready-to-hand, *zuhanden*) and the traditional conception of physically-present-objects (present-at-hand, *vorhanden*). Thus, he argues that we normally use things in a tacit, skillful way without being explicitly aware of what we are doing. This tacit understanding may under special conditions (e.g., breakdowns in understanding) become explicitly interpreted. However, even when we have explicit understanding this is only possible on the basis of tacit pre-understandings that serve as preconditions for it. Thus, our ability to have explicit knowledge of physically-present-objects is derivative of our tacit skills with artifacts-in-use. The ontological distinctions correspond to transformations of our understanding.

This dissertation has hypothesized that *computer support of innovative design must overcome the problem that designers necessarily make extensive use of situated tacit understanding while computers can only store and display explicit representations of information*. This is termed the problem of tacit and explicit understanding in computer support of cooperative design.

The ontological transformation described by Heidegger provides the solution to the problem of computer support by indicating the forms into which tacit knowledge can be transformed. Heidegger's analysis of the preconditions of understanding stresses that the representations used in computer systems are derivative of tacit human understandings and are the products of interpretation based on those understandings. The transformations of tacit to explicit understanding will be analyzed in Section 5.3 and will be developed into a theory of computer support in Chapter 6.

5.2. The Social and Human Grounding of Interpretation

This section will locate Heidegger's philosophy historically in order to highlight its contribution. It will show how his analysis addresses the key issues underlying a theory of computer support:

1. Heidegger's emphasis on the priority of the tacit over rationalist philosophers' stress on the explicit should be understood through a recognition of his place in the history of philosophy. The view that the world is interpreted—*socially constructed*—and not simply known is a result of modern philosophy.

2. Tacit preunderstanding is intimately related to the issue of *intentionality*. This issue, in turn, is critical for a theory of computer support, providing the ultimate argument for a people-centered approach to computerization.

3. Given that computer support relies upon the appropriate application of representations to innovative situations, the problem of *application* arises as a central issue. Gadamer has addressed this issue as integral to Heidegger's philosophy of interpretation.

4. The problem of application leads to the related and more general problem of *relevance*, which pervades attempts at computer support for design.

1. The social construction of reality. The interpretation of Heidegger's philosophy in this dissertation bears directly upon the problem of tacit and explicit understanding in computer support of cooperative design. His philosophy makes particularly clear the basic ways in which (fundamentally tacit) human interpretation differs from (necessarily explicit) computer representation. This is in contrast to the rationalist philosophy of functionalism[15], which is usually assumed to provide a basis for AI. Functionalism proposes that human cognition and computer computations share a common functional structure, i.e., that mind is adequately modeled as software running on the brain's hardware. If one reviews the history of philosophy leading up to Heidegger, one can see clearly the roots of AI's belief that computer representations could correspond to the structure of human understanding. One can also see that this belief is misleading and based on antiquated philosophical positions.

In philosophical terms, the problem with the traditional AI approach is that it assumes that a single interpretive framework can, at least in theory, be formulated that will be adequate for all representations within a given domain. That is, most influential AI systems define a representation for the domain of knowledge they are dealing with and then proceed to compute solutions to problems in the domain by manipulating elements of the representation. In contrast, this dissertation argues that problem solving is typically situated in ways which require the representation of the problem to be interpreted based upon the interpreter's unique situation, perspective, and language.

The assumption that problem-solving intelligence is based on mental representations that can be known *a priori* can be traced back to Kant. In his *Critique of Pure Reason* (1787), Kant argued that the human mind imposes a set of elements or categories on sense data in order to understand the external world. These elements or categories of space, time, quantity, quality, etc. that Kant derived were claimed to be universal *a priori*. The idea in AI is to capture such objective categories in a representation scheme that could be determined in advance to be valid of necessity, in analogy with the example from mathematics or physics that within certain geometric domains all objects can be represented with Cartesian spatial coordinates. Kant's approach was revolutionary in that he located the source of the objective representations or categories that we use to make sense of our world in the human mind, rather than in some divine or natural order. The

---

[15] This position was most prominently formulated by Putnam (1967), although he has more recently (1988) renounced functionalism and moved much closer to Heidegger in the sense that he recognizes the ultimate necessity of founding any formalism upon unformalizable human interpretation.

objectivity of these categories derived from the view that all minds necessarily used the same categories.

However, Kant's claim for the universality of our interpretive framework was soon criticized by Hegel, who argued that reason evolved through history. In the *Phenomenology of Mind* (1807), for instance, Hegel laid out the logical stages of reason's development in terms of a review of human history. So, for Hegel, our interpretation of reality depends upon the developmental stage reached by reason in our times. While there is a logic to the unfolding of reason, it happens historically (contingently). Therefore, the appropriate representations for understanding things change with socio-historical conditions.

Marx, in turn, tied this idealist history to the social development of production relations in *Capital* (1867). The basic categories for representing social phenomena within capitalist society—private property, exchange value, labor time, etc.—were themselves products of the historical development of capitalism and had to be interpreted through a hermeneutic process by people living within that society in order to avoid ideological conceptualizations. (See Stahl, 1975a, for a detailed discussion of the hermeneutic character of Marx' method.)

Subsequent writers in the human and social sciences have shown many other aspects of how our representations and conceptualizations of reality are necessarily determined by our situation. Freud (1917), for instance, related an individual's understanding to the person's formative history of inter-personal relationships. Anthropologists and other theorists show how interpretation is necessarily embedded in rich traditions of social, cultural, and personal histories.

Finally, Heidegger (1927) generalized these historical perspectives by saying that we always understand from within the situation in which we find ourselves already thrown as a result of our past. The social, cultural, and personal traditions are part of the background that we bring to interpretation as part of our preunderstanding of the world. But Heidegger also added a second important dimension to this critique of Kant. Our interpretive perspective, he argued, is not simply a matter of categories that can be made explicit and stated in propositions. More fundamentally, it is a matter of understanding what it means to be a person and what it means for other things to be encountered in the world. This background knowledge is fundamentally tacit. It is not only tacit in fact (most background knowledge has never been expressed explicitly), but also in principle (tacit knowledge is the necessary foundation for having explicit knowledge at all). Dreyfus

(1985) claims that Heidegger was the first in the history of philosophy to point out the tacit nature of pre-understanding.

It is only in terms of our ontological pre-understanding—which can be seen in the intentionality of our actions, in our grasp of linguistic meaning, in bodily adeptness, and in our interpersonal skills—that we can in the first place make things explicit and formulate propositional knowledge. Our understanding of our world, of artifacts in it, of ourselves, of other people, and of problems we have meeting our goals are structured by skills, preconceptions, and traditions that make up a social construction of reality. From the historical nature of understanding and its basis in tacit pre-understanding it follows that understanding develops through the hermeneutic circle of interpretation, in which the categories of understanding cannot be taken as pre-given but must evolve out of preconceptions, the situational context of meaning, and the process of iteratively interpreting the artifacts of interest.

The notion that our perception of reality is a social construction that fundamentally involves acts of interpretation that are essentially structured by our socio-historical context has had a profound impact upon contemporary thought and has driven the critique of traditional, rationalist outlooks.[16] As Resnick (1991) points out, both Mead (1934) and Vygotsky (1978)—two of the most important analysts of the social basis of human understanding—proposed that mechanisms of individual thought are best conceived as internalizations of ways of interacting socially with other people. Extending the ideas of Hegel and Marx, Mead and Vygotsky claimed that to understand the psychological development of an individual one must understand the social relations in which the individual has developed and operated. Resnick (1991, p.2) concludes, "as Vygotsky (1978) and Mead (1934) have independently suggested, social experience can shape the kinds of interpretive processes available to individuals."

2. The problem of intentionality. Given the complexity and subtlety of the social situatedness of human categories of understanding, the representations proposed for AI systems look primitive and rigid indeed. Even if large amounts of commonsense background knowledge could in principle be represented in a computer system, as proposed by the CYC project (Smith, 1991), there are three major limitations to computer systems carrying out the interpretive tasks autonomously:

---

[16] The entrenched rationalism of AI is just starting to be subjected to such critique: see the collection of articles in Floyd, et al. (1992), based on a 1988 conference on Software Development and Reality Construction.

* The "background knowledge" for interpretation consists largely of procedural skills and ontological understandings that cannot effectively be made explicit. For instance, people know how to interact with broad ranges of artifacts (e.g., specialized tools) and how to behave in cultural settings (which involve recognizing the intentions of other people). They can identify different kinds of beings and are able to interact with them appropriately.

* Interpretation is not an algorithmic process. Although we know that interpretations are conditioned by various factors in the situation, we cannot say that a certain interpretation will arise given certain inputs. Interpretation seems to be an emergent phenomenon from a holistic context. Heidegger's analysis argues that interpretation is a response to an open-ended set of preconditions and situational factors, but it gives no suggestion of causal effects that could be programmed into an autonomous computer system.

* The *problem of intentionality* probably presents the greatest barrier to defining an autonomous computer system for interpretation. Searle (1980) convincingly argues that computer software does not (and never can) understand the semantics of what is represented symbolically. Even a thorough cognitivist (functionalist) like Fodor (1981) must concede that the symbol systems of programs must be interpreted by people.

One useful way of stating the problem of intentionality is as the "symbol grounding problem" (Harnad, 1993). This refers to the fundamental principle of model theory, that regardless of the formal syntactic relations among symbols in a model, their truth or meaning depends upon a mapping to things in the real world. This mapping is not part of the model itself, but is a matter of the human *interpretation* of the model. Even if one takes a functionalist view of human thought and hypothesizes that thought takes place by the manipulation of formal or formalizable symbols, one must in addition assume that the thinking person has *grounded* the symbols of thought in some kind of understanding of their meaning.

The term *intentionality* has the same implication as the term *grounding*. They both indicate that when a person uses a word, sentence, or symbol that refers to something, then that person "intends" the thing referred to. In other words, the person's understanding of the word is "grounded" in the thing. Very few philosophers have much idea about how this grounding takes place. Searle makes vague references to biology. Marx would locate the grounding in social practice. Wittgenstein speaks of a "form of life." For Heidegger (1927 and 1975; see also Dreyfus, 1991), the structure of being-in-the-world provides the solution to the problem of intentionality. The fact that people are in-the-world in Heidegger's sense means precisely that they have direct, meaningful, semantic access to—are grounded in—things in the world. The situation is the network of the understood things with which one is more or less involved. The disclosure of the world as preunderstood is what makes interpretation possible. This is very different from a simplistic argument that knowledge is often "in the world" rather than "in the head." Whether we are understanding an artifact in our physical environment or one represented mentally, we rely on preunderstandings that are grounded in our interpretive situation.

Computers lack being-in-the-world. They merely manipulate ungrounded symbols. As Searle (1980) argued, even if computers are placed in robots that move among and interact with things in physical space, they lack intentionality of those things. This means that when computers are used in tasks like innovative design that involve interpretation, they cannot accomplish the entire task autonomously, but can at best support people in the required interpretations.

Computers lack intentionality. They can only manipulate explicit, ungrounded symbols; they have no tacitly-based sense of the semantics of the formal symbols. This has been identified in the present dissertation as the fundamental problem of tacit and explicit understanding that must be addressed by a theory of computer support for interpretation in design. Suchman (1993) has formulated this problem as a lack of access by computers to "semantic resources" and has agreed on its centrality. She summarized her book (Suchman, 1987) as an attempt to locate the "sense-making ability for machines in the limits of their access to relevant social and material resources, and identify the resulting asymmetry as the central problem for human-machine communication" (Suchman, 1993, p.73).

The problem of intentionality or symbol grounding underlies the problem of tacit and explicit understanding. The asymmetry in the relationship of people to computers—the fact that people have intentional understanding but computers do not—means that computers can only support the interpretive processes of people. This means that (at least within application domains like innovative design) a theory of human-computer interaction should be framed as a theory of computer support for (human) interpretation. People's intentional grounding is, according to Heidegger's analysis, primarily a matter of tacit situated understanding. Computers, on the other hand, can only operate with explicit symbolic representations. This poses the core problem for a theory of computer support: how the computer's manipulation of explicit symbols can support people's fundamentally tacit understanding.

3. The problem of application. Decontextualization of knowledge presents problems for the subsequent application of that knowledge in new contexts of interest. Because hermeneutic theory claims that all interpretation is situated in concrete circumstances, the problem of application of knowledge is an important issue. In particular, the theory of computer support of interpretation must address the question of how the explicit, formalized, and decontextualized information that can be provided by computer systems can be applicable to the human tasks of tacit interpretation that this information is supposed to support. For instance, in Section 3.2 this problem arose in the context of how to apply specific patterns from Alexander's pattern language to particular decisions in the design of a lunar habitat.

Gadamer (1960) addresses the problem of application as a central issue for his hermeneutic theory of interpretation. Although Gadamer is primarily interested in the human sciences and bases his discussion of application on examples of ethics, law, and theology, his characterization of the role of application in interpretation has broad generality. Schön (1983) makes similar arguments concerning the application of scientific principles in design and engineering.

Generalizing from his analysis of Aristotelian ethics, Gadamer (1960) concludes that application is not a secondary phenomenon of understanding, but an essential determinant of understanding as a whole from the start. That is, a textual statement in ethics or some other subject matter of interpretation cannot be interpreted in the abstract first and then subsequently applied to the situation of the interpreter:

> The interpreter dealing with a traditional text seeks to apply it to himself. But this does not mean that the text is given for him as something universal, that he understands it as such and only afterwards uses it for particular applications. Rather, the interpreter seeks no more than to understand this universal thing, the text; i.e., to understand what this piece of tradition says, what constitutes the meaning and importance of the text. In order to understand that, he must not seek to disregard himself and his particular hermeneutical situation. He must relate the text to this situation, if he wants to understand at all. (p.289 / S.307)

Granted, historical texts arose within situations that are different from the situation of the current interpreter. This is particularly clear in stories from the Bible or legal case law. Here the moral or precedent of the story was originally situated in a context that could be removed by thousands of years and vast cultural distances from the person who tries to understand it now.

But for Gadamer, a religious proclamation is not to be understood strictly as an historic document, but is to be taken in a way that exercises its religious effect upon the interpreter. Similarly, a legal case is not simply an historic fact, but needs to be made concretely valid as a precedent through being interpreted in a contemporary context. Gadamer claims, "The text, whether law or gospel, if it is to be understood properly, i.e., according to the claim it makes, must be understood at every moment, in every particular situation, in a new and different way. Understanding here is always application" (p.275 / S.292).

The term *application* may be misleading because of its rationalist innuendoes. Gadamer is not talking about taking a decontextualized meaning and applying it to some set of particular conditions by somehow adjusting this pre-given meaning the way one thinks of applying a scientific law to a practical problem by adjusting parameters or taking into account confounding factors like friction. As discussed in Section 4.3, according to Heidegger understanding always takes place within the preconditions of prepossession, preview, and preconception. Application of a text to an interpretive situation in Gadamer's sense means that the text is necessarily interpreted within the preunderstanding of the current interpreter. This preunderstanding includes an anticipation of what the text is all about. For instance, if we are reading a text from the Bible, then our background knowledge and prejudices concerning the Bible come into play. These include the results of a long history of biblical interpretation and religious traditions through the ages, which has sedimented in our preunderstanding. So, for Gadamer, our "openness to the text" always includes placing its meaning in relation to the whole of our own understandings.

In this sense of application, the problem becomes not one of somehow adjusting a pre-given meaning to our circumstances, but of making sure that our preunderstanding provides access to the text as something that transcends (i.e., can surprise) our preunderstanding of it. This is the role of interpretation: to start from a preunderstanding and to go beyond it on the basis of it. This involves a process of critiquing the assumptions of the preunderstanding in terms of the text (as revealed by that preunderstanding): "Methodologically conscious understanding will be concerned not merely to form anticipatory ideas, but to make them conscious, so as to check them and thus acquire right understanding from the things themselves" (p.239 / S.253). This is why interpretation must be a critical reflection upon its presuppositions. The restructuring of the network of significance (the situation) that takes place in interpretation takes place on the basis of the anticipatory preunderstood situation but questions its adequacy in the face of discoveries made of the text as disclosed by that preunderstanding. This dialectical process of anticipation and discovery—and not some objective viewpoint—provides the foundation for the validity of interpretation. Thus, validity and rigor of interpretation are situated in the process of application.

4. The problem of relevance. The problem of application is related to the larger question of *relevance*. Given a task—whether a design task or a task of textual interpretation—the question arises as to what past experience is relevant to the accomplishing of that task. Once the relevant past experience has been selected, it can then be applied to the task at hand.

There are basically three ways a computer system can "know" what information is relevant to a given design situation: First, there are often useful heuristics that can be programmed into a system for use in strictly delimited domains. Second, people can be in control of crucial aspects of the system's decision making and can use their human interpretive powers to determine what is relevant. In this case, the computer may be able to provide support for the person's decisions and it can store representations of the decisions for future reuse. Third, the computer can present these stored past decisions for a person to approve reusing in the current case.

In general (excluding the narrowly confined domains where appropriateness can be algorithmically defined in advance), the judgment of what is relevant to a particular task at hand requires the tacitly-based judgmental skills that require the involvement of people. As suggested above, the decision of relevance involves carrying out to some extent the process of interpretation in which experiences recalled from the past are applied to (interpreted within) the current situation. Being based on tacit preunderstanding, this process cannot be carried out in explicit computer algorithms. Furthermore, as already discussed, the judgment of relevance relies upon an understanding that is intentionally grounded in being-in-the-world with the artifacts of the current task and of the past experience. Without human intentionality and interpretive powers, questions of relevance are intractable. The explicit nature of computerized knowledge means that computers may be able to support human judgments of relevance, but they cannot replace them. The following chapter explores how computers can support interpretation in domains of non-routine design such as lunar habitat design.

5.3. Transformations of Tacit to Explicit Understanding

Definition of tacit and explicit. In formulating the central problem for computer support, it has been repeatedly stated that human understanding is at bottom tacit while computer representations are necessarily explicit. In this claim, the terms *tacit* and *explicit* have been tacitly assumed to mean something like "unverbalized" and "verbally expressed", respectively. In order to address the problem of tacit and explicit understanding in computer support of interpretation, it is now important to make the usage of these terms more explicit.

The dictionary (Merriam-Webster, 1991) provides the following definitions:

tacit: expressed or carried on without words or speech; implied or indicated but not actually expressed.

explicit: fully revealed or expressed without vagueness, implication, or ambiguity; leaving no question as to meaning or intent; verbal plainness and distinctness such that there is no need for inference and no room for difficulty in understanding.

Comparing these definitions, it seems that there is a continuum of verbal expression, whose extremes are defined as tacit (not expressed) and explicit (fully expressed). The analysis of understanding as a result of the iterative hermeneutic circle suggests that understanding indeed progresses along such a continuum of gradual explication. The discussion of the hermeneutic *as* indicates that what becomes explicit in an individual step of interpretation is not a complete understanding of a whole state of affairs, but rather one particular aspect (the thing considered *as* such and such).

A taxonomy of tacit and explicit information. The interpretive movement from tacit to explicit is only the first of several possible transformations of understanding that Heidegger is interested in explaining. Ultimately, he wants to show how the formalized and codified scientific knowledge (which the rationalist tradition took as fundamental) is founded in tacit being-in-the-world. Section 4.3 above summarized Heidegger's discussion of the role of language in expressing understandings. He uses the term *discourse* as the basis for verbal expression. Discourse does not necessarily mean that an understanding is spoken out loud, but simply that it is verbalized, if only in the mind of the person who understands. This qualifies as making explicit. Discourse makes the interpretive step from an understanding that has not been verbalized (but can be inferred from a person's understanding of related things or from the person's behavior) to one that is revealed to the person who has the understanding. So far, the discussion remains at the level of an individual person.

Discourse can be *asserted*: spoken out loud. This makes it available to other people. An assertion produces an externalized expression. According to Heidegger's analysis, assertion can mean *pointing out, predicating,* or *communicating.* With assertion, shared knowledge is possible through one person pointing it out or communicating it to others. Furthermore, it is possible to codify knowledge in canonical forms through *predication.* This formalizes the structure of the knowledge and paves the way for preserving the knowledge in media of external memory, including representing it in a computer symbolism. *Capturing* the knowledge in a computer provides a stored representation of the knowledge. If the computer system is flexible, this captured knowledge can evolve through modification of the stored representations for use in computer modeling of innovative situations.

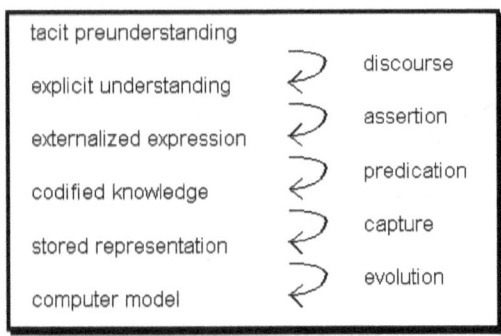

Figure 5-3. Successive transformations of knowledge.

The left-hand column lists consecutive forms of information. The right-hand column indicates the transformation processes from one form to another.

Figure 5-3 shows the sequence of possible transformations of understanding. Moving down the progression, the knowledge becomes increasingly explicit and formal. Through this sequence, Heidegger's theory connects the grounding of knowledge in tacit preunderstanding with the potential for evolving computer representations of knowledge. This provides the epistemological foundation for a theory of computer support for interpretation.

Each transformation involves a reinterpretation of the informational content in a new medium of expression. This entails both gain and loss. Not only is there a gain in precision and clarity with the increasing explicitness, but new discoveries are made along the way. On the other hand, there is a loss of contact with the experiential grounding in the tacitly understood situation. For instance, when the lunar habitat designers first began to interpret privacy in their design, they began with a tacit feeling that they had discovered a problem in the adjacency of the bathroom to the ward room. This feeling was grounded in their personal experiences (e.g., Desi's memory of the location of the bathroom at his office) or their imaginations of life in the habitat. The tacit preunderstanding of this problem was *interpreted* in the *discourse* of privacy. Then Desi and Archie made *assertions* about privacy in the habitat. This externalized their understanding in language so it could be communicated. If they wanted to preserve their interpretation, they could have *predicated* it as design rationale, using some semi-formal or formal method such as IBIS. Using a computer support system like HERMES, they could then proceed to *capture* their concern with privacy in a computer representation that could subsequently be *evolved* into a useful computer model of privacy for future design efforts.

Figure 5-4 presents a vocabulary of different forms of information for the theory of computer support. All the forms of understanding or knowledge discussed above may be considered forms of *information*. These are divided into the forms of human knowledge (which are hermeneutically grounded in the intentional *presence* of the understood situation) and forms of computer *representation* (formal symbol systems). The taxonomy moves from information forms that are appropriate to *individuals* to those that form data for *computer* manipulations. In the middle are forms of *shared* knowledge. They can be shared by several human designers, or by designers and a computer system.

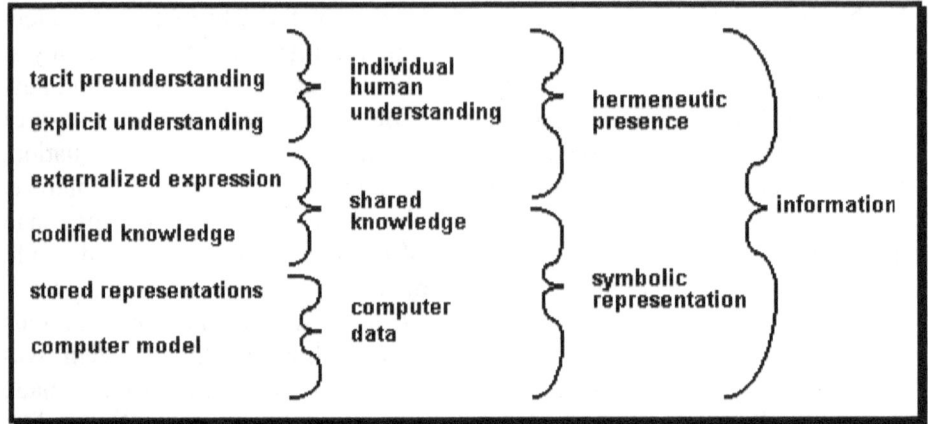

Figure 5-4. A taxonomy of classes of information.

This taxonomy is meant to provide a vocabulary for discussing a theory of computer support founded on the analysis of interpretation as the transformation of tacit understanding to increasingly explicit knowledge. A taxonomy draws conceptual distinctions. In practice, the categories may be blurred and inter-mixed. A designer dealing with privacy while using HERMES with privacy critics already represented may be working with an understanding of privacy that synthesizes all these forms of information.

The taxonomy is laid out along the dimension of explicitness. This is not the same as formality. Formal information is structural (syntactic); it may be processed by computer. Explicitness is a precondition of such formality, not its equivalent. Consider for instance the semi-formal information of design rationale in an IBIS format. An `issue`, stated in English text, may have an `answer`, also in English. The structural relationship between the `issue` and its `answer` may be formal in the sense that computers can process this information algorithmically. At the same time, the semantics of the texts of the `issue` and `answer` are informal: they cannot be processed by the computer, but require human interpretation. Nevertheless, all the design rationale information has been stated explicitly in order to be entered into the computer.

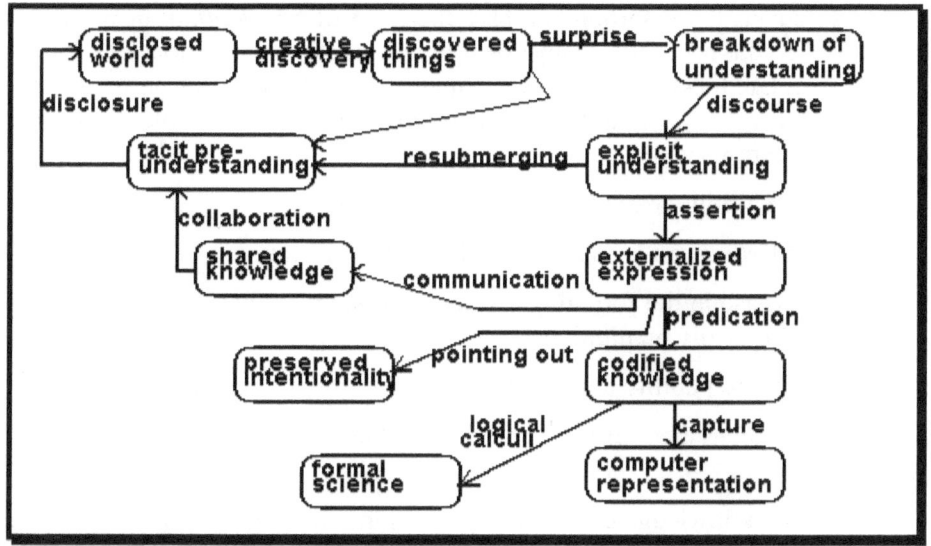

Figure 5-5. Successive transformations of information.

Successive transformations of tacit and explicit information. Figure 5-5 expands the model of interpretation in design (Figure 5-2) to include Heidegger's three-fold analysis of assertion. At the end of Chapter 6 (Figure 6-2), it will be further expanded to include the transformations of knowledge capture and representational evolution. This will provide a model of the theory of computer support for interpretation in design.

Here, the subsequent transformations of assertion have been included in the diagram: (i) communicating, (ii) pointing out, and (iii) predicating:

(i) The externalized expression that has been asserted can be used for *communication* with other people. This makes possible the shared knowledge that forms the basis for collaboration in activities like designing. Understandings that have been made explicit in the process of interpretation can affect the tacit understanding that enters into future activity, either directly as part of the individual's understanding or indirectly as a social process involving a change in the shared knowledge of a communicating community.

(ii) Alternatively, the externalized expression can serve as a *pointing out* of the object of the underlying intentionality. When something is put into words there is a potential that it will become reified and lose its semantic grounding; but the act of assertion can be used to counteract this tendency.

(iii) Moreover, the assertion can take the form of *predication*, in which the reference to the meaning is subsumed in a syntactic formulation. The loss of personal relatedness to that which is understood is traded for an increase in the intersubjective availability. Predication leads to the multiple advantages of codified knowledge:

*   An increase in the explicitness of the knowledge.

*   A standardization of the formulation in a more canonical form.

*   An increase in the formality of the expression, so that it can more easily be syntactically manipulated.

*   An increased ability to preserve the knowledge in external media.

These characteristics are essential for the development of scientific knowledge.

The *codified* knowledge can be transformed into the logical calculi of formal science. Heidegger was interested in this transformation because it allowed him to tie scientific knowledge to tacit, commonsense, background knowledge in a way that shows that the formal knowledge is only possible on the basis of the tacit. This, of course, counters the rationalist assumption that one should analyze tacit knowledge as a partial and faulty expression of underlying formal, precise, symbolic, intersubjective, or objective scientific knowledge. For Heidegger, the successive transformations of understanding from tacit knowledge to explicit, externalized, codified, and formalized knowledge is an ontological transformation. Tacit knowledge has to do with our understanding of artifacts-in-use. As the knowledge is transformed through explicit interpretation, externalized assertion, codified predication, and formalized calculi, the artifact becomes a physically-present-object, something observed from an objective status rather than used transparently. With this ontological transformation, the artifact/object becomes decontextualized.

Codified knowledge can also open the opportunity for *computer representations*. The transformations from tacit preunderstanding to successively explicit forms of information provides a basis for the theory of computer support in the following chapter.

CHAPTER 6. A THEORY OF COMPUTER SUPPORT

While Heidegger's analysis of understanding provides the opportunity for a theory of computer support of innovative design, his analysis must be operationalized if it is to guide the development of useful software systems. This task of operationalizing Heidegger's categories will be undertaken here, resulting in the outline of a theory of computer support for interpretation in design.

What does it mean for a computer system to *support* the processes of interpretation that designers use in their work? Chapter 6 addresses a number of the central issues of this question:

6.1. As argued in the previous chapter, a *people-centered approach* is needed in which designers using software are in control of determinations of relevance, application of representations, modifications of reused structures, and other matters of judgment that cannot be reduced to computational mechanisms. The analysis of interpretation in Part I distinguished three characteristics of interpretation: (a) its situated, (b) perspectival, and (c) linguistic nature. Each of these three characteristics involves the modes of (1) reuse and (2) innovative modification. Computer software should provide support for each of these three characteristics of interpretation in both modes.

6.2. (a) Experience with graphical and textual tools for designers has shown that computer systems can be useful for capturing explicit understandings of design *situations*. Additional media—including pen-based sketches, pictures, videos, and audio commentary—can also be useful for this. With each of these media it is important that they be sufficiently expressive to meet the demands of designers. Ideally, computer control of the media should not be much more intrusive than use of a hand-held pen. The advantage of the computer is that it can coordinate representations of the situation in these media in computationally powerful ways in order to support the designers' interpretations. (b) One way a computer system can help organize information is through systems of *perspectives*. Each designer, design team, or design case can have its own perspective for gathering related information. A general perspectives mechanism can provide computational support for storing and viewing information in categories defined by the designers to support their organizational and collaborational needs. (c) *Language* is as important a means of externalizing design ideas as is sketching. It serves to make the ideas explicit and to communicate them, so their problems and opportunities can be discovered. A computer-based language facility can help to store and communicate definitions and interrelationships of terms. To the extent that the language can be processed by the computer, it can serve as a means for communicating with the computer and defining or refining mechanisms of control and operation.

6.3. Plasticity of knowledge representations is critical for offering designers the necessary control over the computer system and over their designs. As mentioned in the preceding paragraphs, the media, perspectives, and language must all be expressive and malleable. This facilitates reuse of previous design constructs, because approximate solutions to an innovative need can be reused from computer memory and modified by the designer for application to a current case. By capturing past design elements and allowing them to be flexibly modified and reused in new designs, the computer support system in effect embodies *a model of the process of interpretation*. Each characteristic of the interpretive process is modeled in computer representations and mechanisms: the situation, perspectives, and language. The explicit nature of the computer model aids the designer's reflection, offering objects to make discoveries with.

These issues of support spell out in practical terms the kinds of mechanisms needed to support interpretation in design. These points determine what related systems to consider in Chapter 7 and what features to look for in those systems. Then, Part III describes HERMES, a substrate for design environments that implements illustrative instantiations of these support mechanisms.

6.1. A People-Centered Approach

HERMES is a *people-centered* computer system, designed with the nature of human understanding foremost in mind. People and computers have different strengths. If one accepts Heidegger's principles of human understanding and contrasts them with traditional AI analyses of computer computation, it follows that people process information very differently from computers. So if one wishes to use computers to support humans doing difficult cognitive tasks like designing then it is necessary to distinguish the roles of computer and human carefully and to define a "cooperative problem solving system" (Fischer, 1989) in which they can work together most effectively.

While much attention has been paid in computer science to the theory of computation and to the mechanics of making computers perform efficiently, little work has been devoted to a theory of the human understanding that is necessary to make sense of computer output and to extend the domain of computer application beyond routine algorithmic computations. Computer scientists tend to leave the analysis of the human partner in human-computer interactions to cognitive psychology, which generally ignores Heideggerian ideas in favor of functionalist approaches. There have been some notable exceptions to this rule, which have provided much of the inspiration for this dissertation and that have covered much of the argumentative background that therefore does not have to be detailed here—e.g., Winograd & Flores (1986), Suchman (1987), Ehn (1988), Budde & Züllighoven (1990), Dreyfus (1991), Coyne & Snodgrass (1991), Schön (1992). Unfortunately, these exceptions have not included convincing examples of software as models for a people-centered approach.

HERMES is an example of people-centered software. It grew out of a recent tradition of domain-oriented design environments (discussed in Chapter 7) that tends toward a person-centered approach. This tradition was a practical response motivated by breakdowns in autonomous expert system approaches. The present dissertation is a reflection on the theoretical framework implicit in that tradition, aimed at repairing the breakdown at the conceptual as well as the practical level.

The systems that HERMES evolved from are people-centered in various ways. Fischer & Nakakoji (1992), for instance, argue that the JANUS system empowers the human designers who use it. Similarly, McCall, et al. (1990) point out that the PHIDIAS system allows the use of an open-ended set of domain categories so that designers are not restricted to a predefined representation of relationships. The previous chapter tried to sketch a philosophical justification for these ideas. It argued that tasks like innovative design require acts of application and judgments of relevance that require interpretive powers and intentionality that come naturally to people but cannot be programmed for computers. A reasonable conclusion to draw from this argument is that computer systems for non-routine design should be people-centered.

People-centered software in the sense proposed here is computer software that provides information to people and then lets the people make the judgments. Rather than incorporating heuristic tricks that allow the computer to make decisions that in most cases look like reasonable human judgments, the software is structured to involve the people using it in a decision-making partnership. The partnership is based on the asymmetry in which computers excel at searching large information spaces and people excel at making judgments of relevancy. In other words, designers interpret and computer systems like HERMES support this interpretation in design.

The term "people-centered" is intended to extend the approach of "user centered system design" (Norman & Draper, 1986). That was an attempt to view interface issues from the user's perspective, not necessarily to include system users in either the software design process as in participatory design (Ehn, 1988) or in the computational decision-making as in the people-centered approach. User centered system design views people as information processors, not as interpreters; it seeks to adjust the software interface to the parameters of human processing characteristics at the periphery of the computation rather than trying to support human interpretation as the center-piece of the computation.

The first principle for a theory of computer support that overcomes the problem of tacit and explicit understanding is that the software should be people-centered. Three further principles are given in the next section.

6.2. Supporting Situated, Perspectival, Linguistic Interpretation

The analysis of interpretation in Part I suggests that computer support for design should:

(a) Capture computer representations of tacit situated understanding at the points when it becomes articulated as explicit interpretations.

(b) Provide multiple perspectives for analyzing and understanding designs.

(c) Allow users to evolve and refine interpretive expressions in language without starting from scratch or accepting predefined frameworks.

This dissertation will pursue these possibilities. Accordingly, three hermeneutic principles will be adopted in trying to develop computer-based environments to support the work of designers:

(a) Provide facilities so designers can create representations of the design *situation* during the process of solving the task.

(b) Provide facilities so designers can define multiple interpretive *perspectives* on design problems.

(c) Provide facilities so designers can articulate explicit conceptualizations in *language* expressions for their work and submerge this new knowledge into tacit forms of knowledge for future use.

These principles will be used to select relevant systems from the literature to review. They will also provide a framework for critically evaluating the systems in Chapter 7. Then, in Chapters 8, 9, and 10, the design of HERMES will be discussed. HERMES is a prototype software substrate that extends the functionality of the domain-oriented design environments and knowledge representation languages that are reviewed so they can support interpretation. The three hermeneutic principles will be used to justify the primary features of HERMES :

(a) An extensible *computational medium for representing and evolving* artifact constructions, design rationale, computational critics, and other forms of design knowledge.

(b) A mechanism for sharing *group and personal interpretive perspectives* to support collaboration and deliberation.

(c) A *language for explicitly defining computations* and for hiding information that can then function in a tacit way.

Capturing explicit understandings of the situation. Human cognition is a complicated business. A recent analysis of its structure by Donald (1991) based on anthropological, neurological, and linguistic evidence suggests four stages in its historical development, all of which remain still active in contemporary cognition: (i) *episodic* memory that is case-based; (ii) *mimetic* memory that is tacit or gestural; (iii) *mythic* memory that is social and linguistically founded; and (iv) *extended* memory of modern thought that relies heavily on using external media such as pictures, writing, and computers. Heidegger's (1927) philosophical analysis of the logical structure of human being-in-the-world can be seen as a parallel to this sequence: (i) there is the preunderstanding of the world as *disclosed* to us and of meaningful things *discovered* in the situation; (ii) through *interpretation* we use our tacit skills to make things stand out *as* what they are; (iii) *discourse* allows us to talk about and thereby share things; and (iv) with *assertion* we can form *predications* and externalize our knowledge. In both Donald's theory of the evolution of the consciousness of the species and Heidegger's theory of the development of an individual's cognitive acts, increasingly explicit understanding emerges out of and on the basis of primordial tacit understandings that remain active under the surface.

A system for computer support of human cognitive activities such as innovative design should at least take this complexity into account, recognizing the role of tacit preunderstanding at the origin of all true understanding. That is the reason for the person-centered emphasis: to keep the intentionality of people in the decision-making loop. Ideally, one would hope to provide support for the various levels of explicitness that continue to play a role in even the most sophisticated understanding. For instance, (i) one might try to provide a computer representation of case-based memory to stimulate human episodic memory and intentionality. (ii) Direct manipulation of graphical icons might be used as an analog to mimetic understanding. (iii) A language facility for people using the computer system to make assertions about objects in the domain in which they are working could provide the ingredients for mythic-linguistic comprehension of that domain. (iv) Finally, the computer can provide a computationally active medium that can extend human mental abilities by storing and manipulating vast quantities of symbolic information.

The successive transformations of information from tacit preunderstanding to increasingly explicit forms of expression result in codified knowledge, as shown at the bottom of Figure 5-5, above. As Heidegger pointed out, this form of knowledge provides the possibility of formal science. By the same token, it puts knowledge into a state that can be *captured* for the physical symbol systems of computer representation.

In particular, if a computer system is being used to provide a medium of external memory for people, then the representations they are using in that medium are available for retention by the computer system for future use. This suggests that computer systems to fill this role need to be structured to provide an enticing and useful medium in which people will represent and solve their tasks. They should also be structured to capture representations as they are developed and used for future reuse and modification. Given the cyclic nature of interpretation, this works well, because the logical source of building blocks for representing the situation of a given task is traditional representations used in the past for representing similar tasks. The abstract chicken and egg problem is solved by starting with a seeded (to shift the metaphor a bit) database. The seed is, of course, generated on the basis of (real or imagined) previous tasks in the domain.

In general, what one wants to capture in the database that grows out of the seed is a palette of symbols for supporting the various forms of interpretation used by people working in the given domain. In particular, it is necessary to support the representation of *situated understanding*. The situation is a network of significance. Computer representations of the situation might include icons with defined behaviors that are semantically meaningful to people who will be manipulating them. It could also include domain terminology—perhaps structured as a semantic network to reflect interrelationships among terms—to help people formulate meaningful assertions about their work. For a field like design, it would likely include tools for sketching and catalogs of sample designs.

If design is a constructing of reality as argued in Chapter 5, then a computer system to support interpretation in non-routine design is a medium to facilitate such construction. The social construction of reality generally—of what we call the "real world" we all live in—takes place largely through the mediation of artifacts. Design as the design of artifacts (e.g., habitats) is therefore the construction of the artifacts through which reality is, in turn, constructed. The computer systems—as media for design—construct a reality in which this design can take place. In designing approaches (e.g., people-centered) to such systems, one is formulating a theory for building systems (e.g., HERMES), for providing representations (e.g., graphical design components, rationale issues), for designing artifacts (e.g., lunar habitats), for mediating the social construction of reality. This is an example of a high-level design task and illustrates the open-ended character of the tasks that human cognition sets for itself and that exceed the capability of the unaided individual mind.

Organizing perspectives on shared knowledge. Complex design tasks require collaboration. The design of lunar habitats, for instance, began in the 1960's and may continue for one or more additional decades before the first lunar habitat is ever lived in. This design process relies upon many teams of professionals, from numerous fields of expertise. The teams that continue working over long periods of time change their membership. Designs pass from team to team, developing from requirements documents, to design concepts, to drawings for technical reviews, to mock ups, to construction, and so on. The designs change and earlier stages are iterated. Ideas, explorations, and rationale from one team or one design are reused in others or eventually forgotten.

At one level of analysis, the design of lunar habitats is an unfathomably intricate social process involving hundreds of people, shifting political priorities, changing technologies, financial constraints, and management headaches. But at another level, each actual act of designing is ultimately carried out by an *individual* person. Some concrete individual must make the suggestion that the wardroom table be shaped a certain way. Other individuals must either agree with or argue against that decision. Each time an individual comes up with an idea or considers a proposal, an act of *interpretation* takes place. Such acts of interpretation are grounded in the interpreting person's situation, perspective, and language. People are necessarily the cognitive atoms of collaborative design because only individual people can ground interpretation in intentionality. So the overall social process is dependent upon many individual *perspectives* interacting in a process of deliberation.

A computer system to support such social processes of interpretation, involving deliberation among multiple perspectives, should provide mechanisms that reflect and aid this process. First, designers using the system need to be able to represent their own ideas and their design rationale. If teams of designers are to use the system, then there should be ways for team members to represent their personal ideas, sketches, arguments, and conceptualizations. The representations of one person need to be kept distinguished from those of other designers. At the same time, design is a collaborative process. The purpose of a design team is to share each other's ideas, to bring different perspectives on a problem together and to arrive at a consensus through argumentation. A system to support this must allow separate definitions, but also facilitate bringing these differing views together and resolving the differences. Consensus or resolution may not always be possible, so one might also want mechanisms for maintaining minority or competing opinions, by means of which it can easily be determined who supports which ideas and why.

The concepts and design rationale for complex design projects *evolve*. The contents of individual perspectives must be easy to change. In addition the structure of perspectives must be able to evolve fluidly, defining, for instance, what shared group perspectives include which personal perspectives, or include which particular contents of various personal perspectives. It might be useful to be able to chart the history of evolving ideas, establishing "snapshot" *versions* of designs in particular personal or group perspectives.

The suggestion is that all representations of design knowledge should be stored in system-defined perspectives because all interpretation is situated in perspectives. This notion transforms the idea of traditional knowledge-based systems that there exists a single body of domain knowledge in the minds of domain experts and that there should be a corresponding fixed knowledge representation. Now the knowledge represented in the system is (1) always relative to the selection of a perspective and (2) continually evolving. The design environment must provide tools to support this view of knowledge and to facilitate the evolution of networks of perspectives and of their knowledge.

Linguistic tools for collaboration. Language plays an undeniable role in collaborative design. Even the individual designer engages in *discourse* when conducting innovative design. As previously discussed, all acts of interpretation essentially involve explication, which depends upon discourse. Design in teams involves the use of language for the deliberation of design rationale from various perspectives. Much of the work of teams takes place linguistically through group meetings and written reports. These media rely on *assertion* for the communication of ideas. Language forms the basis for the sharing of knowledge, which is the hallmark of collaboration. The formulation of understandings in language makes possible the formalization of knowledge in methodologically-based systems and the representation or capture of knowledge in external media such as documentation.

As seen in the videotaped lunar habitat design sessions, the design process relies heavily upon concepts, rules of thumb, and constraints. Each of these can be more or less formulated in sentences. To some extent they can even be codified, formalized, operationalized, computerized; to some extent they remain tacit, out of either necessity or practicality. In providing computer support, it is important to analyze the use of techniques like conceptualization, rules of thumb, and constraint formulation. One should support the explication of these to enhance their sharing, retention, and reuse. At the same time, one should recognize that the advantages of explicit knowledge are offset by costs in time, cognitive effort, rigidification, and loss of intuitive control. Designers may wisely decline to make their understanding explicit in many cases. Systems should encourage a flexible mixing of knowledge in the head with knowledge in the machine, of tacit and explicit, of intuitive and verbalized.

When it is deemed desirable to capture knowledge in a computer support system, then language can play a major role. According to the theory proposed here based on Heidegger's analysis, the capture of knowledge is a refinement of the process of putting tacit preunderstanding into language. One way to make this process explicit and to help people exert control over it is to provide a language facility to support the expression of knowledge for computer capture. Because people need to relate explicit assertions to their tacit preunderstanding, it is important to tie the language facility to people's natural modes of expression as much as possible. So, for instance, the computer-based language could use terms from the design domain chosen by the designers actually using the system. This means having most of the vocabulary user-defined and easy to extend or modify. The appearance of the language can be made similar to natural language also, to ease the translation back to the level of original discourse in which the intentional content is less alienated than in codified and formalized expressions of logical calculii. This can be accomplished to some extent by careful design of the syntactic appearance of the language facility, keeping this naturalness a priority.

Linguistic tools to support interpretation and collaboration in design should support the interplay of tacit and explicit understanding in the interpretation of the language. While it may be necessary to structure an end-user programming language in a way that can be used to control the computer like traditional programming languages, one wants to avoid the cognitive costs of using these languages as much as possible. Although it may be important to include some of the basic functionality of traditional programming concerns such as variables, recursion, types, control structures, etc., it is desirable to avoid requiring the users to keep the associated doctrine in mind. One wants a programming language in which most of these structures are kept tacitly behind the scenes most of the time.

At the same time, the user still needs to be able to analyze the structure of the representations explicitly and formally (e.g., as a hypermedia node and link structure) and have expressions in the language reflect that. For instance, if one wants to capture a rule of thumb involving the separation of public and private areas in a lunar habitat, then one must think through a scheme for operationalizing and representing the notion of privacy that is involved. This is an extension of the process of explication that is involved in all interpretation of innovations that are not adequately comprehended by situational preunderstanding. However, once the rule of thumb has been expressed (written) in the language, the explicit understanding should be able to resubmerge into a more tacit comprehension. That is, when the rule is used in the future—whether by the original creator or by a subsequent designer using the system and its language—it should be available (readable) in a more tacit way.

The problem of tacit and explicit understanding pervades the design issues for a system of computer support of cooperative design. The design of a language facility for computer support must particularly address this problem because discourse is the medium through which one moves back and forth between tacit and explicit understanding within the process of interpretation.

6.3. A Model of Computer Support

The goal is to support the situated, perspectival, linguistic character of interpretation in cooperative design. This requires plasticity (flexibility, malleability, or adaptability) of representation. For each of the many individual designers involved, their situation is somewhat unique. They have different trainings, traditions, formative experiences, areas of expertise, skills, priorities, interests, motivations, and so on. For each of them to represent what they take the design situation to be requires a toolbox of representation elements and techniques that can be customized to their individual needs. Their different perspectives also have crucial commonalities, without which collaboration would be impossible. These interrelationships can usefully be modeled in a network of perspectives for organizing knowledge representations by individual and group owners. Group perspectives need to combine knowledge from multiple other perspectives, selectively deleting, modifying, or adding to particular items. The hierarchical structure of perspectives must be able to evolve fluidly over time. The language, too, must be flexibly expressive so that it can generate innovative locutions. Like natural language, it must be capable of spawning infinite variations and arbitrarily complex structures from a manageably finite syntax.

In Figure 6-1, the schematic of computer support from Figure 1-1 in Chapter 1 has been expanded to depict the dimensions of interpretation as (a) situated, (b) perspectival, and (c) linguistic. The upper-left-hand rectangle, which stands for tacit preunderstanding, includes these three dimensions. The figure has also been expanded to depict the need for (1) reuse and (2) plasticity of representation in its lower portion.

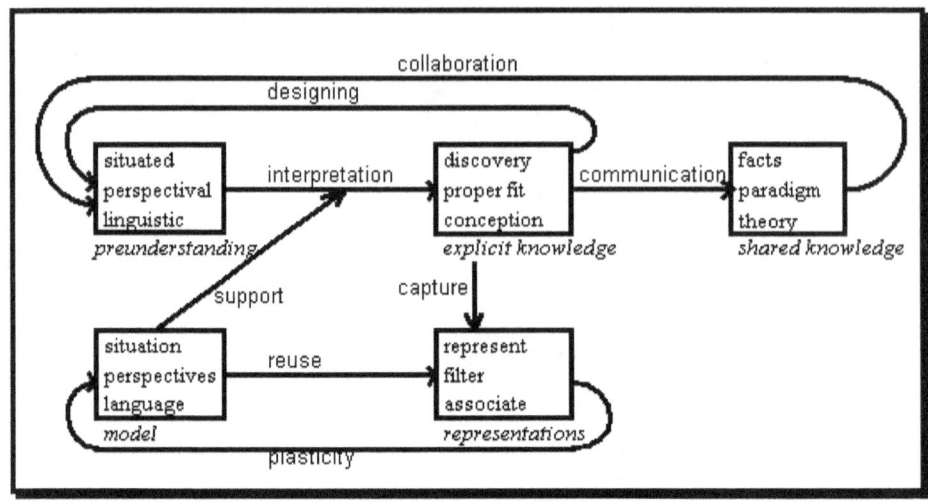

Figure 6-1. Computer support for interpretation in design.

The process of interpretation is depicted across the top of this figure. The movement of the hermeneutic circle from preunderstanding via interpretation to explicit understanding and from there via communication to shared knowledge has been detailed: (a) The disclosure of the situation leads to discovery. (b) Perspectival anticipations move to an appropriate fit of the understanding to what has been discovered. (c) The linguistic preconceptions express themselves in explicit conceptualizations. In the realm of shared knowledge, the discoveries can take the propositional form of facts, perspectives can become paradigms or worldviews, and conceptualizations can be elaborated as theories.

In addition to following the communication path to interpersonal knowledge, the externalized expressions of assertion and predication can be captured in a computer system. In this case, the representations that capture the codified knowledge can provide (a) representations of the interpretive situation, (b) filters for selecting knowledge belonging to specific interpretive perspectives, and (c) associations among related conceptions in a personal sub-language.[17] Once captured, this knowledge can be stored for future use in the computer knowledge base as models of the situation, perspective, and language of a specific instance of understanding.

---

[17] Wittgenstein (1953) would term these personal sub-languages "language games" corresponding to the individual's "form of life".

Future use is not confined to simply retrieving and displaying frozen knowledge. This knowledge is intended to support new and innovative design work. While even frozen knowledge has an important role to play in reminding designers of past solutions, the ability to reuse and modify the past solutions by applying them to new tasks is desirable as well. For this, the representations of the situations must be malleable, the perspectives should be capable of evolving, and the language must be generative. Knowledge can be *applied* to support interpretive tasks, in the sense discussed in Chapter 5, only when the representations of knowledge have the plasticity to allow them to be adapted flexibly enough to represent innovative interpretations.

The computer process in the bottom part of Figure 6-1 mirrors the upper loop of interpretation. That is, the computer system constitutes a model of the human interpretive process. The three-fold structure of interpretation as situated, perspectival, and linguistic is modeled in the ability of the computer system to represent these with, for instance, hypermedia, perspectives, and a language as in HERMES. The possibility of creating such a model is based in the fact that the understanding in the interpretive process can be explicated to the point where it can be captured on a computer. This possibility of knowledge capture is added to the sequence of successive transformations of information in Figure 5-5 from Section 5.2 to produce an expanded model in Figure 6-2. In addition, the computer support process in the bottom loop of Figure 6-1 is added as well. (An expanded view of the hermeneutic circle from the top of Figure 6-1 had already been incorporated.)

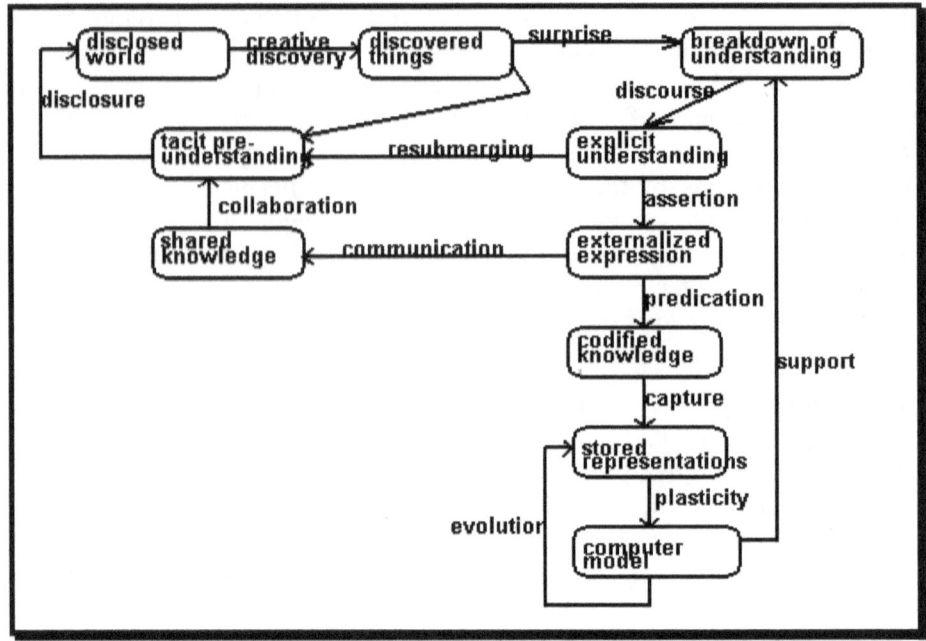

Figure 6-2. A model of cooperative interpretation and its computer support.

The rectangles represent classes of information. The arrows represent transformations from one class to another.

Now Figure 6-2 presents a complete model of the theory of computer support for interpretation in cooperative design. The information in tacit preunderstanding is successively transformed through disclosure, creative discovery, surprise, discourse, assertion, predication, capture, plasticity, and evolution. Then it is available to support new acts of interpretation by providing candidates for the interpreted meaning that is needed to repair situational breakdowns of understanding. The many transformations are necessary to produce representations that may be truly helpful, given the nature of human interpretation. Of course, the final judgment of which representations are relevant and how to apply them requires human judgment, based on intentional grounding in the world. Such grounding cannot be captured symbolically. The computer can only supply tools for the ultimately human project of constructing a meaningful understanding of reality.

This model shows the interplay of tacit and explicit understanding in the process of interpretation. The path of assertion and predication opens up the possibility of knowledge capture in a computer system. A properly designed computer system oriented toward evolution of knowledge and plasticity of representation can provide support for human interpretation in the form of an external medium for representing the situation, displaying alternative perspectives, and articulating linguistic expressions.

CHAPTER 7. RELATED COMPUTER SYSTEMS FOR DESIGN

The theory of computer support in the previous chapter has suggested that systems to support interpretation in innovative design should be oriented toward the evolution of domain knowledge and should provide for plasticity of knowledge representations. It suggests that such systems should be people-centered and should offer—among other things—(a) a computationally active form of external medium for representing the situation, (b) a mechanism for displaying alternative perspectives, and (c) a language for articulating interpretations. Above all, it stresses that such functionality should be implemented so as to support a healthy mix of tacit and explicit understanding. This mix is required to support the process of human interpretation as the explication of tacit understanding. This chapter will look at software systems that have been developed to support designers and see what techniques they incorporate for meeting these suggestions. These related systems provide many of the ideas that led to the mechanisms, functionality, and concerns of the HERMES substrate.

The approach of this dissertation is within the tradition of *situated cognition*. A number of influential works in this tradition have addressed the question of computer support for design. They are uniformly opposed to the approach of expert systems like MYCIN (Buchanan & Shortliffe, 1984) for innovative domains. Rather than endorsing systems that automate the decision making process, they call for systems that provide media in which people can exercise their design skills while benefiting from computational supports. Unfortunately, these writings have proposed little in the way of detailed proposals for alternative software techniques to support situated interpretation in design.

Dreyfus (1972), for instance, makes some high-level suggestions about designing software to augment human understanding. But Dreyfus is a philosopher and not a computer scientist, so he does not propose any software prototypes. Similarly, Schön (1992) is not a programmer and can, in the end, merely hope that better work will be put into building "designer assistant" programs than has been in the past, rather than into expert systems. The architects Coyne and Snodgrass (1991) propose a hermeneutic philosophic basis for AI, and they too make general recommendations along the lines of Dreyfus and Schön.

Suchman (1987) emphasizes the contrast between rationalist plans and situated action. She also stresses the role of language in constituting human interpretation of situations. But she is concerned with human-computer communication in which the computer must understand and act (produce Xerox copies), rather than with the computer as external memory or as a medium for shared human cognition. Instead of proposing an alternative programming approach, she fine-tunes traditional programs with more hardware sensors of the human situation and with more situated testing of the human-computer communication.

Another forceful critique of expert-system style AI from a Heideggerian perspective is presented by Winograd and Flores (1986), who call for a new approach to software design. They note that the computer is ultimately a structured dynamic communication medium and they stress the central role of language in coordinated action. They propose the COORDINATOR program as an example of new software as a medium for Computer Supported Cooperative Work. They note its limitation: "In many contexts this kind of explicitness is not called for, and may even be detrimental" because language is ultimately an "open-ended domain of interpretation." Despite this recognition, they propose software that initially failed to be accepted in many social settings because it imposed a rigid, explicit, public structure where people often want to remain implicit. In such cases it did not empower personal interpretations because it misjudged the balance between tacit and explicit.

Participatory design, as described by Ehn (1988), is a method for developing software in partnership with the end-users, so it can be designed to support skillful work and democratic workplace relations, in contrast to traditional automation approaches like those reported by Noble (1984). The idea is to design computer tools for experts that support and extend their situated skills, including their tacit know-how. As an example, the Utopia project worked with graphic layout professionals to pioneer a desktop publishing toolkit, as an alternative to the automated systems that were putting graphics professionals out of work. This toolkit approach may have been innovative at the time, but is now considered mainstream. Participatory design proposes alternative approaches to design, but offers little in the way of recommended software functionality for supporting interpretation.

The situated cognition literature has not made it clear what kinds of differences the alternative theory makes at the level of software techniques. Therefore, this chapter must look elsewhere and define its own answer to this question. It will do this by turning for ideas to two traditions of system building in AI that do provide alternatives to expert systems. While these traditions have not produced adequate systems for supporting interpretation, they have prototyped mechanisms for supporting either tacit or explicit understanding. The traditions to be considered are: *design environments* and *knowledge representations*. These "traditions" will be caricatured here as distinct and contrasting approaches, although there are significant cross-influences and confluences.

To represent the tradition of design environments, a series of systems developed during the past several years at the University of Colorado will be reviewed: especially JANUS (Fischer et al., 1989) and PHIDIAS (McCall, et al., 1990a). These systems provide tools for designers to construct design artifacts and to reflect upon them. PHIDIAS and JANUS serve as the particular focus because the development of the HERMES system was intimately influenced by them. The tradition of knowledge representations will be taken to include a series of knowledge representation languages and a series of design rationale capture systems. The knowledge representation languages include PLANNER (Hewitt, 1971), CONNIVER (Sussman & McDermott, 1972), KRL (Boborow & Winograd, 1977), and PIE (Boborow & Goldstein, 1980a). The design rationale capture systems include IBIS (Kunz & Rittel, 1970), PHIBIS (McCall, 1987), GIBIS (Conklin & Begeman, 1988), and DRL (Lee & Lai, 1991).

The caricature of these two traditions consists in taking the design environments as systems that support *tacit* designing and the knowledge representation languages as systems for supporting *explicit* documentation of argumentation. This is an exaggeration, because the design environments include explicit knowledge structures and the knowledge representation systems have made efforts to support tacit usage. Nevertheless, the major thrusts of these traditions (at least as they are distinguished in principle) is usefully characterized this way. Moreover, the real question is not simply whether some mixing of tacit and explicit understanding is supported, but precisely how that mixture is defined. That is, the previous chapter called for support of the movement between tacit and explicit understanding based on the particular sequence of transformations of understanding that are outlined in the analysis of human interpretation and in the corresponding theory of computer support. The question is how to take the two traditions' ideas for supporting tacit and explicit understanding respectively and to "apply" them in an integral approach to supporting interpretation.

This chapter will argue that the traditions of design environments and knowledge representation languages call for the following functionality to support interpretation in innovative design:

* an external medium for design (Section 7.1);

* perspectives for deliberation (Section 7.2);

* a language for human problem-domain communication (Section 7.3).

Each of these realms of functionality should support the designer's movement back and forth between tacit and explicit understandings of the design artifact.

While design environments strive to provide tools for doing the design work, knowledge representation systems focus on tools for explicating the knowledge—e.g., as formalized design rationale. They both overlook the importance of the dynamic interpretive cycle. Developers of design environments claim that their knowledge bases capture rules of the domain, and the design rationale system developers ignore the grounding of arguments in human understanding. In this way, both groups of systems understate the role of human interpretation. However, together they provide mechanisms that can be integrated into systems for supporting interpretation. This integration is prototyped in HERMES, as described in Part III. Systems that properly merge the ideas of the two traditions have the potential to be both expressive and usable by exploiting the synergy of tacit and explicit, human and computer.

7.1. External Media for Design

Expert systems—which incorporate domain knowledge in a set of explicit computational rules and infer solutions to problems in the domain automatically from these rules—do not represent the only approach developed in AI. There have always been some researchers who sought ways to use technology to *augment* human problem solving (e.g., Bush, 1945; Engelbart, 1963), rather than to model, simulate, or replace it. The characteristics of design found in the studies of lunar habitat design suggest that computer systems for innovative design in such exploratory domains should be structured to capture evolving design rationale and other design knowledge during actual design processes. That is, at critical moments during design work the understanding which is normally tacit takes on some form of explicit expression, permitting it to be captured in external media or computer representations for future use. Computer systems that take advantage of this can support human designers, rather than trying to automate design on the basis of heuristics and knowledge representations formulated in advance. The idea is to keep the human designers in control, but to extend their ability to reuse knowledge gained in past design work (by themselves or by others).

There are two difficult aspects to this approach: (1) how to capture knowledge (i.e., design concepts, terminological refinements, critiquing rules) without imposing inappropriate representations and without requiring excessive effort, and (2) how to retrieve and present to the designers knowledge that has been stored but that is now timely and relevant. Issues of design capture and retrieval have been addressed by design environments. PHIDIAS and JANUS are prototypical design environments, both originally developed using the sample domain of the layout of kitchen floor plans. They address knowledge capture by proposing a process of seeding, evolutionary growth, and reseeding of the knowledge base. They address timely knowledge retrieval by the use of triggers and critics. These systems will be discussed in this section.

The PHIDIAS design environment. PHIDIAS[18] combines a hypertext issue-based information system with a CAD-style construction kit. The issue-base contains issues that are important for designing in the domain, along with possible answers to the issues and arguments supporting those answers. The issue-base is motivated by Rittel's view of design as an argumentative process (see Section 2.2). Designers can add their own answers and arguments, which can contradict alternatives already in the issue-base. The graphical construction kit facilitates the designer in constructing a solution to the task at hand. It provides an external representation of the design concept with which the designer can enter into dialogue.

---

[18] PHIDIAS has undergone continuous development for many years. Most recently, it has been re-implemented on top of the HERMES substrate. The version discussed here is prior to that conversion and is described by McCall, et al. (1990a).

The integration of graphical construction with this textual deliberation is seen by the developers of PHIDIAS (and JANUS) as a way of operationalizing Schön's theory of reflection-in-action or breakdown-and-repair, in which designers construct, observe, reflect, and respond (see Section 2.3). PHIDIAS embodies knowledge of its domain in the hierarchy of information in the issue-base and in the palette of design items for the construction. Relevant knowledge is displayed through a *trigger* mechanism, which presents issues related to what palette item to select and where to place it. The designer can trigger this information by clicking on a button during the selection of a palette item. The designer is free to navigate through the hypertext from these displays to explore related issues. The trigger mechanism provides the designer easy access directly to the knowledge in the issue-base that is most relevant to the current decision of what to place where.

A simple query language is also available for displaying information from the issue-base. The query language—which is PHIDIAS' most important contribution to the problem of tacit and explicit understanding—will be discussed in Section 7.3 below.

The JANUS design environment. JANUS[19] takes a similar approach, with significant differences in the details and implementation. Knowledge about kitchen design is encoded in the various components of JANUS' multi-faceted architecture (see Figure 7-1): A *palette* of kitchen appliances provides a kit of parts for a *graphical construction* of a layout.

---

[19] JANUS has gone through many versions. The most advanced prototype system, called KID (Nakakoji, 1993), is the one discussed here. An end-user modification component was developed in a version called MODIFIER (Girgensohn, 1992). The view of JANUS as a communication medium has been stressed in the INDY version (Reeves, 1993).

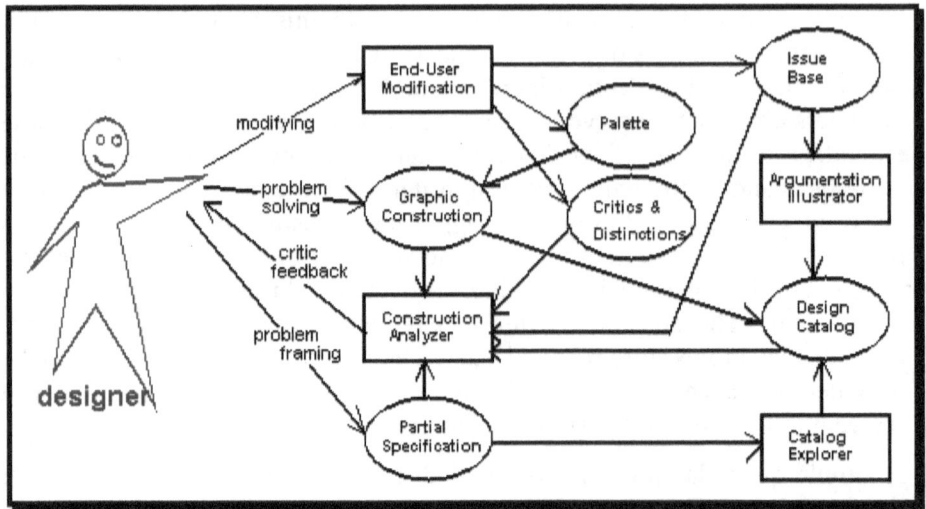

Figure 7-1. The multi-faceted architecture of JANUS.

The major components of the system (shown in ellipses) each use a different data representation. Other components (shown in rectangles) are used to bridge between these representations. Designers alternate between problem framing (altering the partial specification) and problem solving (altering the graphic construction).

Sets of *critics* embody rules of thumb about the placement of these appliances—such as that the stove should be near but not next to the refrigerator—and domain *distinctions* provide a vocabulary for expressing these rules. A *specification* checklist prioritizes client concerns, like whether the kitchen should be child-proof. An *argumentation* issue-base contains discussions of rationale for kitchen design, including deliberation related to the critic rules. There is also a *catalog* of past kitchen designs, which can be used as starting points for new designs or illustrations of abstract rules.

A number of additional components in JANUS are used to link the major components together, translating the data representations used in one component to those in the other. For instance, the Catalog Explorer prioritizes items in the catalog according to the decisions made in the specification, and the Argumentation Illustrator displays catalog items that relate to a given topic in the argumentation.

Perhaps the most powerful computation in the system is carried out by the Construction Analyzer, which critiques the construction using a set of *critic* _rules._ These rules can be modified by decisions in the specification as well. For instance, if there is a stove and a refrigerator in the construction, then their distance apart is calculated and used in rules about minimum and maximum distances. The critics "fire" automatically when one of their rules is violated by the placement of items in the construction. If the construction does not meet the critic rules, a message is displayed alerting the designer to a possible problem. The designer can then view the relevant section of the issue-base. Like the triggers of PHIDIAS, the critics of JANUS present knowledge from the issue-base that is most relevant to what is taking place in the design construction, but now as analyzed actively by the system.

Despite the progress that systems like JANUS represent in meeting the needs of designers, they still fall short of supporting interpretation. Consider the forms of knowledge in such a system. The paradigm is still that the programmer who built the system obtains pieces of knowledge from books and from domain experts, and enters it all in the system. Users benefit from being guided by the knowledgeable system (e.g., the critic rules). When designers want to, they can also explore the rationale for critic rules and defined characteristics of the standard appliances. But the bulk of the knowledge exists independently of the personal concerns of the user or the specifics of the task at hand.

Recently, an "end-user modification" component was created for JANUS (Fischer & Girgensohn, 1990). This allows users to add new appliances (e.g., when microwave ovens become popular they can be added to the palette) and to modify existing definitions and critic rules. However, this is not intended as a mechanism for continual redesigning of components under alternative interpretations: it does not support multiple simultaneous definitions for different users or different interpretations. Nor does it provide a medium for designers to articulate and explore innovative interpretive perspectives. The ideal of support for an evolving knowledge base requires the ability to partition the knowledge base for alternative modifications, but JANUS provides only a homogeneous knowledge base.

The reliance on standardized components and non-controversial rules of thumb in JANUS may work in the realm of kitchen design because this domain is, in fact, well-defined and well-understood. Stoves, sinks, and cabinets come in standard sizes and raise few issues for the designer. By ignoring broader issues of aesthetics, sociability, and architectural interactions with the rest of the building, JANUS is free to concentrate on rules that are independent of the interpretive perspectives of designers or their clients. For instance, the implemented critics have to do with distances between appliances, the size of the work triangle, the placement of the sink under a window, or the separation of the stove from the refrigerator. However, this approach needs to be extended for domains like lunar habitat design that are less well understood and less "tame".

JANUS and PHIDIAS are still like expert systems in their reliance on encoding domain knowledge in representation systems that are fixed in advance at the level of domain representations. They go beyond expert systems in two significant ways: (1) they recognize that most interesting design tasks cannot and should not be automated so they provide user-centered support systems, and (2) they recognize that domain knowledge evolves so they provide user-extensible systems. However, if one wants to have a design environment that, for instance, recognizes different people's definitions of privacy—and helps users explicate and share these definitions—and critiques designs using these multiple definitions, then one must extend the domain-orientation of PHIDIAS and JANUS to allow divergent interpretive perspectives, as discussed below in Section 7.2.

In a sense, the idea of a design environment is to open up an environment, or to disclose a world in which designs can come to be. In other words, a design environment provides a software model of the design *situation*, in Heidegger's sense (see Section 4.1). The modeled situation includes the developing design of the artifact (modeled by graphical figures), rules of thumb (modeled by critic rules), the designer's concerns (issues in the issue-base), design goals (specifications), domain concepts (issue-base distinctions), available parts for the design (palette), and past experience (the catalog of prior designs).

The theory of *human problem-domain communication* underlying the JANUS system corresponds roughly to Heidegger's insistence on the tacit nature of the understanding of the situation that is modeled. According to Fischer, et al. (1989),

> To shape the computer into a truly usable and useful tool, users must be able to work directly on their problems and tasks. The goal of human problem-domain communication is to eliminate computer-specific programming languages and instead to build layers of abstraction with which domain specialists—such as kitchen designers—can feel comfortable. Human problem-domain communication provides a new level of quality in human-computer communication because the important abstract operations are built directly into the computing environment. (p.5 f)

The idea is to replace (for the users) general purpose computer programming languages with domain-specific media that represent or model elements of the problem-domain situation. Then kitchen designers can communicate their ideas about kitchen appliances in terms of tacitly comprehended representations of these appliances (e.g., icons of stoves and refrigerators) rather than by means of abstract and explicit statements in an abstract language like LISP.

In order to turn the computer system into an "invisible instrument" that can be used tacitly in this way, Fischer (1989) calls for a layered architecture in which the "transformation distance" between the problem domain (e.g., kitchen layout) and the underlying system (e.g., LISP) is in effect reduced for the designer by building intermediate layers of abstraction (i.e., the design environment).

The existence of a series of intermediate layers supports end-user modifiability because if a modification is needed at one layer it can probably be made at the next lower level, without requiring the designer to descend to (and understand) the lowest level of implementation. For instance, if there is no microwave in the palette of the Kitchen Design Environment, then procedures in the Architectural Design Environment (MODIFIER) allow a microwave to be defined.

Fischer, et al. (1989) argue convincingly that it is important to relieve designers of the burden of "mastering the many details inherent in general purpose programming languages" (p.6). Designers have enough to keep in mind without learning and applying the complex knowledge required by sophisticated programming languages. However, the question is whether the palette of icons offered by JANUS has sufficient expressiveness for creative, professional, innovative design. Even with its end-user modification component, there is only limited plasticity in JANUS' representations. Ironically, use of the modification component itself requires at least some knowledge of LISP. The question of how to provide adequate expressivity without overwhelming the design task with extraneous programming tasks will be taken up in Section 7.3.

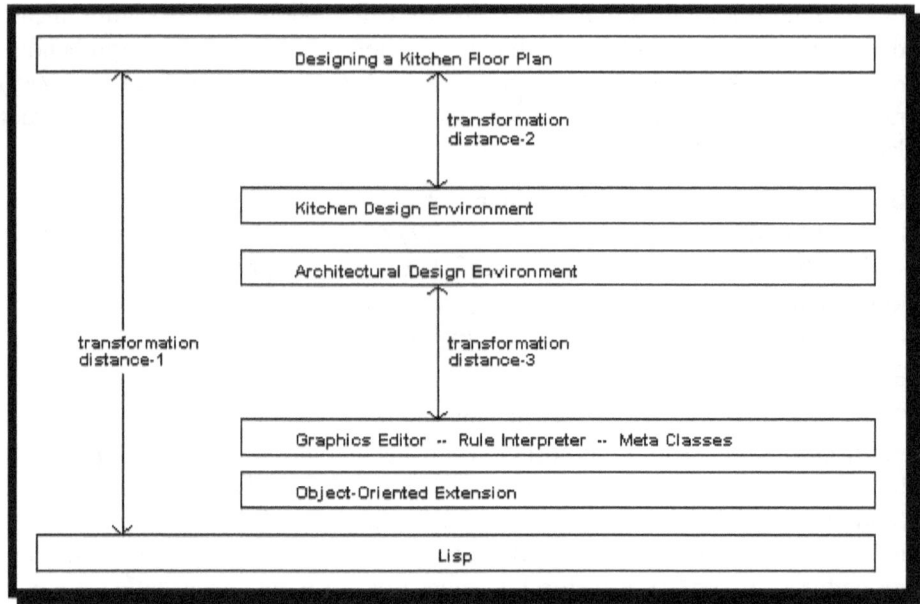

Figure 7-2. A layered architecture

The design environment provides a layer of abstraction between the problem domain and the implementation language, reducing the transformation distance-1 for the designer to transformation distance-2. From (Fischer, 1989, p.15).

One way to think about this problem is to ask whether JANUS has gone far enough with the layered architecture. There are two major gaps in Figure 7-2. Transformation distance-2 is certainly smaller than the original transformation distance-1, but it may be possible to build additional intermediate levels to further reduce the average effective transformation. Also, transformation distance-3 could be filled in to relieve at least two kinds of problems: (i) the difficulty for system developers of building new components and (ii) the fact that end-users of MODIFIER are often forced to use LISP to define modifications. HERMES will address these gaps by introducing new layers in both of these areas. The perspectives mechanism allows designers to build their own hierarchies of layers of knowledge between their specific task and the design environment, filling in transformation distance-2 with arbitrarily many levels. The HERMES substrate fills transformation distance-3, providing high-level functionality for system developers to use in building new components and providing a language for designers to use in making their modifications (see Part III).

Design environment support for interpretation. A final question must be raised during this look at the computationally active media that PHIDIAS and JANUS propose for supporting design. To what extent do they support the designers' *interpretative* processes?

The developers of PHIDIAS and JANUS justify their systems by appeal to Schön's description of design and the process of breakdown. They are anxious to operationalize this theory in system mechanisms. In order to operationalize the analysis of breakdown, they construe it as breakdowns in action, rather than the underlying breakdown in situated understanding. For instance, McCall, et al. (1990a) write:

> Reflection-in-action takes place when *action* breaks down. There are at least two major types of breakdowns. One is when the designer's *action* results in unanticipated consequences—either good or bad. The second is when the designer is stuck and simply does not know how to *act* or which *action* to take. To apply Schön's theory to environmental design we operationalized his concepts by dividing design into construction and argumentation. . . . To support reflection-in-action, the section of the issue-base relevant to a particular construction task must not be brought to the designer's attention in such a way as to interfere with construction. There are two ways this can be accomplished: by allowing immediate retrieval of this section of the issue-base when construction produces surprising side-effects or by allowing such retrieval when the designer is deciding how to *act*. The former strategy is used by JANUS; the latter by PHIDIAS. (p. 156f; italics added)

In operationalizing Schön's concepts of knowing-in-action and reflection-in-action, the developers of JANUS and PHIDIAS have squeezed out much of the interpretive content. Interpretation—the basis for innovative design—has been reduced primarily to a choice among pre-interpreted actions. Rather than supporting interpretation, these systems propose alternative actions.

The innovative interpretive tasks have been replaced by choices among limited actions listed in an issue base. Of course, it is necessary to drastically limit the set of palette icons and their possible locations in order to make it feasible to supply a manageable list of answers for their selection or a computationally tractable set of rules for critiquing them. But this restricts design to the level of routine design. It allows for more flexibility than automated expert systems because human designers are "kept in the loop" to make the choices among alternative actions and because new actions can occasionally be added to the system. However, this approach to operationalizing Schön's theory does not fully support interpretation or the repair of breakdowns of interpretations.

The triggers of PHIDIAS do provide partial support of interpretation in the sense that the issue base that is displayed can include alternative options and rationale for them. A designer can explore this rationale and use it to revise his or her understanding of the design situation. PHIDIAS even allows the designer to add new options that arise in this deliberation. The shortcoming of this approach is that it takes little advantage of the computational power of the computer system. It goes beyond a paper system only in the indexing of information for display and linking of it for browsing.

JANUS adds the power of computational critics. Fischer & Nakakoji (1991) point to Schön (1983) as the major theoretical influence behind their use of critics, but then claim to "move beyond Schön's work":

> Schön's framework is based on the cycle of 'seeing-drawing-seeing'. However, Schön's notion of seeing is 'not good enough'; as Rittel pointed out, 'buildings do not speak for themselves'. Non-expert designers (and this is what designers are, in almost all realistic situations) do not have the complete knowledge and experience to understand fully the conversation with the materials of the situation. Critiquing mechanisms serve as '*interpreters*' that support designers in seeing and understanding the 'back talk' of the situation. When a critic fires, reflection does not occur on the simple basis of the message. Designers 'listen to' the design material with the help of the *interpreter* in the form of a critic (p.27; italics added).

In what sense do the critics serve as interpreters? A critic may act as a reminder to focus one's seeing, but scarcely as an in*sight*ful interpreter. The only sense in which a critic provides an interpretation of the design situation, is that it provides the abstract, decontextualized interpretation of whoever programmed the critic rule. This is someone else's interpretation, far removed from the designer's situation. The programmer may have been considerably less expert than many users in terms of domain knowledge, having expertise in the area of programming. Like a knowledge engineer for expert systems, the programmer may have relied on generally accepted rules. These rules were then "interpreted" by the programmer in the sense of being expressed in a formalism that JANUS could execute. They were not interpreted within the context of a concrete design situation because they have to apply to all designs.

The MODIFIER (Girgensohn, 1992) and KID (Nakakoji, 1993) versions of JANUS move further toward supporting interpretation. MODIFIER allows a designer to modify critic rules and other domain knowledge. However, this feature is intended more to support changes in the domain (e.g., the invention of new appliances) or in generally accepted domain knowledge (e.g., new rules of thumb or building codes), than to support tailoring knowledge to an individual designer, a particular design case, or a technical viewpoint. In addition to selecting critic rules based on the selection of design units that are placed in the construction area, KID selects rules based on a series of specification questions that the designer answers for a specific design project. KID derives "specific rules" by adapting the generic critic rules to the choice of specification answers. In these ways, the system of critics is tied to the specifics of the construction, the specification, and the evolving knowledge base. Furthermore, the critics merely display information which the designer can reflect upon; they leave the decision to the designer.

Triggers and critics have been shown to be useful, even powerful mechanisms for design environments. JANUS and PHIDIAS have recognized the need to support the repair of breakdowns in designing. However, their mechanisms fall short of offering the necessary support of interpretation. Nor is it a matter of scaling up the prototypes, for their approach to operationalizing the concept of breakdown is itself the problem. The representations proposed are simply not expressive enough to model the situations, perspectives, and languages of designers in order to support their interpretations in more than a partial way. Mechanisms for customizing domain knowledge to the situations of individual designers and teams are called for (such as the perspectives discussed in Section 7.2). Also, more expressive knowledge representation systems are needed (such as the languages in Section 7.3). As shown in Section 10.3, HERMES extends the trigger and critic mechanisms with its perspectives mechanism and end-user language to provide *interpretive critics*. These more fully support the capture, reuse, and modification of critic rules.

7.2. Perspectives for Deliberation

An adequately expressive system of knowledge representation for supporting interpretation in design requires (among other things) *a perspectives mechanism*. This is a conclusion that can be drawn from many of the related systems considered in this chapter. The general need to mix tacit and explicit support means that the perspectives must be easy (natural, transparent, tacit) for designers to select, change, create, and merge, while providing an explicit structure (e.g., a browsable hierarchy of well-defined inheritance relationships) for organizing alternative versions of domain knowledge.

The systems reviewed suggest three ways in which alternative versions of domain knowledge must be distinguished in order to support design:

* Domain knowledge is different in different times and conditions. For instance, kitchen design is different on the Earth, on the moon, and on a space station due to gravity and atmospheric conditions. Each of these can be captured in a design *tradition*. Domain knowledge also changes as technology develops and as new ideas come along. Design traditions can evolve along multiple branches, creating a tree of alternative versions of knowledge.

* In their work, designers view various *aspects* of their task or their partially designed artifact. There are, for instance, various technical aspects of a design (plumbing, electrical, structural, aesthetic), as well as a wealth of different theoretical or argumentative aspects from which to interpret the task. Each of these aspects brings different domain knowledge into play.

* In collaborative design, several people each elaborate their own personal *viewpoints*. The individual viewpoints incorporate shared knowledge and also contribute to a shared group viewpoint. Much of the detailed work of a design team is done by individuals working within their own viewpoints. The deliberative processes of groups then consider ideas from the individual viewpoints and create a shared viewpoint that modifies those individual viewpoints to provide a basis for continued work.

Systems for design that do not support interpretation by providing a perspectives mechanism in effect proclaim that there is a single body of domain knowledge. That is, they make an implicit choice of a tradition, an aspect, and a viewpoint from which design is to be carried out. Of course, they may include alternative choices in an issue-base or in a catalog of design suggestions, but they do not support the designer in making a decision about what tradition or aspect to view things from. More importantly, they do not allow the designer to build an individual viewpoint and to select what other viewpoints to share knowledge from. A perspectives mechanism provides the means with which to build alternative versions of the knowledge base corresponding to traditions, aspects, and viewpoints. A number of perspectives mechanisms to support traditions, aspects, and viewpoints have been proposed in the literature. The three classes of perspectives are considered one at a time in this section.

Perspectives for traditions. Recent work on design environments indicates a strong need for support of alternative traditions. The end-user modification capability of JANUS (Girgensohn, 1992) allows designers to add new kitchen appliances to the palette and to define new critic rules. This allows for a cumulative growth in the represented domain knowledge. But, suppose that different designers want different definitions of the same critic rule. For instance, they may think that the work triangle should be different for residential kitchens, kitchens for disabled people, and commercial or industrial kitchens. To *support these variations simultaneously without causing a proliferation of alternatives* that the designer must cope with explicitly, a perspectives mechanism would be useful. Such a mechanism would allow the development of various traditions of kitchen design, like "disabled", "commercial", etc. Then all the palette items, catalog examples, issue-base entries, domain distinctions, and critic rules relevant to a given tradition would be grouped together in their own perspective. Section 9.1 presents a scenario showing how lunar habitat designers can use HERMES to work with information in multiple perspectives for traditions.

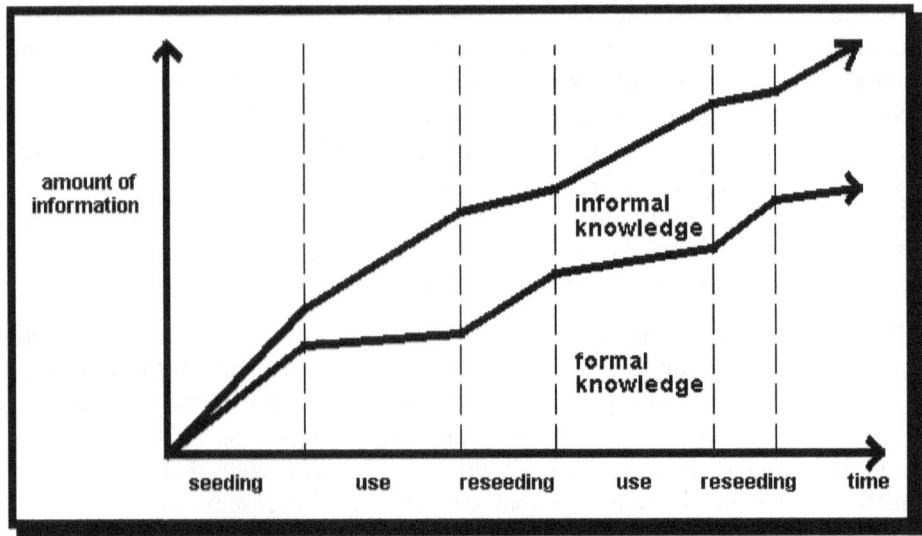

Figure 7-3. Growth in total and formalized information.

From Fischer, et al. (1993c, p.5).

A perspectives mechanism for traditions would facilitate the evolution of the knowledge base. Developers of design environments have proposed a model of evolutionary growth that mixes tacit and explicit development by means of alternating phases of system usage and reseeding (Fischer, et al. 1993c). (See Figure 7-3.) They think of the use phases as periods in which knowledge is entered in predominantly informal formats (e.g., natural language text). Then, during a phase of reseeding of the knowledge base, knowledge engineers would help to formalize this new knowledge, explicating and operationalizing it in, for instance, formal (computer interpretable) critic rules. (Shipman, 1993). A perspectives mechanism would allow new knowledge to be organized into alternative traditions by defining perspectives in which to group related information. To some extent, the use of perspectives for these traditions would allow users to add their informal knowledge within the appropriate perspectives in which they were working, so that the organization would take place naturally. Section 9.3 describes mechanisms in HERMES for supporting knowledge evolution by creating and merging perspectives.

A mechanism for supporting perspectives for traditions was proposed by Mittal, et al. (1986) as part of the PRIDE design environment. They called their technique "virtual copying of networks." They noted that in many systems knowledge is represented by networks of inter-connected sets of objects. Closely related alternative versions of these networks can be created efficiently by using the original network as a prototype and defining alternatives by pointers to this original where there are no changes. Only differences have to be represented by new data in memory. This "copy-on-write" strategy is a standard approach in many versioning systems, CAD graphics, and even operating systems (Fitzgerald & Rashid, 1986). In Pride, domain knowledge is represented in a design net, from which alternative virtual copies (of different traditions) are made. Design work can then proceed in different versions of the knowledge base:

> Specific designs are created by making a virtual copy of this design net. . . . Alternative designs can be explored by making a number of virtual copies of a partially completed design, and continuing operations in the virtual copies. Versioning in this way allows comparison of alternative designs, something not supported by all versioning systems. (Mittal, et al., 1986, p.164)

Most versioning mechanisms are file based. They can save the historical state of a design at a given time to a file on disk for later reference. In contrast, a perspective mechanism must maintain alternative versions of a knowledge base or of a particular design within the design environment, so designers can move from one tradition to another. This is achieved by the virtual copying technique. Unfortunately, the mechanism described by Mittal, et al. is specific to the LOOPS programming language and involves modifying the implementation of this language. McCall (1991/92) proposed a technique for implementing this approach to virtual copying of issue-base networks in hypermedia to support perspectives for traditions. This proposal has been worked out in the HERMES substrate (see Chapter 9).

Perspectives for aspects. Rittel argued that people bring different interests to bear on design tasks and view the problems under these different aspects (see Section 2.2). Deliberation requires the confrontation of arguments made by people with these different interests. So Rittel's IBIS and its subsequent versions have put the conflicting arguments into one structure where they can be compared. But this makes it hard to see which arguments belong together within a common perspective. If one wants to suspend deliberation for a while and work within a commitment to a given perspective, that is not supported by IBIS. The IBIS structure also does not represent *relationships among perspectives as such* (since the perspectives are not themselves represented, but only their elementary arguments). Thus, one cannot determine if one perspective incorporates others or modifies only particular arguments of another perspective. In HERMES, perspectives can be defined to organize any collection of knowledge in the system. Inheritance relations can be established among perspectives so that information is virtually copied from one to another.

The discussion of design in Part I repeatedly stressed the importance of viewing aspects of a design problem. In Chapter 2, Schön particularly emphasized that designers continually move from focusing on one aspect of a design artifact to another. In Chapter 3, the aspect of habitability and privacy became determinant of the designing—the problem with the NASA knowledge base was that it largely ignored this aspect. In Chapter 4, the idea of interpretive perspectives is key to Heidegger's analysis of interpretation; all interpretation, according to this analysis, takes place focused on a certain aspect of that which is interpreted.

It has been experimentally demonstrated that it is often helpful to consider one aspect of a problem at a time. Redmiles (1992) showed the usefulness of this for the interpretation of examples in computer programming problems. His EXPLAINER system allows a user to switch between several alternative aspects of problem explanations: graphical, mathematical, programming language representations, etc. The system uses a perspectives mechanism for viewing the knowledge base under a given aspect. While the user can select which of several perspectives to view, the choice is limited to a fixed set of perspectives. The mechanism here does not allow users to create new perspectives as versions of existing ones and modify them in line with their interests.

KRL (Boborow & Winograd, 1977)—a sophisticated computer language for representing knowledge—provides a more flexible perspectives mechanism. KRL is based on the following principles (among others):

*   A knowledge representation language must provide a flexible set of underlying tools, rather than embody specific commitments about either processing strategies or the representation of specific areas of knowledge.

*   Reasoning is dominated by a process of recognition in which new objects and events are compared to stored sets of expected prototypes.

*   A description must be able to represent partial knowledge about an entity and accommodate multiple descriptors that can describe the associated entity from different viewpoints.

KRL provides a syntax for describing things in terms of prototypes having default characteristics (slot values). For instance, a lunar habitat ward room could be described as a public area, a meeting space, or a large room. In each of these descriptions, different characteristics would be specified. Users of KRL can define new aspects of things by defining prototypes. This does offer a flexible, extensible system for describing things from aspects. However, it is too fine-grained to provide a mechanism for organizing systems of perspectives. It allows users to view different aspects of a given object, but does not support the defining of perspectives which apply to many or all objects, as in HERMES.

Perspectives for viewpoints. In the first versions of JANUS, the issue-base component was named "Viewpoints". By this, the developers recognized the need to support perspectives for aspects. However, JANUS has never had a mechanism for *distinguishing or organizing different people's viewpoints.* While the PHIDIAS project recognized the need for supporting perspectives for traditions, neither JANUS nor PHIDIAS have considered supporting the perspectives of individuals or design teams. As seen in Chapter 9, this is an important use of perspectives in HERMES.

It is clear that collaborative work in innovative areas involves dynamics among individual and group perspectives. The SPIDER system (Boland, et al., 1992) is a software environment for enriching communication within "learning organizations", i.e., less hierarchical, more network-like organizations able to cope with changing tasks, technologies, and environments. The developers of this system argue for the importance of mechanisms to support the sharing of perspectives:

> The impromptu, ad hoc nature of the understandings the decision makers wish to represent requires flexibility in both the representational structures made available and in the ways these structures can be created, shared, and modified. In creating an environment to foster richness of communication through the sharing of perspectives, there are two primary representational issues to be addressed: 1. What are the structures to be used in the formation of a perspective? 2. In what ways and through which tools should users be able to present their perspective for their own introspection and for the use of others? (p.309)

They claim that structured decision aid systems like IBIS and DRL, which provide powerful representational tools, "orient the user to a mathematical modeling paradigm that is neither conducive to flexible, impromptu thinking nor amenable to the rich communication between colleagues" (p.310). Rather, what they think is needed is a set of mechanisms that allow the user to easily build and modify a layered understanding of the situation. SPIDER provides a set of tools to do this within the domain of organizational management, producing linked networks of spreadsheets, graphical browsers, and textual annotations. These networks are considered perspectives. The contribution of SPIDER is to emphasize the need for some kind of perspectives mechanism and to stress the importance of making its interface easy enough to support tacit thinking rather than just explicit, mathematical modeling. Unfortunately, SPIDER is not in the domain of design.

Perhaps the most concerted effort to represent design alternatives was that of the PIE system (Goldstein & Boborow, 1980). Focusing on design in the domain of software programming, the authors of PIE call for a "contexts" mechanism to support the flexible examination of alternative designs:

> All designers create alternative solutions, develop them to various degrees, compare their properties, then choose among them. Yet most software environments do not allow alternative definitions of procedures and data structures to exist simultaneously; nor do they provide a representation for the evolution of a particular set of definitions across time. It is our hypothesis that a context-structured database can substantially improve the programmer's ability to manage the evolution of his software designs. (p.19)

The context mechanism in PIE is complicated in two ways. (1) Contexts (which support perspectives for viewpoints) are sequences of layers, where layers are saved states (versions). (2) Layers can be saved by the user or by the system. Once saved, a layer cannot change, although contexts can evolve by adding new layers. The contexts and the layers are nodes in the knowledge representation network itself, rather than separate files, so they can be accessed during the retrieval of information.

PIE supports personal viewpoints through the convention that different designers place their contributions in separate layers. Shared viewpoints can be created through the merging of two designs in a new layer. The designers of PIE do not claim that such a merger is trivial for complex designs. PIE does not eliminate the complexity and the need for extensive user intervention, but "it does provide a more finely grained descriptive structure than files in which to manipulate the pieces of the design. Layers created by a merger have associated descriptions in the network specifying the contexts participating in the merger and the basis for the merger" (p.5).

The context mechanism of PIE provides support for perspectives, but at the cost of increased cognitive overhead, i.e., a demand for more explicit understanding of relationships among contexts. The developers tried a number of responses to this problem through interface features: (1) a way for a user to view two contexts simultaneously, with differences highlighted; (2) the use of a metadescription to specify default selections of contexts for saving and retrieving information; (3) the option to turn off the context mechanism. They conclude that "all three of these strategies have proved useful in some circumstances, but it remains an important research goal to make the context machinery available to the user in a convenient fashion" (p.15). This is similar to the approach in HERMES, except that HERMES perspectives are less complicated and rigid than the PIE layers. Also, a number of system methods have been defined for supporting the merger of information from multiple perspectives (see Section 9.2).

Systems like PRIDE, SPIDER, and PIE have responded to the need to develop mechanisms to support perspectives. In each case, they provide a formalism that raises and addresses certain important issues of functionality. They also point to the difficulty of making it easy (i.e., natural, transparent, tacit) to take advantage of the perspectives mechanism. None of these systems has solved the problem of how to support perspectival interpretation in cooperative, innovative design within a domain like lunar habitat design. However, all of them have contributed ideas for the perspectives mechanism in HERMES (Chapter 9).

7.3. Languages for Human Problem-Domain Communication

As discussed in Section 7.1, a central thrust of design environments like JANUS is to eliminate the need for designers to "master the many details inherent in general purpose programming languages" (Fischer, et al., 1989, p.6) by supporting "human problem-domain communication." For example, JANUS provides a palette of icons that represent key objects in the problem domain of kitchen design. These icons can be manipulated tacitly with a mouse, with no need for the designer to express decisions in an explicit programming language. Similarly, the designer views discussions in the issue-base and messages from the critics in natural language statements that are formulated in the language of kitchen design, not that of computational operations.

However, it has also been noted that this kind of human problem-domain communication is insufficiently expressive for supporting interpretation in innovative, cooperative design. This section will discuss three arguments for supplementing human problem-domain communication with some form of programming language: (1) Recent versions of JANUS have come up against the limit to expressivity in various ways that call for an end-user programming language. (2) PHIDIAS and other systems have successfully incorporated end-user programming languages to different degrees. (3) Discussions of knowledge representation languages provide strong arguments for the utility of general purpose programming languages for communicating with the computer more flexibly. Once more, the point is to find the right mix of tacit and explicit support. It may be necessary to include an end-user programming language within design environments for designers to use in extending the current vocabulary of human problem-domain communication. However, the need to use that language should be minimized to where it is truly necessary to express things explicitly. Furthermore, the structure of that language itself should be designed to promote tacit usage as much as possible, in order to minimize the number of details of the language that must be mastered.

Increasing expressivity. The need for increased expressivity of communication in design environments is greatest when it comes to modifying existing knowledge representations. As long as one can express one's ideas adequately with the given representations (for instance, the defined palette items, domain distinctions, critic rules), there may be no need to go beyond them. This follows from the analysis of interpretation: explication is triggered by breakdowns in one's understanding. Only when the nexus of signification of one's current tacit preunderstanding is inadequate for the understanding of something is there a need to make one's understanding more explicit. However, when one's understanding does have to be extended innovatively, then one needs linguistic resources to make things explicit. The degree to which things must be made explicit and the length of time for which they must remain explicit before being resubmerged into a revised tacit understanding depends on the particular circumstances. It is the same with interpretation within a design environment (which is, after all, a model of the designer's understanding). When the current representation is inadequate, there must be a way of analyzing that representation more explicitly, modifying its structure or significance, and then re-submerging the new representation in a form that can once more be used tacitly.

The end-user modification component of JANUS (Girgensohn, 1992) failed to provide a smooth transition to the explication of palette items and critic rules that needed to be modified. It provided extensive interface support for creating new representations in the form of examples, context-sensitive help, checklists of required steps, and even critics of the modification process. But it provided no means for explicating existing tacit representations short of the LISP code of their implementation. For non-programmers, LISP does not offer a graceful transition from human problem-domain communication. Moreover, although this version of JANUS was completely rewritten to support end-user modification, it's structure severely limits the scope of possible innovation, even using the power of LISP. This is because it is not designed to make use of an end-user programming language to, for instance, define critic rules that are significantly different from the existing seeded rules. As Girgensohn (1992) writes:

> The representation of critic rules in JANUS proved to be difficult to understand for many of the subjects in the user studies. Especially the applicability condition that relates a critic rule to descriptions of design units such as (Cooks Self Food) was a source of problems. The LISP-like format of descriptions and the use of keywords such as Self was a part of these problems. A representation has to be found that is more familiar to users such as natural language and at the same time constrained so that the system can reason with it. Another source of confusion was the mechanism for specifying how many combinations of design units had to be tested. For example, a stove has to be near to only one refrigerator, but it should be away from all windows. . . . A related problem [is] that critic rules [to] check for the absence of design units cannot be formulated in the current representation. For example, it is impossible to check whether a kitchen has a door or whether the window area is at least 10 percent of the floor space. Stahl (1992) proposes to tackle problems of this kind by formulating critic rules with a natural-language-like query language in which the user can formulate queries. (pp. 79f)

This statement lists some of the kinds of issues that an adequate end-user language would need to be able to express: applicability conditions, self-reference, combinatorics, absence of units.

There is no reason why these issues could not be stated in a format more natural to designers than abstract LISP syntax—particularly since LISP itself is designed to build up more application-specific languages. As suggested in this quotation, what is needed is a language that can represent the explicit relationships that are implicit in the tacitly used critic rules and design units in a way that makes sense both for the designer and for the computer. The HERMES language (discussed in Chapter 10) tries to do just this. It builds up an end-user language for defining critic rules and other design knowledge in formulations which are as close as possible to domain terminology. Through the generality of its syntax, the HERMES language permits designers to define a much less constrained set of critics than those in JANUS.

A similar limit to expressivity is found in X-NETWORK (Shipman, 1993). This design environment employs agents to "search for information with certain attributes within the system and perform operations based on what, if any, objects they locate. Agents consist of a trigger, a query, and an action" (p.32). By basing the agents on queries of the current database, the system allows all actions and displays to be dynamic. The power of the agents is largely determined by the expressivity of the queries, which determine what kind of information the agents can respond to. In particular, if a designer wishes to modify the way a given agent is operating, the designer is dependent upon the expressivity of the query expressions for extending or innovating the agent behavior.

Currently, the queries in X-NETWORK (Shipman, 1993) are limited to the specifying of a conjunction of attributes:

> The query defines the information that must be located before the agent will execute its action. The query definition area within the agent editor is similar to the property sheet used to attach attributes to objects in the information space. This interface limits the expressiveness of the query to the location of objects matching attribute patterns but allows for the transfer of skills acquired in using the property sheets. Use of a more powerful query language based around a hypermedia model, such as that found in HERMES (Stahl, this dissertation), would allow greater expressiveness but with the added cost of the users being required to learn the syntax and semantics of the formal language. Beyond such traditional query mechanisms, query definitions should also be allowed to use built-in primitives that do complex analysis (p.34).

An end-user language such as that in HERMES could express more than conjunctions of attributes without requiring a forbidding syntax and semantics. It could also include primitives for the complex analyses mentioned. As noted in this passage, the concern is with the trade-off between increased expressivity and mounting cognitive overhead. The ideal would be to partially end-run this trade-off by minimizing the cognitive overhead that comes from making things explicit by keeping even the use of the language as tacit as possible.

Incorporating end-user programming languages. PHIDIAS (McCall, et al., 1990a) incorporates a query language for its issue-base. That is, the issue-base consists of a hypertext network in which each issue, answer, or argument is a distinct node connected with labeled links. In order to display part of the issue-base, PHIDIAS evaluates a query. Thus, if issue-234 is "What should be the location of the refrigerator?", then the issue-base discussion of the proper location of the refrigerator would be generated with the query:

```
issue-234 with answers with arguments
```

The PHIDIAS query language began in an earlier version named MIKROPLIS (McCall, 1989). This was primarily a system for constructing and using issue-bases for designing. It was based on McCall's (1987; 1991) variant of Rittel's IBIS: Procedurally-Hierarchical-Issues (PHI). A PHI issue-base consists primarily of issues, answers, arguments, and resolutions connected by links based on the "serves" relation. PHIQL, the PHIDIAS Query Language was developed to meet the needs of someone using a PHI issue-base. Its primary use was to display subtrees of the issue-base hierarchy, such as:

```
answers of subissues to issue-105
answers of issues with arguments
issues containing "doorway"
```

The original PHIQL language was based on a number of observed regularities in the formulation of queries in natural language. It was hoped that by incorporating these patterns of natural language in the computer language it would seem more natural and "English-like" than existing programming languages. In particular, it was noted that the procedure of following links of type L from node N was expressed by the phrase L of N in English. N was considered to be the *subject* of this expression and L to express a *relationship* applied to that subject. Successive relationships (i.e., link traversals) could be applied by adding additional phrases to the front of the query: L3 of L2 of L1 of N. Various conditions, such as containing a given substring, could follow the subject (McCall, 1989). By means such as this, a query language was defined with a simple syntax that could be easily parsed and that appeared English-like. The *Mikroplis User Manual* (McCall, et al., 1983) noted:

> The Mikroplis command code is similar to natural English. It is, however, a code, and as such must be learned and followed. The intention in imitating natural language—for instance, the fact that a variety of prepositions and articles is allowed, or that the syntax generally follows the subject/predicate conventions of English— was to minimize learning effort and to essentially eliminate the kind of opaque codes often found in other command sets (n. p.).

A number of limitations were imposed to maintain the workability of this approach: issue, topic, and document nodes had to have standardized names like `issue-123`; other nodes could not be direct subjects of a query; and the syntax was kept simple.

Query input was done through a prompted command line interface, so users simply typed in the query like a sentence. Incidental words like articles and prepositions were allowed, but ignored by the parser. Users could think about the information they wanted in the same terms that PHIDIAS accepted as a query. This made the query language easy to learn and to use. In proposing to use PHIQL for defining queries in virtual structures, McCall (1990/91) continued to emphasize the English-like character of the language:

> PHIQL is a highly English-like language which has been in use by end users for more than six years. This experience has consistently shown PHIQL to be learnable within a single day—often within an hour. . . . Though it appears purely declarative to end users, PHIQL is in fact an applicative (functional) language . . . [yet] statements in PHIQL almost always appear to be ordinary (declarative) English expressions. (p.6)

McCall (1990/91) proposed extending the original PHIQL to help make PHIDIAS a viable alternative to expert systems. This proposal focused on adding the functionality of virtual structures, that is expressions in the query language embedded in hypertext nodes. When a node that has been defined as a virtual structure is evaluated, it returns the results of the embedded query in place of its textual contents. This mechanism was seen as a way of embedding computational power in the very nodes of the hypertext database. (See Appendix B for a discussion of how this idea has been developed in the HERMES language.)

To give significant inferencing power to virtual structures, the PHIDIAS query language needed to be extended to include several new operations. The technical section of the proposal (McCall, 1990/91) detailed the planned modifications as follows:

> 1. Addition of comparison operators: PHIQL now only uses substring matching. It will need other comparison operators, including >, <, and =.

> 2. Addition of existential and cardinal (numerical counter) quantifiers: These will allow queries which ask for such things as nodes having no children.

3. Addition of negation operator ("not").

4. Addition of a true "if" statement, so that conditional queries can be stated more naturally.

5. Addition of capability for conjunction of conditions.

6. Addition of capability to compare the contents of a pair or more of retrieved nodes. This will allow the comparison of user-input nodes, whose contents cannot be known in advance by the system (p.7).

These extensions were implemented in an initial version of the HERMES language. They were tested by developing an application in the text-based domain of academic advising. This domain was chosen because it took good advantage of the inferencing capability. It also provided a basis for comparison with a hypertext system lacking inference (Peper, et al., 1990) and with expert system approaches. This version of the language is reported on by Stahl, et al. (1992). Appendix A reports on a programming walkthrough of this language and Appendix B discusses the academic advising application.

To support a wide range of inferencing, the language had to be extensively expanded to include true/false conditionals, numerical calculations, comparison operations, and nesting of phrases. A typical request in the new language—taken from the test domain of academic advising—might look like the following:

```
courses of sandra that have studio_types and that
   also have less than 3 prerequisites, with their
   prerequisites.
```

To evaluate this statement, the system would navigate from the student node, `sandra`, across all its `courses` links; check which nodes arrived at had at least one `studio_types` link and also had less than three `prerequisites` links; and output a list of the course nodes that satisfied these conditions, along with a sublisting of their prerequisites. Here is the output:

```
***COURSES:
1. ENVD 2110 Architectural Studio
   *** PREREQUISITES:
   1. ENVD 1000 Environmental Design Studio
   2. ENVD 1014 Intro to Environmental Design
2. ENVD 2120 Planning Studio
```

```
*** PREREQUISITES:
1. ENVD 2110 Architectural Studio
```

The structure of statements in this language and their method of evaluation are based on the structure of hypermedia. The queries investigate the node and link structure, rather than the content of a relational database, and their evaluation proceeds by navigation across the links from initial nodes. In this sense, the research represents an effort within the hypermedia paradigm. The thrust of the effort is to exploit hypermedia mechanisms to achieve certain functionality of artificial intelligence and information retrieval technologies. Thus, the goal was to expand hypermedia to include:

* Some of the inferencing capability of PROLOG, but without the comprehension difficulties of predicate calculus and explicit variables;

* Some of the querying ability of SQL, but applied to an object-oriented, hypermedia database;

* Some of the advantages of semantic databases, but allowing semantic relationships to be defined between instances as well as types by labeled links; and

* Some of the utility of semantic networks, but without restriction to a pre-defined set of link types or to semantic relationships.

The PHIDIAS query language illustrates a number of important principles: (1) It shows one approach that has proven successful for defining an end-user programming language that minimizes the cognitive overhead by modeling its syntax and semantics on that of natural language. (2) While the syntactic structure of queries follows a standard subject/predicate order, the vocabulary of terms is taken from the problem-domain (e.g., the node names and link types for issue-base queries are user-defined). (3) Moreover, the vocabulary is easily extensible by the users, so they can develop terminology for expressing their innovative interpretations of the structure of the issue-base. (4) The advanced version of the language includes logical and computational operations for specifying complex conditions. (5) Additional computational primitives can be included that would be useful in a design environment for a specific domain. (6) The language is based on the hypermedia structure of the database that it queries and expressions in the language can be incorporated in the nodes of the hypermedia as virtual structures.

The HERMES language is based on the PHIDIAS query language. It significantly extends the computational power and flexibility in order to support interpretation in design. It retains the idea of a constrained syntax, that made the PHIDIAS language easy to use, and it provides additional interface supports for its much larger syntax. However, the HERMES language moves away from the "English-like" emphasis in PHIDIAS as a result of issues that arose in programming walkthrough evaluations of intermediate forms of the language. Rather, the HERMES language normally hides much of the computational details to support tacit usage while allowing users to make the structure of expressions more explicit as needed for modification and interpretation.

The PHIQL language suggests the possibility of including an end-user programming language in a design environment. Such languages have proven useful in other computer applications. Many commercial products like CAD systems, spreadsheets, word processors, database management systems, MATHEMATICA, and HYPERCARD include macro languages, scripting languages, or end-user programming languages. While these languages are not always easy for non-programmers to use (Nielsen, et. al., 1991), they often provide a middle ground between canned applications and programming environments in which non-programmers can gradually learn to customize operations and local developers or local-site super-users can help people go beyond the limitations of standard applications (Nardi & Miller, 1990).

Another advantage of a language for design environments is to integrate the knowledge representations of various components. Even if some effort is involved in learning to use the language, if the same language applies uniformly to many or all of the system's components then once it is learned it provides the power to modify and extend all knowledge in the system. The language can impose a unity on a complex system. For instance, the KID version of JANUS is the most multi-faceted implementation of that system, with many components and linking subsystems. The developer of KID has remarked that "now that all these components have been prototyped with different knowledge representations it is time to integrate them with a unified substrate, and the HERMES language would be a great way to do that." (K. Nakakoji, personal communication, June 7, 1993.)

Of course, the inclusion of a language does not change a design environment's knowledge representations, but *the decision to use a language across components imposes a design constraint that favors an integrated system built on a consistent knowledge representation*. Part III discusses the role of the language in the HERMES integrated substrate.

Communicating more flexibly with the computer. For a design environment that is centrally built around an end-user language, the design of the language and the design of the knowledge representation are intimately linked. The developers of the design rationale language, DRL (Lee & Lai, 1992), for instance, point out that "a large body of research in the last two decades or so points to the importance of choosing the right representation for a given task (e.g., Brachman & Levesque, 1985; Winston, 1984). The task of using and reusing design rationales is no different." They argue that the common perception that the capturing of design rationale is not worth the effort may be based on a representation problem. It may be that a different representation system or language would allow people to represent more easily what they want to represent in a way that can provide significant benefit.

Many research programs in AI have concentrated on designing knowledge representations and languages that had maximal computational power based on formal schemes. Only afterward did they attempt to add a user-friendly interface facade. However, it may make more sense to start out from an effort to design a language oriented toward tacit understanding and then to gradually extend its computational power, always keeping in mind its usability. Systems like KRL, PIE, and DRL demonstrate the importance of sophisticated programming languages in knowledge-based systems. However, they require a high level of explicit, abstract analysis to use. The PHIDIAS Query Language, in contrast, proved to be rather natural to use, but it had limited power.

The ACE project took the alternative approach to combining computational power with usability by starting with a consideration of how to empower non-programmers and then worrying about formal computational issues. The ACE developers studied the programming language needs of end-users and local developers, and attempted to develop end-user languages for them. This resulted in ACE, an Application Construction Environment (Johnson, et al., 1993). ACE provides a set of frameworks for defining application-specific programming languages. These languages allow end-users and local developers to extend the functionality of applications by adding behavior to their systems without their having access to source code and without recompilation (p.47). ACE adopts the model of spreadsheets, by focusing on a well-thought-out set of primitives and avoiding complex explicit control structures, such as "for" loops and recursion. Thus, it goes beyond the superficially user-friendly style of HYPERTALK, which requires iterations and conditionals to be explicitly expressed rather than being implicit in application-specific operators. ACE is intended to "foster a methodology more like that fostered by spreadsheets. It puts users at the center of the development process" (p.53). That is, users are seen as the primary implementors of applications; they assemble the main components of their application and get it working. To support this, users are supplied with application componentry in the form of reusable, extensible software libraries, and components are self-describing so that new ones can be easily added to the system.

The HERMES language adopts much of the ACE approach, starting with a consideration of the user's (interpretive) needs. The HERMES language provides a computationally active medium in which designers can build up their own behaviors and supports. Systems of defined language expressions can evolve, be organized in perspectives, and be shared by different designers of different skill levels.

Programmable design environments. The idea of combining design environments with the approach of programmable applications (Eisenberg, 1992) has been explicitly proposed by Eisenberg and Fischer (1992). They motivate this combination on pragmatic grounds, hoping to integrate the best features of each approach and overcome their respective weaknesses. While they do not address many of the issues that arise in actually implementing a programmable design environment, they recognize the advantages of extending a direct manipulation system with an appropriately designed end-user language. HERMES can be seen as a first instantiation of the idea of a programmable design environment, moreover one that is motivated by principles of human understanding.

The system suggested by Eisenberg and Fischer (1992) consists of two independently conceived halves (as mirrored in the structure of the paper, which discusses the notions of programmable applications and design environments separately, and then worries about their interactions). However, the indications are already present in their discussion that the attempt to implement such a system would lead to an integrated approach, as it did in HERMES. For instance, they suggest that, "the programming environment 'half' of the application should be constructed around a domain-enriched language (which might be a newly-constructed language or an application-specific 'dialect' of some existing general-purpose language)" (p.81). This distinction between a new language and a dialect of an existing one underestimates the extent to which the language must be integrated with the structure of the design environment's knowledge representations. Any language useful for extending the expressibility of the design environment will be severely constrained by (i) the need to incorporate primitives that refer to the elements of the design environment, (ii) the need to incorporate functionality that corresponds to the structure and tasks of the design environment (e.g., navigating hypermedia links and filtering by specific kinds of criteria), and (iii) the goal of making the language accessible to designers. Whether or not an end-user language that meets these constraints is built on top of an existing language like PASCAL, FP, LISP, or SCHEME it will look like a new language. On the other hand, any flexible end-user language would want to incorporate much of the power of programming languages and would do well to build upon or model itself after a successful language at the computational level. So, in the end the proposed alternatives come down to roughly the same thing and the important point is the integration of the language with the structure and goals of the design environment. Chapter 10 will show how the HERMES language was designed specifically to satisfy these constraints.

Design rationale is a particular concern of Eisenberg and Fischer (1992). They want the user to be able to reuse design examples from the catalog and to copy and modify the associated rationale. They recognize that this puts a general requirement on the system to support incessant reuse and plasticity: "The upshot of all this is that our systems must support users in creating, retrieving, browsing, modifying, storing, and reusing information structures that capture design-related decisions—and the systems must moreover support this type of activity interactively, in the broader context of creating new artifacts" (p.86). Unfortunately, they never suggest mechanisms to achieve such system-wide plasticity of representation or to organize the proliferation of different versions of rationale and other kinds of knowledge. The substrate in HERMES (see Chapter 8) is designed to maximize the ability of users to modify all forms of knowledge and the perspectives mechanism (Chapter 9) is available for users to organize their versions of knowledge and reuse design examples with their associated rationale through virtual copying.

The HERMES perspectives also solve another problem raised by Eisenberg and Fischer (1992), that of maintaining "historical" information. Versions of a design at a given state can be saved in their own perspectives. The issue of whether something was created by direct manipulation or by programming does not arise in HERMES, because the HERMES language does not change state; it only displays, analyzes and critiques the current state—which is created via direct manipulation and dialog boxes. Although the SCHEMEPAINT (Eisenberg, 1992) programmable application showed that a programming language could be useful in creating precise, complex graphics, there is little sense in Eisenberg and Fischer (1992) how the language would be used in the creation of designs in other domains.

The example given for use of the language in a programmable design environment for graphs does not create new graphs, but queries the hypermedia database. It is to "write a procedure to find all catalog entries of a particular graphical type within two links of a particular entry" (p.87).

This example is not worked out, but could be accomplished in the HERMES language. Say the particular catalog entry was named `mike's graph` and the particular graphical type of interest was `pie graph`. Then the following expression would return the desired results:

```
all associations of all associations of mike's graph
    that are of kind pie graph
```

If the only kind of link type of interest is that of `similar example` links between catalog entries, then one could define `list of pies` as:

```
similar examples of similar examples of mike's graph
    that are of kind pie graph
```

and then evaluate the expression,

```
deliberation of list of pies
```

to display the design rationale attached to all the catalog entries in the list.

Note that in order to carry out this task, all the relevant knowledge must be in an integrated knowledge representation, linked together by hypermedia links. That is, the catalog items (graphical representations), the specification elements, and the design rationale (text and pictures) must be compatible nodes that can be linked together in a way that the language can navigate. Both by the nature of the tasks that are proposed as desirable by Eisenberg and Fischer (1992) and by the necessity of having a single language refer to and analyze all knowledge in the system, an argument is implicitly made for the use of an integrated substrate to define a hypermedia structure and its accessibility via the language and perspectives. As Part III will show, this is precisely the role of the HERMES substrate as a basis for programmable design environments.

There are good reasons to incorporate programming languages in design environments in order to go beyond the limited expressivity of human problem-domain communication as suggested by the notion of a programmable design environment. Systems like KRL, PIE, and DRL have shown the utility of languages to define sophisticated knowledge representations and design rationale capture systems that can be supported with powerful computational means. Each of these systems has, however, run into the need to make the systems more usable by supporting tacit understanding. The PHIDIAS query language has suggested an approach to syntax and semantics that promises to reduce the explicit cognitive overload of formal programming languages for non-programmers. ACE suggests additional techniques for keeping computations tacit and for designing languages that help promote plasticity of knowledge representation. HERMES tries to incorporate ideas like these to achieve an adequate mix of mechanisms requiring tacit and explicit understanding on the part of designers using an end-user language in a design environment. Thereby, it hopes to go far toward overcoming the problem of tacit and explicit understanding in the computer support of interpretation in design.

Part III. Computer Support of Cooperative Design

"The philosophers have only *interpreted*
the world in different ways;
the point would be to *transform* it."

Karl Marx

Theses on Feuerbach

(1844, S.192)

The chapters of Part III discuss the three major features of HERMES: the hypermedia knowledge representation, the perspectives mechanism, and the language. HERMES is an instantiation of the theory of computer support proposed in Part II. The discussion of these features of HERMES is intended to illustrate how a system based on the theory might look—a set of mechanisms for supporting the situated, perspectival, linguistic character of interpretation. While the theory suggests the usefulness of a language and a perspectives facility, many very different kinds of languages and perspectives mechanisms are possible. The particular mechanisms in HERMES that have been prototyped as part of this dissertation, suggest one possible approach. The discussion of these mechanisms should illustrate the application of the theoretical framework previously developed to the concrete design of software; these mechanisms represent an attempt to *transform the philosophical interpretations into practice*.

In this Part, Chapter 8 discusses the integrated hypermedia structure. This provides the medium for representing the design *situation* using the many media of design. The *perspectives* mechanism of Chapter 9 provides for flexible organization of all knowledge in the system in order to support collaboration. The *language* presented in Chapter 10 offers designers increased power for interpreting, communicating, and capturing their tacit understandings more explicitly.

Each of these chapters is divided into three sections. The first reviews the needs which must be addressed by the mechanisms discussed in the chapter. The second describes in some detail the implementation of the mechanisms in the HERMES prototype. The third illustrates how the explicit mechanisms are actually used by designers working in HERMES. Generally, the interfaces to these mechanisms encapsulate their computations so that they normally function behind the scenes of relatively tacit usage by designers, only becoming more explicit when the designers must articulate their understanding.

Together, the three mechanisms that are detailed here are intended to support interpretation in design. Specifically, they support the situated, perspectival, linguistic character of design. The kind of design they are meant to support is that of exploratory domains like lunar habitat design, which can be characterized as innovative in nature and collaborative in structure. The computer support proposed has been developed particularly to help designers move back and forth along the spectrum of tacit and explicit understanding. The description of each mechanism will show how it promotes tacit usage as well as facilitating more explicit understanding when that becomes temporarily necessary.

CHAPTER 8. REPRESENTING THE DESIGN SITUATION

Many forms of knowledge are required to support design. The lunar habitat designers in Chapter 3 used sketches of previous designs, graphical representations of design components, discussions of design rationale, terminology for thinking about the design, information from experiences of former space missions, drawings from references, and guidelines from NASA documents. They viewed problems from alternative perspectives and they deliberated issues using concepts that were redefined in the process. Rather than simply constructing a solution from these many pieces of retrieved knowledge, the designers continually modified the knowledge, trying numerous variations. They continually reinterpreted their task, candidate solutions, and the knowledge that went into the solutions.

To support what Part I of the dissertation described as the process of interpretation in design with a computer-based design environment requires a system that provides many media of representation. Furthermore, the representations of knowledge in the media must be designed to support incessant modification, tailoring, customizing, or plasticity by end-users.

According to Part II, a design environment should be people-centered, supporting the human designer's ability to interpret and make judgments. It should support tacit usage as well as allowing designers to make knowledge successively more explicit to meet their specific interpretive needs. This suggests incorporating an end-user language for explicating terms and a perspectives structure for organizing different people's customized versions of knowledge. To take advantage of the computational power of the computer, a design environment should provide a computationally active medium in which the designers can work individually, communicate with the computer, and collaborate with other designers on team work.

The HERMES system described in Part III attempts to meet these requirements by providing a substrate of functionality that can be used by all components of a design environment. It defines a multi-media structure in which all elements of knowledge can be defined and interconnected. All knowledge is represented as data that can be retrieved and modified by the end-user. The knowledge representation structure integrates a perspectives mechanism so that all representations of knowledge are organized into hierarchies of user-defined contexts. It also integrates a language that designers can use for defining and modifying representations of knowledge, including definitions of computer agents such as critics, queries, and displays.

Section 8.1 describes the characteristics of the HERMES substrate. It discusses how it meets the requirements from the analysis of design as interpretation presented in Part I and from the theory of computer support for interpretation in design proposed in Part II. Section 8.2 shows how the substrate is defined at a more technical level. It discusses the knowledge storage, retrieval, modification, and interconnection mechanisms. Section 8.3 then illustrates how a lunar habitat design environment with multiple components can be built on top of the HERMES substrate. In addition to outlining how components for construction, rationale, specification, and catalogs can be built, it highlights the usefulness of the hypermedia, perspectives, and language in defining these components.

8.1. A Computationally Active Medium for Designers

The HERMES substrate. HERMES is a *substrate* for building design environments to support interpretation in innovative design. Many of the previous design environments discussed in Chapter 7 got along without primary attention being given to a substrate level. This is because those systems prototyped functionality specific to individual components. However, recently there has been a proliferation of efforts related to JANUS to introduce functionality that spans all the components of a design environment. KID (Nakakoji, 1993) pushes the non-substrate, multi-faceted approach to its limit, integrating design decisions made in one component with displays in others by "linking mechanisms" to bridge different knowledge representations. But even here, the beginnings of an integrating language are established with the formulations of specification-linking rules, which tie together several major components (critic rules, specification, catalog, domain distinctions). MODIFIER's (Girgensohn, 1992) approach to end-user modifiability of data in all components was an effort that naturally led to integration. The components whose knowledge became modifiable (e.g., the palette and its critics) were, in effect, redesigned to be based on a minimal common substrate of LISP tools for using property sheets. INDY (Reeves, 1993) proposes history capture mechanisms and embedded annotation techniques that apply to events in all parts of the system. In order to implement this, it was necessary to rewrite JANUS to represent all events in the system uniformly. Similarly, the idea of a "programmable application" (Eisenberg, 1992; Eisenberg & Fischer, 1992) suggests the applicability of an end-user programming language throughout a system, as noted in Chapter 7.

An explicitly designed substrate is a way to have various special components implementing multi-faceted functionality while at the same time providing a base of common functionality that is shared by all these components. Certainly, a construction component needs to provide some special supports that are not appropriate to a design rationale component. However, it may be useful to have hypermedia linking, partitioning of knowledge by perspectives, and definition of expressions in an end-user language available in many or all the components. An architecture based on an integrated substrate can support the multi-faceted functionality required for a design environment.

X-NETWORK (Shipman, 1993), for instance, has hypermedia linking, multi-user access, and incremental formality mechanisms that must apply to multiple components; it implements these within a hypermedia object system substrate. HERMES is also a substrate that can provide functionality that applies to all parts of a design environment built on it. Its language supports end-user-programmability of all components and its perspectives affect all knowledge used in the system. Its critics, palette, catalog, construction, and argumentation displays are all programmable in the language and their definitions or contents are dependent upon the selected perspective.

There are several benefits to creating a design environment substrate. As shown in Section 8.3, it facilitates creating new components within an integrated, high-functionality system by exploiting powerful existing data structures. It permits adding additional trans-component functionality (e.g., for supporting learning, collaboration, interpretation, evolving formality, or agent mechanisms) by enhancements at the substrate level. It provides an integration that helps both developers and end-users because the various components now use standardized structures, mechanisms, and interfaces, so techniques learned in one component transfer well to others.

The layered architecture of HERMES has the following structure (see Figure 8.1):

(1) *Programming environment.* This layer includes commercial object libraries for list processing, graphics, B+ indexing, windowing user interface, etc., as well as the PASCAL source code compiler.

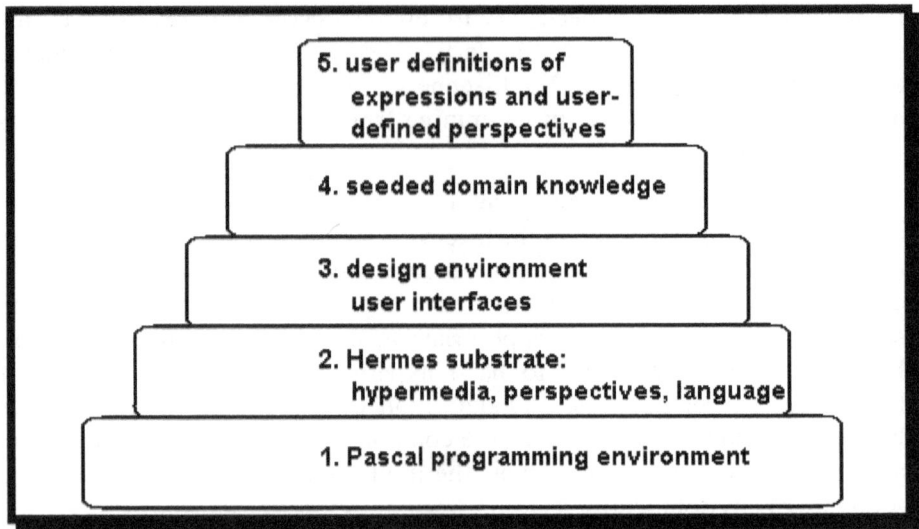

Figure 8-1. Layered architecture of HERMES.

(2) *HERMES substrate.* In addition to the hypermedia structure, the language definition, and the perspectives mechanism, this substrate level includes an efficient, scalable object-oriented database management system for persistence of the hypermedia data structure. With the language interpreter, this substrate alone consists of about 200 object classes (roughly 20,000 lines of code). The power and flexibility of HERMES for empowering users to represent, manipulate, and interpret domain knowledge comes from the complex interactions of the functionality of the substrate—much more than from the higher-level components of the multi-faceted user interface built on top of it.

(3) *Design environment user interface.* Components like adaptive palettes, design catalogs, and adaptable argumentation are defined as specialized window objects (graphical user interface features). They use the functionality of the substrate to retrieve hypermedia nodes in the active perspective using queries in the language. Some interface components are necessary for user access to the language and perspectives; others are

specific to an application, like lunar habitat design. User interface components can take advantage of terms defined in the language, so that end-users can modify the behavior by redefining the terms.

(4) *Seeded domain knowledge.* The system is initially seeded with knowledge specific to the domain for which the system will be used, such as lunar habitat design. This includes definitions of useful terms and queries in the language and an initial hierarchy of perspectives for organizing knowledge. This seeded information is represented using mechanisms defined in the substrate and is stored in the database.

(5) *User definitions and perspectives.* Users can read, modify, and add to any of the domain knowledge. They can organize alternative versions of text, graphics, and language definitions (e.g., domain distinctions, critics, and queries in the language) by perspectives. The substrate is designed to empower users of various skill levels to reuse, modify, and extend all forms of information stored in the knowledge base and to reorganize it into meaningful perspectives.

A hypermedia system. The HERMES system is built on an extended form of *hypermedia.* Hypermedia can be understood as a system of *nodes* having content of various kinds connected together by *links* to form a network or graph structure. Alternatively, if one focuses on the language elements and their interconnections, the HERMES hypermedia can be viewed as an extended form of semantic network (Woods, 1975). In HERMES, the content of nodes can take the form of various media, such as text (e.g., for the issue-base), graphics (for the construction area), or expressions in the HERMES language (like critic rules). In this way, everything that needs to be represented in the computer to support design can be represented in an appropriate data structure that is still part of an integrated system. Each element of information can be interconnected with other elements as needed.

The media requirements for a system to support design are extensive. As mentioned in the introduction to this chapter, the lunar habitat designers in the transcripts used the following: sketches of previous designs, graphical representations of design components, discussions of design rationale, terminology for thinking about the design, information from experiences of former space missions, drawings from references, and guidelines from NASA documents. In order to represent these in the HERMES system, the hypermedia substrate defines the following media for the content of nodes: character (text), number (reals), conditions (boolean-valued expressions), graphics (vector graphics), images (bitmaps), pen-based sketches, sound (recorded voice), and video recordings.

Because HERMES *needs to display information in accordance with interpretations that are not pre-defined but are defined by the user, all displays must be computed dynamically.* This is done with dynamic displays, in contrast with the page-based approach of most hypertext systems. In a program like HYPERCARD, a presentation of design rationale might contain a pre-formatted page of issues. Embedded with an issue might be a button for its justification. Clicking on that button brings up another page of text presenting the justification. Similarly, in JANUS a page of design rationale contains highlighted terms; clicking on one of them displays information about that term, allowing one to browse through pages of related textual information. In HERMES, however, the justification must be recomputed based on the current interpretation. This is done by executing a query specifying the information desired (e.g., `justifications of answers of a certain issue`) and based on the currently active interpretive perspective. The results of the query are then displayed, in place of a pre-formatted page. This approach was adopted from the PHIDIAS design environment, which featured a limited query language for allowing the user to structure textual displays (McCall, 1989). Because in this approach design rationale is generally stored at the relatively fine granularity of sentences rather than pages, it can be modified either by changing or adding short sentences, or by modifying the definition of the query.

The HERMES language provides the means of navigating the links of the HERMES hypermedia. Links between nodes have *types*, like an `answer` link to connect an issue with its answers. In addition, as described in Chapter 10, the language defines processes of information retrieval, analysis, filtering, display, and critique, which make link traversal more dynamic than just following static link types. Expressions in the language can be incorporated in computational agents or in interface features of a design environment. All terms and expressions defined in the language are stored as nodes of the hypermedia. The language can also be embedded in the hypermedia structure in various ways. For instance, nodes and links can be made conditional on an arbitrary expression in the language that evaluates (at run-time) to true or false. The content of a node can also be defined by the result of an expression in the language that evaluates to a list of other nodes. These two uses of the language to make the content of nodes dependent upon the run-time evaluation of expressions are known as *conditional nodes* and *virtual structures*, respectively. (See Halasz, 1988, and McCall, et al., 1990a.)

The hypermedia system also defines and incorporates HERMES' perspective mechanism. The links between nodes maintain lists of which perspectives can or cannot view the connected nodes. When the link is traversed during the evaluation of an expression in the language (which is, at an implementation level, the only way that the node the link leads to can be retrieved or displayed), the currently active perspective is compared with this list.

Active media. The HERMES hypermedia provides a computationally active medium for designers to work in. All information retrieval, display, analysis, and critique is performed by navigating the hypermedia network of nodes and links. The content of the nodes may be dynamically dependent upon other content in the network, as in conditional nodes and virtual structures. Whether or not such nodes are involved, the retrieval of information depends upon an expression in the language, which may in turn be composed of many other terms, whose definitions can be changed. Furthermore, information retrieval and display is always dependent upon the current perspective and the list of perspectives from which it inherits. All of these dependencies are under the control of the person using the system. However, the synergy of the various dependencies (definition of the retrieval expression, content of nodes, definition of language terms, choice and structure of perspectives) quickly exceeds the ability of people to foresee the results in detail. Rather, users of the system proceed with a largely tacit understanding and the computer works out the details. In this way, people can concentrate on the interpretive tasks while the computer takes care of the detailed but routine bookkeeping. This exploits the advantage of a computational medium over passive external media like paper.

People-centered system. The language provides a central control mechanism over computational processes in the HERMES system. As such, it makes the control over all computations ultimately available to designers using the system. The language is a means of communication between the computer and its users, through which end-users can specify in as much detail as they wish how information is to be stored, retrieved, analyzed, displayed, and critiqued. At the same time, the system is seeded with default definitions so that designers do not have to be concerned with these matters in any more detail then they need to be as a result of their design tasks.

Because HERMES is designed for exploratory domains like lunar habitat design, however, a seeded knowledge base is only a starting point and source of reusable definitions. Design requires incessant modification and tailoring of definitions of all relevant knowledge based on the particular design situation, the active perspective, and the linguistic frameworks and terminology in use. This means that all information in the system must be flexibly modifiable.

It is not only that there are no longer any experts in the traditional sense because systems of knowledge have become too extensive and too rapidly changing for individuals to master (Fischer & Nakakoji, 1992). Beyond this, in exploratory design tasks like lunar habitat design, there is no such thing as an objective body of domain knowledge that could even in principle be defined once and for all. So-called domain knowledge arises through processes of interpretation that are situated, perspectival, and linguistic. This certainly does not mean that such knowledge is arbitrary or that it cannot be justified. On the contrary, it is grounded precisely in the situations, viewpoints, and traditions that provide its background knowledge and in the deliberations that importantly accompany it. But, the point is that alternative versions of the knowledge are applicable under different conditions and only designers can determine relevance.

Evolving knowledge base. The plasticity of HERMES' language and other media takes off from the ideas of PHIDIAS. In PHIDIAS, node and link types were user-defined. This was a simple matter of allowing users to define new names for types of nodes and links. Then, new nodes and the links between them could be labeled with any one of these types. The importance of this came in its effect upon the PHIDIAS query language (discussed in Chapter 7). This language consisted largely of options for combining node and link types. So by careful choice of type names, query expressions could be made to read descriptively and the language could be extended to include new terms. The HERMES language is far more complex, but it retains the principle that all semantic elements should be user-definable and namable. In fact, this principle is extended to the various media as well, so that everything in the knowledge base can be named and modified.

All representations of knowledge in the HERMES system are maintained as data in the hypermedia information base on disk. This makes it easy for the system builders who define components for design environments built upon the HERMES substrate, for knowledge engineers who seed or reseed the knowledge base, as well as for end-users who tailor the information to their own needs. Standard interfaces are available for browsing, editing, and extending knowledge in all media.

The HERMES substrate is designed to support constant tailoring of all information in the knowledge base. All nodes in the hypermedia can be browsed, modified, annotated, or deleted within the current perspective. Much knowledge is defined by language expressions, which can likewise be edited. The terms used in expressions can also be edited, and so on recursively. Knowledge is organized by perspectives. Together, the hypermedia, perspectives, and language provide considerable control over all knowledge in the system by designers using it. The following chapters will detail how this works.

8.2. Knowledge Representation in the Hermes Substrate

Figure 8-2 shows how the functionality of the most important objects in the HERMES substrate is built up. Starting at the top is the generic *HERMES named object*. Any object descended from this can optionally have a name and can be stored on the object stream (file) that functions as the database for HERMES. The objects below it in the hierarchy successively accumulate data slots (indicated in parentheses) and methods.

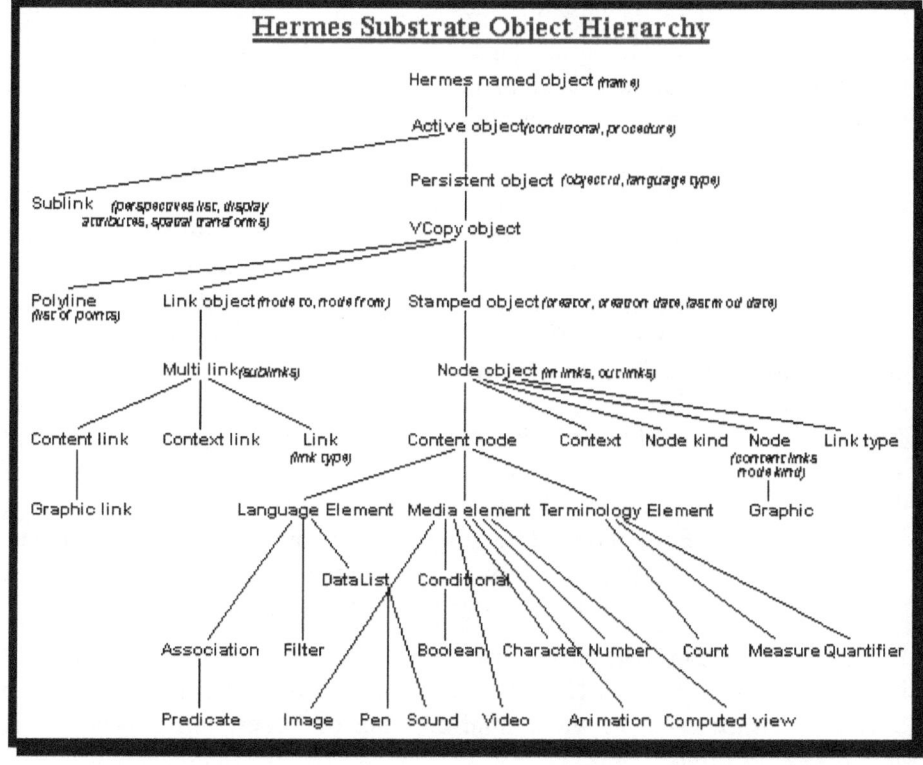

Figure 8-2. The HERMES substrate object hierarchy.

The *Active object* adds two features that provide considerable power for the advanced user: conditionals and procedures. Any object that inherits these (for instance, all varieties of nodes and links and language elements) can be made conditional upon a language expression or can incorporate an arbitrary procedure. A conditional can be any boolean expression defined in the HERMES language. When an object with this conditional is encountered in traversing the hypermedia, the conditional is evaluated. If it evaluates to true, then the link can be traversed or the node evaluated and displayed, otherwise, the object is ignored. A procedure is a user-defined procedure written in any commercial programming language that supports WINDOWS dynamic link libraries (DLLs), e.g., PASCAL or C++. HERMES includes a DLL with ten procedure identifiers, so that users can define and compile up to ten procedures. The procedure identifiers can then be attached to HERMES objects. When the object is encountered during hypermedia traversal, the procedure is run. This mechanism of procedural attachment has also been used internally to implement one of the procedures for the HERMES perspectives mechanism (see the implementation of "lazy virtual copying" in Chapter 9). With these mechanisms, procedures written in either the HERMES language or in a general purpose programming language can be embedded anywhere in the hypermedia database.

Persistent objects can be retrieved from the HERMES database. They have a unique object id, which is used internally for direct random access to the stream on disk. A set of methods for persistent objects defines an efficient database management system that performs buffered reads from disk. Once accessed, objects are cached in memory by these methods since they are likely to be traversed again. For objects that have user-defined names, a B+ index is used to retrieve the internal object id for object retrieval. This means that even when the database is scaled up to millions of objects, any object can be retrieved from disk either by user-defined name or by internal id with no appreciable increase in the number of disk accesses. The index to the stream maintains the node kind of each stored node, so lists of nodes of a given kind can be generated. Similarly, the index of named objects maintains the object type, so lists of named objects of a given language type can be displayed quickly for pick lists in the interface.

VCopy objects can participate in the virtual copying mechanisms that implement perspectives in HERMES. A set of ten object methods (defined in Section 9.2) are used for the virtual copying of nodes, links, hypermedia networks, and subnetworks.

Stamped objects are time-stamped with the name of the person who was logged in when the object was created, the date and time of creation, and the date and time of the last modification. This information is useful for browsing the knowledge base with queries in the language. It can also be used for security systems built on top of HERMES.

Node objects are the "first class objects" of the HERMES hypermedia system. They can all be interconnected in the hypermedia, referred to by the language, and organized into perspectives. This is the basis for the interlinked hypermedia structure. Any node objects can, for instance, have annotations or arbitrary features attached to them. A node object maintains a tree of links coming in to it and a tree of links going out. The trees of links consist of lists of link lists, where each link list contains links of a given link type. This list of lists is sorted by link type. The link lists contain the object ids of the individual links. This structure makes for efficient access of a node's links for traversal and language expression evaluation.

Links are stored independently of the nodes that they connect, because they may contain considerable data and may be accessed, traversed, or modified without needing to read in their attached nodes (which may be very large for bitmaps, video, etc.). A link consists of a list of *sublinks*, which maintain information about perspectives, display attributes (e.g., color, font), and spatial transforms (e.g., scaling or rotation for 3-D graphics). By combining a list of sublinks between a given two nodes into one link rather than having multiple links between the same two nodes, the number of links that need to be read in from memory is minimized. Combining all links between two nodes is important because there may be very bushy trees of sublinks due to the perspectives mechanism's implementation. For many functions, one needs to look at all or many of the sublinks. Also, often one only wants to cross one sublink of a link (the first one), otherwise one would get multiple copies; this is efficiently done with a for-each or for-first method on a list of sublinks.

Contexts, node kinds, and *link types* are very simple node objects. They just have user-defined names. Contexts are linked in a hierarchy that defines the perspectives and their inheritance relations (see Chapter 9). Node kinds and link types can have synonyms defined. When they are created, the HERMES interface suggests a plural form to be defined as a synonym. This is useful for making language expressions smoothly readable.

Nodes have no content themselves. Rather, they have content links that connect them to content nodes that contain the content (e.g., characters, numbers, language elements). This separation of the named nodes from their content is useful and efficient in a number of ways. It allows a given node to have multiple contents. It may have a different content in different perspectives; it may have several contents of the same or different media; or it may be part of a hierarchy of graphical objects, from a complex lunar habitat, through its components and subcomponents, down to its ultimate polylines of points in 3-D space. The separation of nodes and contents allows perspectives information (as well as display attributes and spatial transforms) to be stored in the intervening links. There are also accessing efficiencies that result from the separation.

Content nodes provide the knowledge representation media. The *language elements* and *terminology elements* are explained in Chapter 10 and in Appendix C. The *media elements* provide the various media required for supporting design. These media elements are traditional objects of hypermedia systems. However, as part of the HERMES substrate their retrieval, modification, display, and analysis take place through mechanisms that are standardized across components, allow integration, are fine-grained, are organized in perspectives, provide for plasticity, and are computed dynamically.

8.3. Lunar Habitat Design Environments

This section will indicate how design environments built on top of HERMES can achieve goals that have long been set for JANUS and PHIDIAS but not previously achieved. In particular, it will argue that the combination of a powerful, integrated hypermedia substrate, a perspectives mechanism, and an end-user language facilitate the desired functionality.

Figure 8-3 shows a screen view of five open windows that are typical of the HERMES interface. This screen view is taken from a prototype Lunar Habitat Design Environment (LHDE) built on top of HERMES. From left to right, the windows are:

1. A control dialog for navigating hypermedia. It shows the selection of the discussion predicate for navigating the out-going links from an issue, "What are the design considerations for bunks?" Discussion is an expression in the HERMES end-user programming language, defined as an indented hierarchy of issues, subissues, answers, and arguments. The results of the query, discussion of the selected issue, is displayed in the next window.

2. The Design Rationale window shows the results of the query evaluated in the *privacy* perspective. The query was defined in the previous control dialog window by choosing a predicate relevant to the `issue` link type going out of the selected issue.

3. The Critique window displays the result of the critics analyzing the construction of a lunar habitat. The critics were evaluated as defined within the privacy perspective. The user initiated critiquing with a button (not shown) in the next window.

4. The Drawing window or construction area displays the current design. This window has buttons (not shown in the Figure) to change perspective, save the drawing in the current context, navigate links connected to the drawing (its rationale), and critique the construction.

5. The Context selection window (partially shown) allows the user to change to a new interpretive perspective in the context hierarchy. This affects contents of textual nodes, definitions of elements of the language used for expressing queries and critics, and contents of drawings.

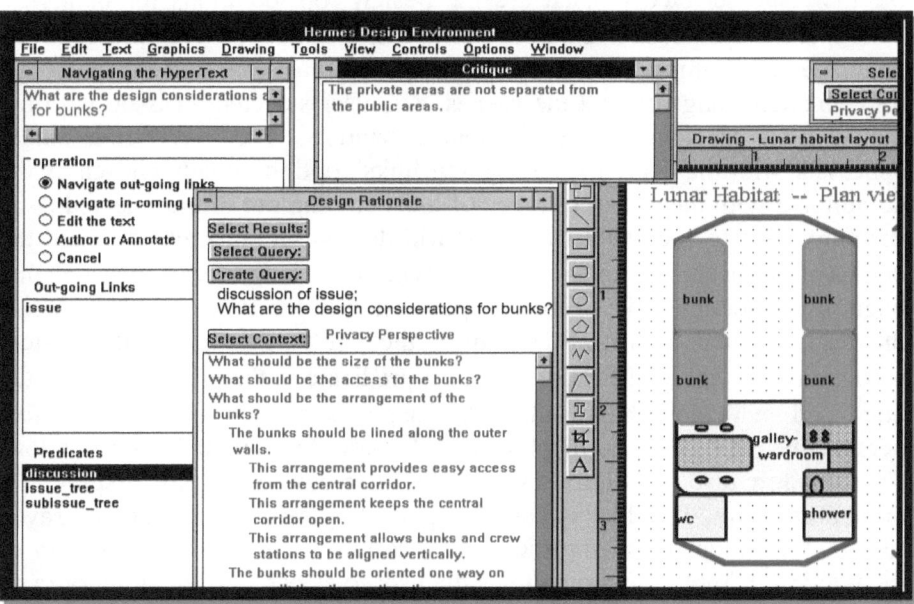

Figure 8-3. A screen view of the LHDE interface.

In this interface to LHDE, one can see a 2-D graphical construction area similar to that of JANUS and PHIDIAS. Subsequently, a version of PHIDIAS II has been built on top of the HERMES substrate by researchers in the College of Environmental Design's CAD lab. It features a very general 3-D construction area, which can be viewed from any angle and distance. It allow a designer to move through the design space and view things at greater or less distance. The LHDE interface shown in Figure 8-3 has a palette of simple geometric shapes along the left edge of the drawing window. The PHIDIAS II interface has palettes of chairs, tables, etc. specifically for lunar habitat designs. In both cases, the palettes are "hard-wired" and cannot be modified by end-users. However, this is not necessary when using the HERMES substrate. Instead, one could define an expression in the language to display a palette. This has not been done because PHIDIAS II's 3-D graphics system is not yet fully integrated with the HERMES substrate. The advantages of an integrated approach will be discussed below.

The LHDE interface shows a view of design rationale. This is dynamically displayed based on the results of the language expression, `discussion of` the issue selected ("What are the design considerations for bunks?"). Note that the system user did not have to worry about "programming" in the language. Everything was done by direct manipulation, and the language implemented things behind the scenes. The user selected an issue with the mouse in a previous Design Rationale window. The Navigation dialog appeared, with the "Navigate out-going links" option already chosen as the default and with the names of types of links coming out of the selected issue (namely, `issue`, i.e., subissues) listed in the Out-going Links box and the names of predicates "relevant" to those types (i.e., language expressions that begin by traversing links of those types) listed in the Predicates box. When the user selected `discussion` from the list of Predicates, the system automatically applied the `discussion` predicate to the previously selected node and evaluated the resulting language expression within the active perspective. The result is displayed in the new Design Rationale window. That window also has buttons so that the user can modify the display in a number of ways. The display can be replaced by selecting previously saved results. (A button for saving the current results is located at the bottom of the window.) Another button allows the user to select a different query to be evaluated; it displays a list of all defined queries. A third button allows the user to create a new query. This is the point where something like programming may enter, although the interface for the language encourages reuse and modification of previously defined expressions (see Chapter 10).

Finally, a last button allows the user to select a different perspective, thereby changing the display.

The PHIDIAS II interface provides an alternative display mode for design rationale and similar displays. Rather than showing an entire indented structure, it displays the top level of the outline form only (the unindented nodes). Every node that has hidden indented material is indicated with a small icon. Clicking on that icon displays the next level of indentation under that node. (This is similar to file directory displays in the Macintosh SYSTEM 7 and WINDOWS 3.1.) What is interesting here is that this mechanism is implemented with the HERMES language, not in a hard-wired, programmed-in way. That is, clicking on a node's icon causes the evaluation of the expression, `all associations` of that node in the result list. The availability of the language made it easy to implement this interface feature, and ensures that the feature can be flexibly modified by simply modifying the definition of the language expression (which does not require recompilation) and can be done by an end-user.

The critics in LHDE are passive agents, similar to the triggers in PHIDIAS. That is, the user must press a button to evaluate the critic rules. In LHDE, the critic rules are expressions in the language. (See Chapter 10 for the LHDE version of JANUS' kitchen critics and for an analysis of privacy critics for lunar habitats.) No additional mechanisms are necessary because the language is designed to traverse and analyze the hypermedia representations of the design situation. In PHIDIAS II, the triggers for displaying design rationale on the selection and location of palette items is implemented using the HERMES language. For instance, the trigger for selection of chairs evaluates the expression, `discussion of chair selection issue`. As `discussion` is defined in the LHDE seed, this goes to the issue named `chair selection issue` in the issue base and displays all the related `issues`, `answers`, and `arguments`.

Of course, one could add additional components to a design environment built on HERMES. For instance, one could make critics fire automatically when a design unit they were defined for is moved, as in JANUS. One could define specification linking mechanisms as in KID, or formalization mechanisms as in X-NETWORK. Even if these mechanisms were borrowed from other systems, the HERMES substrate would pay off. Critic rules would still be defined in the HERMES language, without having to be programmed in LISP, and they could be associated with design units via general-purpose hypermedia links instead of special mechanisms. The specification linking would be greatly simplified in LHDE by defining domain distinctions as well as critic rules in the HERMES language, and then using the language to traverse the specification hypertext. Even the formalization mechanisms would be aided by using the HERMES language for formulating queries (as suggested in Chapter 7) and for providing a medium of formal (computer understandable) expression. The perspectives feature would also come in handy, allowing different versions of critics to be organized into perspectives and using these perspectives for making their critics more specific to the situation corresponding to that perspective (perhaps obviating the need for a separate specification mechanism).

The most important benefit of the HERMES substrate is the synergy possible with the hypermedia network, the perspectives organization, and the language expressivity. For instance, the HERMES substrate provides a useful basis for finally achieving the goals proposed as "future work" in the classic JANUS paper (Fischer, McCall, Morch, 1989), as discussed in the following paragraphs:

> (1) Within the argumentation system there is a pressing need for authoring to be integrated with browsing. (2) Allowing ad hoc authoring during browsing would enable the designer to annotate the issue base, record decisions on issues and generally personalize the argumentation. (3) This in turn would create the need for certain basic kinds of inference mechanisms. (4) For example, if the designer has rejected the answer "dining area" to the issue "What functional areas should the kitchen contain?" then the system should probably not display any issues, answers or arguments that presuppose or assume that the kitchen has a dining area.

> (5) Construction and argumentation might usefully be connected in a number of additional ways. (6) Catalog examples could be used to illustrate argumentation, and argumentation could be used to help in selecting examples from the catalog (p.12; sentence numbering added).

(1) Integrating authoring with browsing. In the LHDE interface, authoring is integrated with browsing. At every step of hypermedia browsing, the navigation dialog in Figure 8-3 gives the user a choice of traversing out-going links, traversing in-coming (inverse) links, editing the current node or authoring or annotating the node. The editing option brings up an editor appropriate to the medium of the current node, with its content ready to be edited. (In cases of multiple contents, the contents are automatically placed in the editor consecutively.) The authoring option allows the user to create a new node and link it to the current node. Annotation is a typical application of this, where one links a text node to the current node with a link of type annotation. Adding the phrase, `with their annotations,` to a predicate will then include all the attached annotations in a given display. Of course, all authoring in LHDE takes place within the current perspective.

(2) Personalizing the argumentation. The authoring option in LHDE is also used for recording decisions in an issue base. Suppose you are browsing through a series of issues that correspond to the issues in KID's specification component. Then when you come to an `answer` that you wish to accept as a specification for your design, you can author a node that you attach to the `answer` with a `resolution` link. You define its content as the boolean value `true`. (This is easier to do in the LHDE interface than it sounds when described because the separation of nodes from their content is never apparent to the user, and the hypermedia linking is generally transparent.) In favoring the personalizing of the argumentation in the preceding quotation, the developers of JANUS did not consider carefully the implications of having many users "personalizing" the same homogeneous issue base. It is one thing for Rittel to have advocated including the deliberations of half a dozen opposing positions in a single issue base; quite another to accumulate the exploratory thoughts of arbitrarily many users, over long periods of time, following diverse and unrelated interests. This may not be a problem for a single-user system; however, LHDE is intended as a repository for extensive exploration. The perspectives mechanism is an important tool that allows "personalization" to scale up in LHDE and to function in a collaborative setting.

(3) Inference mechanisms. In HERMES, the inference mechanism is not some add-on function, but the embedded language itself. While the language does not allow fully general inference across large sets of production rules, it does allow people to encode dependencies. Conditionals, for instance, are used in a number of ways in LHDE. The evaluation of any object in the database can be made conditional upon an arbitrary expression in the HERMES language that evaluates to `true` or `false`. Queries incorporating such conditional expressions can also be defined as the content of nodes. Another approach is used in LHDE to preface display expressions with conditional expressions, as illustrated in point (4).

(4) Adaptive argumentation. In LHDE one can build up a `dining area conditional` as follows:

```
if resolutions of answers of the functional areas
    issue that contain "dining area" are true.
```

As would be clear when building this expression in the language interface (shown in Chapter 10), the phrase, `that contain "dining area",` is applied to the `answers` of the `functional areas issue` prior to checking if the `resolutions` of the `answers` that pass through that filtering condition have the boolean content, `true`. Once this conditional expression has been defined, it can be used in the variety of ways suggested in point (3). For instance, if the design rationale included the display expression, `discussion of dining area issues`, then that expression could be modified to be: `if dining area conditional then discussion of dining area issues`. This would display the `issues`, `answers`, and `arguments` concerning dining areas if and only if the `dining area answer` of the `functional areas issue` had been resolved in the positive.

(5) Connecting construction and argumentation. Because the HERMES hypermedia substrate integrates the construction graphics and the design rationale text, graphical examples from the catalog can be linked to entries in the issue base. Assume that a particular kitchen layout is linked to an `issue` about dining areas with an `examples` link. Then you can amend the display expression above to include `dining area issues with their examples`. Depending on whether the LHDE or PHIDIAS II interface was being used, either the text and graphics would be inter-mixed in the outline indented form, or the graphic examples would be represented by an icon and clicking on that icon would display the graphic in situ or in another window.

(6) Connecting catalog and argumentation. In LHDE, catalogs are not fixed displays. They are defined by language expressions. These expressions can, of course, be modified with conditionals and other inferencing computations. Following are some sample catalog definitions illustrating a filtering of the content of the displayed catalog based on decisions in the argumentation (i.e., the issue base is treated as a specification component):

```
if dining area conditional then kitchens that contain
    dining areas
if safety is important then kitchens that are safe
if privacy is important then habitats that have parts
    that have privacy ratings
if privacy is important then privacy gradient catalog
```

The first of these evaluates the conditional that was defined earlier. If it is true, then `kitchens` are displayed if they contain subparts that are of node kind `dining areas`. The second makes use of an expression named `safety is important`, that checks the resolution of some issue related to safety. It then evaluates an expression that performs an analysis of kitchen layouts similar to the safety-related subset of JANUS' critics. The third again begins with a specification conditional. It then accesses all habitats in the database. For each habitat, it goes through its subparts to see if any of them have a link of type `privacy rating`. As soon as such a link is found, the habitat is added to the list of items to be displayed. The last expression takes the idea of the third one further, critiquing the separation of parts of a lunar habitat based on the privacy ratings attached to its parts (see Chapter 10 for a detailed analysis of this last expression).

These examples of the synergy possible with the HERMES substrate have emphasized the use of hypermedia linking made possible by an integrated substrate. That is, all the objects inherit common functionality, including the ability to be linked together. The role of the language as a tool for traversing the hypermedia has also been emphasized. Expressions in the language can be defined to relate information from different components of a design environment. The utility of the perspectives mechanism has not been stressed as much. However, it can play a powerful role in personalizing the information, in coordinating sets of specifications, and in promoting collaboration. That theme will be taken up in the next chapter.

CHAPTER 9. INTERPRETIVE PERSPECTIVES FOR COLLABORATION

The HERMES substrate includes a mechanism for organizing knowledge in a design environment into a network of *perspectives*. These perspectives provide support for design as a process of interpretation and deliberation. They allow designers to interpret the design situation according to their individual and group interests. Perspectives provide a mechanism for creating, managing, and selectively activating different sets of design knowledge, such as critics, spatial relations, domain distinctions, palette items, and argumentation, so that alternative ideas can be deliberated and either adopted, rejected, or modified.

The perspectives mechanism organizes all the design information in the knowledge base. A designer always works within a particular perspective. At any time, the designer can select a different perspective by name. When a given perspective is selected ("active") then only information indexed for that perspective (or for a perspective inherited by that perspective) can be accessed, traversed, or displayed.

A new perspective can be created by assigning a name to it and selecting existing perspectives for it to inherit. Perspectives are connected in an inheritance network; a perspective can modify knowledge inherited from its parents or it can add new knowledge. Designers switch perspectives to examine a design from different viewpoints. Switching perspectives changes the currently effective definitions of critics, the terms used in these definitions, and other domain knowledge. For example, imagine that Archie was collaborating with Desi using the HERMES computer system. Then he could create `archie's habitat perspective` and select `desi's habitat perspective` to inherit from. This would allow him to build upon and critique Desi's work, without altering what is viewed by Desi in his perspective.

The organization of information by perspectives encourages users to view knowledge in terms of structured, meaningful categories that they can create and modify. It provides an extensible structure of knowledge contexts that can correspond to categories meaningful in the design domain. This eases the cognitive burden of manipulating potentially large numbers of alternative versions of critics, rationale, graphics, language expression definitions, and other design knowledge.

The perspectives mechanism allows items of knowledge to be bundled in various ways, which can overlap orthogonally or inter-connect. Common types of perspectives are:

* personal and group viewpoints of individual designers and teams

* topical groupings by content traditions (e.g., kitchen design)

* technical aspects by specialties (e.g., plumbing)

* historical versions (e.g., Archie's Monday morning habitat design)

For instance, `archie's habitat perspective` might include considerations specific to Archie's design, as well as incorporating many ideas from Desi's. If Desi and Archie are part of a larger team, then the team's perspective could display concepts and rationale from all its members, or it could select from and modify the knowledge inherited from multiple sources. Archie would also want to inherit knowledge from lunar habitat design traditions and related technical specialties. Then, as his design evolved, Archie could define perspectives for archiving versions of his work.

Lunar habitat design takes advantage of information from many technical disciplines and domain traditions: kitchen and bathroom design, low-gravity and vacuum considerations, electrical and lighting expertise, submarine and Antarctic isolation experiences. It can borrow selectively from both space station and Mars habitat prior designs. Each of these bodies of knowledge can be defined within a network of domains and subdomains that inherit, share, and modify knowledge from each other. Perspectives can also be used to save networks of historical versions of developing designs. The HERMES perspectives mechanism is a general—but hypermedia specific—

implementation of contexts[20] that can be used to supply a variety of functionality to a design environment.

This chapter will present the HERMES perspectives mechanism in three sections. First, Section 9.1 offers a scenario to show how a design team using HERMES might approach the task documented in the protocol analysis of Section 3.2, "Perspectives on Privacy." Second, Section 9.2 describes the techniques used to implement the perspectives mechanism in HERMES. This will detail the hypermedia character of the implementation. Third, Section 9.3 discusses how the perspectives mechanism can provide computer support for cooperative work. This will include examples of interface features for displaying, browsing, and sharing knowledge in multiple perspectives representing different people, interests, or domains.

9.1. A Scenario of Cooperation

The work of lunar habitat designers was studied in order to learn about the work process of innovative cooperative design in a complex domain. Lunar habitat design seems to call for computer support because of the volume of technical information and governmental requirements, as well as because of the other-worldly setting in which the designers' tacit skills may be unreliable. It seemed wise to explore how lunar habitat designers work now without substantial computer support in order to envision new ways to support the old goals and to imagine how computer support would transform the tasks involved.[21]

The episode transcribed in Chapter 3 showed an important turning point in a design process: the application of the concept of privacy to the task at hand. The tacit notion of privacy was eventually operationalized with the idea of

---

[20] The terms *perspective* and *context* will be used interchangeably in this Chapter. Technically, the functionality of perspectives is implemented by defining contexts. As M. Gross suggested, perspectives are similar to the notion of "binding contexts" in programming languages: a definition is bound within the perspective in which it was created.

[21] This "dialectic of tradition and transcendence" in work-oriented design of computer support systems is a central theme of Ehn (1988). The transformation of tasks as a result of computer support is also emphasized by, for instance, Hutchins (1990) and Norman (1993).

defining a privacy gradient, according to which public and private areas of a habitat are distributed based on their privacy ratings. The concept of privacy then provided a paradigmatic example for investigating the design rationale issue-base provided to lunar habitat designers by NASA: the Manned Systems Integration Standards (NASA, 1989a). Here it was seen that this important concept of privacy had largely eluded NASA's extensive efforts to provide propositional rules for the design of space-based habitation. Although privacy was acknowledged to be an important issue, NASA failed to provide support for designers to take privacy into account.

The present section will build on the discussion in the transcript and the critic definitions to show how HERMES can respond to the challenge of providing computer support for considerations of privacy. A scenario will show how lunar habitat designers could use the HERMES system to define a powerful set of privacy critics using the hypermedia links, perspectives, and language of HERMES. The detailed explanation of how the critics are evaluated by the system will be saved for Chapter 10.

Desi's perspective. Suppose that instead of sitting down together with pencil and paper, Desi and Archie had been part of a team that worked in a design environment built on the HERMES substrate. Desi, Archie, and two other team members (Phyllis and Sophia) are asked to design a lunar habitat for four astronauts to live in for 45 days. They decide to take turns working on the design in HERMES, starting with Desi.

Desi begins creating a perspective for his new work, which he names desi's habitat perspective. He defines this perspective to include (inherit) the information collected in a number of specialties and domains that he considers relevant to the design task. Then he selects two other lunar habitat perspectives and copies individual items of graphics and design rationale out of them for the lunar habitat shell, bunk-bed crew compartments, and a wardroom (dining and meeting room) arrangement. He inserts these into design rationale and graphics in his perspective. Then he adds some rectangles to represent the bathroom and galley (kitchen). The resulting layout is shown in Figure 9-1 (reproduced from Figure 3-2 of Section 3.2).

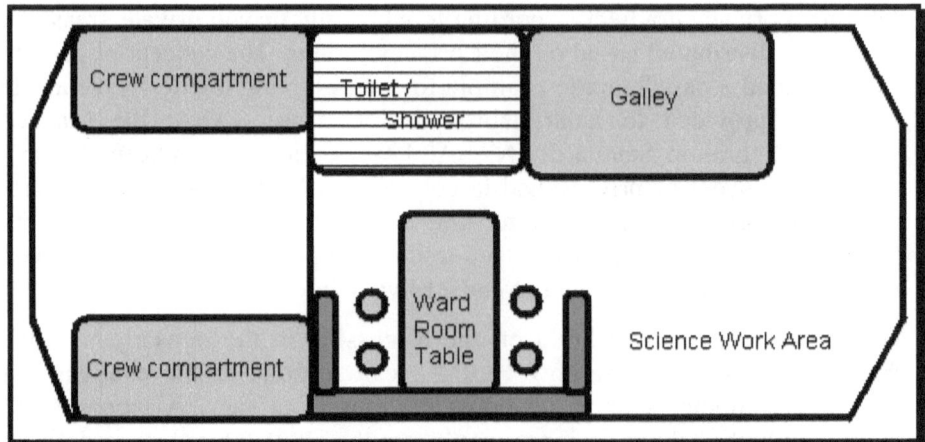

Figure 9-1. Desi's lunar habitat design.

An initial sketch has been proposed for the design team to work on.

The main functional areas of the habitat have been laid out in this sketch. This is an initial design concept. Because other team members will be reviewing this design and wondering why things are arranged the way they are, Desi adds some design rationale, arguing that the bathroom and galley have all been placed together in a "wet wall" configuration to minimize plumbing arrangements. Desi feels his design provides a good start for the team and he goes off to work on other projects.

Archie's perspective. Archie is interested to see what Desi has designed and to critique it from his own viewpoint. However, he does not want to destroy Desi's version. So Archie defines archie's habitat perspective as a new perspective and lists desi's habitat perspective as its inherited perspective. This means that Archie will start off with everything that is in Desi's perspective, but as he makes changes to it the changes will only be in effect within Archie's perspective and not within Desi's. The inheritance is active in the sense that if Desi subsequently modifies something in his perspective that Archie has not changed in his then the modification will show up in Archie's perspective as well (unlike if Archie had simply made his own copy of Desi's design at some given time).

Archie also inherits a number of additional perspectives with useful technical information. The hierarchy of perspectives incorporated in Archie's perspective—including those he inherits via Desi's perspective—are pictured in Figure 9-2.

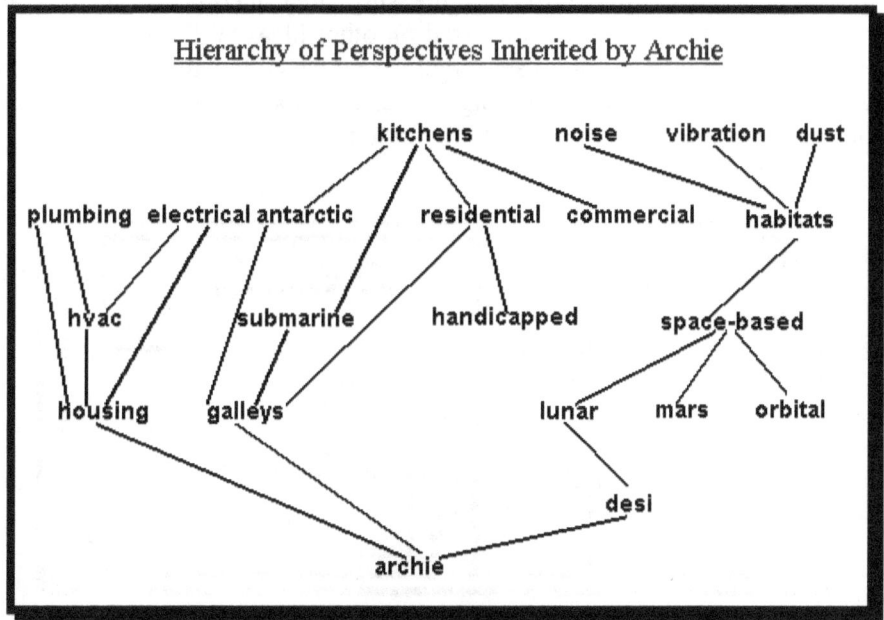

Figure 9-2. The hierarchy of perspectives inherited by Archie.

Note that Archie has access via Desi's perspective to information in the lunar, space-based, habitats, noise, vibration, and dust perspectives, as well as additional information related to housing and galleys.

Archie is concerned with spatial adjacencies. He likes the way the crew compartments have been separated from the rest of the habitat to provide relief from the daily activity. However, he dislikes the acoustic proximity of the toilet (which flushes loudly) to the beds. Even worse, he finds the opening of the bathroom into the eating and gathering area potentially offensive. Archie is unsure of how to handle the bathroom, so he switches to a perspective that he has not inherited, the perspective for residential (terrestrial) bathrooms and browses the issue-base section on the design and placement of bathrooms. This perspective inherits from several other cultural and domain perspectives, including European perspectives. Here he finds the idea that showers and toilets have rather different location and adjacency considerations in the European tradition.

Applying these ideas in his mind to how he projects life in the habitat, Archie concludes that the shower should be near the sleep areas, but the toilet should be near the other end of the habitat, by the entrance. Moving the shower gives him the idea of elaborating the separation of the sleeping and working areas by forming a dressing area incorporating personal stowage. He redesigns the galley based on other ideas he finds and feels he has reached a stopping point. (See Figure 9-3.) He copies the rationale from the bathroom perspective concerning the separate location of the shower and toilet, revising the rationale to apply to the lunar habitat.

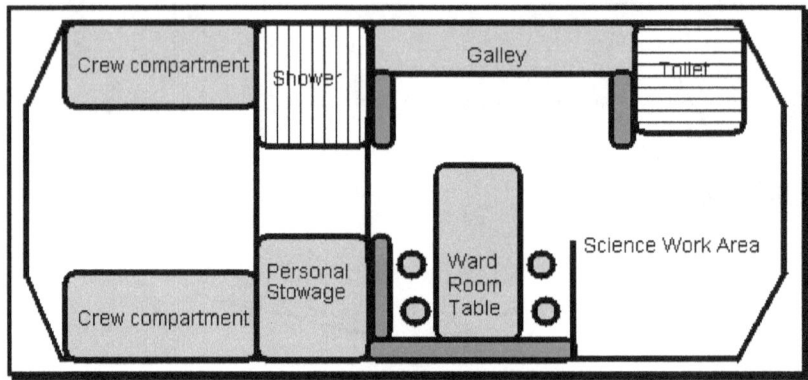

Figure 9-3. Archie's lunar habitat design.

The toilet and shower functions have been separated using the European perspective on bathroom design.

Archie revises the design rationale for the habitat. Within his perspective, he can modify or add to (annotate or author) anything in the issue bases he has inherited from Desi or from the other domains. He does this in preparation for the up-coming team meeting. Before the meeting, the team members each review Archie's design and its rationale by displaying it in HERMES. First, they discuss the over-all design. They like the creation of the dressing area between the shower and the personal stowage, but argue that it blocks traffic flow. A consensus is reached when Phyllis drags the dressing area to the other side of the crew compartments in the HERMES construction area.

As a group they deliberate about the issues in Archie's rationale section and agree that habitation issues must be the primary focus of their designing on this project. In particular, privacy is a key concept. In order to make the notion of privacy operational for evaluation by interpretive critics, they decide to label the parts of the habitat with privacy ratings. They agree on the following scale with values from 1 to 9:

```
very public:          1
quite public:         2
public:               3
somewhat public:      4
neutral:              5
somewhat private:     6
private:              7
quite private:        8
very private:         9
```

They define a link type, `privacy rating`, and use this type to link each area of the habitat to a node with one of the above numeric values (or their equivalent label). This process is facilitated by the HERMES interface: clicking on an area like the shower in the habitat brings up the same *Navigating the Hypertext* dialog seen in Figure 8-3 (in Section 8.3). Selecting the *Author or Annotate* option allows them to define a new numeric node with the value 8 or `quite private` and to connect it to the shower with a `privacy rating` link automatically. Figure 9-4 below shows the lunar habitat design the team has come up with, labeled with the agreed upon `privacy ratings`.

At the end of the meeting, Sophia and Phyllis agree to develop a suite of privacy critics that can be used for this and future lunar habitat design assignments.

Sophia's perspective. Sophia sets up her perspective to inherit all of Archie's work (and, indirectly, Desi's). Now Sophia must define the terminology to be used in her critics. She is interested in determining problem areas in which private areas are too near to public areas. By "too near", Sophia decides she means less than five feet. So she defines a "Measure" in the HERMES language named `too near` as:

```
closest distance is less than 5 feet
```

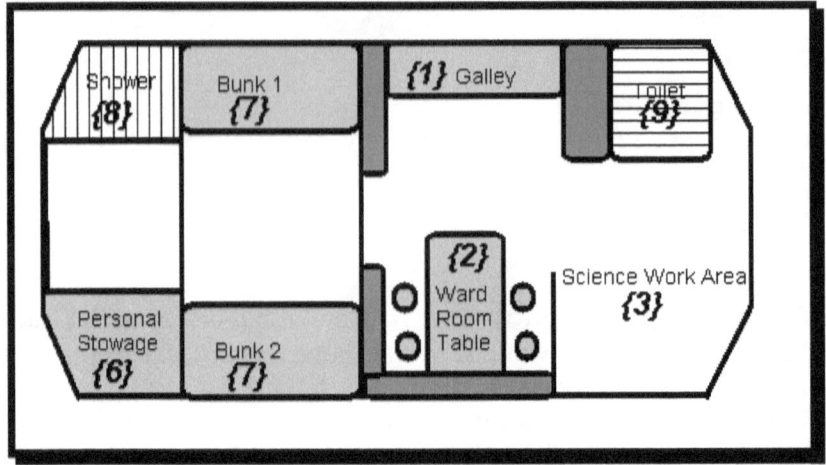

Figure 9-4. Archie's lunar habitat with its privacy ratings.

Then, she defines public and private areas in terms of the ends of the privacy scale:

```
public area: parts that have privacy ratings that are
    less than somewhat public
private areas: parts that have privacy ratings that
    are more than somewhat private
```

Next she defines the problem areas she is concerned with using these terms:

```
problem areas: private areas with public areas of
    that (last subject) that are too near those items
```

Then, Sophia defines a message for her critic to display if no problem areas are found:

```
privacy message: "Public and private areas are
    separated."
```

Finally, she can define her `privacy check` critic:

```
name with either name of problem areas or privacy
    message
```

This critic, `privacy check`, is a predicate that can be applied to any node or list of nodes in the database. When Sophia applies it to her lunar habitat design, it lists the name of the design and then lists all the `problem` areas in the habitat by their names; if no problem areas are found, it displays the privacy message. Figure 9-5 shows the output from applying privacy check to the design of archie's lunar habitat shown in Figure 9-4:

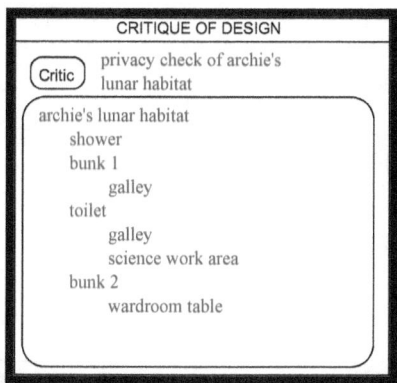

Figure 9-5. Output from the privacy check critic.

Note that all private areas are listed by name. Under each of them are the public areas that are too near to them. The way this critic is defined it supports the designer's review of the information. Sophia gets a complete listing of private areas from which she can check just what problematic adjacencies each has so she can also make sure the critic is doing exactly the computation she wants it to.

Debugging of critics is an important process, particularly since much of the computation is implicit in the language expressions. The privacy check is a fairly complex critic that Sophia has developed and debugged gradually. Once she is sure it is working, she can use it as a basis for more complicated evaluations. For instance, the display of the lunar habitat design in HERMES does not actually include the privacy ratings that were shown in Figure 9-4. So Sophia decides she wants to print these values out along with the listing of areas. To do this, she defines a new critic that prints out both the name and the privacy rating of each listed area:

```
privacy display: name and privacy ratings of problem
    areas
```

The result of applying this critic to `archie's lunar habitat` is shown in Figure 9-6. (The names of the `privacy ratings` are shown in **bold**.)

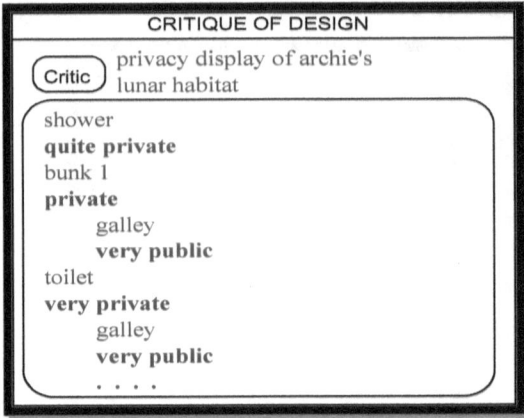

Figure 9-6. Output from the privacy display critic.

Now that Sophia has gotten her critics working the way she wants them to, she decides to make them general enough to apply to lists of objects. Then, as more habitats are developed in the HERMES database and are labeled with privacy values, designers can use Sophia's privacy critics to display catalogs of interesting habitats. This is illustrated in Figure 9-7. This way Sophia can quickly find examples of problem areas in past habitat designs to help her deliberate about when such adjacencies might in fact be acceptable.

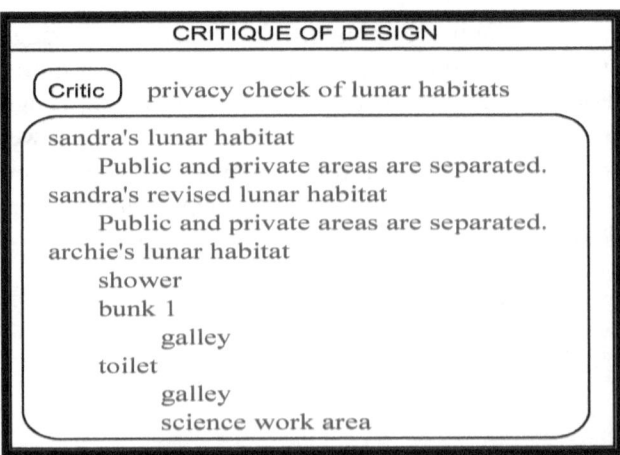

Figure 9-7. The privacy check critic applied to a list of all lunar habitats

Phyllis' perspective. Phyllis is a super-user of the HERMES language. To test its power, she tries to define a critic that involves a complex series of computations. By using an advanced feature of the language (explained in Section 10.3 below), she succeeds. Phyllis recalls previous discussions between Desi and Archie (from Chapter 3) that proposed the concept of a privacy gradient. That meant that the arrangement of the habitat should gradually change from private areas to public areas. To operationalize this notion, Phyllis introduces a test to see if any two areas of the habitat that are near each other differ in their privacy values by more than two.

Phyllis defines the following set of definitions to compute `problem parts` in her sense:

```
are incompatible: have privacy ratings that are more
    than privacy ratings of that (last subject) + 2 or
    are less than privacy ratings of that (last
    subject) -2
too near: closest distance is less than 3 feet
other parts: parts of inverse parts that do not equal
    that (last subject)
problem parts: name and privacy ratings of other
    parts that are too near that (last subject) and
    that are incompatible
```

These definitions illustrate the limits of the HERMES language, calling upon advanced features of the language that only experienced users of HERMES would feel comfortable using to create new expressions. The wording of some of Phyllis' expressions are no longer intuitive because their computations refer outside of the expressions used to define them. In fact, the wording in such cases is designed to interrupt tacit understanding and to stimulate reflection on the explicit computational relations. Fortunately, this complexity is generally encapsulated in the names of the expressions so future users need not always be concerned with it.

Note that Phyllis has defined a measure with the same name (`too near`) as one of Sophia's, but with a different value. This is not a problem since they are working in independent perspectives (even though they inherit much of the same information from other perspectives.)

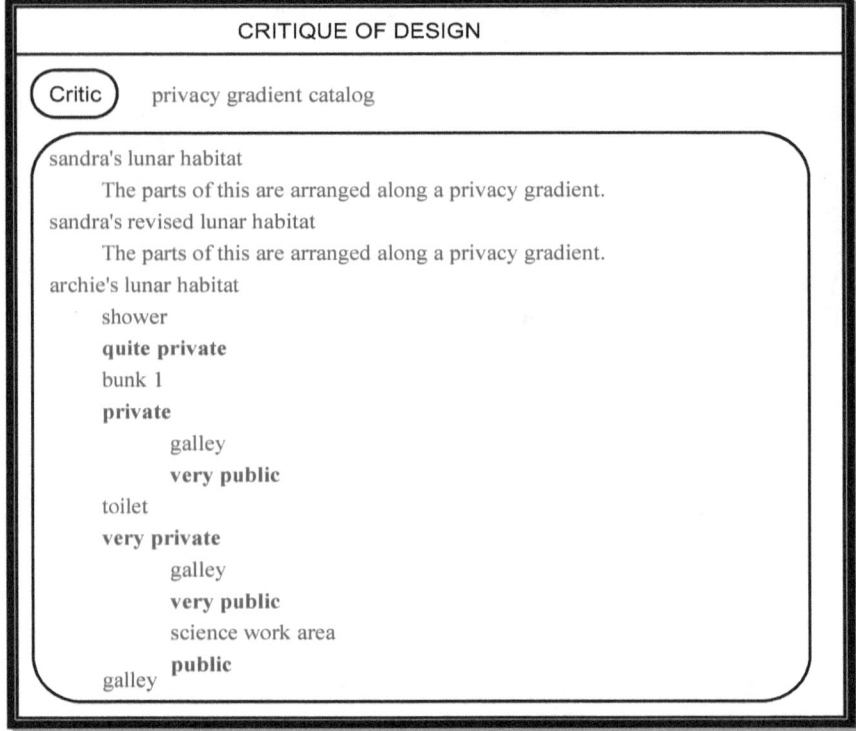

Figure 9-8. Output from the privacy gradient catalog expression.

To complete the `privacy gradient critique`, Phyllis defines a format for listing problem parts and she specifies a message for the case in which no problem parts are found in a habitat:

```
privacy gradient listing: name and privacy ratings
    with problem parts
privacy gradient message: "The parts of this design
    are arranged along a privacy gradient."
privacy gradient critique: either privacy gradient
    listing of parts or privacy gradient message
```

Like Sophia, Phyllis wants to apply her critique to all `habitats` in the database. Note that in the following definition for this procedure Phyllis first filters the list of `habitats` to just those for which `privacy ratings` have been defined. This produces a list of habitats for which issues of designing for privacy are most likely to have been thought through and to provide relevant ideas and rationale.

For these habitats, it is indicated which meet the criteria of following a privacy gradient and where the problem areas are in those that do not. A sample result is shown in Figure 9-8. Here is Phyllis' final critic rule or display expression, `privacy gradient catalog`:

```
name with privacy gradient critique of habitats that
    have parts that have privacy ratings
```

The team perspective. When the team comes back together, they are enthusiastic about the power of the privacy critics to automate some complex analysis of habitats for them. Desi says, "I never tried to define anything in the HERMES language; I just make little adjustments to the display definitions and critics that I find already in the system. They usually meet my needs. But these new critics do things I could never do before. And I think I understand them well enough to use them and maybe even tweak them." "Yeah," chimed in Archie, "I never used the advanced syntax options for dealing with graphics and distances. Maybe I can learn how to do that by playing around with these privacy critics. Can you put them all in a perspective where we can experiment with them?"

Sophia was happy to oblige: "Sure. The thing we need to be careful about is the definition of `too near`, because Phyllis and I disagree on that. Let's make the default for that 5 feet, okay?" She created a perspective called `lunar habitat design team` that anyone could inherit from to experiment with the critics or to pursue their design work further. She had the new perspective inherit from both the `sophia perspective` and the `phyllis perspective`, making sure she listed the `sophia perspective` first so that its definitions would override in case of conflicts, as with the definition of the expression `too near`.

Figure 9-9 shows the dialog box for creating the new perspective. Figure 9-10 shows the new hierarchy of defined perspectives.

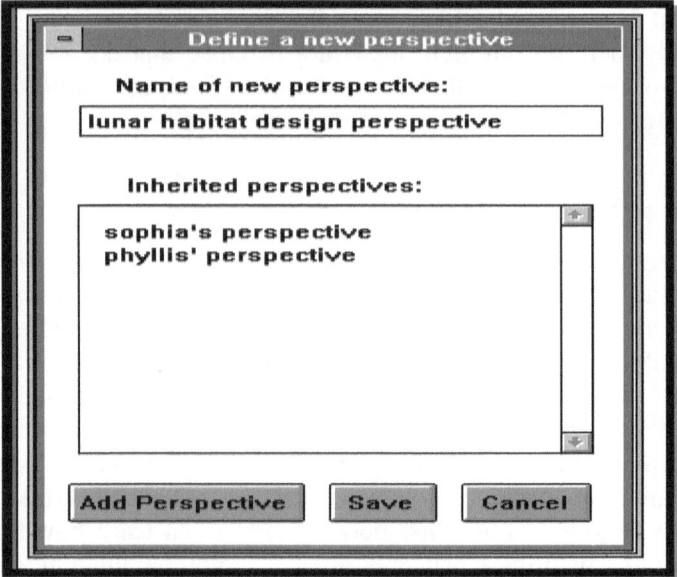

Figure 9-9. Creating a new perspective.

9.2. A Hypermedia Implementation of Perspectives

This section discusses the implementation of the HERMES perspectives mechanism. The ten methods discussed below are used by the HERMES substrate internally. The user never needs to know how they work. Even people who build design environment components on top of the HERMES substrate do not need to be concerned with the details, but can simply call the methods. The purpose of this section is to describe some of the computation that takes place behind the scenes every time a designer retrieves, displays, navigates, modifies, critiques, or analyzes information in the system. It is an example of the active computation that supports the user's tacit design work.

As suggested in Chapter 7, the perspectives (or, equivalently, contexts) mechanism in HERMES is loosely based on the virtual copying of networks approach proposed by Mittal, et al. (1986) and the general copy-on-write technique discussed by Fitzgerald and Rashid (1986). More particularly, it was proposed by McCall (1991/92) for application to hierarchical networks of domain rationale in PHIDIAS. In HERMES, the perspectives mechanism has been expanded and generalized so that all information (e.g., graphics and other media, as well as definitions of language expressions) is accessible relative to the perspectives.

There are two parts to the perspectives mechanism. First, there is a hierarchy of defined perspectives that is maintained as a network of (context) nodes and (context) links. Second, every link in the hypermedia database contains lists specifying which perspectives may or may not be active for the link to be traversed. The question as to what perspective is the "active" one at any given time is answered by reference to a value maintained by the HERMES application.

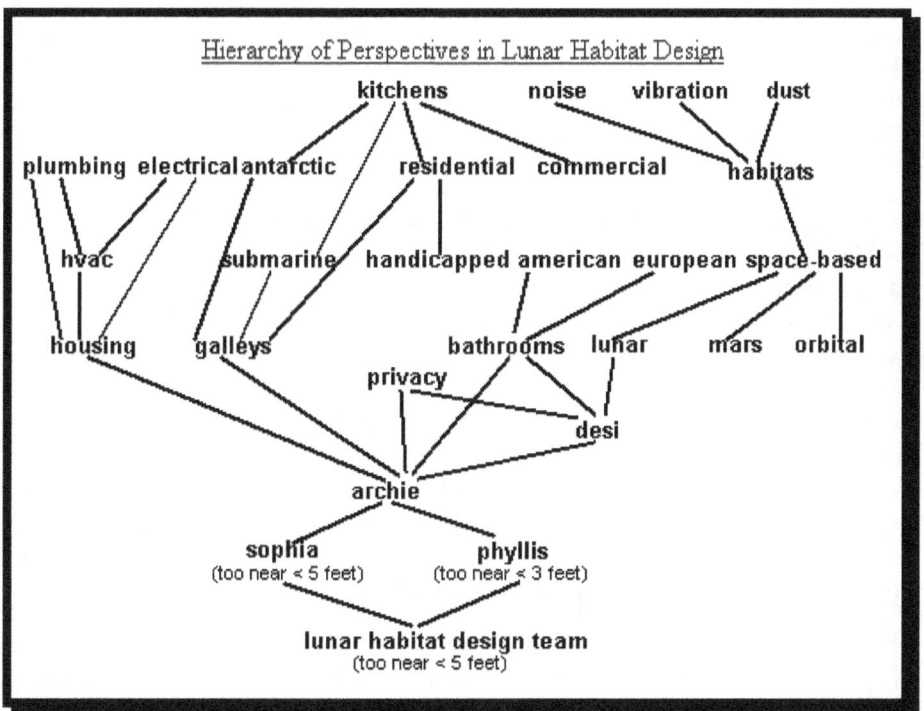

Figure 9-10. Hierarchy of perspectives inherited by the team.

The hierarchy of perspectives is quite simple. It looks much like the nodes and links pictured in Figure 9-10. When a new perspective is defined by a user through a dialog box like that in Figure 9-9, a new context node is created. It is linked to the context nodes it inherits from by a simple context link. As discussed in Chapter 8, context nodes and links are like regular nodes and links except that they have no node kinds or link types. Context nodes have just their names and their links to other contexts. Like any node in HERMES, they can be time-stamped and they can be linked to annotations or other attributes. This linking can be used for documentation or to implement security systems that restrict movement from one perspective to another. However, in the normal HERMES system all information can be accessed by all users; it is organized in perspectives to support timely access. Traversal of the context hierarchy is similar to normal hypermedia traversal, but it has been optimized for efficiency.

Links in HERMES consist of multiple sublinks between a given pair of nodes. Each sublink maintains four items related to the perspectives mechanism: (1) the original context in which the link was created, (2) a list of added contexts in which the link can also be traversed, (3) a list of deleted contexts in which the link should not be traversed, and (4) a "switch" context to which the active perspective should be changed when the link is traversed. This information supports ten methods for the virtual copying of nodes, links, or hypermedia networks, as discussed in this section.

When the system wants to traverse a link, it tests to see if any of the link's sublinks can be traversed. The test proceeds as follows: (a) If the currently active perspective or any of its inherited ancestors matches a context on the deleted list (3), then the sublink cannot be traversed. (b) If the currently active perspective or any of its inherited ancestors matches the original context (1) or a context on the added list (2), then the sublink can be traversed. If there is a switch context (4), then when the link is traversed the active perspective must be changed to the switched context. The inherited ancestors are checked through a breadth-first recursive search with a check for cycles in the inheritance network. Conflicts from multiple inheritance have no consequence since there is no content to the context nodes, the first match halts the search, and alternative paths are equivalent.

Recall from Chapter 8 that named nodes are separated from their contents. So, links connect pairs of named nodes and they also connect named nodes with their content. Because the contexts are checked during link traversal, they control both which named nodes are connected in the active perspective and what contents go with a given named node in that perspective. This is why it is possible for a given named node (e.g., the language expression named "too near") to have different contents (different definitions) in different perspectives.

The following suite of ten methods implement the creation, deletion, and modification of links, nodes, and contents relative to perspectives. They are defined as object methods for VCopy nodes (see Section 8.2). They provide the following functions:

1. Copy the information from one context (perspective) into another.

2. Delete one node in a context that descends from another context.

3. Modify one node in a context that descends from another context.

4. Delete one link in a context that descends from another context.

5. Modify one link in a context that descends from another context.

6. Physically copy one node from one context into another context.

7. Virtually copy one node from one context into another context.

8. Reuse a subnetwork from one context in another context.

9. Virtual copy a subnetwork from one context into another context.

10. Lazy virtual copy a subnetwork from one context into another context.

Method 1: copy an entire context. Given the foregoing apparatus, the ten virtual copying methods can be explained. The simplest is to just copy all the contents of one perspective into a new perspective. For instance, Archie wanted to make his own copy of everything that was visible in Desi's perspective. This is done by defining the new perspective and having it inherit from the old one. Then, when the system checks a link to a node or to a node's contents when the new context is the active one, it will start by trying to match the new context and then will try to match its ancestors. The old context is its ancestor, so a match will be found when the new context is active if and only if it would have been found when the old context was active. Therefore, the same nodes and contents will be visible to Archie as to Desi. Of course, once Archie starts adding, modifying, or deleting nodes or links in his perspective, sublinks will start being labeled with Archie's new context and this will introduce changes between the two perspectives.

This approach is called *virtual copying* because the effect is to make it seem that all the information from one perspective has been copied into the other perspective. However, nothing has in fact been physically copied in the database. In fact, no nodes or links have been changed at all, except the addition of the new context node and its links in the perspectives inheritance hierarchy. Physical changes to the nodes and links only take place when there are changes made to the virtual copies. That is, if Archie deletes or modifies a node or link that was originally created by Desi, then changes must be made to ensure that the modifications or deletions show up in Archie's perspective but not in Desi's. On the other hand, if Desi changes something that has not been altered by Archie, then these changes should show up in both perspectives. Under many circumstances, his last point is an advantage of virtual copying over physical copies—in addition to the great savings of memory and time.

The next four methods are for handling deletions or modifications to virtual copies in a descendant perspective.

Method 2: delete a node in a descendant context. To delete a node, simply add the name of the current perspective to the delete list of the sublink. For instance, to delete in Archie's perspective a named node or a content node that was virtual copied from Desi's perspective, leave its original context (Desi's) alone and add Archie's perspective to the delete list of the sublink of the link leading to the node. Then when traversal of that link is attempted in Archie's perspective, the delete list will prohibit the traversal, although it will still be permitted in Desi's perspective.

Method 3: modify a node in a descendant context. To modify a node, first create a physical copy of it in the new perspective and link it with a new link labeled with the current perspective as its original context. Then delete the old node in the perspective using method 2. Suppose Desi had defined `too near` as `closest distance is less then 5 feet` and Archie modified it to `closest distance is less then 3 feet`; the result is shown in Figure 9-11.

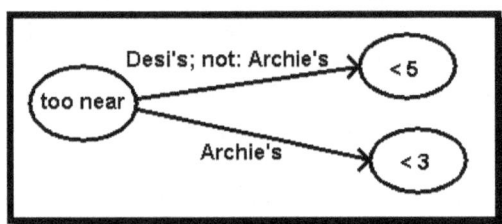

Figure 9-11. The result of modifying the virtual copy of a node.

Method 4: delete a link in a descendant context. This is identical to method 2. To make it so that a link will not be traversed in the descendent context is to make the linked node effectively deleted in that context.

Method 5: modify a link in a descendant context. This is similar to method 3, although no changes to nodes are made. Rather a new sublink of the original link is created. The original sublink and the new sublink are labeled as were the two links in method 3 (and Figure 9-11). Now there are two routes through the link to the node. One will be crossed in the ancestor context(s) the other in the descendent context.

Recall that display attributes and spatial transforms are stored in the sublinks, so which sublink gets traversed can make a significant difference in how the node at the end of the link is displayed. For instance, the node could be the graphics for a brick in a wall. If the wall consists of thousands of identical bricks, it could be made up of thousands of virtual copies of the one graphic node, each reached by a different sublink having different spatial transforms to locate that copy in the wall. Such efficient vector graphics is a major benefit of the virtual copying scheme, although it is not a central concern of this dissertation.

The remaining methods handle cases in which one does not wish to copy an entire perspective, but rather just a single node of a linked network of nodes.

Method 6: physical copy one node into another context. One can always simply make a physical copy of a node from one context to another. The old node is not changed. The link from the new copy of the named node to the new copy of its content is labeled with the new perspective. This option can be used in place of virtual copying in cases where one does not wish the copy to change if its original prototype is changed in its old perspective.

Method 7: virtual copy one node into another context. This method uses the list of added contexts in the sublist. To copy a node from, say, Phyllis' perspective to an independent perspective, like Sophia's, simply add Sophia's perspective to the add list of the link between the node and its content. (The perspective hierarchy in Figure 9-12 is assumed in this and the following methods.)

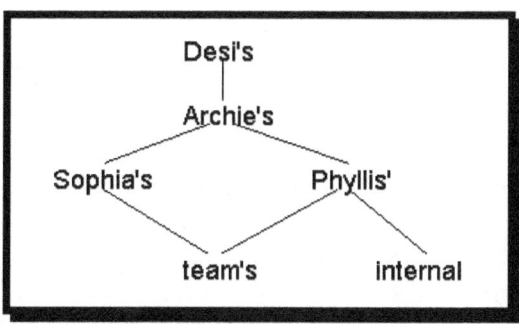

Figure 9-12. An illustrative perspectives hierarchy.

Method 8: reuse a subnetwork in another context. This method uses the switch context in the sublist. To virtual copy a network of nodes in, say, Phyllis' perspective so they can be traversed in an independent perspective like Sophia's, first create a new context and have it inherit from Phyllis' context. This context need not even have a name; since it is used internally, it can always be referenced directly by its internal object id. Although the number of such internally-defined contexts may proliferate with extensive virtual copying, they will never appear to the system users. Then create a link from where you want to enter this subnetwork in Sophia's perspective to the first node you want to traverse to in Phyllis' perspective. This link will have Sophia's perspective as its original context. Define its switch context to be the new internal context as in Figure 9-13. Then, what happens when you traverse this link from Sophia's perspective is that your currently active perspective changes to the internal context. Since this context is a descendant of Phyllis' perspective, you can now freely traverse the subnetwork.

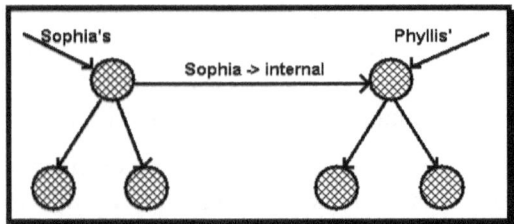

Figure 9-13. Switching contexts to traverse a subnetwork.

The network of nodes on the left is visible in Sophia's perspective; that on the right in Phyllis'. The link between them can be traversed in Sophia's perspective, but it switches the active perspective to an internally defined descendent of Phyllis' perspective so that the right-hand network will be visible.

Method 9: virtual copy a subnetwork into another context. This method is an extension of method 7 and an alternative to method 8. The disadvantage of this method is that it is more computationally intensive to set up. Whereas method 8 involves just adding an internal context to the perspectives hierarchy and creating a single new link with the switch context, method 9 involves inserting the current context into the add list of a sublist in every link of the subnetwork. If the subnetwork has thousands of nodes linked together, this can be an expensive operation, involving many disk accesses.

Method 10: lazy virtual copy a subnetwork into another context. This is a variation on method 9. Instead of traversing the entire subnetwork and inserting the current perspective into all the sublink add lists at once, only the link to the first node is treated. All links coming out of this node are then marked for future treatment. As each of these links is traversed in the future during normal operations, those links are treated and the links further down in the subnetwork coming out of their nodes are then marked for future treatment. This spreads out the costs and delays them until they are unavoidable. A further advantage is that prior to virtual copying each of the nodes as they are encountered, the user can be queried if the node should actually be included in the new perspective. This allows the user to browse through the network and selectively include just those nodes that are really desirable in the new perspective.

Method 10 uses the procedural attachment technique mentioned in Chapter 8. Every node in the system is capable of having an arbitrary procedure attached to it. The nodes to be treated in the future by method 10 are marked by having the lazy virtual copying procedure attached to them. Then when they are traversed, the procedure is executed and it treats them and their further links appropriately. This is a form of delayed recursion.

The ten methods reviewed here (along with the context hierarchy and the procedure for checking links during attempted traversal) suffice for implementing the HERMES perspectives mechanism. They provide an efficient means for organizing information in over-lapping categories, such as hierarchies of personal and group viewpoints, of technical aspects, and of domain traditions. The virtual copying is also useful for efficient versioning schemes, CAD graphics, and information security systems. The following section will touch on some ways this mechanism can be used to support interpretation in collaborative design.

9.3. Evolving Perspectives

Supporting knowledge evolution. As knowledge in the database grows and changes, it must often be reorganized. The evolution of knowledge means that different designers are adding, deleting, and changing information in different perspectives. In a design environment without perspectives all the growth of knowledge would take place within a single, homogeneous knowledge base. When the organization of this knowledge became disorganized and contradictory it might be necessary for a reseeding process to take place. This could involve specialist programmers or knowledge engineers (that is, people other than the designers who normally use the system) to step in and impose order and consistency. They might extend some of the system functionality as well, but their main task would be to straighten out the organization of knowledge.

In HERMES, the perspectives mechanism can be used by the designers themselves to do some of the reseeding process in an on-going way. They can also use the language to extend the functionality of the system, defining, for instance, new analytic computations.

A paradigmatic task for supporting the evolution of perspectives and their knowledge is the merging of two unrelated perspectives. This was also identified as a critical task by the authors of the perspectives mechanism in the PIE system, reviewed in Chapter 7. In Section 9.1, above, the design team decided to merge the privacy critic work in `phyllis'` `perspective` with that in `sophia's perspective`, creating a new `lunar habitat design team` perspective. This is an example of reorganizing evolved knowledge. The new perspective might also be designated the `privacy perspective`. The point is that multiple independent efforts had created new knowledge in separate perspectives. Because the designers decided that this knowledge belonged together, they created a new category (perspective) for it and reorganized the knowledge accordingly.

Figure 9-14 shows the HERMES interface for doing this. It is similar to the schematic in Figure 9-9. Here, the new perspective is created by assigning it a name. Then existing perspectives are chosen from a pick list (either as a sorted list or a hierarchical tree) to specify what information should be inherited. The inheritance takes place using Method 1 described in Section 9.2. In the particular scenario of Section 9.1, there was a multiple inheritance conflict in the definition of the expression, `too near`. Such conflicts are resolved through a breadth-first search of the inheritance tree. So the version of information in the most immediate ancestor perspective takes precedence. In case of two ancestors at the same level, the one named first in the dialog takes precedence. Note that this dialog allows one to review and modify the inheritance tree of existing perspectives as well as perspectives being newly created in the dialog.

Once the new perspective is set up, designers can browse through the information visible in the perspective and modify it. Information can be added, deleted or modified using the methods described in Section 9.2. This process of adding, deleting, and modifying applies to both named nodes and to their contents. It also applies to both individual nodes and to whole subnetworks of nodes. For instance, an issue in the design rationale could be wholly deleted or it could merely have its content changed in the new perspective. Furthermore, the networks of subissues, answers, and arguments underneath a given issue could be copied in from another perspective by one of several alternative methods already described in Section 9.2.

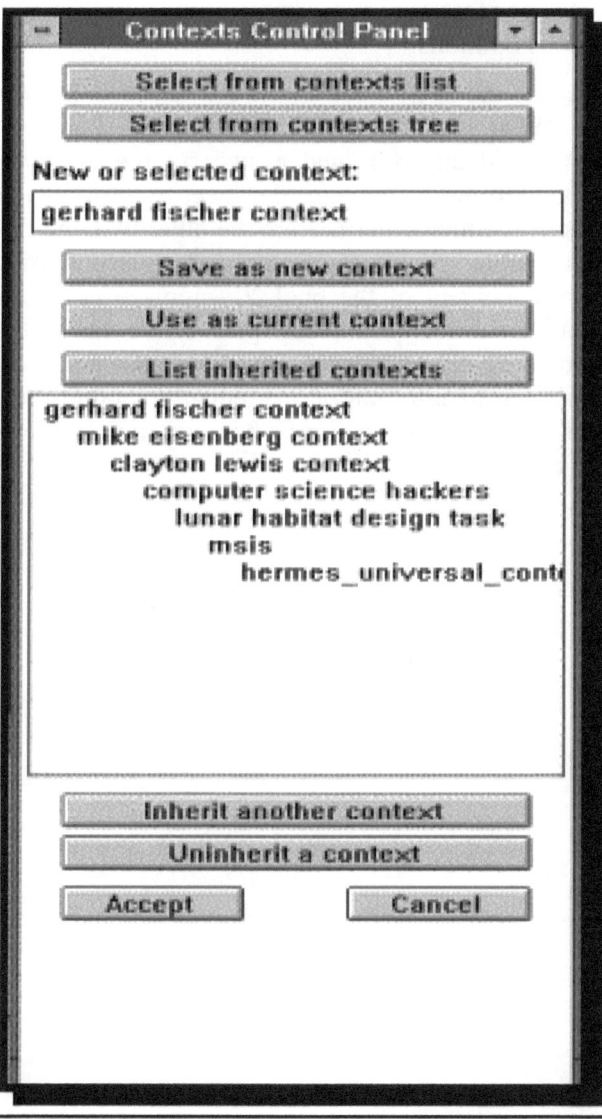

Figure 9-14. Interface for merging existing information into a new perspective.

Of particular interest in merging design rationale and other information from different perspectives is the fact that multiple opinions can be preserved or suppressed at will. Figure 9-15 shows the same segment of design rationale as viewed in three perspectives, which inherit from each other sequentially (right to left). Two kinds of changes have been made in the subsequent perspectives: changes that overwrite the previous opinions and changes that add to the previous opinions.

In each perspective, the same three issues are raised. For the answer to the second issue—"What should be the access to the bunks?"—the middle perspective has added an additional answer to the original one and the perspective on the left has added a third answer to those two answers. So in the final perspective, which inherits from the other two, the three competing answers are all visible. However, the answers to the third issue—"What should be the arrangement of the bunks?"—replace each other. Here, the issue is answered differently in each perspective because the inherited answers were deleted or modified to the new answers. This shows how support for evolution of information can equally support the accumulation and deliberation of historical versions of information or the replacing and modification of information.

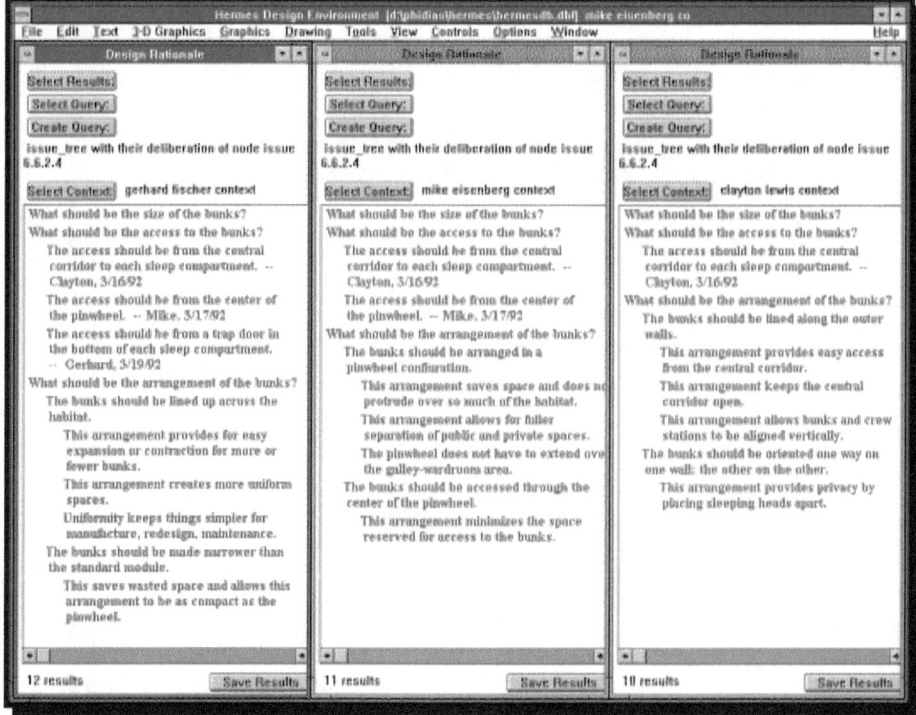

Figure 9-15. Three perspectives on a segment of design rationale.

Another important concern for the evolution of knowledge is the need to support the demotion and promotion of items of information from a given perspective to one that is higher or lower in the perspective hierarchy. Assume that there is a hierarchy of domain traditions such as that on the right-hand side of Figure 9-10. From most general to most specific there are the perspectives: habitats, space-based habitats, and Mars or lunar habitats. Suppose that a particular network of design rationale had been formulated by a designer working in the `space-based habitat perspective` at some point in the past. In reviewing this information within the `lunar habitat design team` perspective the design team members use the language constructs discussed below to determine which context this rationale is defined in and they decide as a group that the rationale is general enough to be placed in the `habitats perspective`. Alternatively, they might decide that some other rationale is too specific to the moon and should be located in the `lunar habitat perspective`. By clicking on the top node of the subnetwork of rationale, they can bring up an interface dialog box (see Figure 9-16) that suggests a number of options for reorganizing the location within the perspectives hierarchy of the node and/or the network of nodes connected to it. These options are implemented with the methods described in Section 9.2.

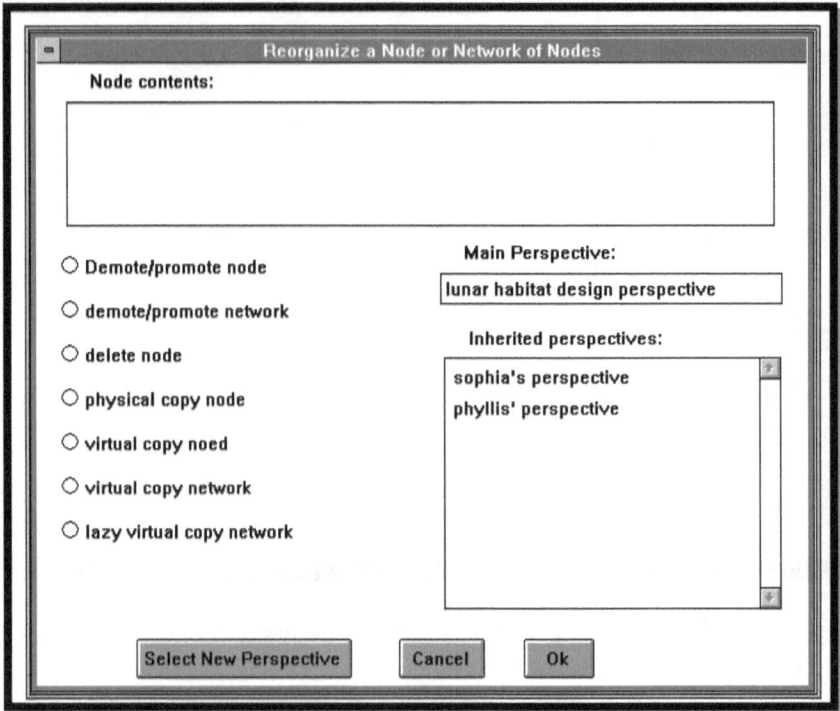

Figure 9-16. Interface for demoting or promoting a node or subnetwork of nodes.

Browsing perspectives. The perspectives mechanism simplifies the task of locating information in the rich knowledge base of an evolving design environment by partitioning the knowledge into useful categories. However, it also adds to the complexity of finding information because the knowledge being sought may not be visible in the current perspective even though it exists in the system. It may not be obvious what perspective to look in. Support must be provided for searching the network of perspectives and for browsing the knowledge available in the different perspectives.

LHDE provides a simple browser with an indented outline representation of the hierarchy of perspectives or a sorted list of the perspectives names as part of the interface for perspectives selection and new perspective creation.

This may be adequate for people who are only interested in a handful of perspectives whose names they recognize. It may also suffice as long as the hierarchy makes intuitive sense, perspectives have descriptive names, and knowledge is distributed among the perspectives in a clear and systematic manner. As the knowledge base evolves, extended by multiple users, these conditions will likely not persist. Of course, users can switch to different perspectives and explore the information there with display queries and hypermedia navigation. Also, more sophisticated graphical browsers can be added to the system interface to better represent the network of perspectives.

The HERMES language also offers a more flexible and expressive solution to the problem of browsing the perspectives hierarchy and the knowledge bases in the various perspectives. As discussed in the next chapter, the language syntax falls into three primary classes: DataLists, Associations, and Filters. Each of these classes supports the formulation of expressions providing information about perspectives or contexts. (a) One can produce DataLists of objects that are visible in some arbitrary context other than the current active perspective. (b) One can list context information associated with a given object in the database. (c) One can filter a list of contexts in terms of their inheritance relations to other contexts or in terms of what objects are visible within them. This provides a useful suite of language functions for browsing the perspectives and exploring how they partition knowledge. Examples of these functions will now be given.

(a) The first function allows one to, in effect, switch perspectives within the evaluation of a language expression. For instance, if Phyllis wants to see what habitats are visible from Sophia's perspective then she can request a display of the following DataList:

```
habitats in sophia's perspective
```

This produces the same effect as if she had first switched contexts and then evaluated the expression, `habitats`. The same function allows Phyllis to apply her privacy critic to the habitats in Sophia's perspective rather than in her own:

```
privacy gradient catalog of habitats in sophia's
    perspective
```

By including this capability in the language, it can be used as part of a complex computation that may involve several context switches. Once defined, such a computation can be given a name and subsequent users of the expression do not have to worry about doing all the switching or remember what nodes are in which contexts.

(b) The second language function related to perspectives provides a special report on the context information associated with an item or a list of items. For each item, it provides the original context that it was defined in, the list of all added contexts in which it also appears, the list of all deleted contexts in which it does not appear, and the optional switch context. (Only named—user-defined—contexts are listed, not internally defined ones.) This way, one can find all the perspectives in which a given item is visible. In the following example, the `contexts` Association is applied to the result of a query:

```
contexts of habitats in hermes_universal_context
```

This example uses the function discussed in the previous paragraph to first switch to the special perspective, `hermes_universal_context`. This special perspective allows all knowledge in the database to be visible: it by-passes the context checking. So first all the habitats in the system are found, and then their context information is displayed.

(c) The third language function defines three Filters for lists of contexts. These filters allow only the contexts to be listed that inherit from a given context, are inherited by a given context, or allow a given item to be viewed. The following expressions illustrate the use of these three Filters:

```
contexts that inherit from desi's perspective
contexts that are inherited by archie's perspective
contexts that view more than five habitats
```

These expressions allow one to explore the structure of the perspectives hierarchy and of the way it organizes knowledge.

Perspectives fill in the layered architecture. Users of a design environment with a perspectives mechanism can build new structures for partitioning the knowledge base as it evolves. Thereby, the inheritance network of perspectives provides a mechanism for end-users to extend the effective structure of the layered architecture of the system. As discussed in Chapter 7, there is a gap (transformation distance-2) in the traditional design environment architecture (e.g., in JANUS and PHIDIAS) between the seeded representations of situations and the concrete task that is addressed during a given use of the system.

As shown in Figure 9-17, this gap is much smaller than that between the implementation programming language and the actual task domain, but it is not negligible.

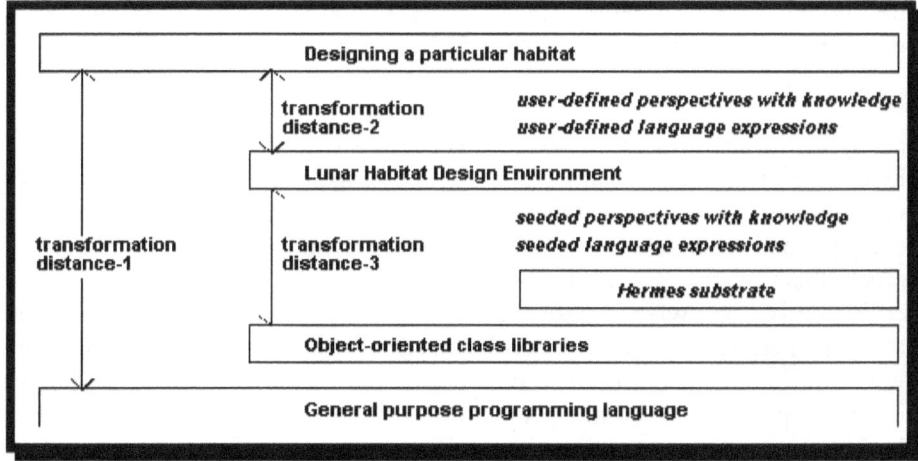

Figure 9-17. The layered architecture of design environments and HERMES.

This figure extends Figure 7-2 in Chapter 7.

In addition to providing palette items, catalog examples, and design rationale for the general problem domain, the seeded knowledge base in HERMES can partition this knowledge in a hierarchy of perspectives. Some of these perspectives can include knowledge that is specific to certain concrete tasks. This mediates between the general domain knowledge and specific tasks. In addition, end-users can extend the hierarchy to close the gap between the generic domain knowledge and novel tasks that arise. The extensibility of the perspectives hierarchy allows the gap to be narrowed as much as is needed to support interpretation in design by eliminating gaps in understanding that cause problems. As problems and knowledge evolve, the perspectives hierarchy can evolve under end-user control to meet the new demands and fill the shifting gaps.

In Chapter 10 it will be argued that the HERMES language can also be used as an extensible mechanism for end-users to progressively fill in the gap in the layered architecture. Definitions in the language exist within perspectives, so these two solutions work in tandem. Together, the HERMES substrate, its perspectives, and its language allow the major gaps in the layered architecture to be filled in to an arbitrarily fine degree and in an end-user extensible manner. Figure 9-17 illustrates this. From left to right in the figure are the original transformation distance between a general-purpose programming language and a task, the two problematic gaps in the traditional layered architecture of a design environment, and the fully layered architecture supported by HERMES.

Many of the features discussed in this section were originally suggested by lunar habitat designers and other NASA employees who have reviewed versions of HERMES. They have responded very favorably to the potential of the perspectives mechanism—as well as the hypermedia and language—to meet their everyday needs as designers facing complex, innovative, collaborative, knowledge-based tasks. To really know the extent to which the perspectives mechanisms can be used tacitly under realistic conditions will require extensive interface refinement and workplace testing. However, it seems plausible that the perspectives mechanisms can be effective in letting the computer manage a significant amount of the complexity of knowledge organization behind the scenes of the task at hand in which the designer is immersed.

CHAPTER 10. A LANGUAGE FOR SUPPORTING INTERPRETATION

The language presented in this chapter is designed as an integral part of the active computer support of human interpretation in design. It is structured for maximal plasticity so that designers can create and modify terms that express their ideas and their interpretations of their developing designs. At the same time, it must serve as a programming language used to instruct the computer in what computations to make. As part of a hypermedia substrate for design environments, it needs to provide expressive functionality useful for building user interface components and for exploring the hypermedia database.

If one thinks of a computationally active medium for design as incorporating a variety of "agents" that respond to events by computing information for messages and displays, then the HERMES language must serve as a *language of agents*. It must be able to analyze information in the database—using the customized terminology that particular designers defined within their perspectives—and format the results of computations on that information for display to the designers using the system. In the people-centered HERMES system, the agents do not change stored information, because such changes are left to the direct control of the human designers.

A central question addressed during the development of the HERMES language was how to make the language appropriate to the nature of the human-computer interaction that should take place in a design environment. The HERMES language grew out of the query language of the PHIDIAS design environment, discussed in Chapter 7. The PHIDIAS language was an attempt to provide a language that was "English-like" in appearance in the hope that it could be used by designers who had only a tacit understanding of what expressions in the language meant (i.e., what the expressions accomplished computationally). However, Part II argued that tacit understanding by itself was often insufficient; that interpretation required making some things explicit. That was one reason a language is needed at all. Designers cannot rely exclusively on pre-linguistic "human problem-domain communication" as illustrated by the JANUS system, but must sometimes be able to articulate their understanding in words. Language and explicit understanding are required to discover innovative interpretations, to share ideas with collaborators, and to create computer representations. On the other hand, explicit knowledge must be founded on tacit understanding and it is only required during creative interpretive acts, not when tacit understandings meet the needs. So PHIDIAS' approach to a tacitly understood language provides a promising alternative to traditional programming languages that require a sustained high degree of explicit awareness; but it is not sufficient by itself.

Of course, the scope of the original PHIDIAS query language was quite limited. The HERMES language extended that functionality to meet more of the expressive needs of design environments and of the designers who use them. During this process, the evolving language was subjected to a series of programming walkthroughs (Bell, et al., 1991) to evaluate its usability for writing programs. A primary result of these walkthroughs—which are documented in detail in Appendix A—was the conclusion that significantly more support was needed for explicit understanding of computational issues. However, previous evaluations of the MODIFIER system summarized in Chapter 7 had shown that a purely explicit approach—even with significant support mechanisms in the interface—was not the answer either.

The theory of computer support from Chapter 6 suggests that *an adequate language must support a dynamic movement between tacit and explicit understanding*. (1) Routine *reuse* of expressions can be largely *tacit*. (2) Innovative *modification* requires a certain amount of *explicit* analysis. But even here, only the domain relationships and certain features of the representations need to be made explicit. Much of the computational "doctrine"[22] associated with general purpose programming languages does not need to be made explicit because it would only distract from the

---

[22] The term *doctrine* refers to guiding knowledge that must be understood in order to use a programming language. For instance, most general purpose programming languages require that programmers know doctrine about when and how to use iteration control structures. The programming walkthrough methodology is designed to assess what doctrine is required for a given task in a language.

problem-domain concerns. Much of this can be kept tacit. The HERMES language represents an attempt to relieve the end-user of such programming doctrine as much as possible.

Relieving the end-user of technical doctrine of programming does not mean that designers using HERMES never need to worry about the explicit structure of the knowledge they are taking advantage of. On the contrary, the analysis of interpretation in this dissertation stresses the necessary role of explication in furthering normally tacit understanding. Rather, the attempt is merely made to minimize the amount of doctrine that must be learned that is unrelated to design. Designers are often predominantly visual, holistic, intuitive thinkers; the symbolic, detail-oriented, precise, mathematical character of programming language doctrine is particularly burdensome for many skilled designers.

Section 10.1 elaborates on the *principles* that have gone into the development of the HERMES language, including the necessity of supporting both *tacit* and *explicit* understanding. The uniqueness of the HERMES language is the way in which it strives to combine the problem-domain centered communicative goals of domain-specific design environments like PHIDIAS and JANUS with the computationally expressive goals of general purpose programming languages like PASCAL and LISP through this mix of tacit and explicit understanding.

Section 10.2 shows at an in-depth level how a number of the basic *mechanisms* of programming languages are available in the HERMES language in ways that require minimal explicit understanding of technical doctrine by system users: *Abstraction* is accomplished by ordinary naming, with no assignment statements. *Iteration* takes place automatically without control structures. *Typing* is maintained by the implicit organization of the syntax options. *Recursion* is defined without explicit concern for halting conditions. *Variables* are generally avoided in favor of the application of successive operators; where necessary, deictic pronouns can be used to reference computational elements. *Quantification* operators can be applied directly to lists without use of explicitly bound variables. Other examples of the encapsulation of explicit mechanisms of computation in tacitly understandable forms are developed in Appendix B, where sample applications using them are also described. Of course, users of the HERMES language need to learn doctrine specific to the use of this language, but that is at a higher level of representation (closer to concerns of the problem domain) than doctrine for a general purpose programming language. Appendix C defines the complete syntax and semantics of the HERMES language.

Section 10.3 illustrates the use of the HERMES language for defining *interpretive critics*. Interpretive critics provide a final example of the synergy of HERMES' support for interpretation, exploiting the combination of the integrated substrate, perspectives, and the language. First, the *critics* from JANUS are redefined in the HERMES language. Then, the *privacy critics* from Chapter 9 are analyzed computationally. A number of the mechanisms discussed in Section 10.2 are shown at work here. This spells out in some detail one way in which HERMES can respond to the challenge from back in Chapter 3, to represent in a computer system Desi and Archie's concerns about privacy. The advantages of the HERMES approach are: definitions are made at a higher level of representation, the definitions can be more expressive, and alternative definitions can be organized in different perspectives.

10.1. An Approach to Language Design

The HERMES language is the result of following several principles arising from the theory of computer support and the review of design environment needs in Part II. These principles are:

1. Support a mix of tacit and explicit understanding.

2. Provide a people-centered approach.

3. Meet the needs of design environments.

4. Offer an end-user language for non-programmers.

 This section will discuss how the HERMES language adheres to these principles.

1. Support a mix of tacit and explicit understanding. The HERMES language stresses different priorities than traditional computation-centered language designs, resulting in a different set of design decisions and a different character to the language. The contrast between the HERMES language and the FP functional programming language proposed by Backus (1978), on which the HERMES language is formally modeled, or the PASCAL procedural language in which it is implemented makes this point graphically.

Here is a task like that posed for the programming walkthroughs reported in Appendix A: Suppose you have a hypertext database with issues in nodes of two types: `question` and `problem`; answers to the issues in `answer` nodes connected by `answer` links; and arguments for the answers in `argument` nodes connected by `argument` links. (See Figure 10-1.) Now, you want to know: *which issues have four or more arguments associated with them* (via their answers).

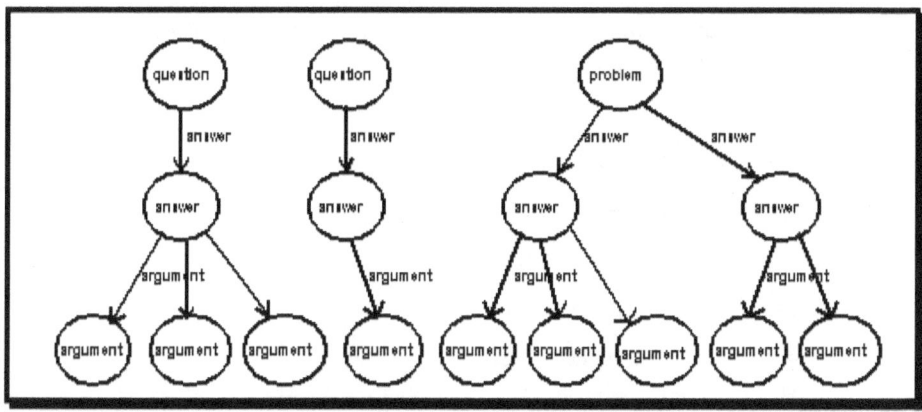

Figure 10-1. A database of design rationale.

This could be accomplished by first defining `issues` as `questions` and `problems` and defining `rationale` as `arguments` of `answers`. Then you could define the query using these newly defined terms as:

```
issues that have more than 3 rationale
```

Notice how this "program" in the HERMES language is a simple statement in domain terms of the desired results. All the computations that the computer must carry out to produce the query results are implicit: iterating through all the `questions` and `problems` in the database, following each of their `answer` links (if any) and their `argument` links (if any), accumulating and counting their `rationale` nodes, filtering out all the `issues` that do not fit the condition.

The statement of the query in the HERMES language contrasts with its formulation in other programming languages. First, it has an appearance that seems easier for non-programmers to understand tacitly than its equivalent in FP, even though the HERMES language is formally close to FP:

```
a(have-Q-R [>3, rationale])  ° issues
```

In this FP declarative statement, much of the computation has been explicitly symbolized in abstract mathematical formalisms of application, composition, and comparison. Even so, the functional approach of FP using successive composition of operators—which HERMES borrows from FP— avoids the step by step detail of a procedural language. The following procedural pseudo-code shows what this query would require in a procedural language, and in fact how it is computed (behind the scenes) even in the HERMES system:

```
begin

list0 := empty list;

list1 := all nodes with Kind = question;

list2 := all nodes with Kind = problem;

list3 := list1 append list2;

for i = 1 to size of list3 do

   list4 := empty list;

   for each link type from node do

      if link type = answer

           then for each linked node do

                   for each link type from node do

                      if link type = argument

                            then add node to list4;

   if count of list4 > 3

      then add node to list0;

return list0;

end;
```

Traditional general purpose programming languages are based largely on mathematical models of fully explicit expressions. To name some of the most popular historical languages, FORTRAN is based on algebraic formulas, COBOL on business arithmetic, APL on matrix algebra, and LISP on symbolic logic. Assembly languages are necessarily closely modeled on the architecture of computer CPUs. Most recent languages are derived from combinations of these prototypes. Even Backus' FP language, which is an attempt to break away from the von Neumann and lambda-calculus models, is strongly influenced by APL—particularly in its outward appearance to the human programmer. All these languages have been developed under severe pressure to optimize usage of computer resources (memory locations and cycle time). This has led to the following problem: programming languages are necessary for empowering people to communicate with and through computers; however, the way in which the predominant languages are closely based on mathematical models make them difficult for many people in many situations to use to express themselves.

Natural languages that societies have historically developed for their own expression and interpersonal communication needs have very different characteristics from these programming languages. They tend to support informal, tacit, contextual, situated expression. Thus, they are very dependent on human intentional comprehension of semantics and communicative intent. They feature a highly generative phrase structure and huge vocabularies that evolve historically. They develop under the constraint of cognitive ease for the human speaker and vocal brevity (Grice, 1975).

Now that computer resources are several orders of magnitude less scarce than in the past while human cognitive resources are being overwhelmed with the complexities of the information age, it seems time to consider designing programming languages or end-user languages in which some of the burdens are shifted to the computer. That is, while a mathematical basis for languages may be important for theoretical reasons, practical considerations of supporting the needs of users without burdening them unnecessarily suggest that the logical computational structure of the language should often be kept tacitly hidden in favor of a higher-level structure close to the user's explicit concerns. Computers increasingly have the power to manage the translation between these levels to relieve the user of that burden.

The goal of the HERMES language is to make communication with the computer system cognitively and interpretively easier for people. It tries to do this by hiding many computational details, leaving it up to the computer software to take care of them. It allows designers to build their own vocabulary incrementally, using terms familiar from their domain of work. The vocabulary can grow through a history of use, with different people developing different meanings for terms (in their own perspectives) and sharing these meanings (in common group perspectives). The language starts out with a shared basic vocabulary, established as a seeded vocabulary by the design environment builders. Terminology in the language can be reused and modified by subsequent system users, just as natural language words can take on new metaphorical meanings. The language is intended to support interpretation, explication, and interpersonal communication, not just formulaic statement. Section 10.2 will detail what is meant by hiding the computational structure of expressions.

2. Provide a people-centered approach. The slogan of a "people-centered" approach means that the computer system should be controlled by the people with whom it interacts at the points where judgmental decisions must be made that involve the exercise of intentionality. The HERMES language is designed to empower people to express their interpretations and judgments in ways that can affect the computer's actions and that can also be communicated to other people. By making the design environment programmable, the language lets designers using the system determine how displays, analyses, and critics used in the active computational environment are to be defined. Terms used in the definitions of these displays, analyses, and critic rules can be defined and modified by designers in accordance with their own interpretive perspectives.

"People-centered" also means that the system interacts with people in ways appropriate to human cognitive (interpretive) styles. HERMES features a language for designers (rather than trained programmers) to use. *The language is defined as a series of subset languages to facilitate learning by new users.* This way, people can work with the language at a level that is comfortable for them. When they need more explicit control in defining revised expressions to capture their precise interpretations, they will have a relatively easy path to exploring language features that are new to them. They can simply move to the next stage of the language in a particular area of the language. For instance, if they need a new definition of a complex expression, they can expand the beginner's dialog box of syntax options to see the additional intermediate options or they can view the definition of an existing expression and modify it gradually. (An interface for doing this is discussed under point 4, below.)

First it should be noted that previously defined terms and expressions are used by designers most of the time. These can be simply selected from lists of relevant terms, even by a *novice*. Then there is a *beginner*'s version of the language that is similar to the PHIDIAS language, which proved easy to use for non-programmer users. This level of the language suffices for defining or modifying most common terms and queries. An *intermediate* level provides access to virtually all features of the language except those related to graphics. Finally, an *advanced* level can be used for graphics-related tasks, like defining interpretive critics. Most system displays and component interfaces are defined in the language, so they can be modified through use of the language. It would be possible to add a fully general *programming* level to the language by providing a programming language interpreter that could treat the syntax options of the HERMES language as predefined functions. This has not been done because the research focus of the HERMES language is to support interpretation in design and to make a language as interpretable as possible for non-programmers. This goal probably does not require a computationally complete language. So, the following levels of usage are supported by the HERMES language:

Novice. Even without defining any new expressions in the language, a novice can still use most of the HERMES system in a flexible way. It is, for instance, possible to define new link Types and node Kinds, although one cannot yet define new computed expressions that refer to them. One can also use all the previously defined (seeded) expressions in the language: DataLists, Predicates[23], conditions, queries, critics, etc. Thus, it is possible to define conditional nodes, conditional links, or virtual structures (queries embedded in nodes) without writing new expressions in the language.

Beginner. This version corresponds roughly to the original PHIDIAS language. It allows the user to define expressions, displays, and critics incorporating Filter clauses. With only 15% of the number of options of the full language, the Beginner syntax provides a good learning experience for most of the features and conventions of the HERMES language. This version of the language features Input Associations, a subset of Associations useful for eliciting design rationale or argumentation. For instance, if an Input Association, `deliberation`, is defined as `issues with their answers with their arguments`, then it can be used to control data entry. A special interface feature is designed to create new nodes following the patterns of user-defined Input Associations. Using the definition of `deliberation`, it will prompt for the text of an `issue` to be entered; then it prompts for one or more `answers` to that `issue`; for each `answer` it prompts for one or more `arguments`. Recursive Input Associations can also be defined that prompt for whole trees of data to as much depth as the respondent is willing to go.

Intermediate. The intermediate version of the language expands the computational power of the beginner version, without, however, including the complications introduced by graphics. This corresponds roughly to the

---

[23] The definition and use of Predicates, conditional nodes, and virtual structures is described in Appendix B. DataLists and other syntax categories are defined and illustrated in Appendix C.

level of complexity implemented for the version of the language used in the programming walkthrough (Appendix A) and in the academic advising application (Appendix B). Here, the simple data-entry Input Associations become a subset of the more powerful and complex Associations. Predicates are a modification of Associations to hide some of their complexity when displayed.

Advanced. This version adds the multi-media capability and more sophisticated programming options. Now all the computational capability of the language can be applied to nodes of any medium (e.g., vector graphics, sound, video, and bitmaps). This is necessary for implementing displays or critics that take into account graphical information (distances, spatial relationships, adjacencies, volumes, etc.). [This level of the language has been designed (see Appendix C), but not yet fully implemented.]

Programmer. Ultimately, one might want to give a user full programming power. In a research prototyping environment, one could simply hand over the source code. In a LISP environment, one can allow the user to enter programs as data that are then interpreted. However, in realistic cases where the source code is not made available and where speed is too much of a concern to use an interpreted language for building the system itself, other mechanisms must be developed. HERMES provides a form of procedural attachment implemented via dynamic link libraries (DLLs) in WINDOWS. This lets the user define a certain number of pre-named functions, using the full power of object-oriented PASCAL or C++. These functions can then be attached to nodes or links in the hypermedia database (see active objects in Section 8.2) and referred to by expressions in the HERMES language. [This level of the language has not been explored extensively, but is meant to be suggestive as a response to the limits of programming complex algorithms in the HERMES language.]

These levels of the language extend the idea from JANUS of a layered architecture, as discussed in Chapter 7. The layers of the language fill in the two gaps that appeared in Figure 7-2: the transformation distance-3 between the system building environment (LISP) and the design environment (JANUS), and the transformation distance-2 between the seeded design environment and the actual task domain (laying out a particular kitchen). The first of these gaps is filled primarily for system builders who are constructing a new design environment or adding new components to an existing one. When a design environment is built on top of the HERMES substrate, new components take advantage of the substrate functionality, including the language. As shown in Chapter 8, many functions are implemented as windows or buttons that evaluate expressions defined in the

HERMES language. That means first of all that functionality can be defined using higher level terms in the HERMES language without the system builder needing to work at the lower level implementation language. It also means that future end-users can revise the way those functions work by modifying the definitions of the terms used in the HERMES language, which is available to them at run-time as well. The second gap is filled primarily for designers using a design environment built on HERMES. They can simply use the terms, displays, and critics that have already been defined. If they need to modify something, the Beginner version of the language is available. If this is not sufficient, they can successively try more advanced versions of the language. This provides almost a continuity of layers to support a range of understanding from tacit work in the problem domain to explicit software programming in the underlying programming environment. (See Figure 9-17 in Section 9.3.)

3. Meet the needs of design environments. Chapter 7 cited the idea of programmable design environments proposed by Eisenberg and Fischer (1992). It was claimed there that HERMES could be viewed as the first implementation of this notion. In fact, the design and development of HERMES was driven by the desire to include programmability as a central feature of a design environment in order to empower designers to define, control, and extend the computational power of the software system in which they carry out their design work.

The desire to have the language refer to, analyze, critique, and display all the varieties of knowledge and representations in a design environment— including information from previous designs in a catalog, palette items for use in new designs, specification decisions, design rationale, domain distinctions, critic rules, etc.—forced the system to become more and more integrated. As the power of the language was extended from its original restriction to design rationale (in the original PHIDIAS query language), more of the knowledge was represented as hypermedia nodes that could be linked in one integrated knowledge base. New forms of knowledge were also added. For instance, conditional expressions could be defined to implement conditional links, conditional nodes, and critics. The increased generality of the system made it easy to add new media, like bitmaps, voice, and video as well.

As the language grew in range and power, the number of its syntax options in the language increased rapidly, despite extensive efforts to generalize and simplify the syntactic structure. In the end, the number of options increased by an order of magnitude. Most of these syntax options (those called "simple" options) directly reflect elements of the multimedia knowledge representation substrate. Many other syntax options (called "computed" options) define combinations of the primitives that are needed for useful computations. The appearance of expressions in the language is dominated by user-defined terms: names of objects, link types, node kinds, names of defined sub-expressions. Otherwise, there are just a few "helper" words that remind people of the functionality of the options. Little is left in its external appearance of the language's computational internal nature. Thus, the HERMES language appears to be a "new" language, although it is really basically the result of adapting a stripped-down functional programming approach to meet the needs of a design environment.

Despite its adherence to the notion of a programmable design environment, the HERMES language is very different from a programmable application like SCHEMEPAINT (Eisenberg, 1992). In SCHEMEPAINT, the language is used for creation of new objects. In contrast, the HERMES language is "non-imperative" (Schmidt, 1986). Evaluation of expressions in the HERMES language do not change state: they do not *create* anything new. They navigate through the hypermedia database and collect lists of existing objects. Of course, by means of user interface features, these lists can themselves be saved as new objects. Also, interface features can be designed that use language expressions to organize, modify, or even create objects. For instance, a design rationale prompting component in the interface can elicit and store new argumentation using the Input Association syntax options as explained in Appendix C. *The language is primarily geared to the diverse information retrieval needs of designers.*

Design environments have a variety of data retrieval, manipulation, and display needs. In a hypermedia-based system like HERMES, these needs can generally be categorized into three groups: (a) to generate lists of information, (b) to selectively choose items from lists, and (c) to navigate through the inter-connected network of the database. This corresponds to the three categories of operations that Abelson & Sussman (1985) emphasize for functional computer programs: to enumerate, map, and filter lists or streams of information.[24] The HERMES language syntax provides three primary classes of terms to operationalize these functions: DataLists, Filters, and Associations, as indicated in Table 10-1:

---

[24] The suggestion to interpret operations in the HERMES language as the processing of streams of information in this sense was suggested by both C. Lewis and M. Eisenberg, independently.

Table 10-1. Correspondence of language uses, operations and classes of terms.

	uses	**operations**	**HERMES language**
(a)	generate lists	enumerate	DataList
(b)	selectively choose	filter	Filter
(c)	navigate network	map	Association

(a) Many forms of lists must be *generated* (enumerated) in a design environment. In a system built on top of the HERMES substrate, virtually all displays in the user interface are constructed dynamically from such lists. The HERMES language is designed above all to provide a flexible means for defining lists of items stored in the database and useful for interpretive tasks in the represented domain. In this sense, the HERMES language is a database query language. The HERMES language is optimized for expressing queries in this environment and for retrieving the requested information efficiently in useful formats. Unlike SQL (a general purpose query language for relational databases), it is designed for an object-oriented, multimedia database in which items are linked together in hypertext style. It differs from SQL in being non-relational and hypermedia-specific. Among the information listings available through the HERMES language are general queries and the basic displays used in design environments, such as design rationale issue-base views, catalogs of past designs, palettes of design components. An example of a DataList that computes the items for a display of some rationale created by Archie is:

```
issues that have creator archie
```

(b) *Filtering* functions of the language are important for implementing critics and for making all displays relative to design decisions encoded in specifications, constructions, or design rationale. For instance, using the language one can define a display of all catalog items that pass a Filter referring to the existence of specific palette items in a certain construction, answers resolved in the design rationale, or selections made in a specification listing. Perspectives provide another filtering mechanism in HERMES, allowing only nodes that are defined in the currently active perspective to be processed by the language. The two filtering mechanisms can be combined in expressions in the language like:

```
issues in context desi's habitat perspective that
   have creator archie
```

(c) *Navigation* through the hypermedia database (mapping) is also accomplished with the HERMES language. A good example of such navigation is shown in Figure 10-1 with the expression:

```
issues that have more than 3 rationale
```

Here, the expression `rationale`, defined as `arguments of answers`, navigates from each `issue` node across its `answer` links to new nodes and across their `argument` links.

The three major syntax categories of the HERMES language (DataLists, Filters, Associations) provide the three primary functions required for design environments: (a) definitions of lists of nodes, (b) expressions for filtering out nodes not meeting stated criteria, and (c) operations to traverse various kinds of associations. These support the situated, perspectival, and linguistic character of interpretation by naming representations of things in the design situation, filtering out objects for display based on viewing criteria, and providing expressions for exploring semantic associations. Objects in each of these three categories can be either (1) reused or (2) refined by combining expressions in useful ways. This defines the six primary syntactic classes; four other classes provide auxiliary terms and features. The syntactic classes are listed with brief descriptions in Table 10-2.

Table 10-2. Major syntactic classes of the HERMES language.

	syntactic class	*description*
a-1	Datalists	options for identifying hypermedia nodes.
a-2	Computed Datalists	permitted combinations of language elements that determine sets of nodes
b-1	Filters	operations characterizing nodes for selection
b-2	Computed Filters	permitted combinations of language elements that define filter conditions
c-1	Associations	links and other associations of nodes
c-2	Computed Associations	permitted combinations of language elements that determine non-primitive Associations
d-1	Media Elements	nodes of various media: text, numbers, booleans, graphics, sound, video, etc.
d-2	Computed Media Elements	permitted combinations of media elements, e.g., arithmetic or boolean computations
e-1	Pre-defined Terminology	connective terms, measurement primitives, fixed values for attributes and types
e-2	Computed Terminology	namable quantifiers and numerical comparisons

The central *syntax classes* of the HERMES language are (a) *DataLists*, (b) *Filters*, and (c) *Associations*. In addition, (d) the Media elements define several syntax classes, one for each kind of allowable multimedia content in the hypermedia database that is traversed by the language: *Character, Number, Boolean, Graphic, Image, Pen, Sound, Video, Animation,* and *ComputedView*. (e) The Terminology options provide the connective terms for joining multiple items together and for counting items, as well as certain definitions useful for graphical computations; these include three syntax classes for user-definable options: *Count, Quantifier, Measure*; and eight syntax classes that are system-defined: *Connective, Combination, Distance,*

Units, Dimension, Attribute, Value, and *LanguageType.* In addition there are three hypermedia classes that are part of the syntax: *Contexts, NodeKinds* and *LinkTypes.* The syntax classes are divided into Simple and Computed options. The Simple options define a single operation for producing a result. The Composite options define legal combinations of applying one operation to another. This defines the operator algebra that is at the heart of the HERMES language. It is discussed below. Table 10-3 (below) provides sample options from each of the classes listed in Table 10-2 (above).

Table 10-3. Examples of syntactic options for the HERMES language.

	syntactic class	example
a-1	Datalists	all database items of a specified NodeKind
a-2	Computed Datalists	items of a *DataList* that pass a specified *Filter*
b-1	Filters	items that are of a specified NodeKind
b-2	Computed Filters	items that pass *Filter1* and also pass *Filter2*
c-1	Associations	a Link Type (e.g., children)
c-2	Computed Associations	*Association1* with their *Association2*
d-1	Media Elements	a real number (e.g., 3.14)
d-2	Computed Media Elements	the total of all numbers in a specified *DataList*
e-1	Pre-defined Terminology	closest distance between two graphic items
e-2	Computed Terminology	a *Distance* is greater than a specified *Number* (e.g., too near: closest distance is less than 5 feet)

The DataList, Filter, and Association options constitute the majority of the syntax options. The Simple options are all defined as primitive operators. For instance, Simple DataLists return a node or list of nodes as their result. DataList, Filter, and Association (both Simple and Computed) evaluation functions all take a DataList as input and return a new DataList as a result. This DataList result format acts as a stream of data items that passes through the operators to generate new items, filter out items that were there, or map from the old items to associated new items. Because of this uniform format, any of the operators can be applied successively to the results of any other operators. This allows the unlimited nesting of phrases and application of operators that makes the HERMES language highly generative.

In HERMES, only certain combinations of applications are permitted, as defined by the Computed options. If the Simple options were incorporated as predefined functions in a general programming language like FP or SCHEME, then any combinations of operators could be evaluated. However, a judgment has been made in designing HERMES to limit the combinations to semantically meaningful and useful options. That accounts for the seeming proliferation of options. In fact, however, the majority of options are nothing but combinations of other options applied to each other. For these combination options, the semantics are trivially defined, as shown in Appendix C in which the denotational semantics and the corresponding implementation code for the evaluation function of one such combination option is shown. The HERMES language is a carefully *constrained* language, designed to promote relatively tacit usage by structuring the choice of operation combinations to avoid many problematic expression definitions and to guide the language user.

4. Offer an end-user language for non-programmers. The use of the language in HERMES can be made appropriate for non-programmers in many ways through interface features. Some examples were already given in Chapter 8. Consider how *navigation* through the hypermedia database (mapping) is accomplished with the HERMES language. An example of such navigation is shown in Figure 10-2. A textual node has been selected in a *Design Rationale* window by clicking on it. This brings up the *Navigating the Hypertext* window. The selected node has been displayed in the top of this window and the default option of "Navigate out-going links" has been chosen. The list of "Out-going Links" displays "issue", indicating that the selected node is associated with out-going links of type issue to other nodes. The list of *Predicates*[25] displays three terms that have previously

---

[25] Predicates are a special form of computed Association. They are explained in Appendix B.

been defined in the HERMES language; these terms are all defined with expressions that include issue as their initial traversal, so they are relevant to the selected node that has issue links. If the user had selected "issue" under "Out-going Links", then a new Design Rationale window would have been displayed listing all the nodes navigated to by following issue links from the original selected node. In the case shown in the figure, the user has instead selected the Predicate discussion. Discussion is defined in the HERMES language (either in the seed or by a previous user) as a series of link navigations beginning with issue links. So the display produced in the new window is an indented list resulting from the navigations defined by the language expression named discussion.

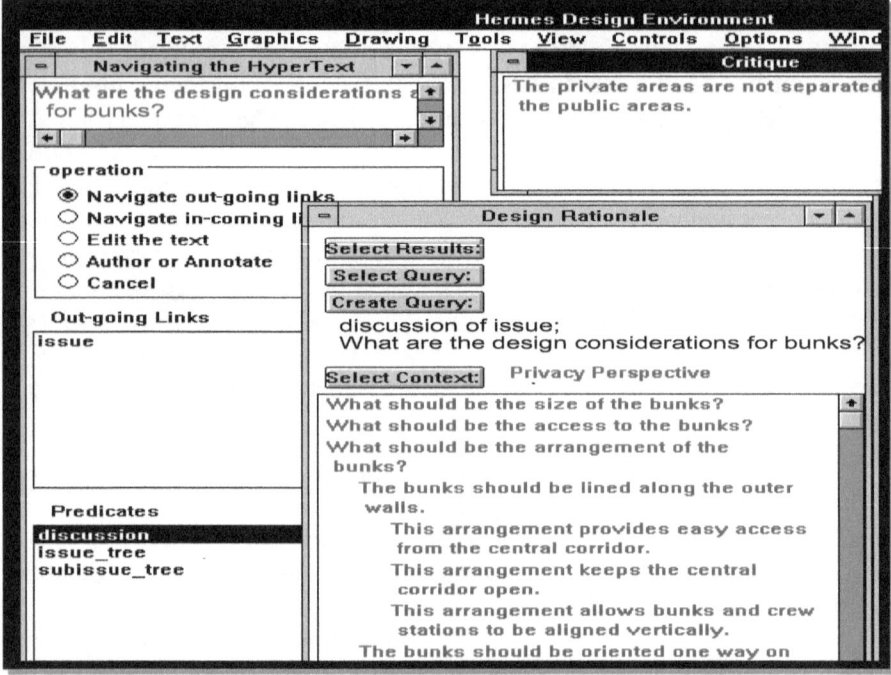

Figure 10-2. An example of hypermedia navigation.

The example just given illustrates a number of points about language usage in HERMES. First, expressions (like discussion) can be reused without explicit concern for their detailed definition, particularly if their name indicates their function adequately. Second, rather complex displays can be defined relatively easily. If one wanted to, one could modify the definition of discussion or define a new term based on it. The new term could use Filter conditions to eliminate items selectively as well. For instance, one could define a new Predicate bunk discussion as: discussion that contains 'bunk'. Then the list of Predicates displayed in the *Navigating the Hypertext* window would include bunk discussion and selection of this option would result in a display that only listed items including the word "bunk". Third, language usage can be integrated into the user interface so that it feels like tacit navigation through hypermedia rather than explicit querying with a language. The use of this language need not have the look and feel of programming, even when new expressions are being defined for accomplishing arbitrarily complex computations.

When an expression must be explicitly programmed, interface support is available to reduce the cognitive burden of recalling syntax options, strict formats, expression names, or terminology spellings. As part of the attempt to reduce programming errors that would frustrate a non-programmer, a direct manipulation interface is provided for use, reuse, modification, and creation of expressions in the HERMES language. Strictly speaking, this is not part of the HERMES substrate, but belongs to the interface of a design environment built on top of the substrate. It is presented here simply to suggest one solution to the problem of supporting people to use the HERMES language with minimal cognitive overload.

* By presenting all relevant options on the computer screen at each stage and requiring expressions to be built up by choosing from these dialog options, the user is relieved of having to remember the various legal options.

* Similarly the problem of entering the precise proper format and spelling is solved. Novice programmers are particularly frustrated by punctuation and spelling errors during program input.

* The interface presents definitions of terms in a readable format. Given that expressions in the HERMES language often read much like English, it is important to avoid the impression that the system can understand arbitrary English formulations. The restriction to a visible menu of choices makes the restrictions clear and unavoidable.

* The same dialog boxes that are used for defining new expressions encourage the reuse of previously defined expressions. Old definitions can be reviewed with the dialogs to see their internal structure, and the definitions can then be modified and reused.

Figure 10-3 shows the three dialog boxes for defining a DataList expression. This is typically the starting point for defining expressions in the language, such as queries or critics. It is also possible to start with other dialogs to define conditional expressions, numerical computations, and so on. The leftmost dialog, labeled "DataList options," is the first dialog to appear under conditions in which one needs to define a new DataList. If one wants to select a previously defined DataList expression—whether defined as part of the HERMES seed, by other system users or by the current user—then a pick-list of the names of all defined DataLists is used instead.

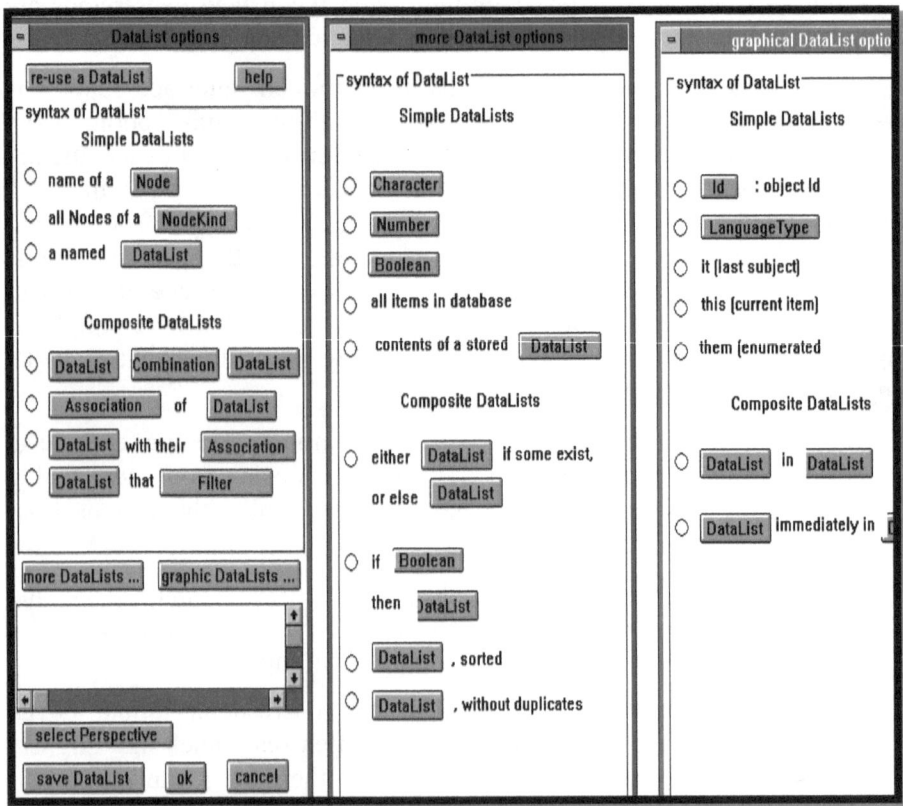

Figure 10-3. Dialog boxes for defining DataList expressions.

This programming interface incorporates the breakdown of the language into a series of levels for users with different degrees of experience in using the language. This is an example of the mixture of support for tacit and explicit understanding. Even when the system user needs to make interpretations explicit and state them in the programming language, this burden is softened by providing a direct manipulation, construction kit interface for defining expressions and by providing a layered architecture of many levels of successive complexity.

The leftmost dialog presents the *Beginner's version of the syntax*. The heart of this dialog is the list of seven small circles, the radio buttons for selecting one of the three Simple DataList options or one of the four Composite DataList options. The first of these options allows the user to simply select a node from a pick-list, which will be displayed when this option is chosen. The second option defines a DataList consisting of all nodes in the database that are of a specified NodeKind. If this option is selected (by clicking the mouse on its NodeKind button), a pick-list of the names of all defined NodeKinds is displayed. The third option retrieves a DataList expression that has been previously defined and saved.

The Composite DataList options lead to other dialog boxes to define constituent parts of the composite expression. The first of these, for instance, has three buttons: "DataList", "Combination", "DataList". If this option is selected, then each of these buttons must be pressed with the mouse before the new expression can be saved. Pressing the first (or the third) of these buttons brings up another copy of the same dialog box so that the constituent DataLists may be selected. For instance, to define a DataList named issues as questions and problems, use this option and press the first button. When the new DataList dialog appears, select the first Simple DataList option and choose questions from the pick-list that appears. Then click the "ok" button at the bottom of the new dialog to confirm this choice. The new dialog will disappear. Then press the "Combination" button. This will bring up a dialog listing the five Combination options. Simply select the and option and click the "ok" button. Then define the DataList for the third button as problems. Now the expression questions and problems will show in the small window near the bottom of the DataList dialog box. Press the "save DataList" button below there. A small dialog will ask for the name of the new DataList that has just been defined. Type the word issues and the new expression will be part of the HERMES system.

Below the list of options in the DataList dialog are buttons labeled "more DataLists" and "graphic DataLists". These bring up the dialogs with the *Intermediate and Advanced DataList options*, respectively. They are also shown in Figure 10-3. They work the same way as the options in the first dialog, which remains on the screen and controls the overall expression definition process. This is how a user advances from the Beginner to the Intermediate or Advanced levels of the language based on their specific needs.

One more button should be mentioned in the basic "DataList options" dialog box. That is the uppermost button: "reuse a DataList". Pressing this button brings up a pick-list of defined DataLists. When one is selected from this list, the list disappears and the definition of the selected DataList appears in the dialog. First it appears in the display window in its narrative format. But it also appears in the options in the sense that the option that was used for defining it is now selected in the dialog. Pressing the buttons for that option will bring up dialogs that are also already displaying the constituent parts. This provides a way of exploring the structure of a defined expression. If anything is changed on the subsidiary dialogs and confirmed and saved, then the definition of that expression will be modified accordingly (within the currently selected perspective).

While the foregoing description and its accompanying figure may seem complicated, that is partly because it is harder to describe this process explicitly in words, covering most of the various possible actions, then it is to use the direct manipulation interface to make selections needed to accomplish a specific task.

The HERMES language represents an attempt to push a particular approach to language design as far as possible. This is what makes the HERMES language distinctive. The approach is motivated by the theory of computer support of interpretation. It includes an effort to balance support for tacit and explicit understanding, promoting tacit activity whenever possible, even during the accomplishment of explicit programming tasks. It tries to develop an expressive and extensible programming language for people like designers who may not be experienced at computer programming. To do this, it hides many of the computational mechanisms (as described in the following section), and constrains the syntax of the language. Of course, there are trade-offs involved in keeping mechanisms hidden and in limiting options to enforce meaningfulness of expressions. The HERMES language has great flexibility and expressivity. It is infinitely generative and arbitrarily complex. But it is far from being Turing complete. There are many definitions of lists that cannot be expressed in it, but that are relatively straight-forward to program in PASCAL or LISP, for instance. Subsequent examples and analysis in the remainder of this chapter and in the Appendices should show the language's ability to formulate easily and tacitly the expressions most useful for design environments, as well as pointing out the limitations that can arise in more complex circumstances.

10.2 Encapsulating Explicit Mechanisms in Tacit Forms

The HERMES language has been designed to minimize the amount of programming language doctrine required as explicit knowledge by people writing and reading expressions in the language. This has been accomplished by hiding a number of programming language mechanisms in the syntax options of the HERMES language so they can be used with only a tacit understanding of their functioning. This section illustrates what is meant by this approach. A number of important areas of programming language doctrine that require explicit understanding for the use of languages like LISP or PASCAL are incorporated in the syntax options, evaluation processes, and user interfaces of the HERMES language in ways that can be used without explicit understanding.

1. Abstraction in HERMES takes place by simply giving a name to an expression that has been defined; there is no explicit assignment statement. All expressions in the HERMES language can be named and the names may be used wherever the corresponding expression could be used.

2. Iteration is implicit in HERMES. For instance, in the example of displaying the `discussion` of an item from the Design Rationale window, all the `issue` links from the item's node were followed. Normally, this would be expressed in a traditional programming language as some form of iteration (a `for`-loop or a recursion). However, in the HERMES language it is not expressed at all, but merely assumed in the declaration calling for a list of the issues.

3. Typing of expressions is enforced by restrictions on the allowable syntax options, without the user needing to be aware of this.

4. Recursion is an important technique for navigating successive links in hypermedia networks using the HERMES language, but users need not be aware of it or worry about halting conditions.

5. Variable binding occurs as a natural result of the syntax of expressions, but explicit variables are not used.

6. The syntax allows one to quantify expressions by asking for all items, checking for at least one item, and so on, but the computational implementation of these is hidden from the user.

7. Conditionals can be stated in explicit if / then format or implied through more tacit formats.

1. **Abstraction**. The importance of *abstraction* has been emphasized by many leading language designers (e.g., Liskov, et al., 1977; Cardelli & Wegner, 1985; Abelson & Sussman, 1985; Wirth, 1988). From a people-centered perspective, the importance of abstraction in definition of expressions in a programming language is that a complex expression can be hidden under an easy-to-use name that corresponds to terminology in the application domain. That means that the name can be used in a relatively tacit way once it has been defined explicitly.

To use an example from Chapter 3, it may be quite difficult to define an operational definition of privacy for lunar habitats. Such a definition must be spelled out in complete and explicit detail (see Section 10.3 below for such a definition) so that the computer system can use it. However, once defined, the definition can be stored under the name privacy. From then on, designers using the system can make use of the term privacy without being concerned about all the computational details. In fact, the term may have been defined as part of the system's knowledge seed by the software developers or by some intermediate knowledge engineer, so that the lunar habitat designers never need to be concerned with (or develop the skills to understand) the technical details of implementation. This is a case in which the analysis of interpretation provides a new argument about the role of abstraction, an old technique. Based on this argument, HERMES in fact places considerable emphasis on this form of abstraction in the design of the HERMES language, allowing every object stored in the computer memory— including all defined expressions and sub-expressions in the language—to be referred to by user-defined names.

The use of abstraction in HERMES supports extensibility of the language. Not only can link Types and node Kinds be user-defined (as they already were in PHIDIAS), but so can the language's namable terminology elements: Count, Quantifier, and Measure. For instance, a new Count term, several, could be defined as: more than 2 and less than 7. By naming the expression "several," a user can then make use of this term without worrying about its precise definition. Of course, if another user interprets the term several differently, the definition can always be explored and modified through the interface to the language. Similarly, Measure terms can be added to the language, like "set off from": central distance is less than 24 inches and closest distance is more than 4 inches

In Section 9.1's scenario in which the notion of privacy is made operational, the scale of privacy values from 1 to 9 was abstracted by the definition of the following Number terms:

```
very public:          1
quite public:    2
public:               3
somewhat public:      4
neutral:         5
somewhat private:     6
private:         7
quite private:   8
very private:    9
```

These definitions allow designers to think in tacit problem domain terms rather than in the explicit quantitative terms required by the computer. The abstractions are constructed tacitly by simply supplying a name when an expression is defined; there are no explicit assignment statements in the language.

2. **Iteration**. Much traditional programming language doctrine has to do with iteration: `for` loops versus `while` control statements, recursive list processing, sequential comparisons, etc. In HERMES, there are no explicit control structures for iteration. Yet, iterating through lists (e.g., all the nodes of such and such a description, or all the links of a certain Type from a node) is ubiquitous in its central task of navigating through hypermedia. In the HERMES language, the various iterative tasks of the design environment and of its hypermedia substrate are encapsulated in primitive syntax options.

A Simple DataList can be defined by a NodeKind or LanguageType; these options iterate through the database index to retrieve all nodes of the specified category. A Simple Association can be defined by a Link Type; this option iterates through all the links of the specified Type from a given starting node. The option, `all associations`, iterates through all of a node's out-going links; `inverse Association` iterates in-coming links; `parts` iterates content links. Each of these options returns the list of all nodes at the other end of these links. The options are implemented with iteration control structures, but the user need not be aware of this.

Simple Filters also iterate through lists of nodes. They test each node successively to see whether it meets some condition. The nodes that meet the condition are returned. For instance, the expression, `arguments of answers of the bunk locations issue that are of kind pro-argument`, will be evaluated by iterating through all the nodes at the ends of the specified argument links and testing which of them are of node Kind `pro-argument`.

Several of the Number options are also implicitly iterative, returning a count of elements in a list, a minimum, maximum, total, or product of the values. One Number option even iterates through all combinations of two or three graphical objects to return a list of the distances between them. To test for an acceptable work triangle in a kitchen, a designer can simply take the minimum value of this list of distances, without needing to worry about the details of iterating through all the combinatorial possibilities if there are multiple stoves, sinks, or refrigerators in the kitchen.

3. **Typing.** The constrained syntax of the HERMES language provides an implicit typing system. Like the strong typing system of languages like PASCAL, it avoids syntactic combinations that would be meaningless or cause conflicts. However, it is enforced "behind the scenes" so users do not have to be aware of it as a typing system. Types are not declared explicitly by the user.

The Simple syntax options are categorized in the syntax classes discussed in the previous section, such as DataList, Filter, and Association. These 25 classes are the *types* of the HERMES language. A typical Computed syntax option combines terms from several of these classes. For instance, one Computed DataList option is: DataList Combination DataList. This joins any two expressions of type DataList with any expression of type Combination, like `and` or `or`.

Notice that each of the computed syntax options listed in Appendix C refers to one or more syntax classes (or types). Legal combinations of these types are defined by the options of the syntax. This is a convention of the language; it would be possible to define combinations of individual options or to distinguish between categories of options like Simple and Computed— but that would be a different language. For instance, example a-2 in Table 10-3 allows a DataList to be defined as a Filter applied to a DataList. This means that any expression of type Filter can be applied to any expression of type DataList and the result will be a legal expression of type DataList. The DataList used as a component in this definition may itself be a Computed DataList composed of several components. By applying these rules repeatedly, one can build up well-defined expressions of arbitrary nested complexity.

The set of defined legal options has been carefully designed to permit the construction of a broad range of expressions to meet the needs of people using a hypermedia-based design environment. While generality of expression has been a priority, an attempt has also been made to exclude combinations that would lead to problems for the users. Another constraint has been to keep the sheer number of options as small as possible. Of the 110 options defined, only a small number will be used most of the time; many are for advanced techniques primarily necessary for internal use building interface functionality or for complex graphical computations.

4. **Recursion**. Recursion was already available in the PHIDIAS query language. A simple example is the definition of issue trees as: issues with their issue trees. Here, the definition recursively incorporates its own name. This is useful for navigating hypermedia networks to arbitrary depth. The evaluation proceeds from a node across all its issue links to new nodes, across their issue links, etc. The recursion terminates at nodes that have no issue links. This graceful termination condition is built into the implementation of the Simple Association option, Link Type. Therefore, users of the language do not need to be concerned about explicitly stating a halting condition for the recursion, a step that frequently causes bugs for novice programmers. The implementation supports what a naive user would tacitly expect, or at least what one would come to expect after having been exposed to some sample recursive definitions in the language.

5. **Variables**. The HERMES language experiments with how far a programming language can go without the use of explicit variables. Variables are perhaps the first serious barrier that most programming poses for people who are not mathematically inclined or experienced. Lack of explicit variables differentiates the HERMES language clearly from procedural languages (that use variables for iteration counters, subroutine parameters, array indices, etc.), functional languages (that use variables for lambda parameters), and logic languages (that use variables for quantification).

HERMES makes use of operator application, applying successive operations directly to the results of previous operations without need for abstract variables to relate the operations to the operands. This works smoothly in simple cases and supports tacit expectations. When expressions are nested several levels deep, the relations of what operations are to be applied to which operands can become confusing. (Several examples of this are given in Section 10.3 and in Appendix B, in which moderately complex applications in the HERMES language are discussed.) For these cases, three special "deictic variables" have been defined. These are not abstract variables, but terms that perform much the same concrete role as deictic pronouns in natural languages.

The deictic variables of HERMES are the following Simple DataList options: `that (last subject)`, `this (expression)`, and `those items`. They are used within an expression to refer to a node or list of nodes that has been previously computed. They disambiguate the application of Predicates and allow intermediate results of computations to be displayed or reused without recomputing them. Examples of the use of the `it` and `them` deictic variables will be seen in the analysis of the privacy critics in the following section. The `this (expression)` variable can be useful in defining recursive terms; `issue trees` can be defined as: `issues with their this (expression)`, where `this (expression)` refers to the term `issue trees` that is itself being defined.

It should be noted that the lack of variables is a trade-off in the design of the HERMES language. It is intended to reduce the cognitive overhead of the use of explicit variables. However, it probably introduces the most severe restriction in the expressibility of the language for relatively complex computations, making critics like the `privacy gradient critique` in Section 10.3 and the `advice` critic in the academic advising application in Appendix B difficult to construct and comprehend. However, the language is not meant primarily to be used for building computationally complex systems, but rather for supporting the incessant reuse and modification of relatively simple definitions of terms needed for displaying, analyzing, and critiquing hypermedia representations of designs.

6. **Quantification**. The HERMES Quantifier type is provided to support quantification. As just discussed, it does not use the explicit bound variables of predicate calculus or PROLOG. Three examples show how it is used:

```
chairs that are near to at least one table in
    archie's habitat
issues that have no answers that include "bunk"
if all privacy ratings of parts of archie's habitat
    are more than quite private
```

As should be clear from these expressions, the computation of a quantity like *all* is carried out internally by the implementation of this syntax option and need not be an explicit concern of the user.

7. **Conditionals**. Conditionals are important in a design environment. They are, for instance, used for critic rules, conditional links, and conditional nodes. In addition to the standard syntax form for conditionals, `if Boolean then DataList1, else DataList2`, HERMES offers the

following form: either `DataList1` or `DataList2`. The second format is more supportive of a tacit approach. Its evaluation first computes DataList1. If it returns something, that is returned as the result of the whole conditional expression; if it returns no nodes, then DataList2 is computed and its results are returned for the conditional. For instance, if one wants to list the answers to an issue if there are any and give a warning message otherwise, one can define the following conditional expression:

```
either answers of my issue or "There are no answers
    to my issue."
```

The implementation of this option takes care of the checking of whether there are any results of the first part and deciding whether or not to compute and return the results of the second part.

10.3 Defining Interpretive Critics

Interpretive critics. Interpretive critics in the Lunar Habitat Design Environment (LHDE) built on HERMES play much the same role as critics in JANUS and triggers in PHIDIAS, as discussed in Chapter 7. In LHDE the critics are not active the way that JANUS' critics were, although a different design environment built on the HERMES substrate could make use of the same mechanisms as JANUS to activate critics associated with a design unit whenever an instance of that unit is created or moved in a design construction. In LHDE and PHIDIAS II (which is also built on HERMES), critics are tied to user interface buttons to provide PHIDIAS-style triggers. Interpretive critics can be used whenever a user has them evaluated by means of any interface mechanism. That is, designers can define and evaluate interpretive critics very freely, without necessarily having them tied to design units in a palette component or to predefined buttons in a construction interface. Interpretive critics are, thus, more general than the critics and triggers of the related systems they were inspired by.

Interpretive critics are defined using the HERMES language. They can take advantage of all of the expressive power of the language. Basically, a critic is any expression in the language that analyzes the state of the hypermedia database. Typically, a critic looks for certain features in a graphical construction and displays a message or takes some other action depending on whether the feature is found or not. The message can include design rationale or examples explaining the reasoning behind the critic definition. It might, for instance, include a selection of items from the design rationale, through which the designer can browse, e.g.:

```
privacy check of habitats and deliberation of privacy
    issue
```

By using the HERMES language, interpretive critics can be more general, more expressive, and more complex than JANUS critics. They are not restricted to spatial relations of individual design units in the palette or to a single construction area. They can analyze, for instance, multiple habitats in the database, evaluate global characteristics of designs (like number of parts or absence of particular parts), and make their analysis dependent on other conditions in the database. Examples of complex critics are the privacy critics described in Chapter 9 and the academic advising critic discussed in Appendix B.

Because the whole language can be used and the whole database accessed, critics can be made dependent upon information in other designs, in an issue base, or in a distinct specification component (as indicated in Chapter 8). The critics can play an important role in integrating diverse pieces of information in the system.

Critics in HERMES are called *interpretive* because of the synergy which they engender between the HERMES language and the mechanism of interpretive perspectives. This is best explained with an example. Suppose Desi defined a critic named `refrigerator access` as:

```
if refrigerators are too near doors then refrigerator
    access message
```

Now, if Desi had defined `too near` as `closest distance is less than 5 feet` but Archie had modified `too near` to be `closest distance is less than 3 feet`, then the `refrigerator access` critic will be "interpreted" differently in Archie's perspective then in Desi's. Since the language allows critics to be built up to arbitrary levels of complexity, a critic like the `academic advising` critic (in Appendix B) may be dependent upon the definition of many sub-expression, which may be defined differently in different perspectives. The point in the example is that Desi and Archie have different interpretations of what it means for something in the kitchen to be too close to something else. In another domain (e.g., molecular chemistry or astronomy) the term `too near` might need to be redefined more drastically. The perspectives mechanism assures that the evaluation of an interpretive critic will always interpret the terms and sub-expressions of the critic's definition within the context of the current active perspective.

Comparison with JANUS critics. HERMES critics are defined in the high level representations made available through the language. That is, they can be defined using vocabulary that is close to the problem domain, without needing to think in the explicit functional manner of the LISP syntax used by MODIFIER. All of the critics used in systems like JANUS and MODIFIER can be concisely stated in the HERMES language. Following are definitions of terms used for defining these critics:

```
next to:    closest distance is less than 4 inches

far from:   closest distance is more than 30 inches

close to:   central distance is less than 60 inches

near:       closest distance is less than 12 inches

set off from:   close to and not next to

work triangle distances:   list      of      closest
    distance in feet among sink, stove, refrigerator
```

Using these terms, the equivalent of JANUS' critic rules can be concisely and readably defined as follows in the HERMES language:

```
all stoves are set off from sinks

no stoves are next to refrigerators

all stoves are far from all doors and windows

all dishwashers are next to sinks

all refrigerators are far from all windows

refrigerators are close to doors

sinks are near windows

the minimum work triangle distances are less than
    23
```

In MODIFIER, the critic rules are meant to be available to and modifiable by the end-user. However, they are written in LISP. Thus, a designer wishing to modify a critic rule in MODIFIER must be at least somewhat familiar with the complexities of LISP doctrine, including its non-intuitive Polish notation. In addition, conventions of MODIFIER's property sheets must be understood and used to make explicit computational decisions. For instance, the HERMES critic,

```
all stoves are set off from sinks
```

appears in MODIFIER's property sheets as:

```
not_next_to (stove , sink )        apply to: all
near (stove, sink)                 apply to: one
```

The parentheses of LISP in MODIFIER's critics are replaced in HERMES by an implicit nested phrase structure that is familiar to people from natural language. This nesting is unambiguously determined at definition time through the tacit use of the interface to the language discussed above. Figure 10-4 shows the explicit phrase structure for the critic rule just discussed. Note that this diagram not only expands the definition of set off from (which has been abstracted in the rule statement), but also indicates the clauses at least one and in kitchen, which are computationally important but are implicit in the expression that the user sees and manipulates. That is to say, both the structure of the critic and substantial contents of it are kept implicit and are hidden from the user's explicit understanding, in much the sense that the explicit phrase structure of normal speech is not usually an object during ordinary communication.

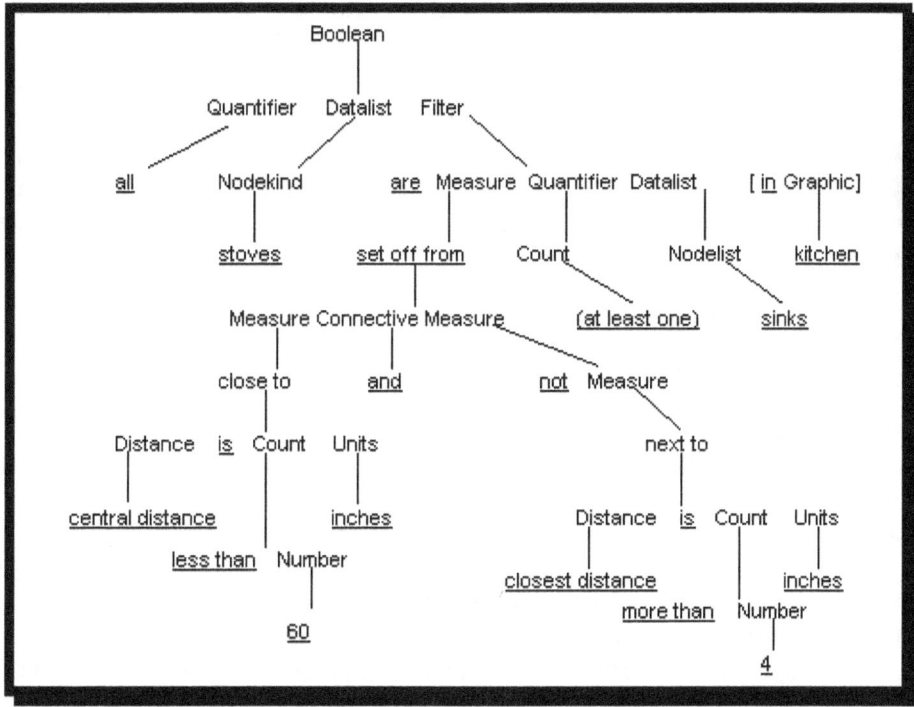

Figure 10-4. Phrase structure of a HERMES critic rule.

The critic rule can be read from the leaves of the tree: `all stoves are set off from [at least one] sinks [in kitchen]`. *Phrases in brackets are implicit. The phrase* `set off from` *can be expanded as:* `central distance is less than 60 inches and not closest distance is more than 4 inches`.

The point of this diagram is not to show how complex interpretive critics are internally, but on the contrary to show how rules that are inherently quite complex can be expressed in apparently relatively simple expressions (like, `all stoves are set off from sinks`), which hide much of the complexity that the user ordinarily does not need to be concerned with.

Analysis of the privacy critics. The privacy critics developed in the scenario of Chapter 9 provide a good example of a complex definition in the HERMES language. A close look can reveal both some of the advantages of using the language and also some of the difficulties.

The task of the privacy critic is to determine if public areas of a lunar habitat are too near to private areas. So first the notions of privacy and nearness must be operationalized and applied to areas within habitats. A `privacy values` scale from 1 to 9 is established and these Number values are given names from `very public` (1) to `very private` (9). Links of type `privacy rating` are attached to various parts of the habitats and connected to nodes with appropriate `privacy values`. The Measure term `too near` is defined as:

```
closest distance is less than 5 feet
```

Now it is possible to define public and private areas:

```
public area: parts that have privacy ratings that are
    less than somewhat public
private areas: parts that have privacy ratings that
    are more than somewhat private
```

These are Computed Associations or Predicates. They look at all the parts of whatever DataList they are applied to. These parts are then Filtered by checking if they have `privacy ratings` links and furthermore if the nodes connected by such links lead to values greater or less than the values named `somewhat private` or `somewhat public`. Any parts found that have at least one such link will be returned by these expressions.

It would be more efficient to make these definitions for `immediate parts` (i.e., top level parts of the habitats) rather than all `parts` (including subparts, all the way down to primitive graphical polygons). That would save considerable traversal of the hierarchies of graphical objects making up the habitats. However, that would require that the person defining the expression knew that all the relevant public and private parts were defined as top level parts of the habitats. If the designer defining this expression had also constructed the habitat graphic this would be possible. For the sake of generality that has not been assumed in this discussion.

Note that a given part might have multiple `privacy rating` links (even in the same perspective). The definitions above only require one such link meeting the Filter condition. Thus, a given part could be returned as both a `public area` and a `private area`. Such an anomaly would quickly show up as a `problem area` in the critic results. In general, the ability of the definitions to deal reasonably with such multiple-definitions is an aspect of robustness in the HERMES language. It is discussed in Appendix B under the topic of defeasible reasoning.

The next step is to create a display of problem areas, that is, private areas that are too near to public areas. This can be accomplished with the following definition of problem areas:

```
private areas that are too near public areas of that
(last subject) with those items
```

The idea here is to select one private area of a habitat at a time and for each one to then iterate through all the public areas of the same habitat and list the public areas that are too near to the selected private area. Both private areas and public areas are Associations that operate on the same habitat (DataList) when the overall problem areas Association is applied to a habitat or a list of habitats.

The Filter syntax option used in the definition of problem areas has the following form: Measure [Quantifier] DataList [in Graphic]. The Measure has already been defined and stored with the name too near. The optional [Quantifier] defaults to an implicit "at least one". The DataList that the private area is to be measured to is each public area of whichever habitat is currently being operated on by the problem areas Association. To define a DataList consisting of these public areas, the deictic variable, that (last subject), is used to refer to the habitat to which the problem areas Association is applied. This deictic refers to the most recently defined "subject" to which operators are being applied, namely the "subject" of the problem areas Association. Here the term "subject" refers to the DataList that is the input to the evaluation of an expression. A stack of recent subjects is maintained in order to implement this deictic variable. The parenthetical explanatory phrase, "(last subject)", departs from the tacit feel of the language in order to alert the reader to think explicitly about the computational structure of operator application in this case because a reference is being made to some term outside the immediate expression—namely to the subject to which this expression will be applied.

The optional [in Graphic] phrase defaults to in that (last subject), which, again, refers to the "subject" of the problem areas Association. That means that the measurement of distance between the private area and the public area is computed within the graphical habitat. Unless a graphical object is explicitly named as the context for distance measurements, the assumption is made that the last explicitly named subject should serve this role. The necessity of naming (tacitly or explicitly) a graphical context for measurements arises from the generality of the HERMES language, which can be referring to any object in the database, rather than to the content of a unique construction area as assumed in JANUS and PHIDIAS.

Finally, in the definition of `problem areas` the deictic variable `those items` refers to the most recently enumerated items, namely the `public areas` that are enumerated for each `private area` and that satisfy the Filter condition. During the testing of the Filter condition, the successful enumerated items are stored on a special list that can be referenced by the special deictic variable "`those items`". Thus, the `with those items` phrase following the Filter phrase retrieves the list of `public areas` that are `too near` a given `private area` and adds them to the result list of the critic following that `private area` and indented under it.

Now that the computational heart of the `privacy check` critic has been defined, the critic can be assembled. First, a privacy message is defined to be displayed in the case that no problem areas are found for a given habitat. This is simply a Character node with the contents:

```
"Public and private areas are separated."
```

This node can be named `privacy message` or it can be linked to the `privacy check` critic itself. If it is named, the critic is defined as:

```
name with either name of problem areas or privacy
   message
```

If it is linked with a link of type `message`, then the critic is defined as:

```
name with either name of problem areas or message of
   this (expression)
```

In the latter case, the reference to the `privacy message` is replaced by a computation, `message of this (expression)`, using the deictic variable `this`. The variable `this (expression)` refers to the current object itself, so `message of this (expression)` follows the `message` link from the definition of this critic to the Character node whose content is the required message. Again, the use of parentheses signals the need for some explicit reflection by the reader.

The `privacy check` critic uses the implicit if / then construction, `either / or`, in which the first phrase is used if it produces any results, otherwise the second phrase (in this case, simply displaying the message) is used. The principal work done by the definition of `privacy check` is to display the names of graphical objects, rather than displaying them as graphics. `Privacy check` is a Computed Association that is applied to a DataList of one or more habitats. So it first displays the name to the habitat to which it is being applied, then (indented under that name, because of the `with` conjunction) it computes the list of `problem areas` of that habitat and displays the names of all the items in the resultant list (including the names of the `public areas` that are indented in the list under the `private areas`). If the resultant list was empty for a given habitat, the `privacy message` is displayed instead.

In the scenario, a variation on `privacy check` named `privacy display` was defined:

    name and privacy ratings of problem areas

This critic displays the `privacy ratings` as well as the `names` of all items in the list computed by the `problem areas` Association.

Recall from Chapter 3 that the lunar habitat designers eventually settled on a concept of *privacy gradient* in the transcribed session. That meant that they wanted the arrangement of the habitat to change gradually from private areas to public areas. To operationalize this notion, one could introduce a test to see if any two areas that are near each other differ by more than a value of, say, plus or minus two. This introduces explicit arithmetic computations into the definitions of a critic. It also introduces a complicated comparison of each habitat part with all the other parts of the habitat. The following set of definitions can be used to compute habitat parts that are incompatible in this sense of a privacy gradient.

In the Chapter 9 scenario, the designers ended up with a critic called `privacy gradient catalog`. It goes through all habitats in the database, selecting those for which `privacy ratings` links are attached to some parts. For those habitats, it displays their name and an analysis of how they meet the defined privacy gradient considerations:

    name with privacy gradient critique of habitats that
        have parts that have privacy ratings

For each habitat that has privacy ratings, the `privacy gradient critique` is displayed. This is similar to the `privacy display`, above, in that it computes `problem parts` using a `privacy gradient listing` Association, or else displays a `privacy gradient message`. Here are the definitions to handle this:

```
privacy gradient critique: either privacy gradient
    listing or privacy gradient message
privacy gradient listing: name and privacy ratings of
    parts that have privacy ratings with their problem
    parts
privacy gradient message: "The parts of this design
    are arranged along a privacy gradient."
```

The privacy gradient listing Association iterates through the parts of a habitat and for each part lists (indented) their problem parts. The definition of problem parts is the tricky part. It uses three further definitions: too near, other parts, and are incompatible. The Measure, too near, is the same as it was in the privacy check critic, except that in the current perspective it has been modified from 5 feet to 3 feet:

```
problem parts: name and privacy ratings of other
    parts that are too near that (last subject) and
    that are incompatible
too near: closest distance is less than 3 feet
other parts: parts of inverse parts that do not equal
    that (last subject)
are incompatible: have privacy ratings that are more
    than privacy ratings of that (last subject) + 2 or
    are less than privacy ratings of that (last
    subject) -2
```

The definition of other parts requires some explanation. Within the privacy gradient listing expression, the Association problem parts must be applied to parts (of a habitat). The definition of problem parts centers on the definition of other parts. However, what is wanted is "other parts" of the habitat, not other parts of the selected part of the habitat, which is what would result from the application of problem parts to parts. Therefore, within the definition of other parts, the computation must get back to the habitat by tracing backwards the part link between the habitat and its part. This is accomplished by the construction, inverse parts. Once the computation is back at the habitat, it can find the other parts by navigating all the parts (i.e., graphical content) links of the habitat. Of course, the computation of "other parts" should exclude the part from which the computation began in order to avoid comparing that part with itself. This is accomplished with the Filter, that do not equal that (last subject), in which the deictic variable that (last subject) refers to the last "subject" of application, namely the original `part` iterated in the `privacy gradient listing` expression.

The definition of the Filter, `are incompatible`, uses the same `that` (`last subject`) variable in order to compare each of the `other parts` with the original `part`. This Filter also introduces explicit arithmetic in order to judge whether the `privacy ratings` of these two parts differ by more than 2 on the privacy scale. This comparison completes the operationalization of the idea of a privacy gradient as it occurred in the lunar habitat design transcript.

The definition of `privacy gradient catalog` with all its preliminary definitions is a relatively formidable task. If one undertakes figuring it out from scratch, it might well seem that the task is easier to do in a traditional programming language. This seems especially true to people who are experienced in programming. It may well be that such a task pushes the HERMES language to near its limits. On the other hand, a design environment built on the HERMES substrate might support reuse and modification sufficiently to make the HERMES alternative preferable. First, much of the defining could have been done in the seeded set of language definitions, providing a well thought-out collection of building blocks for complex tasks involving privacy. If this was not available in the original seed, a reseeding process could take place when the privacy issue is raised as an important concern. Then an experienced programmer or a HERMES local developer could step in and provide a set of privacy-related definitions for everyone to use.

As stated at the outset of this chapter, the HERMES language has been developed to push its approach to supporting a mix of tacit and explicit understanding as far as possible and to explore its limits. The `privacy gradient critique` expression provides an important test of these limits. On the one hand, it shows that the task that appeared extremely challenging back in Chapter 3 can in fact be accomplished using the HERMES language. On the other hand, it shows that such a task may strain the limits of the language. The limits of the language are explored further by examples in Appendix B. More thorough experience will have to await the building of robust design environments on the HERMES substrate and their use by a community of designers.

Conclusion

"I propose that men and women be returned to work
as controllers of machines, and that the control of people
by machines be curtailed. I propose, further, that the effects
of changes in technology and organization on life patterns
be taken into careful consideration, and that the changes
be withheld or introduced on the basis of this consideration."

> Kurt Vonnegut, Jr.
> *Player Piano*
> (1952, p. 285)

CHAPTER 11. CONTRIBUTIONS

The topic of this dissertation has been the problem of providing computer support for cooperative design given the nature of tacit and explicit understanding. But at a meta-level, an important theme has been the role of theory in software design. Often, work in cognitive science and artificial intelligence proceeds with little reference to philosophy, which is given lip service as one constituent of these interdisciplinary endeavors. Of course, preconceptions abound in such work, but they are either treated as self-evident common sense or addressed through discussions of individual concepts whose inner coherence remains outside the investigation.

This dissertation is an attempt to take *theory* seriously in computer science. Rather than first creating a software artifact whose theory is at best only tacitly available retrospectively,[26] and then subjecting the artifact to controlled user testing to determine its effectiveness, the approach followed here is to formulate a set of explicit theoretical principles to motivate an approach to computer support of design and then to present a package of prototyped functionality to illustrate that approach. Together, the theory and the examples are meant to provide cogent arguments for the deliberation of

---

[26]Carroll and associates have made a case for considering artifacts as themselves implicit expressions of theories, as though guiding philosophies were unnecessary. This case has been made specifically in terms of software artifacts in the realm of human-computer interaction, and has even been related to hermeneutics (Carroll & Campbell, 1989; Carroll & Kellogg, 1989). While they persuasively point out problems with the traditional assumptions about the relation of psychological theory to design practice, they overlook the spiral character of understanding, in particular the guiding role of (often tacit) philosophical beliefs and conceptual frameworks.

central issues in software design of systems to support innovative, collaborative design work in exploratory domains.

Of course, several preconceptions have been at work here, too. However, the major assumptions have been systematically reflected upon in the process and explicated or modified as need be. It has been assumed, for instance, that software to support professional designers should be based on an understanding of the structure of their work processes. As a guiding idea, the design process was viewed (or pre-viewed) as a process of interpretation (Chapter 1). Two approaches were then taken to explore this work process: one by looking at some of the best available descriptions of the way designers work (by Alexander, Rittel, and Schön in Chapter 2), and the other by looking at a concrete example of designers working (on lunar habitat design in Chapter 3). To make this theory even more explicit and general, it was then put into the framework of a philosophy (Heidegger's hermeneutics in Chapter 4). An explicit theory of computer support for interpretation in design was built on top of the results of the preceding investigations (Chapter 5 and 6). The theory developed in this way was then used to evaluate related software systems meant to support design (Chapter 7). Finally, the theory served to motivate and justify design decisions in the HERMES software (Chapters 8, 9, and 10).

While this approach stresses theory, it does not ignore the need for empirical grounding or iterative testing. The design methodologies reviewed all grew out of either reflection on professional practice or consideration of experimental findings. The study of lunar habitat design pursued as part of the dissertation took on the flavor of participatory design (Ehn, 1988; Greenbaum & Kyng, 1991) by having the software designers and the design professionals working together on a lunar habitat design, and by involving the two groups in dialogue about the design work and about possibilities for computer-based support of this work. Although it was never reflected in the Chapter 3 transcripts, the lunar habitat designers have been involved in on-going evaluation of the HERMES system and its functionality as part of their role as corporate sponsors of the funded research. In addition, the design of HERMES is a response to empirical experience with the related design environments on which it is based, as well as on a series of programming walkthroughs to evaluate the HERMES language design (reported in Appendix A).

Evaluation and refinement of the Lunar Habitat Design Environment (LHDE) and PHIDIAS II built on top of the HERMES substrate are expected to continue indefinitely. Clearly, the greatest need for future work is to build a robust design environment that exercises all of the functionality of the

HERMES substrate and to gain experience in the utility of this functionality through use by professional designers. Unfortunately, that is beyond the scope of the present effort. For one thing, it will involve identifying real-world projects in which a system like LHDE makes commercial sense in order to get professionals to invest significant time in using preliminary versions. The support of lunar habitat design has served as a fruitful application domain in developing HERMES, but a specific project must now provide a practical context for further participatory development and workplace evaluation.

It is useful to view the unfolding of this dissertation as a hermeneutic process, in which a vague preconception of interpretation in design becomes increasingly clearer through precisely the kind of interpretive process that has been analyzed in the dissertation. The concept of interpretation has been elaborated through an investigation of the role of interpretation in design. The guiding perspective was the intuition that *interpretation is the central category for founding a theory of computer support*. This perspective was tied through a process of reflection to its explicit roots in Heidegger's philosophy, but also to the almost forgotten role of interpretation in the related systems that HERMES grew out of. In a sense, the dissertation embodies a moment of reflection in which the effort to build systems of computer support ran up against the limits of multi-faceted, domain-oriented, knowledge-based systems; made explicit the role of interpretation in design; and then, using this, proposed a system that *integrates the facets in a hypermedia substrate, extends the notion of domain-orientation with perspectives*, and uncovers the basis of explicit computer knowledge representations in the *expressing of tacit human preunderstanding in language*.

In looking back over what has been accomplished in this dissertation, it is clear that no final answers have been given. The analysis of interpretation remains unclear and incomplete in many ways. The theory of computer support is no more than a beginning in an attempt to provide rationale for a new direction in artificial intelligence. The design of HERMES is suggestive of promising functionality, but this promise remains largely untested. Nevertheless, whatever the limits of this work, it does seem to have made significant contributions on three primary levels: on a philosophical level (11.1), on a theoretical level (11.2), and on a system building level (11.3).

11.1 Contributions to a Philosophy of Interpretation

At least since Dreyfus (1966; 1972; & Dreyfus, 1986), the relevance of Heidegger's philosophy to AI has been debated. Unfortunately, most of the discussion by computer scientists has relied on secondary sources, especially pre-publication drafts of Dreyfus' (1991) commentary on Heidegger. So one contribution of this dissertation has been to return to the original text of Heidegger (1927) and to systematically apply that text to the context of computer support for interpretation in design. The result has been an *analysis of interpretation* that is frequently more detailed and rigorous than alternative presentations. This represents a contribution to Heideggerian scholarship as such, not just from a computer science perspective.

Of course, according to the philosophy there is no "correct" interpretation of a text unrelated to a background of concerns. The confrontation of the Heideggerian text with the problematic of design and computer support for design had important consequences. Examples from design methodology and from lunar habitat design provided not only a concreteness to Heidegger's abstractions, but a more realistic context than Heidegger's own craft-oriented glimpses of the lonely carpenter absorbed in his hammering. Design shifted the emphasis to collaborative work. It also moved (thanks largely to Schön's insights) from use of the physical artifact to the more conceptual design of artifacts. In particular, this brought to the fore the role of discovery over that of laying out what was implicitly disclosed. This clarified and extended the analysis of interpretation, removing certain ambiguities that Heidegger glossed over.

Perhaps most importantly, the effort to apply Heidegger's philosophy to computer system building not only forced a precision of concept, but resulted in the operationalizing of many of the ideas. This is, of course, a common benefit to philosophy of mind when it is applied in AI. In this case, the result was a computer model of human interpretation as situated, perspectival, and linguistic. However, in addition to the model, there is an extensive recognition of the limits of the model and the need to involve people in the operation of the model. These limits are shown to be consequences of the Heideggerian analysis. So philosophy benefited from its meeting with computer science.

11.2 Contributions to a Theory of Computer Support

The central contribution was to identify the key concept for a theory of computer support: interpretation. Although Winograd & Flores (1986), for instance, talked a lot about interpretation, they ranged across Heidegger's (1927) framework and focused on its critique of technical rationality. Ironically, their proposed software example, the COORDINATOR program, suffered from a lack of respect for the importance of interpretative control by the users. They failed to take seriously the fact that there is no objective structure to a domain and that people should be supported in defining their own analyses, interpretations, and terminologies from their own perspectives. Support for interpretation is the ingredient missing from most traditional AI programs. This dissertation contributes the antidote: a *recognition of the central role of interpretation and the impossibility of fully automating it*. It is difficult to convey the potential importance of this contribution; that is why so many pages of the dissertation have been devoted to this theme.

The proposed theory of computer support is built squarely on the analysis of interpretation. This gives the theory a coherence and consistency missing from other theoretical frameworks in computer science (other than those based on strictly formal logical grounds). It demonstrates how philosophy (again, other than logic) can be put in the service of computer science.

Knowledge-based system design inevitably raises the question of the nature of knowledge. Some contributions have been made here. First, *the varieties of knowledge or information have been categorized* in terms of their origins in various phases of the process of interpretation. This includes not only tacit and explicit understanding, but also shared understanding and captured computer representations. Second, the idea of domain knowledge has been critiqued. Not only does knowledge in a design domain change as the related technologies and styles change and as the expertise of the field matures and grows, but every designer and every design team has their own domain knowledge. It is not simply that they each have different pieces of an underlying knowledge. Rather, to know is to know from a perspective, so *there is no objective body of domain knowledge independent of what people know in their own ways*, within their many perspectives. Third, the role of language in expressing knowledge has been emphasized. *The emergence of interpersonal or operationalized knowledge from tacit experience takes place through discourse and assertion* within situated interpretation.

Correspondingly, an end-user language has an important role to play in computer support.

11.3 Contributions to a System for Innovative Design

The effort to illustrate the functionality called for by the theory resulted in three major contributions to building computer support for innovative design: (a) a hypermedia knowledge representation substrate, incorporating: (b) a system of perspectives and (c) an end-user language. The design of each of these features has been thought through, both in terms of the functionality required by the theory and in terms of their usability in a practical computer system for design professionals. Each has also been prototyped in executable code and subjected to testing to confirm the implementability of the ideas. Various versions of these features, along with auxiliary functionality have also been incorporated in a series of design environments that have been shown to lunar habitat designers for feedback.

(a) The *hypermedia substrate* incorporates the power of the fine-grained hypertext in the original PHIDIAS system, provides an efficient and scalable object-oriented database for persistence, incorporates multi-media nodes, and integrates the perspectives and language into the fundamental node and link structure. This hypermedia offers an extremely powerful and flexible knowledge representation system, whose control by the user is limited primarily by the lack of a fuller user interface. Adaptability by the user—or plasticity of representation—is critical according to the theory. The HERMES hypermedia contributes an example of a substrate for supporting such adaptability.

(b) The *perspectives mechanism* is a contribution to Computer Supported Cooperative Work. It allows individuals to organize their own versions of knowledge representations and to share them. This provides a tool for supporting the evolution of knowledge by starting with systematically organized domains and allowing users to inherit and modify these and to organize meaningful new domains. The virtual copying approach is an inherently efficient mechanism, which encourages consistency by eliminating unnecessary duplication of representations in multiple copies.

(c) The *HERMES language* is a contribution to end-user programming languages and programmable design environments. It suggests ways of reducing the programming doctrine that users have to learn or keep in mind. Much of the traditional programming language doctrine is suppressed by keeping the corresponding features tacit in the HERMES language. Also, the appearance of expressions in the language supports tacit understanding by making heavy use of user-defined domain terminology and by following several syntactic conventions of natural language. At the same time, when the computational structure of an expression must be made more explicit to be understood or modified, this can be done to some extent through interface displays and to some extent by exploratory execution. A programming language paradigm that was implicit in PHIDIAS' query language has been pushed forward, extended, and modified to the point of a powerful end-user language that can play key roles in a system to support interpretation.

Computer technology can contribute to human emancipation. By providing computationally active media of external memory, it can significantly extend cognitive capabilities within an increasingly complex world. However, that requires a people-centered approach in which machine computations are at the service of human judgments and interpretation. Mainstream software approaches have developed within a social context dominated by the interests of military, government, and multinational corporations, resulting in computer applications that replace people or that dictate how they think and work. This dissertation has tried to present design rationale to oppose the bureaucratic interests, a theory to guide people-centered software development, and example mechanisms for giving people innovative, shared control over software computations.

BIBLIOGRAPHY

Abelson H, Sussman G (1985) *Structure and Interpretation of Computer Programs*. Cambridge: MIT Press.

Adorno TW (1964). *Jargon der Eigentlichkeit: Zur deutschen Ideologie.* [The Jargon of Authenticity]. Frankfurt am Main: Suhrkamp.

Adorno TW (1966). *Negative Dialektik* [Negative Dialectics]. Frankfurt am Main: Suhrkamp.

Alexander C (1964) *Notes on the Synthesis of Form*. Cambridge: Harvard University Press.

Alexander C (1971) The State of the Art in Design Methods. In Cross N (1984). 309-316.

Alexander C, Ishikawa S, Silverstein M, Jacobson M, Fiksdahl-King I, Angel S (1977) *A Pattern Language: Towns, Buildings, Construction*. New York: Oxford University Press.

Alexander C, Poyner B (1966) The Atoms of Environmental Structure. In Cross N (1984). 123-133.

Backus J (1978) Can Programming be Liberated from the von Neumann Style? A Functional Style and Its Algebra of Programs. *Communications of the ACM. 21.* (8). 613-641.

Bell B, Citrin W, Lewis C, Rieman J, Weaver R, Wilde N, Zorn B (1992).The Programming Walkthrough: A Structured Method for Assessing the Writability of Programming Languages. Technical Report CU-CS-577-92 January 1992. Department of Computer Science. University of Colorado.

Bernstein B (1992) Euclid: Supporting Collaborative Argumentation with Hypertext. Technical Report CU-CS-596-92 January 1992. Department of Computer Science. University of Colorado.

Bluth BJ (1984) *Space Station/Antarctic Analogs*. Washington, D.C.: NASA.

Bluth BJ (1986) Lunar Settlements—A Socio-economic Outlook. *37th Congress of the International Astronautical Federation*, Innsbruck, Austria, October 4-11. Oxford: Persimmon Press.

Boborow DG, Goldstein IP (1980a) *An Experimental Description-Based Programming Environment: Four Reports.* Technical Report CSL-81-3. Palo Alto, CA: Xerox Palo Alto Research Center.

Boborow DG, Goldstein IP (1980b) Representing Design Alternatives. In Boborow & Goldstein 1980a. 19-29.

Boborow DG, Winograd T (1977) An Overview of KRL, A Knowledge Representation Language. *Cognitive Science* 1 (1), 3-46. In Brachman & Levesque (1985).

Boeing Aerospace Company (1983) *Space Station/Nuclear Submarine Analogs.* Granada Hills, CA: National Behavior Systems.

Boland RJ Jr., Maheshwari AK, Te'eni D, Schwartz DG, Tenkasi RV (1992) Sharing Perspectives in Distributed Decision Making. *CSCW '92 Proceedings.*

Bourdieu P (1977) *Outline of a Theory of Practice.* Oxford: Oxford University Press.

Bourdieu P (1991) *The Political Ontology of Martin Heidegger.* Stanford: Stanford University Press.

Brachman R, Levesque H (1985) *Readings in Knowledge Representation.* San Mateo: Morgan Kaufmann.

Buchanan BG, Shortliffe EH (1984) Human Engineering of Medical Expert Systems. In Buchanan BG, Shortliffe EH (Eds.) (1984) *Rule-Based Expert Systems: The MYCIN Experiments of the Stanford Heuristic Programming Project.* Reading, MA: Addison-Wesley. 599-612.

Budde R, Züllighoven H (1990) *Software-Werkzeuge in einer Programmierwerkstatt: Ansätze eines hermeneutisch fundierten Werkzeug- und Maschinenbegriffs.* [Software Tools in a Programming Workshop: Approaches to an Hermeneutically-based Concept of Tools and Machines]. München: Oldenbourg Verlag.

Bush V (1945) As We May Think. *Atlantic Monthly.* 176 (1), 101-108. Reprinted in Greif I (1988) *Computer-Supported Cooperative Work.* San Mateo, CA: Morgan Kaufmann.

Cardelli L, Wenger P (1985) On Understanding Types, Data Abstraction, and Polymorphism. *ACM Computing Surveys. 17.* (7). 471-522.

Carroll JM, Campbell RL (1989) Artifacts as Psychological Theories: the Case of Human-Computer Interaction. *Behavior and Information Technology.* Vol. 8, no. 4, 247-256.

Carroll JM & Kellogg WA (1989). Artifact as theory-nexus: hermeneutics meets theory-based design, *Proceedings of the Conference of Human Factors in Computing Systems*, Austin, 7-14.

Compton WD, Benson CD (1983) *Living and Working in Space: A History of Skylab.* Washington, DC: NASA.

Conklin J, Begeman M (1988) gIBIS: A Hypertext Tool for Exploratory Policy Discussion. *Proceedings of the Conference on Computer Supported Cooperative Work*. New York: ACM. 140-152.

Coyne R (1991). Inconspicuous Architecture, *Gadamer Action & Reason: Conference Proceedings*. Australia: University of Sydney. 62-70.

Coyne R, Snodgrass A (1991) What Is the Philosophical Basis of AI in Design? Working paper. Faculty of Architecture, University of Sydney.

Cross N (1984) *Developments in Design Methodology*. New York: Wiley.

Dayton T, et al. (1993) Skills Needed by User-centered Design Practitioners in Real Software Development Environments: Report on the CHI '92 Workshop. *SIGCHI Bulletin. 25* (3) 16-31.

Design Edge (1990) *Initial Lunar Habitat Construction Shack*. Design control specification. Houston, TX.

Descartes R (1641) *Meditations of First Philosophy*. Indianapolis: Hackett. 1979

Donald M (1991) *Origins of the Modern Mind: Three Stages in the Evolution of Culture and Cognition*. Cambridge: Harvard University Press.

Dreyfus H (1966) *Alchemy and Artificial Intelligence*. Rand paper P3244. The Rand Corporation.

Dreyfus H (1967) Phenomenology and Artificial Intelligence. In Edie J (ed.) (1967) *Phenomenology in America*. Chicago: Quadrangle. 31-47.

Dreyfus H (1972) *What Computers Cannot Do*. New York: Harper and Row.

Dreyfus H (ed.) (1982) *Husserl, Intentionality, and Cognitive Science*. Cambridge: MIT Press.

Dreyfus H (1985) Holism and Hermeneutics. In Hollinger R (Ed.) (1985) *Hermeneutics and Praxis*. Notre Dame, IN: University of Notre Dame Press. 227-247.

Dreyfus H (1990) Heidegger's History of the Being of Equiptment. In Dreyfus H, Hall H (eds.) (1991) *Heidegger: A Critical Reader*. Oxford: Basil Blackwell. 173-185.

Dreyfus H (1991) *Being-in-the-World: A Commentary on Heidegger's Being and Time, Division I*. Cambridge: MIT Press.

Dreyfus H, Dreyfus S (1986) *Mind Over Machine*. New York: Free Press.

Ehn P (1988) *Work-Oriented Design of Computer Artifacts*. Stockholm: Arbetslivscentrum.

Eichold A (1992) Lunar Base Planning Criteria. NEA grant final report. Washington, DC: NEA.

Eisenberg M (1992). SchemePaint: A Programmable Application for Graphics. Technical Report CU-CS-587-92. Computer Science Department, University of Colorado at Boulder.

Eisenberg M, Fischer G (1992) Programmable Design Environments and Design Rationale. AAAI'92 Workshop on Design Rationale Capture and Use. San Jose, CA. July 15, 1992. 81-90.

Engelbart D (1963) A Conceptual Framework for the Augmentation of Man's Intellect. In Howerton, P (Ed.) (1963) *Vistas of Information Handling.* (Vol. 1). Washington, DC: Spartan Books. Reprinted in Greif I (Ed.) (1988) Computer-Supported Cooperative Work. San Mateo, CA: Morgan Kaufmann.

Ericsson KA, Simon HA (1984) *Protocol Analysis: Verbal Reports as Data.* Cambridge: MIT Press.

Fischer G (1989) Creativity Enhancing Design Environments. *Proceedings of the International Conference "Modeling Creativity and Knowledge-Based Creative Design".* Heron Island, Australia. 127-132.

Fischer G (1991) Supporting Learning on Demand with Design Environments. *Proceedings of the International Conference on the Learning Sciences August 1991.* Evanston, IL. 127-132.

Fischer G, Girgensohn A (1990) End-User Modifiability in Design Environments. *Human Factors in Computing Systems, CHI '90 Conference Proceedings (Seattle, WA).* New York: ACM.

Fischer G, Grudin J, Lemke A, McCall R, Ostwald J, Reeves B, Shipman F (1991a). Supporting Indirect, Collaborative Design with Integrated Knowledge-Based Design Environments. Submitted to *Human-Computer Interaction.*

Fischer G, Lemke A, McCall R, Morch A (1991b) Making Argumentation Serve Design. *Human-Computer Interaction* (Special Issue on Design Rationale). *6,* (3 & 4), 393-419.

Fischer G, McCall R, Morch A (1989) Janus: Integrating Hypertext with a Knowledge-based Design Environment. *Proceedings of Hypertext '89.* Pittsburgh, PA: ACM, 105-117.

Fischer G, McCall R, Ostwald J, Reeves B, Shipman F (1993c) Seeding, Evolutionary Growth and Reseeding: Supporting Incremental Development of Designs and Design Environments. Submitted to *AAAI'93.*

Fischer G, Nakakoji K (1992) Beyond the Macho Approach of Artificial Intelligence: Empower Human Designers—Do Not Replace Them. *Knowledge-Based Systems Journal. 5,* (1), 15-30.

Fischer G, Nakakoji K, Ostwald J, Stahl, G, Sumner T (1993a) Embedding Computer-Based Critics in the Contexts of Design. *Proceedings of InterCHI '93. Conference on Human Factors in Computing Systems.* Amsterdam. April 1993. 157-164.

Fischer G, Nakakoji K, Ostwald J, Stahl, G, Sumner T (1993b) Embedding Critics in Design Environments. *The Knowledge Engineering Review*, Special Issue on Expert Critiquing. Fall 1993.

Fitzgerald F, Rashid R (1986) The Integration of Virtual Memory Management and Interprocess Communication in Accent. *ACM Transactions on Computer Systems, 4*, (2), 147.

Floyd C, Züllighoven H, Budde R, Keil-Slawik (1992) *Software Development and Reality Construction*. Heidelberg: Springer Verlag.

Foley J, van Dam A, Feiner S, Hughes J (1990) *Computer Graphics: Principles and Practice*. Reading, MA: Addison-Wesley.

Fodor J (1981) Methodological Solipsism Considered as a Research Strategy in Cognitive Psychology. In Haugland (1981). 307-338.

Freud S (1917) *A General Introduction to Psychoanalysis*. New York: Washington Square Press. 1952.

Gadamer H-G (1960) *Wahrheit und Methode*. Tübingen: Mohr. Translation: Gadamer H-G (1988) *Truth and Method*. New York: Crossroad.

Gadamer HG (1966) Die Universalität des hermeneutischen Problems [The universality of the hermeneutic problem]. In Gadamer HG (1967) *Kleine Schriften I Philosophie Hermeneutic*. Tübingen: Mohr. 101-112.

Gadamer HG (1967) Rhetorik, Hermeneutik und Ideologiekritik [Rhetoric, Hermeneutics and Ideology Critique]. In Gadamer HG (1967) *Kleine Schriften I Philosophie Hermeneutic*. Tübingen: Mohr. 113-130.

Girgensohn A (1992) *End-User Modifiability in Knowledge-Based Design Environments*. Ph.D. dissertation. Department of Computer Science. University of Colorado at Boulder.

Goldstein IP, Boborow DG (1980) Descriptions for a Programming Environment. *Proceedings of the First Annual Conference of the National Association for Artificial Intelligence*, Stanford, CA. 1-6.

Greenbaum J, Kyng M (1991) *Design at Work: Cooperative Design of Computer Systems*. Hillsdale, NJ: Lawrence Erlbaum.

Greif I (Ed.) (1988) *Computer-Supported Cooperative Work*. San Mateo, CA: Morgan Kaufmann.

Grice HP (1975) Logic and Conversation. In Cole P, Morgan J (1975) *Syntax and Semantics 3: Speech Acts*. New York: Academic Press. 41-58.

Habermas J (1967) Zur Logik der Sozialwissenschaften [On the Logic of the Social Sciences]. *Philosophiphische Rundschau*. Beiheft 5, February, 1967.

Habermas J (1968) *Erkenntnis und Interesse* [Knowledge and human interests]. Frankfurt a. M.: Suhrkamp Verlag.

Habermas J (1985) *Der philosophische Diskurs der Moderne: Zwölf Vorlesungen* [The Philosophical Discourse of Modernity]. Frankfurt am Main: Suhrkamp.

Halasz F (1988) Reflections on Notecards: Seven Issues for the Next Generation of Hypermedia Systems. *Communications of the ACM*. Vol. 31, No. 7. 836-852.

Harnad S (1993) Grounding, Situatedness, and Meaning. In *Proceedings of the Fifteenth Annual Conference of the Cognitive Science Society*. Boulder, CO. 169-174.

Haugland J (Ed.) (1981) *Mind Design*. Cambridge: MIT Press.

Hegel GWF (1807) *Phänomenologie des Geistes*. Translation: Hegel GWF (1967) *Phenomenology of Mind*. New York: Harper & Row.

Hegel GWF (1833) *Grundlinien der Philosophie des Rechts* [Principles of the philosophy of right]. Leipzig.

Heidegger M (1927) *Sein und Zeit*. Tuebingen: Niemeyer. Translation: Heidegger M (1962) *Being and Time*. New York: Harper & Row.

Heidegger M (1947) Brief Über den "Humanismus" [Letter on Humanism]. In Heidegger M (1967) *Wegmarken*. Frankfurt a.M.: Klostermann.

Heidegger M (1950) Ursprung des Kunstwerks [The origin of the work of art]. In Heidegger M (1950) *Holzwege*. Frankfurt a.M.: Klostermann.

Heidegger M (1951) *Erläuterungen zu Hölderlins Dichtung*. [Commentary on Holderlin's Poetry] Frankfurt a.M.: Klostermann.

Heidegger M (1953). Wissenschaft und Besinnung [Science and reflection]. In Heidegger M (1954) *Vorträge und Aufsätze*. Pfullingen: Neske.

Heidegger, M. (1971) *Poetry, Language, Thought*. Trans. A. Hoftadter. New York: Harper & Row.

Heidegger M (1975) *Der Grundprobleme der Phänomenologie* [Basic problems of phenomenology]. *Gesamtausgabe* vol. 24. Frankfurt a.M.: Klostermann.

Heidegger M (1979) *Prolegomena zur Geschichte des Zeitbegriffs* [Introduction to the history of the concept of time]. *Gesamtausgabe* vol. 20. Frankfurt a.M.: Klostermann.

Hewitt C (1971) *Description and Theoretical Analysis (Using Schemata) of PLANNER: A Language for Proving Theorems and Manipulating Models in a Robot*. Ph.D. Thesis. June 1971. Reprinted in AI-TR-258 MIT-AI Laboratory, April 1972.

Hinton G, Anderson J (1989) *Parallel Models of Associative Memory*. Hillsdale, NJ: Lawrence Erlbaum.

Hutchins E (1990) The Technology of Team Navigation. In Galegher P, Kraut R, Egido C (Eds.) (1990) *Intellectual Teamwork*. Hillsdale, NJ: Erlbaum. 191-220.

Illich I (1973) *Tools for Conviviality*. New York: Harper & Row.

Johnson JA, Nardi BA, Zarmer CL, Miller JR (1993) ACE: Building Interactive Graphical Applications. *Communications of the ACM. 36* (4). 41-55.

Kant I (1787) *Kritik der reinen Vernunft*. Translation: Kant I (1929) *Critique of Pure Reason*. New York: St. Martin's Press.

Kazmierski M, Spangler D (1992) Lunatechs II: A Kit of Parts for Lunar Habitat Design. Unpublished project report, College of Environmental Design, University of Colorado at Boulder.

Kolodner J (1984) *Retrieval and Organizational Strategies in Conceptual Memory*. Hillsdale, NJ: Lawrence Erlbaum.

Kuhn T (1962) *The Structure of Scientific Revolutions*. Chicago: University of Chicago Press.

Kunz W, Rittel H (1970) Issues as Elements of Information Systems. Working paper 131. Center for Planning and Development Research, University of California, Berkeley.

Kunz W, Rittel H (1984) How to Know What is Known: Designing Crutches for Communication. In Dietschmann HJ (Ed) (1984) *Representation and Exchange of Knowledge as a Basis of Information Processes*. North-Holland: Elsevier. 51-60.

Lakoff G (1987) *Women, Fire, and Dangerous Things*. Chicago: Univ. of Chicago Press.

Lee J (1990) SIBYL: A Tool for Managing Group Decision Rationale. *Proc. CSCW*. LA: ACM Press.

Lee J, Lai K-Y (1991) What's in Design Rationale? *Human-Computer Interaction*. 6. 251-280.

Lefebvre H (1991) *The Production of Space*. Oxford: Blackwell.

Liskov B, Snyder A, Atkinson R, Shaffert C (1977) Abstraction Mechanisms in CLU. *Communications of the ACM. 20*. (8). 564-576.

Marshall C, Halasz F, Rogers R, Jannsen W (1991) Aquanet: A Hypertext Tool to Hold your Knowledge in Place. In *Hypertext '91*. 261-275.

Marx K (1844) *Texte zu Methode und Praxis II*. Germany: Rowohlt. 1966.

Marx K (1867) *Das Kapital*. Hamburg: Meissner. Translation: Marx K (1977) *Capital*. New York: Vintage.

Mead GH (1934) *Mind, Self, and Society*. Chicago: University of Chicago Press.

Merriam-Webster (1991) *Webster's Ninth New Collegiate Dictionary*. Springfield: Merriam-Webster.

Merleau-Ponty M (1945) *Phenomenologie de la Perception*. Paris: Gallimard. Translation: Merleau-Ponty M (1962) *Phenomenology of Perception*. London: Routledge & Kegan Paul.

McCall R (1986) Issue-Serve Systems: A Descriptive Theory of Design. *Design Methods and Theories*. Vol.20, no. 3, 443-458.

McCall R (1987) PHIBIS: Procedurally Hierarchical Issue-Based Information Systems. *Proceedings of the Conference on Architecture at the International Congress on Planning and Design Theory*. New York: American Society of Mechanical Engineers. 17-22.

McCall R (1989) Mikroplis: A Hypertext System for Design. *Design Studies*, 10 (4), 228-238.

McCall R (1991) PHI: A Conceptual Foundation for Design Hypermedia. Design Studies. 12 (1), 30-41.

McCall R, Bennett P, d'Oronzio P, Ostwald J, Shipman F, Wallace N (1990a) Phidias: Integrating CAD Graphics into Dynamic Hypertext. In Rizk A, Streitz N, Andre J (eds) (1990) *Hypertext: Concepts, Systems and Applications* (Proceedings of ECHT '90). Cambridge: Cambridge University Press. 152-165.

McCall R, Morch A, Fischer G (1990b) Supporting Reflection-in-action in the Janus Design Environment. In Mitchell W, McCullough M, Purcell P (eds) (1990b) *The Electronic Design Studio*. Cambridge: MIT Press. 247-260.

McCall R, Schaab B, Schuler W, Mistrik I (1983) *Mikroplis User Manual*. Heidelberg.

McCall R (1989/90) Development of a Design Environment Integrating Dynamic Hypertext with CAD. Funded proposal to Colorado Institute for Artificial Intelligence.

McCall R (1990/91) Intelligent Hypertext as an Alternative to Expert Systems. Funded proposal to Colorado Institute for Artificial Intelligence.

McCall R (1991/92) Virtual Copies of Hypermedia Networks in a System for Design of Space-based Habitats. Funded proposal to Colorado Institute for Artificial Intelligence.

McCall R (1992/93) Intelligent Hypermedia Graphics in the Design of Space-based Habitats. Funded proposal to Colorado Advanced Software Institute.

McCall R (1993/95) Computer-Supported Knowledge Capture for the Design of Space-based Habitats. Proposal to Colorado Advanced Software Institute.

Minsky M (1985) *The Society of Mind*. New York: Simon and Schuster.

Mittal S, Boborow DG, Kahn KM (1986) Virtual Copies At the Boundary Between Classes and Instances. *OOPSLA '86 Proceedings*. 159-166.

Miyake N (1986) Constructive Interaction and the Iterative Process of Understanding. *Cognitive Science*. *10*. 151-177.

Moore GT, Fieber JP, Moths JH, Paruleski KL (1991) Genesis Advanced Lunar Outpost II: A Progress Report. In Blackledge RC Redfield CL Seida SB (Eds.), *Space—A Call for Action: Proceedings of the Tenth*

Annual International Space Development Conference. San Diego, CA: Univelt, 55.

Nakakoji K (1993) *The Role of a Specification Component*. Ph.D. dissertation. Department of Computer Science. University of Colorado at Boulder.

Nardi B, Miller J (1990) The Spreadsheet Interface: A Basis for End User Programming. *Proceedings of Interact '90*. 977-983.

NASA (1989) *Space Station Freedom Man-Systems Integration Standards*. NASA-STD-3000 Volume I. Revision A. December 14, 1989. NASA.

NASA (1989) *Space Station Freedom Man-Systems Integration Standards*. NASA-STD-3000 Volume IV. Revision A. December 14, 1989. NASA.

Nielsen J, Frehr I, Nymand NO (1991) The Learnability of HyperCard as an Object-oriented Programming System. *Behavioral Information Technology. 10* (2) 111-120.

Nilsson N (1980) *Principles of Artificial Intelligence*. Palo Alto: Morgan Kaufmann.

Nobel DF (1984) *Forces of Production: A Social History of Industrial Automation*. New York: Knopf.

Norman D (1993) *Things That Make Us Smart*. Reading, MA: Addison-Wesley. In preparation.

Norman D, Draper S (1986) *User Centered System Design: New Perspectives on Human-Computer Interaction*. Hillsdale, NJ: Lawrence Erlbaum.

Palmer R (1969) *Hermeneutics: Interpretation Theory in Schliermacher, Dilthey, Heidegger and Gadamer*. Evanston: Northwestern University Press.

Papert S (1980) *Mindstorms: Children, Computers, and Powerful Ideas*. New York: Basic Books.

Plato (348 BC) *The Collected Dialogues of Plato*. E Hamilton & H Cairns (Eds.). New York: Pantheon. 1961.

Polanyi M (1962) *Personal Knowledge*. London: Routledge & Kegan Paul.

Putnam H (1967) The Nature of Mental States. In Block N (Ed.) (1980) *Readings in Philosophy of Psychology* (Vol. 1). Cambridge: Harvard University Press. First published as Psychological Predicates. In Capitan WH,. Merrill DD (Eds.) (1967) *Art, Mind and Religion*. Pittsburgh: University of Pittsburgh Press.

Putnam H (1988) *Representation and Reality*. Cambridge: MIT Press.

Quillian MR (1967) Word Concepts: A Theory and Simulation of Some Basic Semantic Capabilities. *Behavioral Science 12*, 410-430. In Brachman & Levesque (1985).

Raybeck D (1991) Proxemics and Privacy: Managing the Problems of Life in Confined Settings. In Harrison AA, Clearwater YA, McKay CP (Eds.) (1991) *From Antarctica to Outer Space: Life in Isolation and Confinement.* New York: Springer Verlag. 317-330.

Redmiles D (1992) *From Programming Tasks to Solutions—Bridging the Gap Through the Explanation of Examples.* Ph.D. dissertation. Department of Computer Science. University of Colorado at Boulder.

Reeves B (1993) *The Role of Embedded Communication and Embedded History in Collaborative Design.* Ph.D. dissertation. Department of Computer Science. University of Colorado at Boulder.

Resnick L (1991) Shared Cognition: Thinking as Social Practice. In Resnick L, Levine J, Teasley S (Eds.) (1991) *Perspectives on Socially Shared Cognition.* Washington, DC: APA. 1-22.

Richardson J (1991) *Existential Epistemology: A Heideggerian Critique of the Cartesian Project.* Oxford: Claredon Paperbacks.

Rilke RM (1912) *Duino Elegies.* Translation: Boston: Shambala. 1992.

Rittel H (1972) Second-generation Design Methods. In Cross (1984). 317-327.

Rittel H, Webber M (1973) Dilemmas in a General Theory of Planning. *Policy Science. 4,* 155-169. Alternative version as Rittel H, Webber M (1973) Planning Problems are Wicked Problems. In Cross (1984). 135-144.

Rorty R (1977) *Philosophy and the Mirror of Nature.* Princeton: Princeton University Press.

Schaab B, McCall R, Schuler W (1984) Mikroplis -- ein Textbank-Management-System. *Nachrichten für Dokumentation. 35* (6). 254-259.

Schank R (1982) *Dynamic Memory.* Cambridge: Cambridge University Press.

Schön D (1983) *The Reflective Practitioner.* New York: Basic Books.

Schön D (1985) *The Design Studio.* London: RIBA Publications.

Schön D (1992) Designing as Reflective Conversation with the Materials of a Design Situation. *Knowledge-Based Systems,* **5**, (3). 3-14.

Schutz A (1970) *Reflections on the Problem of Relevance.* New Haven: Yale University Press.

Searle J (1980) Minds, Brains, and Programs. *The Behavioral and Brain Sciences, 3.*

Searle J (1983) *Intentionality: An Essay in the Philosophy of Mind.* Cambridge: Cambridge University Press.

Shipman F (1993) *Supporting Knowledge-Base Evolution Using Multiple Degrees of Formality.* Ph.D. dissertation. Department of Computer Science. University of Colorado at Boulder.

Simon H (1973) The Structure of Ill-structured Problems. *Artificial Intelligence. 4.* 181-200.

Simon H (1981) *The Sciences of the Artificial.* Cambridge: MIT Press.

Smith, BC (1991) The Owl and the Electric Encyclopedia. *Artificial Intelligence. 47.* 251-288.

Smolensky P, Fox B, King R, Lewis C (1987) Computer-Aided Reasoned Discourse, or How to Argue with a Computer. In Guindon R (Ed.) (1987) *Cognitive Science and its Implications for Human-Computer Interaction.* Hillsdale, NJ: Lawrence Erlbaum.

Snodgrass A, Coyne R (1990) Is Designing Hermeneutical? Working paper. Faculty of Architecture, University of Sydney.

Stahl G (1975a) *Marxian Hermeneutics and Heideggerian Social Theory: Interpreting and Transforming Our World.* Ph.D. dissertation. Department of Philosophy. Northwestern University.

Stahl G (1975b).The Jargon of Authenticity: An Introduction to a Marxist Critique of Heidegger. *Boundary 2, III,* (2). 489-498.

Stahl G (1976) Attuned to Being: Heideggerian Music in Technological Society. *Boundary 2, IV,* (2). 637-664.

Stahl G (1991) A Hypermedia Inference Language as an Alternative to Rule-Based Expert Systems. Technical Report CU-CS-557-91. Computer Science Department, University of Colorado at Boulder. 1-23.

Stahl G (1992) A Computational Medium for Supporting Interpretation in Design. Technical Report CU-CS-598-92. Computer Science Department, University of Colorado at Boulder. 1-39.

Stahl G (1993a) Supporting Situated Interpretation. *Proceedings of the Cognitive Science Society: A Multidisciplinary Conference on Cognition.* Boulder. CO. June 18-21, 1993. 965-970.

Stahl G (1993b) Supporting Interpretation in Design. Submitted to *Journal of Architecture and Planning Research.* Special issue on Computational Representations of Knowledge.

Stahl G, McCall R, Peper, G (1992) Extending Hypermedia with an Inference Language: An Alternative to Rule-Based Expert Systems. *Proceedings of the IBM ITL Conference: Expert Systems (October 19-21, 1992).* 160-167.

Suchman L (1987) *Plans and Situated Actions: the Problem of Human Machine Communication.* Cambridge: Cambridge University Press.

Suchman L (1993) Response to Vera and Simon's Situated Action: A Symbolic Interpretation. *Cognitive Science. 17.* (1). 77-86.

Suchman L, Trigg R (1991) Understanding Practice: Video as a Medium for Reflection and Design. In Greenbaum & Kyng (1991). 65-90.

Sussman G, McDermott D (1972) *From PLANNER to CONNIVER: A Genetic Approach*. Montvale, NJ: AFIPS Press.

Tafforin C (1990) Relationships Between Orientation, Movement and Posture in Weightlessness: Preliminary Ethological Observations. *Acta Astronautica. 21.* 271-280.

Toulmin S (1958) *The Uses of Argument*. Cambridge: Cambridge University Press.

Vonnegut K (1952) *Player Piano*. New York: Avon.

Vygotsky LS (1978) *Mind in Society*. Cambridge: Harvard University Press.

Weizenbaum J (1976) *Computer Power and Human Reason: From Judgment to Calculation*. New York: Freeman & Co.

Winograd T, Flores F (1986) *Understanding Computers and Cognition: A New Foundation for Design*. New York: Addison-Wesley.

Winston PH (1981) *Artificial Intelligence*. Reading, MA: Addison-Wesley.

Wirth N (1988) From Modula to Oberon. *Software—Practice and Experience. 18.* (7). 661-670.

Wittgenstein L (1953) *Philosophical Investigations*. New York: Macmillan.

Wixon D, Holzblatt K, Knox S (1990) Contextual Design: An Emergent View of System Design. *CHI '90 Proceedings.*

Woods WA (1975) What's in a Link: Foundations for Semantic Networks. In: Brachman RJ, Levesque HJ (1985) *Readings in Knowledge Representation*. San Mateo, CA: Morgan Kaufmann. 217-242.

APPENDIX

A.   **Programming Walkthrough of the HERMES Language**

B.   **Tacit Usage of the HERMES Language**

C.   **Explicit Structure of the HERMES Language**

A. Programming Walkthrough of the Hermes Language

Two programming walkthroughs (Bell, et al., 1991) were conducted of the HERMES language after an initial version of the language had been implemented and its functionality tested. The purpose of the programming walkthrough method is to evaluate the "writability" of a programming language during its design phase by carefully considering the steps that a programmer must go through in order to complete a programming task in the language. In particular, note is made of the "doctrines" (or pieces of knowledge) that one must have mastered in order to use the language. The method pinpoints factors in the design of the language that require large amounts of background knowledge.

In a series of sessions during April, 1992, the programming walkthrough methodology was carefully followed for a sample task in the HERMES language. The language designer defined the task, briefly described the language with several simple examples and a copy of the BNF syntax, served as a resource about the language, and indicated whether or not progress was being made with the task. A professor of computer science who is particularly interested in end-user programming languages worked through the task. A Ph.D. student in computer science who had investigated the programming walkthrough methodology and had conducted many sessions with it, assisted in carrying through the programming walkthrough methodology.

In August, 1992, the walkthrough was repeated with a similar set of participants. This second walkthrough substantially confirmed the findings of the first one. For the sake of logical presentation, results of the two sessions will be merged together in the discussion here. First, the various steps in solving the task will be laid out and the potential problem areas that were uncovered will be described. Then a list of redesign decisions will be presented, describing the rationale of the version of the language that emerged in response to these evaluations.

The task. The task for the programming walkthrough was to write a query statement in the language to accomplish the following: *list people with four or more grandchildren*. The participants in the first walkthrough were given a copy of the BNF syntax of a simplified form of the language.[27] Those in the second walkthrough were given a screen image of the interface to the language (similar to Figure 10-3 in Chapter 10). Both groups were told that the database consisted of six kinds of hypertext nodes (`cats`, `dogs`, `boys`, `girls`, `men`, `women`) connected by four types of links (`parents`, `owners`, `likes`, `dislikes`).

Step 1. Construct a Query. The language being evaluated still retained PHIDIAS' query language structure. It had a syntactic category named "Query" (which no longer exists in the revised language). Thus, the first step when working in the language used in the Walkthrough is to realize that a Query must be constructed. This is the first piece of doctrine about the HERMES system and its language that is needed to create the list of people. Non-programmers (for whom this language is intended) may not be familiar with the term "query" as it is used in computer database jargon. They might not know that queries are the mechanism to search a database and return a list of the items specified by the query. In practical terms, this issue means that the user of HERMES must know how to find the menu option for constructing a query in the HERMES language. In the walkthrough, this corresponds to focusing on the language options for a Query in the syntax.

The syntax for `Query` is the following (Capitalized terms here are non-terminals further defined in the syntax. Note that this syntax included a number of operators that no longer exist in the language or that have different names as defined in Appendix C.):

```
disclose  Article  Relationship  Preposition  Article
    Subject   which    Filter    as    How,    with    their
    Relationship, if Boolean, else Query.
```

The walkthroughs emphasized several problems with this syntax. Interestingly, the problems pointed to were very similar in both walkthroughs, even though in the first sessions this syntax was displayed textually (as an explicit BNF formalism) and in the other session it was displayed as a dialog box with buttons for each term (for tacit direct manipulation). In both cases, the Query option was considered visually

---

[27] A BNF of the current HERMES language can be found in Appendix C. The version used for the Walkthrough had a similar structure, but many of the terms used in that language and discussed in the present Appendix have been changed, primarily as a result of the Walkthrough. These changes may cause some confusion in reading the following discussion.

confusing in its overall impact as well as in some of its details. Above all, there were simply too many terms to deal with at once.

This complaint had several aspects. First, the number of terms was too great. It turned out that these terms fell into three categories: operative syntax options, glue words, and fillers. The syntax terms which represented computational mechanisms were the terms: `Relationship, Subject, Filter, How, Relationship, Boolean, Query`. The glue words were `Article` and `Preposition`, which could take on values of articles and prepositions to make queries read more like flexible English without changing the computational meaning—e.g., `all arguments about those answers` instead of just `arguments of answers`. The filler words were `disclose, which, as, with their, if, else`; they make the syntax more meaningful to the human reader, but play no role computationally. It was felt that the word "`disclose`" is unnecessarily obscure, and might best be replaced by something like "show" or "list", or be eliminated.

The glue words seem to just get in the way. They add unnecessary work, looking up their possible options, and they clutter the query statement. Operator options like `Article` and `Preposition` require an extra level of look-up in addition to the main language syntax options. While they add a marginal degree of smoothness to the reading of the query, they are simply in the way during the writing of the query. Moreover, they obscure the functional structure of the query, making it difficult to determine what is operational in the query and what is not. The other filler words are less of a problem because they do not require any action by the query formulator and they make the structure and function of the query clearer even during the writing stage. Nevertheless, it was suggested during both walkthroughs that a radical rethinking of the language (e.g., in a LISP-style functional notation or in a visual programming graphical notation) might well do away with the fillers and lay the structure of the query bare. Here, the trade-off between supporting tacit and explicit understanding was already clearly coming into play.

Given the complex definition of the query, a programmer has little guidance on where to begin and how to proceed. The terms in the syntax template appear equally important. In fact, in this version of the language all of the terms are optional. Any subset of them can be defined in any order, giving the one template great generality and allowing it to stand for many possibilities. However, this gives little guidance to the programmer. It is not clear to a novice user how the system would compute a Query without a

Subject, or one without an `if Boolean` but with an `else Query`. A more general problem is that there is little support for the person constructing a query step by step: where to start, what order to proceed in, what has been defined so far, how to test partial queries, how to re-use existing queries and already defined complex terms.

Step 2. Define the Subject. To build effective queries in a hypertext system like HERMES, one must begin by defining a Subject of the query that corresponds to the starting point of the search that is to be defined. For instance, in the query, `arguments of answers`, the computer will start with a set of answers and follow their `argument` links to the set of their arguments, which will be the result of the query. Similarly, in `people that have more than 3 grandchildren`, the system will start from a set of people and traverse links to discover which of them have more than three grandchildren. However, this was not obvious in either walkthrough. Both attempts went astray at this initial step. In the April session, analysis began with the grandchildren and tried to compute their grandparents (eventually getting stuck trying to trace back which of the grandparents had more than three grandchildren). In the August walkthrough, the idea that the Subject of a query like `arguments of answers` was `answers` seemed counter-intuitive. In fact, it seemed counter English-like. In English, "of answers" is a phrase modifying the noun (subject) "arguments".

Another way of putting the problem of choosing the Subject is that the user might assume that the Subject is that which is to be disclosed or listed. So, in `arguments of answers`, the Subject might be taken to be the arguments that are sought. In fact, however, the Subject of the query must be the answers, from which the search for arguments begins.

The walkthroughs fundamentally questioned the assumption that had been taken over from the original PHIDIAS query language that the starting point of hypertext navigation corresponded to what people would naturally name as the "subject" of a query. The strategy of the PHIDIAS language had been to model the language as much on the structure of English as possible. This strategy worked well for the readability of the language. However, the walkthrough began to uncover problems with the strategy when one wanted to write innovative expressions.

The people who originally used the PHIDIAS query language would formulate a query like `answers of issues with their arguments` to instruct the computer to start at each of the `issues` and then list its answers with sublists of all the arguments of each of those answers. It was assumed that this was the "English-like" phrasing, and the query language's syntax corresponded to it nicely. But consider the following equally natural requests for the same output:

```
*   answers with their arguments of the issue.
*   for each issue list its answers and for each of
    them list the arguments.
*   each issue's answers and their arguments.
*   arguments for each answer of the issues.
*   arguments for each issue's answers.
```

It seems that any of the three operative terms can come in any position in English and that a variety of equally plausible alternatives are available for even the simplest queries. The users of PHIDIAS had, perhaps, been accustomed to think in the PHIDIAS programming language. The fact that this may have happened without anyone realizing that learning of a new language was taking place may speak well for the readability of the language, but it covered up the writability issues. The PHIDIAS queries seemed "English-like" not because they represented the obvious way to formulate the queries, but because once formulated their meaning (semantics) seemed intuitively clear. That is, a query that would procedurally navigate the hypertext sounded like an English language description of the results that would thereby be produced.

What worked for the original PHIDIAS language cannot work for the considerably more complex HERMES language. The PHIDIAS language was syntactically limited to simple query statements. In fact, most queries formulated in practice instantiated a handful of patterns. Moreover, these patterns were part of a culture existing among the people who worked together on PHIDIAS. The HERMES language, in contrast, is highly generative, allowing an unbounded variety of expression forms. While it is assumed that some training will be necessary for its use (in fact, considerably more than was given to the walkthrough participants), the language is supposed to be usable by designers in workplaces who have arbitrarily complex and innovative information retrieval needs.

A serious confusion arose in determining the correspondence between nodes or links and Subjects or Relationships. In the PHIDIAS culture, a phrase like answers of issues corresponded to answer links coming out of issue nodes. The nodes at the other end of the answer links would, it was assumed, be answer nodes. In a standard PHI issue-base hierarchy this was a reasonable assumption. However, in the general case, a link of Type x might point to a node of Kind y. So the original assumptions of how node and link structures correspond to English descriptions and query syntax no longer necessarily obtain.

An issue also arose in the step of defining the Subject having to do with conjunctions. The Subject, people, had to be defined as a conjunction of boys, girls, men, and women. In ordinary English, one might say "men *and* women who ...." But the computer combines nodes using set operations, so one has to say "men or women who ...." Whereas a native English speaker would use "men *and* women who ...." to group all the men and all the women together, the computer would interpret this as people who are men and who also are women, i.e., the null set. The first aspect of this problem is that the query writer must leave tacit common English and think in explicit set terms; the second part is that the syntax options redundantly included and and or along with the set operations for union and intersection—and the relationships among them are unspecified.

A more general point that came up concerning the presentation of the syntax is that the overall structure is not clear. The syntax looks like an arbitrary listing of many possible syntactic templates. What are the important primitive (or first class) elements here and what are the rules for combining or abstracting them? If Query is a primitive object, can one request: disclose queries that ...? Are there general principles for combining Subject, Relationship, Filter, etc. that underlie the definitions of the templates? Is so, could these principles be given instead of the seemingly arbitrary proliferation of template options?

Again, the question of structure goes back to the tension between the English language perspective and the hypertext navigation perspective. The underlying structure of the language as a computer programming language for hypertext querying has to do with the structure of nodes and links in the hypertext. However, the appearance of the language is tuned to the rather different structure of English language descriptions of results desired, as stated using terms of the domain (grandchildren, answers, wardrooms). This tension became explicit in Step 3.

The list of syntax templates arose from a series of trade-offs. The Operator options allowed the collapsing of several language options into one: e.g., Subject and Subject, Subject or Subject, ... into Subject *SOperator* Subject. This reduced the overall number of options, but added another layer of options (*SOperator*) to go through. Another trade-off has to do with providing templates that correspond to common queries versus maximizing the generality of the options. Adding options increases the likelihood that a need can be met immediately without the extra effort of building up from several options or specializing from a complex, generalized option. The trade-off is that this proliferates options, making it harder to locate the correct one.

Step 3. Think through the computation process. At some point early in the formulation of a non-trivial query, one must focus on the computational process needed to get the desired results starting from the given information. For instance, given nodes for various kinds of people and links to parents, how can a list of certain grandparents be defined? In the walkthrough task, one must first generate a list of people by generating lists of men, women, etc., and then combining these lists. Then one must perform a mapping from these people to their grandchildren by crossing the parent links coming into them to get to their children and then repeating this to get to the grandchildren. For each person, the number of their grandchildren is computed and compared to 3. Those people who do not meet this condition are filtered out of the list of people, and the remaining list is the desired output. It may be useful to conceive of the sets or lists of nodes as "streams", and the computational process as consisting of operations on this stream such as generation, mapping, filtering, performing conjunctions, applying predicate tests, etc. (see Abelson & Sussman, 1985). Such an abstract scheme would provide a way of analyzing a task. If the language's syntax was organized this way, then the procedure of formulating a query might be more straight-forward. It is even conceivable that a query formulated on the basis of this scheme could then be translated into an English-like format to enhance future readability.

The point is that for any non-trivial query the writer will need to think through the computational process in terms of operations on nodes and links. For each operation, the writer will then have to select the proper syntax option. So the selection of query terms will be made on the basis of a conceptualization in terms of nodes and links, not directly in terms of domain concepts (answers, grandchildren, etc.). The domain concepts have to be translated into system concepts (i.e., into the terms according to which the hypertext database is organized) before the structure of a query can be determined. This implies that the syntax should correspond to the system view which the user must develop, rather than to the user's native English formulation of the task.

This consequence applies to the writing of queries, not the reading of them. If a query has already been stated in an English-like way so that it reads like a statement of the general task that it indeed carries out, then the user may not need to think in the system terms of nodes and links at all. This would relieve the user of a considerable cognitive burden and justify the approach of supporting tacit understanding.

However, even if one anticipates that the language will be used almost exclusively in a read mode by most users, one should not underestimate the concern for the language's writability. Both programming walkthroughs underlined the inadequacy of the "English-like" approach for programming queries, and the strongest implication of both was the necessity to redesign the syntax to reflect more closely a system view of computations. That is, there are important times when it is necessary to think in explicit computational terms and the language should support this as well as tacit readability.

Step 4. Formulate the query based on the computation. Once the necessary computation has been understood, the query can be formulated. A first step might be to consider alternative starting points for the computation based on the structure of the data. In the given task, for instance, both walkthroughs got side-tracked by following parent links from people to their grandparents. To complete the task, one must add up each person's grandchildren, which means following the links in the other direction to each person's children and to their children, so that each grandparent will be associated with the set of his or her grandchildren.

This raised a question about backwards links, called "converse" links in the syntax. It may not be obvious to users that links can be traversed in both directions. In fact in PHIDIAS they could not be. So this is intended as a new feature in HERMES, and the converse Relationship option (along with its explanation in a User's Manual or training session) is meant to point out this possibility. In fact, the given task could not be performed without the ability to traverse links in both directions. However, even if one wants to retain this functionality, "converse" may not be the best term to use.

Once alternative strategies for achieving the task have been worked out, the programmer of the query might optionally try to estimate the relative computational efficiency of the alternatives. For instance, in the given task one might reason that only adults could have grandchildren. So, instead of starting from a set of people that included boys and girls, one might start from a set of people defined as men or women.

The analysis of the task in terms of defined nodes and links implies the selection of Subjects and Relationships. These must be built from the given kinds of nodes and types of links, using whichever syntax templates produce the desired results from the primitives. Thus, the Subject option, Subject SOperator Subject can be used to combine men and women with the appropriate connective selected from the list of SOperator options. Similarly, the best Filter option can be chosen by a pattern matching process: the option have COperator Number Relationship ... allows a numeric comparison, where COperator is matched to "more than", Number to "three", and Relationship to "grandchildren". Unfortunately, another option, have QOperator Relationship, also almost seems to match, necessitating extra analysis.

The walkthroughs uncovered a technical problem with having the user always choosing from lists of defined options. For instance, to choose a primitive link type the user selects from a pick list containing all defined types. The advantage of this is that spelling mistakes are avoided and long names can be entered with a click of the mouse. The problem is that the type must always be defined before it is used. This creates a problem in two situations: top-down design and recursive definitions. Suppose one wants to define a Relationship, issues and discussion, before one has defined discussion. In top-down design it makes sense to use a subcomponent before figuring out its definition in detail—as long as it gets defined before actual program execution. With the HERMES graphical user interface, one would at least have to define discussion with a simple, nominal definition prior to referring to it in a higher-level definition. (Then one could always come back later and refine the lower-level definition.) In the case of recursive definitions, one could not define discussion as: issues with discussion, because when one went to select the last term in this definition the Relationship discussion would not yet be on the list. This is a problem arising from the HERMES interface. In PHIDIAS, the user simply typed any character strings into the command-line interface. Of course, one could work around this problem too by first defining a dummy discussion Relationship and then redefining it with the recursive definition.

Step 5. Test and refine the query. Ideally, one should be able to build up complex queries iteratively, testing as one goes. This was not possible during the walkthroughs because the HERMES language and its interface were not completely implemented. The interface should be designed to make the testing of query components as easy as possible.

In addition, the construction of modular queries should be supported. One should be able to define a Subject as men or women, save it with a name people and then subsequently use it in queries. Similarly, one should be able to define a Relationship converse parents of converse parents, save it with a name `grandchildren`, and use it later in the final Query:

```
disclose people that have more than 3 grandchildren.
```

This kind of modularity promotes top-down and incremental design. It also hides the complex details and provides building blocks for other queries in the future.

Finally, once the task is solved and the query has been shown to work properly, the user may want to check the appearance of the query for readability. In the above example, care has been taken to name terms like `people` and `grandchildren` with descriptive names in the plural, so they make sense and sound reasonable in the query syntax. Also note that the awkward and non-English-like phrases have been hidden within secondary definitions that are represented by these carefully chosen names.

The revised language. In response to the findings of the programming walkthroughs, an extensive redesign effort was undertaken. In particular, many of the "English-like" analogies of the original PHIDIAS query language were eliminated in favor of a mixing of support for tacit and explicit understanding. The primary redesign decisions resulting from the walkthroughs are discussed below: [28]

Decision 1. Provide for multiple skill levels. The programming walkthroughs highlighted the problematic nature of *writing* expressions in the HERMES language. Experience using the language on more complicated tasks than that tried in the walkthrough suggests that, in fact, it would sometimes be easier to use a general programming language like PASCAL or LISP than to apply the HERMES language. This suggestion is closely related to the difference between the natural language model of the task and the node-and-link system model. That is, if one arranged programming tasks along a spectrum from trivial examples like `disclose boys`, through typical PHIDIAS queries like `answers of issues with their arguments`, to more complex computations like `display people that have more than 3 grandchildren`, and finally to small applications like the academic advising example (Appendix B) used to test the unrevised language, or to even more complex computations (like the

---

[28] It should be noted that the HERMES language continued to evolve after these revisions, so that the syntax in Appendix C and the examples throughout the dissertation do not correspond exactly to the revised version of the language discussed here.

privacy critics in Part III), then they would progress from being easy in PHIDIAS to being do-able in the HERMES language to being easier to do in a general programming language. The advantages of the ties of the HERMES language to natural language become less helpful and more of a burden the more one needs to concentrate on intricate computations at the node and link level.

At the same time, an expression in the HERMES language has the great advantage of being very easily understood by a reader (assuming it has been carefully programmed with that in mind). For a design environment that is not restricted to use by people trained in programming, this is a great advantage. Even for trained programmers, use and re-use are promoted by having expressions be self-documenting at the surface English level. Perhaps the best solution is to recognize that people defining complex computations will need to think explicitly in system terms and use programming skills, but to shield most users from these demands as much as possible. With this in mind, the HERMES language has been divided into a number of skill levels, defined in Chapter 10:

*   novice: read-only

*   beginner: entry and display of data trees

*   intermediate: hypertext computations

*   advanced: multi-media critiquing

*   programmer: general programming language

Decision 2. Replace Queries and Subjects with DataLists. The biggest problem uncovered by the walkthroughs was the complexity of the syntax. This complexity was due primarily to two factors: the sheer number of syntactical options and the lack of an apparent organizing principle based on the computational structure. The first strategy for dealing with the complexity was to provide different levels of the language for users of different skill levels. This should help users to adjust incrementally to the language. The second strategy is to structure the syntax more clearly along computational lines. This turns out to have the additional advantage of reducing the number of options.

The hardest part of completing the task in the walkthroughs was the start up. This required the most knowledge of background doctrine. It was the most confusing; once one was started along the right track, the rest was much clearer. The determination of the computational starting point is the key— not an analysis of the English description of the task or of the desired results. The starting point is always a list of nodes (people, issues, etc.).

Once this list is generated, the task is solved by successively performing a series of operations on this list. If one looks carefully at the syntax, one finds three inter-related terms for lists of nodes: Query, Subject, and DataList. A Query consists of the resultant list of nodes returned by a computation. A DataList is an arbitrary list of nodes, including Query results. A Subject can be a list of one node, all nodes of a certain kind, all nodes in the database, a DataList, a Query result (indirectly, as a DataList), or some combination of such lists. This is unnecessarily redundant.

The revised language eliminates the terms Query and Subject—two terms that caused considerable confusion in the walkthroughs—and consolidates their functions under the term DataList—a term that more clearly represents a system view of its role. The steps in solving a task are no longer to construct a "query" by first defining a "subject", but to compute a desired data list starting from some easily generated data list. The consolidation of these terms substantially lowers the number of options as well as clarifying their structure.

Decision 3. Require all parameters to be defined. Part of the confusion in defining Queries (and other terms) was that all their parts were optional and could be defined in any order. In particular, the main option for a Query (and hence the first one a user confronted) had ten terms, any combination of which could be defined in any order. So this first step offered the user several million permutations. The syntax had been structured with all terms optional in order to make each option as general as possible. However, it turns out that the syntax can be defined with all terms *required,* and the result is much greater structural clarity and simplicity with only a few more options. Compare a slightly cleaned up version of the old definition of Query (where the glue words have been eliminated and `DataList` has been used for Subjects, Queries and DataLists, for the sake of comparison) with part of the new definition of DataList:

```
DataList ::= Association of DataList that Filter as
    How, with their Association , if Boolean, else
    DataList
DataList ::= Association of DataList | DataList that
    Filter | DataList as How | DataList with their
    Association | if Boolean then DataList , else
    DataList
```

In the old definition each capitalized term is optional, in the new they are each required. The five options of the new definition allow one to build up a DataList through the same five operations that are combined in the old definition. The two definitions are formally equivalent because the old one can be converted to any of the new options by dropping optional terms, and the new options can be nested to build the old definition. But look how much clearer the function of each of the new options is. They each define a way of combining a DataList with another syntactical term (Association , Filter, How, or Boolean). Once one of the new options is chosen, there are only two choices: define the first term and then the second or the second and then the first. This new format makes the structure much clearer—for instance, it is now clear that the five operations can be performed in any order, whereas the older format gave the misleading and confusing impression that there was a required order. In fact, exactly the same operations are generally needed regardless of the template formats: to define people that have more than 3 grandchildren, one must press the same number of interface buttons in either version.

Decision 4. Eliminate glue words. The articles and prepositions have been eliminated from the syntax. They may have made sense in the simple, intuitive days of the PHIDIAS query language, but they seemed to get in the way excessively in the walkthroughs. Above all, they obscured the structure of the computations being defined and added to the confusing appearance of the syntax. Too much smoke and mirrors.

Decision 5. Retain filler words. The filler words (of, that, as, with their, ...) have been retained in the syntax to aid in the comprehension of the options as well as increasing the readability of the final expressions. "Converse" has been replaced by "inverse", which is probably more colloquial. Disclose, which used to start all Queries, has been deleted, along with the troublesome terms Query and Subject. These decisions reflect a continued commitment to maintaining the readability of the language. The suggested alternatives of a Lisp syntax or a visual programming approach are not attractive. Lisp requires enormous doctrinal knowledge and cognitive strain for the sake of a somewhat more functional notation. It is not clear that a visual programming approach could retain the functionality of the HERMES language syntax and still improve its clarity or simplicity. One could easily change the appearance of the options from their English-like format to a functional format, for instance:

```
DataList ::= Association(DataList) | Filter(DataList)
    | How(DataList) | Association-sublist(DataList) |
    Boolean(DataList1, DataList2) | UnionOp(DataList1,
    DataList2)
```

instead of:

```
DataList ::= Association of DataList | DataList that
    Filter | DataList as How | DataList with their
    Association | if Boolean then DataList, else
    DataList
```

However, for the non-programmer the filler words make the functional relationships much clearer.

Decision 6. Compress syntax levels. The Operator options had been created to consolidate options like `DataList` and `DataList`, `DataList` or `DataList`, etc. into `DataList UnionOp DataList`, where `UnionOp ::=` and/or (unique sorted union) | and also (intersection) | but not (difference) | or (append). This makes sense where `UnionOp` is used in several places in the syntax. However, the Operator options themselves proliferated, making it difficult to look them up, let alone remember them. In the new syntax, a number of these Operator options have been combined, eliminated or moved back to the higher level options in order to lessen the number of steps involved. Note that the use of "and" and "or" has been tied to the set operations in order to clarify the sense of their computation. The net result of all the changes to the syntax is a significant decrease in the number of options, despite an increase in the clarity of their computational structure, in their ease of use, and even in their functionality. Compared to the previous language, the revised language has only 12%, 55%, and 76% as many options in its Beginner, Intermediate and Advanced versions respectively.

Decision 7. Clarify the computational structure. The *Media* options of the revised language provide the primitive node contents. The *Language* options are functions that take a DataList of nodes and return a DataList of nodes. In particular, *DataList* options generate lists (streams) of nodes. *Association* options (and their subsets, *InputAssociation* and *Predicate* options) provide mappings of each input node to output nodes (based on navigation of links coming out of the nodes). *Filter* options are conditions applied to filter nodes out of a stream. Most of the language options define rules for combining options, the majority of which are forms of application with different semantics, like `Association of DataList` and `DataList with their Association` that both apply the Association to the DataList but return the resultant lists structured differently. In this sense, the new syntax is based on a computational structure, but is displayed in an English-like format. The English-like format is arbitrary for the writing and internal representation of the language (except that it may help the programmer remember the semantics), and merely plays a role in the display (readability) of the language.

Note that many options in each category are defined in terms of options from other categories. All options are stored in the hypermedia and can be referenced by the language itself (see the definition of ObjectType). In many ways, the revised language has some of the characteristics that make LISP useful: it is functional, it is interpreted, and it can treat data as programs.

Decision 8. Improve graphical computations. The treatment of graphics was sketchy and awkward in the language. For instance, to test if a chair was near a table, one could define a `Boolean` as: `((Measure) of Graphic) is COperator Number`, or: `minimum distance to the table of the chair is less than 3`. In the new revised language, one can first define a measure, `closest distance is less than 3`, and name that `near`. Then one can use that term in the Boolean: `Graphic is Measure Graphic`, yielding: `the chair is near the table`. One can then go on to define the kind of Boolean required for graphical queries: `most chairs are near at least one table`. This new syntax has several advantages: users can define their own terms for `Measures` like `near`, the syntax for the graphical `Booleans` is clean, and the expression is smoothly readable. By defining measures in terms of either central distance or closest distance, using the full range of quantity operators, and allowing quantification of both graphical terms, the graphical booleans provide for considerable computational flexibility.

Decision 9. Retain safeguards against errors. The language used scrollable pick lists for choosing Types, Kinds and defined terms. This protected the user from typing errors and from entering undefined terms, as well as reminding the user what terms or options were available. The only keyboarding allowed was to type in names for new terms. This prevented a variety of kinds of user errors that would have required debugging—perhaps the hardest skill to require of a non-programmer. In order to allow recursive definitions of Associations and Input Associations, a `recursive self` option was added to the syntax of these terms. Now if one defines a Relationship as `issues with their recursive self` and then names this `discussion`, the Relationship will automatically be made to read `issues with their discussion`. Similarly, the syntax for Input Associations is entirely designed to protect the user from error. Input Associations are intended primarily for data entry; otherwise they are just instances of Associations. The reason for distinguishing them is that not all

Associations make sense for data entry: i.e., it makes no sense to apply Filter operators to nodes that have not yet been input. Only those options that are meaningful for input are included in the syntax for Input Associations and only Input Associations can be used by the interface mechanisms that prompt the user to elicit sequences of input.

Decision 10. Support the construction of language expressions. The new user interface to the language provides dialog boxes in conformance with the WINDOWS 3.1 conventions. For instance, if one wants to create a DataList, one brings up a dialog displaying all the syntactic options for DataLists. In a given option, each term that has to be defined is represented with a button. Clicking the mouse on that button brings up a dialog with the relevant options for that term. Primitive terms like link Types are chosen from a pick list of defined terms. Dialogs are modal, so that work on a given dialog must be completed (or canceled) before reverting to work on a previous stage. As an expression is built up, it is displayed at the bottom of the dialog box in its English-like format. Control buttons are available on most dialogs for naming and saving a constructed term, for bringing up and editing a previously saved term, and for changing the interpretive context in which terms and expressions are defined. The dialog for DataLists also includes buttons for evaluating the DataList (testing it) and for saving the results to disk (for subsequent processing or viewing).

The construction of expressions in the HERMES language could be supported with a wide variety of other mechanisms beyond the scope of this research. One could have graphical palettes of previously defined expressions, browsers of the hypertext structure, intelligent assistants that suggest new constructions or critique partial constructions, facilities for specifying desired results, checklists for steps to be done, and context-sensitive help. Some of these have been tried in MODIFIER (Girgensohn, 1992). It is hoped that defining expressions in the HERMES language is generally not so difficult as to warrant such extensive support. As Girgensohn implied, the supports he developed were largely required because of a non-intuitive representation of critic definitions, etc. in terms of LISP expressions and property sheets. Although it is likely that certain forms of support, carefully designed and implemented would be extremely useful, Girgensohn (1992) probably turned to providing such supports too early. The HERMES language is carefully designed to provide representations of useful computations for design environments that syntactically support designers tacit and explicit understandings.

Decision 11. Provide training in the use and extension of the language. The walkthroughs made explicit the background doctrine that is required to write expressions in the HERMES language. Clearly, some instruction is needed to explain the purpose, format, implementation, and use of the language to new users. This instruction must include some discussion of navigation and computation across hypertext, as well as a description of the syntax, semantics, and pragmatics of the language itself.

During the year since the development of the revised language, the HERMES language has been further refined to clarify its structure, functionality, and appearance. Its current design is reflected in Chapter 10 and Appendix C.

B. Tacit Usage of the Hermes Language

This Appendix is intended to give the flavor of the HERMES Language *in use*. It describes two small applications that were programmed during the early development of the language—and which actually drove the definition of much of its functionality. It also discusses four computational mechanisms that can be used within the language. In each example application or computational technique, there is a mixture of support for tacit and explicit understanding:

* The example of *family relations* shows how a system of terminology can be defined in the HERMES language for expressing common family relations. However, while these terms may be easy to use once defined, even the definition of a basic term like brother or sister (`sibling`) can require a relatively high degree of explicit reflection.

* The attempt to build a mini-expert-system to automate the job of an *academic advisor* using the HERMES language was instructive. On the one hand, building the application strained the ability of the language to construct complex procedures, requiring explicit programming strategies to be applied in an environment whose only support for that is abstraction. On the other hand, once defined, the application defined a micro-world in which users could browse and pose queries in ways not possible in closed expert systems.

* The definition of *Predicates* as a subtle variation on Associations gives substantial extended power to the language in practice and at the same time nicely hides from the user some of the underlying complexity of definitions that stretch across multiple hypermedia links.

* As programs in the language become more complex, issues of *variable binding* arise that may be confusing to think through. HERMES solves these issues in an intuitive way so that they ordinarily need not come to the attention of the user.

* The use of *recursive procedures* to compute transitive closures—both breadth-first and depth-first—generally requires cognitively burdensome abstract thinking. The HERMES language can support recursion through simple expressions. The problem of the recursive out is handled automatically by a natural convention having to do with hypermedia navigation.

*   *Decision trees* can be set up using hypertext links between nodes that contain conditions expressed in the HERMES language. The links between the nodes model the decision tree in a clear way. This supports the explicit understanding of the logic of the decision tree in an intuitive manner.

*   The options of the HERMES language support *defeasible reasoning* flexibly. They often eliminate the need to think through all the possibilities explicitly and allow the user to state in an understandable way the critical condition.

Programming family relations. A textbook example from logic programming like PROLOG provides a good illustration of how terms can be defined in the HERMES language to break down and solve a typical inference problem. The domain of family relations makes a nice test case because it is easy to compare the use of the HERMES language with one's tacit understanding of these relations and with the need in ordinary conversation to occasionally make these tacit understandings more explicit.

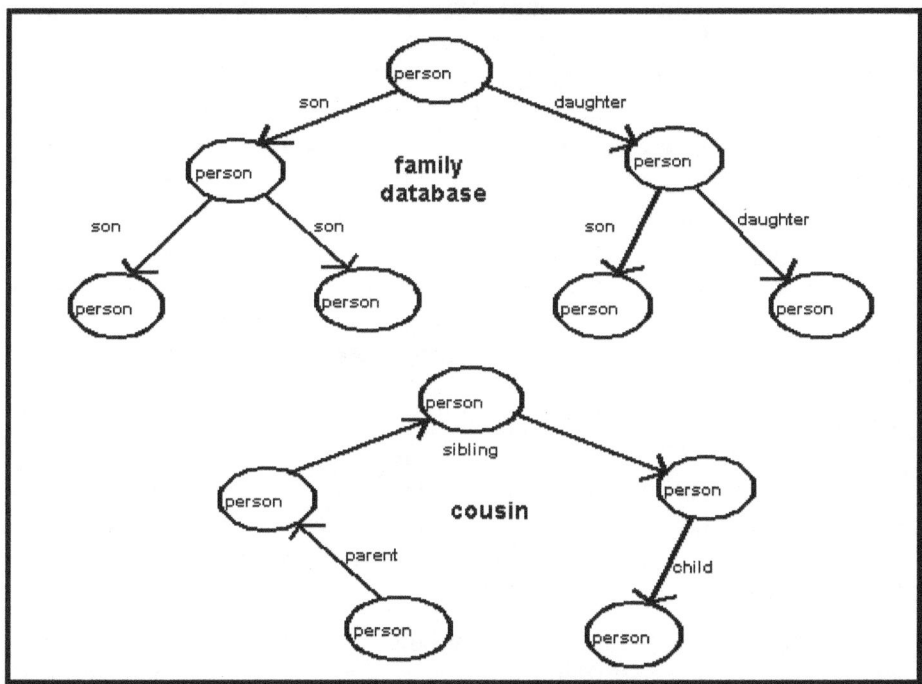

Figure A-1. Family relations.

The definition of cousin *from* son *and* daughter *links.*

Take the problem: given a network of people nodes linked by son and daughter links, infer cousin relationships. Inference is defined as the combining of facts to derive new facts. In Figure A-1, facts about sons and daughters are combined to produce facts about who is a cousin of whom. This is a non-trivial task for humans, generally requiring people to consciously articulate part of the computation (e.g., "Let's see, her mother is my father's sister. . . .")

In the HERMES language, the problem can be solved by the definition of the following terms:

```
children: sons or daughters.
parents:  inverse sons or inverse daughters.
siblings: children of parents that do not equal that
   (last subject), without duplicates.
cousins:  children of siblings of parents.
```

Of course, these definitions require some explanations about the language— although probably less explanation than corresponding definitions in a traditional programming language like LISP or PROLOG. The children predicate includes nodes linked by both sons and daughters primitive links. Inverse links are primitive links traced backwards, like from the son back to the person whose son he is. The definition of siblings is inherently tricky. Most likely, the definer of this predicate would discover an adequate definition through a series of successive refinements. If one defines siblings as just children of parents, one discovers upon first use of the predicate that the original people are always included among their own siblings, because they are sons or daughters of their own parents. Therefore, a condition must be added to exclude the original person (i.e., the last subject, to whom the expression is applied) from the result list. Similarly, there will usually be duplicate names on the list of siblings because they are children of both the mother and the father of the original child. The simplest way of solving this problem while maintaining the ability to handle children of multiple marriages is to simply eliminate duplicates from the final list of results.

The complexity of the definition of siblings is telling. Although the task of determining cousins is difficult for people, the problem does not lie in the definition of siblings but rather in the sequence of steps that must be put together. People naturally exclude the extra results that pop up surprisingly when the siblings term is incompletely defined. This is symptomatic of the fact that programming in any language in any domain is going to require some explicit steps of logical analysis and some efforts at debugging. No computer language can entirely avoid that. The primary advantage of the readability of the HERMES language is that once terms are successfully defined, it is clear what they mean, even for someone with little training in the language. The definition of siblings is about as obscure as any statement in the language need be.

Given the above definitions, the following computations can now be evaluated:

```
cousins of sandra
people that have cousins and have less than 3
   cousins, with those items
```

Furthermore, these definitions have begun the creation of a domain language for family relationships. It is an easy matter to add predicates for brothers, aunts, grandparents, etc.

The academic advising application. To test an early version of the HERMES language, an application was created using information about the curriculum of the College of Environmental Design at the University of Colorado. This information included not only lists of offered courses, but other facts and rules used by the College's official student advisor. Courses were linked to their prerequisites and to their categories, such as which curriculum they belonged to and which elective breadth requirements they satisfied. Other, less formal factors were also included, like which courses were particularly labor intensive.

Primitive nodes and links were defined to correspond to information that students traditionally enter on forms prior to seeking counseling from the human academic advisor. This includes the student's name, curriculum option, semester number, and courses taken in the past, taken currently, or proposed.

The centerpiece of this application was the definition of a term named advice. The expression defining this term was built on a combination of several specific kinds of advice, which in turn used specially defined terms to compute inferences across the hypermedia. The idea was that a student, Sandra, could enter her name, curriculum option, semester number, completed courses, current courses and proposed courses into the hypermedia system (instead of onto a paper form). By clicking on the Advice button, Sandra would initiate the query,

```
advice of sandra.
```

The query critiques Sandra's proposed list of courses. Figure A-2 displays a typical result:

```
Here is some advice on your choice of courses:
The following courses each require a lot of work.
It would be wise not to take them in the same
semester:
 ENVD 3220 Planning Studio 2
 MATH 1300 Calculus

The following courses are not designed for your
curriculum option:
 ENVD 3220 Planning Studio 2

You have not taken the listed prerequisites for the
proposed courses:
 ENVD 3220 Planning Studio 2

With your proposed courses you will not satisfy the
following elective breadth requirements:
 science
It would be wise to take a course in one of these
areas rather than the following proposed courses in
elective areas for which you have already satisfied
the breadth requirements.
 FINE 1012 Art History
```

Figure A-2. Output from the academic advising application.

This Figure shows the actual system output for a sample student. Computations have been performed to check, count, and list courses meeting or not meeting certain conditions. In particular, for instance, the advice about breadth requirements is only displayed if the proposed courses include an elective in an area that has already been satisfied and do not include one in an unsatisfied area. This kind of inferencing facilitates the offering of important information tailored to a particular user in a way that is impossible in a purely navigational hypermedia system. It begins to look like a rule-based expert system, but without many of the problems of such systems.

To give a feel for the computations carried out by the language, the computation of `prerequisite_problems` will be detailed. The query, `advice of sandra`, makes use of a term, `advice`. This term is defined as follows:

```
advice:  advice_intro  and  labor_intensive_advice  and
    option_advice and prerequisite_advice.
```

In this way, the one term combines the terms for the four major computations in advice. The `prerequisite_advice` component is a term defined as follows:

```
prerequisite_advice:  prerequisite_intro and prerequi-
    site_problems if there are prerequisite_problems.
```

This first checks to see if there are problems with prerequisites; if there are, it prints out a message and then lists the problem courses. The checking and listing is done with the following term:

```
prerequisite_problems:  proposed_courses   that   have
    prerequisites_not_taken.
```

This term checks each of the student's proposed courses, using the following term :

```
prerequisites_not_taken:  prerequisites that are  not
    included in courses_taken.
```

For each of the student's proposed courses, this term follows each prerequisite's link and then checks if the node for that prerequisite is in the set of nodes resulting from the query, `courses_taken [of sandra]`. If it is not, then the proposed course for which it is a prerequisite is returned. An example of this was seen in the advice output above, where ENVD 3220 is listed.

Several problems can be noted in this implementation, if considered from a traditional computer science perspective: (i) First, there is a serious efficiency problem. (ii) Then, there is the complexity involved in setting up the application. (i) The efficiency problem is a result of the operator nature of the language. Many computations are done redundantly. For instance, in the `prerequisite_advice` computation the term `prerequisite_problems` is evaluated twice. Even worse, the subquery, `courses_taken` is evaluated many times, although its result is the same each time for a given student. While some cases of redundancy could be eliminated with a more complex syntax, most are caused by the generality required by the design of the language as successive application of modularized operators and the conscious decision to disallow use of explicit variables in the language. The system is also slowed by the fact that the language is interpreted dynamically, rather than being compiled. Nevertheless, the delay encountered for an application of this scale is scarcely noticeable—largely because the data involved is cached in RAM after its first access from disk, so redundant computations require no disk accesses.

(ii) Developing an application of this level of complexity requires considerable system designing expertise. One needs to know how to represent the knowledge in hypermedia and how to build up a sequence of modular definitions. The way to structure a program in the HERMES language is to define a hierarchy of terms with descriptive names. In complex cases like the academic advising application, one must explicitly design a manageable hierarchy and choose meaningful names that will result in readable expressions. This is probably inevitable in any system. Once well designed, however, the system can be significantly easier to understand, modify, and extend than alternative implementations would be. While the result of the `advice` term looks like the output from a traditional expert system, the hypermedia flexibility is still there to explore the underlying knowledge base by navigation. Alternatively, one can reformulate the major query or execute a series of simpler queries using components of the `advice` predicate.

Furthermore, the availability of all the information in hypertext makes it possible for users to browse the database. For instance, information could be linked to each course describing its content, hours, instructor, etc. The advantages of this approach in terms of flexibility probably outweigh the problems in settings like academic advising. The domain of academic advising is subject to frequent changes in rules and to many occurrences of "special cases" in student situations. Characteristics like these make the ability of end-users to revise and explore information important considerations.

Predicates. In HERMES, the language can be integrated into the hypertext node and link structure in a number of ways. The first approach tried relied heavily on the idea of *smart nodes*, in which the inferencing power of the language is embedded in the nodes of the hypermedia. This was conceived primarily in terms of *virtual structures*, an extension of the fixed structures of textual or graphical nodes in traditional hypermedia systems, suggested by Frank Halasz (1988). The navigational (or hypertext) approach to query evaluation was used, as found in the PHIDIAS query language, and the language was embedded in the hypermedia nodes. This was done to avoid simply gluing together two different paradigms (e.g., hypermedia and PROLOG, or hypermedia and SQL, or HYPERCARD and HYPERTALK) and to develop the querying or inferencing capability out of the hypermedia paradigm itself.

The content of a smart node is not limited to the text or graphic originally entered into it. Instead the content is determined by the results of a query or conditional phrase associated with the node. The embedded query traverses the hypermedia network, so its result depends upon the current state of the network: the existence of other nodes, their links and their current content. When smart nodes are displayed, the appearance of the hyperdocument itself changes dynamically.

Two forms of smart nodes were explored: *conditional nodes* and *virtual structures*. A conditional node contains a conditional phrase in the inference language and normal text or graphics. If the condition evaluates to true, the text is displayed. If the condition is false, nothing is displayed. For instance, in the academic advising application a node with the text, `"Are you interested in a studio course?"` might have the condition, `if there are courses that have studio_types`. Then the text would be displayed only if there actually were studio courses for the student to choose from.

A virtual structure differs from a conditional node in that it contains only a query. Instead of fixed text, the system displays the result of the query. So, in the previous example, if there were studio courses and the user responded to the question with a "yes," then the yes response might be implemented as a link to a virtual structure node with the query, `display all courses that have studio_types`. The user would not see the statement of the query, just the results.

Conditional nodes and virtual structures add significant flexibility to hypermedia. They allow specific nodes to be responsive to changing conditions in other nodes of the hyperdocument. For instance, decision trees can be implemented using smart nodes by basing new decisions on nodes that contain the results of previous decisions (see discussion of decision trees below).

However, there is an important limitation to smart nodes. Suppose you had defined an inference computation for a specific node, embedded it in that node, and found that it worked fine. But now you wanted to apply the same computation to other nodes without explicitly entering the condition or query in each of the other nodes. More generally, suppose you wanted to apply the computation as an operation on an arbitrary list of nodes. This turns out to be a critical concern because it is important to be able to do this within the inferencing language itself.

Smart *links*—or *predicates*—solved the limitation of smart nodes. Predicates are different from primitive links or defined link types. When a hypermedia system is designed, a set of link types is defined. For instance, in the academic advising application there are links of type `proposed_courses` from a student's node to his or her chosen course nodes, and other links of type `prerequisites` from course nodes to other course nodes. A smart link is a virtual link that is computed based on the definition of a term. For instance, a predicate might be defined as:

```
required_prerequisites = proposed_courses that have
    prerequisites, with their prerequisites.
```

Here, `required_prerequisites` would not be a primitive defined link type, but a computation or an inference.

This is an example of a query using normal primitive links:

```
display the proposed_courses for sandra.
```

It would be evaluated by following the `proposed_courses` links from the student node `sandra` and displaying the nodes reached:

```
*** PROPOSED_COURSES:
1. ENVD 2110 Architectural Studio
  . . . .
```

This is an example of a query using smart links:

```
display the required_prerequisites for sandra.
```

It would be evaluated by substituting the definition for the computed link type into the query and displaying the result:

```
***PROPOSED_COURSES:
1. ENVD 2110 Architectural Studio
    *** PREREQUISITES:
    1. ENVD 1000 Environmental Design Studio
    2. ENVD 1014 Intro to Environmental Design

    . . . .
```

The idea of substituting a definition for a term in a query is known as *macro expansion*. The definition of smart links as macros turns out to be an extremely powerful mechanism for the inferencing language. Because of the way the substitution is implemented, recursive definitions of smart links are possible (discussed below). This allows simply stated queries to evaluate tree structures and easily display transitive closures, in both breadth-first and depth-first order—an accomplishment not matched by relational query languages like SQL.

The HERMES language distinguishes between macros and predicates. A predicate is like a macro; however, when its results are displayed, they are labeled to appear as though the predicate were a primitive link type. This is critical for the tacit understanding of the user. Now when the user says,

```
display the required_prerequisites for sandra.
```

the user does not need to know that `required_prerequisites` is anything but an ordinary link type. The result is displayed without any indication of the internal structure, like this:

```
*** REQUIRED_PREREQUISITES:
1. ENVD 2110 Architecture Studio
2. ENVD 1000 Environmental Design Studio
3. ENVD 1014 Intro to Environmental Design
 . . . .
```

In HERMES there are three kinds of links:

* Primitive links, which are the traditional link types of hypermedia.

* Macros, which add significant inferencing power by encapsulating computations across multiple links.

* Predicates, which use the power of macros but hide the complexity from the user.

Predicates like `required_prerequisites` had to be defined and the differences between types, macros, and predicates had to be explicitly considered during system development. However, the eventual end-user can take advantage of this computational power without knowing that no primitive links actually exist in the hypermedia between student nodes and their required prerequisites. The predicates look like simple links to the user and can be tacitly used as though they were simple primitive links.

Smart links overcome the limitation of conditional nodes and virtual structures. Because macros and predicates are syntactically equivalent to primitive link types, they can be bound to arbitrary nodes or lists of nodes as if they were actual links coming out of those nodes. Smart links turned out to be so powerful and flexible that the academic advising application was developed almost exclusively with them.

Decision trees. Another important programming technique—particularly for expert system applications—is *decision trees*. A typical example of using a decision tree is categorization of fauna and flora. One proceeds through a sequence of questions posing alternative choices. Based on one's answers, the choices lead down a path through the tree of decisions to the answer, e.g., the name of the animal or plant corresponding to the choices. Here is an example from the domain of academic advising, implemented with virtual structure nodes (nodes containing queries to be evaluated).

Suppose we have the query, `suggestion` (this query consists simply of the name of a node). And suppose the node named "suggestion" contains the following DataList:

```
if  envd_semester  of  student  is  less  than  3  then
    beginner, else advanced.
```

Assuming that the proposition (`envd_semester of student is less than 3`) turns out true, `beginner` is evaluated. It contains the DataList,

```
if   there   are   envd_1000   that   are   contained   in
    completed_courses of      student    then    completed,
    else uncompleted.
```

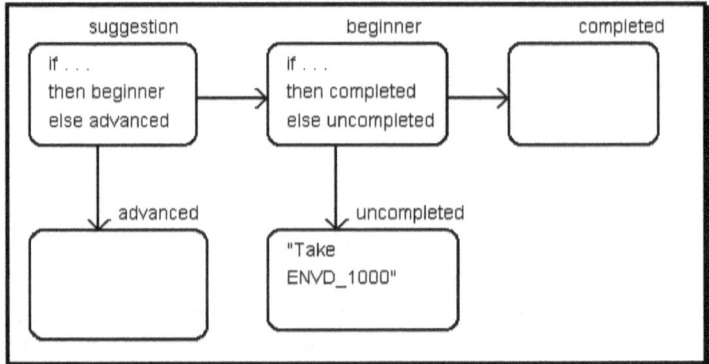

Figure A-3. A decision tree as virtual nodes.

The rectangles are virtual structures. Evaluating node Suggestion produces the message, "Take ENVD_1000."

Suppose we take the branch of the tree (shown in Figure A-3) to the simple `uncompleted`, which contains the text, "`Take ENVD 1000.`" Then this text is displayed in response to the original query.

The virtual structure nodes have implemented a decision tree in a way that is relatively easy to understand and to modify if necessary. The links through the hypermedia defined by the embedded queries reflect in a very straight-forward way the structure of the abstract tree of decisions. Here again, the system requires some analysis to set up, but once defined in the HERMES Language it is rather self-documenting.

Variable binding issues. While the above implementation of a decision tree is appealing, it demonstrates the limitation of virtual structure nodes as well as their power. Note that in the last two queries the node `student` was referred to by name. If one next wants to evaluate the decision tree for another student, the new student information must be substituted in the hypermedia network that contains the virtual structures. The decision tree cannot be simply applied somehow to other existing nodes, let alone to arbitrary lists of nodes (the way predicates can). This is a form of the general binding problem, a consequence of avoiding the use of variables in order to keep the language easy to understand. In the HERMES Language one cannot say "`If envd_semester of X is less than 3,`" except by defining a predicate to encapsulate that computation and applying the predicate to an arbitrary subject. That is why predicates are used so extensively in applications using the language.

However, predicates have their own *binding problem*. Predicates are a form of Association. They must ultimately be applied to (operate on) a DataList in order to produce a DataList result. The input DataList is referred to as the "binding subject". A predicate is like a function, `f(x)`; eventually, its parameter, `x`, must be bound to a variable value in order to be evaluated. When it is used in the evaluation of a query, a predicate is implicitly (automatically) bound to whatever subject it is applied to. Therefore, any unbound relationship in the predicate definition is implicitly bound to that subject as well. However, predicates can have whole queries embedded in them and so a question arises concerning the subjects of these embedded queries. If there is an explicit subject node named in the embedded query, then there is no problem. However, predicates draw much of their power from binding to implicit subjects, as explained in the previous paragraph. Therefore, the HERMES language permits leaving the subject unnamed in an embedded query. In such a case, the implicit subject of the embedded query is bound to the last explicit subject of a query (i.e., to the subject of the query in which the embedded query is embedded, or if that query has no explicit subject then the subject to which its subject is bound). This procedure is based on the usual assumptions of the English language, so that language expressions behave the way English-speaking users would expect them to, without the user having to think in programming terms.

For an example of the two binding mechanisms presented in the previous paragraph, consider the problem of determining what problems a student has with missing prerequisite courses. The query for this (`prerequisite_problems of sandra`) can be based on a predicate named "prerequisite_problems" (`proposed_courses that have prerequisites_not_taken, with their prerequisites_not_taken`) which contains a predicate named "prerequisites_not_taken" (`prerequisites that do not include courses_taken`).

In this query, "prerequisite_problems" is bound to the explicit subject of the query, `sandra`. The other predicate used in its definition, `prerequisites _not_taken`, is applied to `proposed_courses` through composition. So `prerequisites` in its definition is bound to `proposed_courses` (i.e., we are concerned with the prerequisites of the proposed courses). The issue arises with `courses_taken`. These are not courses taken by the proposed courses, but by Sandra. According to the syntax of the query, `courses_taken` is part of an embedded query: `courses_taken of X`. The subject is left implicit, which to English speakers means it refers to the previous main subject, `sandra`. This is in fact the rule used for binding implicit subjects of embedded queries in the HERMES Language as well.

The HERMES language solves the binding problem through the two mechanisms illustrated above. This allows predicates to exercise their power of leaving their subjects implicit, to be bound at runtime. The solution maintains the language's support of tacit understanding by corresponding to the intuitions of non-programmers. While it cannot handle arcane examples requiring binding to multiple or obscure subjects, it handles reasonable, humanly comprehensible examples—including arbitrarily deep embedding of queries. The example of `prerequisite_problems` is a realistic one, occurring in the academic advising application described above. The HERMES language also provides syntax options to specify bindings: the options <u>that</u> (`last subject`), <u>this</u> (`expression`), and <u>those items</u> are part of the language's syntax. These options provide an explicit choice of variable bindings, that can be left to their tacit defaults in many cases. These options fulfill some of the functions of variables using the familiar terminology of deictic reference in English.

Recursive procedures. Recursive programming is a potentially powerful technique. It is particularly useful for processing trees of data, like family trees. In the academic advising application, tree structures appear in the list of course prerequisites. A full set of tree elements is called the *transitive closure*.

A particularly interesting definition from the example domain of family relations is that of descendants:

```
descendants:    children with their descendants
```

A programmer would recognize this to be a *recursive* definition. That is, it not only lists the descendants of the starting node, but the descendants of those descendants, the descendants of descendants of descendants, etc. until there are no more generations. A non-programmer might be able to see that this definition would produce such a result, without having studied recursive function theory in the abstract. Again, the non-programmer might not be able to generate recursive definitions easily from scratch, yet might understand them when seen. Note that the recursive halt condition is implicit: stop when there are no more of the specified links to traverse. This is a convention that is built into the HERMES language implementation. It relieves the end-user from worrying about the recursive out condition that causes so many errors in programming languages that require its explicit statement.

The two primary approaches to enumerating a transitive closure by navigation through a tree structure are *depth-first* and *breadth-first*. Both of these approaches can be programmed in the HERMES Language. The following Predicate and DataList definitions produce a nested, depth-first listing of the transitive closure of course prerequisites:

```
prerequisite_trees:    prerequisites    with    their
    prerequisite_trees.
ENVD_4550       and       ENVD_4560       with       their
    prerequisite_trees.
```

The following Predicate and DataList definitions produce a flat, breadth-first listing of course prerequisites:

```
prerequisite_lists:  prerequisites  and  prerequisite_
    lists of them.
prerequisite_lists of ENVD_4550, without duplicates.
```

The computation through trees has important applications in practical problems. For instance, in a hypermedia design rationale system of issues, subissues of the issues, subissues of the subissues, etc., it is useful to define the issue_trees, a depth-first listing of the whole tree of issues. If the issues can each have answers and arguments for the answers (as in the popular hypertext IBIS systems), then one wants to list deliberations—the tree of arguments on the issue tree. This is straight-forward to do in the language. It is trickier to produce a list of the *terminal* issues, that is subissues at the leaves of the issue tree that have no subissues themselves. This can be done with a Predicate for terminal_issues:

```
terminal_issues: if there are issues of issues then
    terminal_issues of issues, else issues.
```

Defeasible reasoning. The HERMES language is also designed to take advantage of *defeasible reasoning* in an intuitive way. Defeasible reasoning allows a system to be designed with certain default behavior that results unless explicit action is taken to change it. Suppose in a hypertext network of issues and answers one wants to allow a user to accept, reject, or ignore answers by attaching status links to nodes containing words like "accept", "reject", "ignore", "don't care", or no links. One might also want to allow multiple status links from any given answer node. So there may be contradictory information attached to an answer, or no information at all. Suppose further that one wants to display an_important_issue unless all its answers have been explicitly rejected with status links to "reject". This would require defeasible reasoning, a very robust approach. The following query could be used:

```
if there are not answers of an_important_issue that
    have  no  statuses  that  contain  "reject"  then
    an_important_issue, else rejection_message
```

This query has to do with the resolution of answers to issues in the issue-base. This is a critical task for use of a PHI issue-base, yet it has not been supported in design environments like JANUS and PHIDIAS in the past. If issues are explicitly resolved by, for instance attaching status links, then related functions within a design environment like the display of palette items can respond to these decisions with expressions like the preceding query.

Note that defeasible reasoning allows one to ignore all the possible combinations of potentially redundant or contradictory conditions (e.g., multiple `status` links from a given node) and express just the desired condition. This is supported by the Quantifiers in the HERMES language, such as `all, most, no, the only one, at least one,` etc. The end-user can formulate an expression based on a tacit understanding; the explicit computations are left to the implementation of the language.

C. Explicit Structure of the HERMES Language

Syntax of the HERMES language. This is a complete listing of the options of the HERMES language in BNF format. This is the full advanced version of the language, incorporating all the options for the beginner and intermediate levels as described in Chapter 10. All Capitalized Terms are non-terminals. Underlined terms are literal terminals. (Words in parentheses) are comments. Other terms describe terminals. [Terms in square brackets] are optional. The start symbol is DataList.

--------------*language elements*---

DataList ::= SimpleDataList | ComputedDataList

    SimpleDataList ::= a node name | id: an object id | Character | Number | Boolean | NodeKind | LanguageType | items | that (last subject) | this (expression) | those items | contents of ResultList | a DataList name

    ComputedDataList ::= DataList Combination DataList | Association of DataList | DataList with their Association | DataList that Filter | Graphic [immediately] in Graphic | DataList in context Context | either DataList or DataList | if Boolean then DataList [, else DataList] | DataList, sorted | DataList, without duplicates

Association ::= SimpleAssociation | InputAssociation | ComputedAssociation | Predicate

    SimpleAssociation ::= LinkType | name | id | creation date | creator | last modification date | contexts | all associations | [immediate] parts | Dimension | Distance in Units from Graphic [in Graphic] | an Association name

    Predicate ::= Association

InputAssociation ::= LinkType | InputAssociation <u>with</u> <u>their</u> InputAssociation | InputAssociation <u>and</u> InputAssociation | an input association name

ComputedAssociation ::= Association <u>of</u> Association | Association <u>with</u> <u>their</u> Association | Association <u>that</u> Filter | <u>inverse</u> Association | <u>either</u> Association <u>or</u> Association | <u>if</u> Boolean <u>then</u> Association [, <u>else</u> Association] | Association Combination Association | <u>the</u> Number <u>th</u> Association | Association, <u>sorted</u> | Association, <u>without</u> <u>duplicates</u>

Filter ::= SimpleFilter | CharacterFilter | NumberFilter | BooleanFilter | ContextFilter | GraphicFilter | ComputedFilter

SimpleFilter ::= <u>equal</u> DataList | <u>named</u> Character | <u>included</u> <u>in</u> DataList | <u>include</u> DataList | <u>of</u> <u>kind</u> NodeKind | <u>of</u> <u>type</u> LanguageType | a Filter name

CharacterFilter ::= <u>include</u> Character

NumberFilter ::= Counter

BooleanFilter ::= <u>true</u>

ContextFilter ::= <u>view</u> [Counter] DataList | <u>inherit</u> <u>from</u> Context | <u>are</u> <u>inherited</u> <u>by</u> Context

GraphicFilter ::= [<u>immediately</u>] <u>contain</u> Graphic | [<u>immediately</u>] <u>contained</u> <u>in</u> Graphic | Measure [Quantifier] Graphic [<u>in</u> Graphic] | <u>have</u> Attribute <u>is</u> Value | <u>have</u> Attribute <u>is</u> Number

ComputedFilter ::= <u>have</u> Counter Association [<u>with</u> <u>those</u> <u>items</u>] | <u>have</u> Quantifier Association <u>that</u> Filter [<u>with</u> <u>those</u> <u>items</u>] | <u>if</u> Boolean <u>then</u> Filter [<u>else</u> Filter] | Filter Connective Filter | <u>are</u> Filter | <u>are</u> <u>not</u> Filter | <u>do</u> <u>not</u> Filter

----------------*media elements*---

Character ::= SimpleCharacter | ComputedCharacter

SimpleCharacter ::= character string | a Character name

ComputedCharacter ::= <u>substring</u> <u>of</u> Character <u>from</u> Number <u>for</u> Number | Character <u>append</u> Character

Number ::= SimpleNumber | ComputedNumber

SimpleNumber ::= real number | a Number name

ComputedNumber ::= <u>count</u> <u>of</u> DataList | <u>minimum</u> DataList | <u>maximum</u> DataList | <u>total of</u> DataList | <u>product</u> <u>of</u> DataList | Number <u>+</u> Number | Number <u>-</u> Number | <u>-</u> Number | Number <u>x</u> Number | Number <u>/</u> Number | <u>list</u> <u>of</u> Distance <u>in</u> Units <u>among</u> Graphic, Graphic[, Graphic] [<u>in</u> Graphic]

Boolean ::= SimpleBoolean | ComputedBoolean

SimpleBoolean ::= <u>true</u> | <u>false</u> | a Boolean name

ComputedBoolean ::= <u>there</u> <u>are</u> Counter DataList | Quantifier DataList Filter | <u>not</u> Boolean | Boolean Connective Boolean | Graphic Measure [Quantifier] Graphic [<u>in</u> Graphic]

Graphic ::= SimpleGraphic | ComputedGraphic

SimpleGraphic ::= polyline | a Graphic name

ComputedGraphic ::= DataList (<u>of</u> <u>type</u> <u>graphic</u>)

Image ::= bitmap image | an Image name

Pen ::= pen sketch | a Pen name

Sound ::= sound segment | a Sound name

Video ::= video segment | a Video name

Animation ::= animation segment | an Animation name

ComputedView ::=   DataList arranged in a window | a ComputedView name

------------------*network elements*---

NodeKind ::=   a NodeKind name

LinkType ::=   a LinkType name

Context ::=   a Context name

ResultList ::=   name of an evaluated DataList

------------------*namable terminology elements*----------------------------

Counter ::=   (at least one) | more than Number | less than Number | exact Number | not Counter | Counter Connective Counter | a Counter name

Quantifier ::=   no | any | all | most | the (only one) | Counter | a Quantifier name

Measure ::=   Distance is Counter Units | not Measure | Measure Connective Measure | a Measure name

------------------*simple terminology elements*-------------------------------

Connective ::=   and (logical) | or (logical)

Combination ::=   and (unique sorted union) | and also (intersection) | but not (difference) | or (append) | with (and, indented)

Distance ::=   central distance | closest distance | x distance | y distance | z distance

Units ::=   inches | feet | cm | meters

Dimension ::=   length | area | volume | x width | y height | z depth

Attribute ::=   font | color | pen width | brush style | brush width | . . . .

Value ::=   roman | helvetica | red | blue | striped | plaid | . . . .

LanguageType ::=   data lists | associations | filters | characters | numbers | booleans | graphics | images | pens | sounds | videos | animations | computed views | node kinds | link types | result lists | contexts | counters | quantifiers | measures

Denotational semantics of the HERMES language. The semantics of the HERMES Language was formalized using the notation of Schmidt (1986), based on the denotational semantics of Strachey and Scott. The abstract syntax, semantic algebras, and valuation functions provide a formal specification for the HERMES source code implementation. Each option in the abstract syntax is programmed as an object. The semantic algebras are implemented by these objects, which are given methods corresponding to the operations specified for the algebras. Evaluation methods for the objects correspond very closely to the valuation functions specified for the syntactic options. In addition, each object has methods for displaying itself and each object can be given a name by the user when it is defined.

For instance, a typical option in the syntax, DataList ::= Association of DataList, might be programmed as follows in object-oriented Pascal:

```
DataListAofD := object(DataList)
 function    Eval(InList:    DataListPtr):    DataListPtr;
   virtual;
 procedure Display; virtual;
private
 TheAssociation : AssociationPtr;
 TheDataList : DataListPtr;
end;

function    DataListAofD.Eval(InList:    DataListPtr):
   DataListPtr;
begin
 Eval                                                  :=
   TheAssociation^.Eval(TheDataList^.Eval(nil));
end;

procedure DataListAofD.Display;
begin
 TheAssociation^.Display;
 write(' of ');
 TheDataList^.Display;
 writeln;
end;
```

This defines the Association of DataList option as an object that inherits from the DataList object, has data items corresponding to its constituent Association and DataList, and has methods for displaying and evaluating itself. Note how the Eval method follows the same applicative process as the valuation function from the denotational semantics:

$$D[[A \text{ of } D]] = \lambda d. \ \lambda z. \ A[[A]] \ (\ D[[D]] \ z)$$

First it evaluates D, the DataList, (using the hypertext database z, but ignoring the input DataList d) and then applies the evaluation of A, the Association, to this intermediate result. (The notation A[[A]] means the Association valuation of A, that is the evaluation of a given Association instance in accordance with whichever option of the Association syntax it instantiates.) The Display method similarly displays the `Association` using whatever method corresponds to the particular Association instance, displays the character string ' of ', and then displays the `DataList` with the method appropriate to its instance. This approach to polymorphic execution depending upon the particular form of the instances at runtime provides the flexibility to define methods that handle nesting of phrases. In other words, `Association` can take the form of any Association option and `DataList` can take the form of any DataList option. This allows the HERMES Language to have the kind of phrase structure that English has, with arbitrarily deep nesting of phrases.

The denotational semantics of the HERMES language is extraordinarily simple because the language has been designed to minimize the amount of programming doctrine required. In particular, there is no state change and no continuation processing because there are no assignment statements and no explicit iteration constructs. In fact, there is no store because there are no variables.[29] Moreover, there is no explicit typing. This all makes for a simple, straight-forward language structure.

Balancing the structural simplicity of the language is the wealth of individual syntax options. The quantity of options results from the history of design trade-offs detailed in Appendix B. In particular, there was a concerted effort to provide a broad range of useful functionality while restricting the possibilities for creating problematic constructs. There are over a hundred options for the Advanced Version of the HERMES Language. Most of them define permissible and useful combinations of other options and are relatively self-explanatory. A few of them require more explanation.

Informal semantics of the HERMES language.

In the following, the major options listed in the syntax above are explained briefly and examples of their use is given.

---

[29] In fact, there is a very limited state change, implemented with a specific associated store for the DataList options `that (last subject)`, `this (expression)`, and `those items`. The first two of these each require a special stack and the third requires a list to keep track of their changing values. These are simple to implement and can be easily accounted for in the denotational semantics without all the overhead of variable names and assignments.

Simple DataLists. These generate ordered lists of nodes from the database. Most of the Simple options generate a list of one node. The options for DataLists signify that these lists of nodes can be generated in the following ways:

By specifying the name of a node. Names are optional for nodes. For example:

```
archie's lunar habitat
```

By giving the Id of a node. All nodes have unique numeric identifiers that are used internally by the HERMES system.

```
id: 2345
```

By defining a Character node using any of the Character options.

```
substring of privacy message from 1 to 26
```

By defining a Number node using any of the Number options.

```
47
```

By defining a Boolean node using any of the Boolean options.

```
there are more than 3 grandchildren of sandra
```

All nodes in the database of a specified NodeKind

```
lunar habitats
```

All nodes in the database of a specified LanguageType

```
datalists that have authors that contain "Sandra"
```

All nodes in the database

```
items
```

that (last subject) stands for whatever the last explicitly specified subject was during evaluation. This is used in the definition of predicates, where it is not known what will be operated on by an expression

```
parts of inverse parts that do not equal that (last
   subject)
```

this (expression) means the item currently being operated upon. This is similar to a reference to "self" in other languages

```
issue_trees: issues with their this (expression)
```

those items refers to the last list of intermediate result items computed. This option saves intermediate results so they do not have to be recalculated in order to be displayed

```
prerequisite_trees: prerequisites and prerequisite
    _trees of those items
prerequisites and this (expression) of those items
```

The name of a stored DataList whose contents (not definition) is to be used

```
contents of archie's problem areas
```

The name of a defined ResultList whose definition (not stored contents) is to be evaluated

```
sandra's prerequisite problems
```

Computed DataLists. These generate ordered lists of nodes from the database. Most of these apply one operator to another to generate a DataList:

By combining two DataLists with a Combination

```
men and women
```

By applying an Association to an existing DataList (and traversing links to arrive at a new list).

```
answers of the privacy issue
```

By applying an Association to an existing DataList and listing the DataList with the Associations of each item listed under that item and indented. The term "with" indicates that indenting will take place for the results of the Association. Note that the Association operator is applied to the DataList results.

```
answers of the privacy issue with their arguments
```

By applying a Filter to an existing DataList (and eliminating nodes which do not pass through).

```
chairs that are near tables
```

By specifying a Graphic that is internal to a hierarchical Graphic. If the optional term "immediately" is used, then only the first level parts of the Graphic will result, and not the parts of parts, etc. as when the "immediately" keyword is absent.

```
chairs in (graphic) habitats
areas immediately in (graphic) habitats
```

By selecting a DataList as viewed within a context other than the currently active perspective

```
habitats in context lunar gravity
```

By choosing between two existing DataLists depending upon whether the first has any items when evaluated

```
either problem areas or approval message
```

By evaluating a Boolean and choosing between two existing DataLists; the second DataList is optional.

```
if stove is near curtains then flammability issue,
   else default_critic
```

By sorting a DataList

```
men and women, sorted
```

By removing duplicates from a DataList

```
men and boys, without duplicates
```

Simple Associations. These are computations that map or transform one list of nodes into another, based on the links coming into or out of the nodes in the first list. The transformations can take place as follows:

All links of a specified Link Type

```
sons
```

The name of a node. This is a pseudo-Association that allows internally stored names to be referenced in the HERMES language

```
name of sons of sandra
```

The id of a node. This is a pseudo-Association that allows internally stored ids to be referenced in the HERMES language

```
id of sandra
```

The creation date of a node. This is a pseudo-Association that allows internally stored names to be referenced in the HERMES language. Design environments built on HERMES could make timestamping automatic

```
creation   date   of   arguments   of   answers   of   an
   interesting issue
```

The creator of a node. This is a pseudo-Association that allows internally stored names to be referenced in the HERMES language. Design environments built on HERMES could automatically stamp a newly created node with the user's login name

```
creator of an interesting issue
```

The last modification date of a node. This is a pseudo-Association that allows internally stored names to be referenced in the HERMES language. Design environments built on HERMES could make timestamping automatic

```
last modification date of arguments of answers of an
   interesting issue
```

List the contexts in which something is defined. This is a pseudo-Association.

```
contexts that inherit from archie's perspective
```

List every association

```
all associations of the privacy issue
```

Parts of a graphical hierarchy. If the optional term "immediate" is used, then only the first level parts will result, and not the parts of parts, etc. as when the "immediate" keyword is absent.

```
immediate parts of archie's habitat
parts of archie's habitat
```

Any Dimension (see Dimensions below). This is a pseudo-Association

```
length of subparts of archie's habitat
```

Distance from a specified graphical object. When applied to one or more graphical objects, this returns the numeric distance(s). Distances are always measured within some implicitly or explicitly specified encompassing graphic

```
closest   distance   in   feet   from   table   in   archie's
   habitat
```

The name of a defined Association

```
sons
```

Predicates. These are Computed Associations that display their resultant lists differently in order to hide the computations that have been encapsulated in the Predicate definition. Any Association definition can optionally be stored as a Predicate. For instance, the Association

```
discussion:  issues  with  their  answers  with  their
    arguments
```

can be stored as an Association or as a Predicate. The same nodes would appear in the lists generated by the use of either, but the lists would appear differently when displayed. The results of the Association would be labeled as `issues`, `answers`, and `arguments`, and they would be indented accordingly to show the structure of the computation. The results of the Predicate, in contrast, would all be labeled `discussion` and would not be indented. To the user, it would appear that the results of the Predicate were all linked directly to the original nodes by simple links of type `discussion`—so the complexity of the actual computation would be hidden.

InputAssociation. This is a subclass of Associations that is used for formulating macros for input of structured data. Its definitions are identical to the corresponding Association definitions, but they are limited as to the complexity of their structure. In particular, they are limited to forms meaningful for prompting input of new nodes. Any InputAssociation can be included wherever a Association can be used, and it can be saved as an Association or a Predicate. However, the reverse is not true, and only expressions saved as InputAssociation can be used for eliciting the entry of new nodes. For instance, if `discussion` were saved as an InputAssociation, then the user could be prompted to enter a hierarchy of design rationale automatically. First, the system would prompt for an issue. For each issue entered, it would prompt for a series of answers. And as each answer was entered, the user would be prompted for arguments to support it.

Computed Association. These combine Simple Associations with other operations.

Apply one Association to the result of another Association

```
arguments of answers
```

Apply one Association to the result of another Association and list each item of the result of the first Association with its Associations listed under it and indented

```
answers with their arguments
```

First apply an Association and then apply a Filter

```
sons that are contained in siblings of sandra
```

Follow the in-coming Association links instead of the usual out-going links

```
inverse parent
```

Choose between two existing Association results depending upon whether the first has any items when evaluated

```
either sons or daughters
```

Evaluate a Boolean and choose between two existing Associations; the second DataList is optional.

```
if stove is near curtains then arguments
```

Combine two Associations with a Combination

```
sons and daughters
```

Select the n-th Association

```
the 7th son
```

Sort the Association results

```
authors of novels, sorted
```

Remove duplicates from the Association results

```
authors of novels, without duplicates
```

Simple Filters. Filters are conditional operators applied to each node in a DataList; if the condition is true of the node, then the node is retained (from the input list, in the output list). The following filtering operations are defined:

Check if an item is equal to (the same object as) an item specified by a DataList

```
habitats that have chairs that equal archie's
    favorite chair
```

Check if an item has a name specified by a defined Character

```
habitats that are named the secret word
```

Check if an item is included in a defined DataList

```
chairs that are included in habitats
```

Check if an item includes a defined DataList

```
habitats that include chairs
```

Check if an item is of a kind defined by a NodeKind

```
parts of habitats that are of kind chair
```

Check if an item is of a type defined by a LanguageType

```
items that are of type distances
```

The name of a defined Filter

```
are desirable
```

Multimedia Filters. These include filters specific to Characters, Numbers, Booleans, Contexts, and Graphics.

Check if a substring is included that is defined by a Character

```
messages that include the warning string
```

Check if a numeric item equals an amount that is defined by a Count

```
that are more than 3
```

Check if a boolean value equals true

```
test conditionals that are true
```

Check if a specified DataList or Count of the DataList can be viewed in a Context

```
contexts that view more than 7 issues that include
    "bunk"
```

Check if a Context inherits from another Context

```
contexts that inherit from archie's context
```

Check if a Context is inherited by another Context

```
contexts that are inherited by archie's context
```

Check if a graphical item contains the graphical items that are defined by a DataList. The keyword "immediately" restricts the computation to the highest level parts.

```
habitats that contain chairs
```

Check if a graphical item is contained in the graphical items that are defined by a DataList. The keyword "immediately" restricts the computation to the highest level parts.

```
chairs that are immediately contained in habitats
```

Check if graphical items are a distance defined by a Measure from items defined by a DataList. This may optionally be quantified with a Quantifier. Distances are implicitly or explicitly measured within a Graphic

```
that are near most stoves in the kitchen
```

Check if an Attribute value equals Value

```
that have color is red
```

Check if an Attribute value equals Number

```
that have pen width is 5
```

Computed Filters. These include Filters that combine other operators.

Check if there are a certain number defined by Count of Associations. Optionally sublist the intermediate results

```
that have more then 3 grandchildren with those items
```

Check if there are a certain number defined by Quantifier of Associations that pass a Filter. Optionally sublist the intermediate results

```
that have all grandchildren that are of kind boy
```

Check a Filter only if a Boolean is true. Optionally check an alternative Filter otherwise

```
that if test conditional then are red, else are blue
```

Check if items pass both of (or one of) two Filters, depending on the Connective, logical and/or

```
that are more than 3 and (logical) are less than 7
```

Check if items do or do not pass a Filter

```
that are equal "bunk"
that are not named "my bunk"
that do not equal "bunk"
```

The semantics of the remaining media options, network options, namable terminology, and simple terminology options are straight-forward and should be clear from their BNF syntax. The **media elements** provide the primitive values for the content of nodes and the terminal values for the language options. However, they also include computations involving other object types. The **network elements** define the graph structure of the database. Some node kinds and link types have been pre-defined for internal use by the system. They are available to the user, but cannot be modified. The **namable terminology elements** serve mainly to provide choices for the language options. However, they can involve computations. Just like any of the above options, these can be named and saved. For example, `some` and `several` have already been defined in the HERMES seed as supplementary Quantifiers this way. It has been assumed in the examples above that several Measures have been defined, like `too near` or `far away from`. These can be redefined and personalized by users in their interpretive perspectives. In contrast, the **simple terminology elements** are fixed: they cannot be named or redefined and extended by users.

www.ingramcontent.com/pod-product-compliance
Lightning Source LLC
Chambersburg PA
CBHW020723180526
45163CB00001B/80